Pascal
An Introduction
to Methodical Programming

Pascal
An introduction
to methodical programming

Second edition

**William Findlay
and David A Watt**

*Computing Science Department,
University of Glasgow*

Computer Science Press

Printed in the United States of America
First Edition published 1978. Second Edition 1981.

Published simultaneously in the United States of America and Great Britain by:

Computer Science Press, Inc.   Pitman Books Ltd
11 Taft Ct   39 Parker Street
Rockville, Maryland 20850 U.S.A.   London WC2B 5PB
ISBN 0-914894-73-0   Great Britain

1 2 3 4 5 6   86 85 84 83 82 81

Library of Congress Cataloging in Publication Data

Findlay, William.
    Pascal, an introduction to methodical programming. Second edition.

    (Computer software engineering series)
    Includes index.
    1. PASCAL (Computer program language) I. Watt, David Anthony, joint author. II. Title. III. Series: Computer software engineering series (Rockville, Md.)
QA76.73.P35F56   001.6'424   78-11540
ISBN 0-914894-73-0

Preface to the second edition

This book is intended for use in conjunction with a first course in computer programming based on the programming language Pascal. The reader is assumed to have had no previous exposure to computers, and to have only elementary mathematics. Programming principles, good style and a methodical approach to program development are emphasized, with the intention that the book should be useful even to those who must later write programs in a language other than Pascal. Thus one objective is simply to teach readers how to write good programs.

A second objective is to present an introduction to Pascal. In this respect the book should be useful not only to novices but also to readers with some experience of programming in another language.

Pascal was introduced in 1971 by Professor Niklaus Wirth. His aim was to make available a language which would allow programming to be taught as a systematic discipline and in which the techniques of both 'scientific' and 'commercial' programming could be convincingly demonstrated. The adoption of Pascal has been rapid and widespread, to the extent that it has become the *lingua franca* of computing science.

For our present purposes what is really important is the clarity with which fundamental programming concepts may be expressed in Pascal. Most of the book is devoted to a treatment of these fundamentals, presented in such a way that the reader should be convinced of the need for each language feature before he is shown how it is realized in Pascal. Since Pascal contains only a few features which are not truly fundamental, these remaining features are also covered, briefly, for the sake of completeness.

Use of the book

The best way to acquire a methodical approach to programming is subconsciously, by imitation, and the best time to start is right at the beginning. The technique of programming by stepwise refinement is therefore imparted mainly by consistent example throughout the book. Nevertheless, three chapters are devoted exclusively to programming methodology. The first, Chapter 7, introduces the methodology by means of a simple example and a case study, and is placed early enough to encourage good programming habits from the start. The second, Chapter 15, shows how subprograms fit into the methodology, illustrating this with another case study. The third, Chapter 18, applies the methodology to realistically-sized problems involving data structures, by means of two further case studies.

The main text falls naturally into six parts. Part I (First Steps in Programming) aims to bring the novice as soon as possible to the stage of writing and testing complete programs in a methodical manner. This part covers the INTEGER and BOOLEAN data types, input and output, and the basic control structures of sequencing, selection and repetition. Its high-lights are the first complete program, in Chapter 4, and the introduction of a methodology, in Chapter 7. Part II (Further Simple Data Types) covers the data types CHAR and REAL, and ordinal types in general. The chapter on CHAR includes a detailed treatment of text input and output. The chapter on ordinal types also covers the related control structures, FOR and CASE. Part III (Arrays and Strings) introduces the simple data structures common to most programming languages. Part IV (Subprog-rams) introduces functions, procedures and parameters, and demonstrates their importance in program development. This is the pivot of the book—the reader who has mastered the material up to this point can reasonably call himself a programmer. Part V (Further Data Structures) continues the coverage of Pascal's rich variety of data structures with records and files, and relates the choice of suitable data structures to the methodical development of a program. Part VI (Additional Topics) completes the coverage of Pascal with sets, pointers and linked lists, recursion, functional and procedural parameters, and the GOTO state-ment.

Some of the topics could be skipped on a first reading, and are so marked in the list of contents and in the text. These same topics may be omitted altogether if time presses.

Examples

Every non-trivial example used in this book has been tested on a computer. We challenge readers to find any errors in them!

Exercises

Each chapter is followed by a set of exercises. The more difficult exercises are marked with asterisks (*). Some of the exercises are intended to be answered on paper, to provide practice in the use of the language features introduced in the chapter. Answers to a selection of such exercises are provided. The remaining exercises are designated *programming exercises*, which involve the writing of complete programs to be run and tested on a computer. Practical experience of this nature is essential to every programmer. (Not all the programming exercises need be attempted.)

A programming course should be supplemented by a programming laboratory, in which a series of programming exercises selected by the course organizer should be undertaken. The programming exercises herein may be used to assist in such a selection.

References

We have not attempted to write a work of reference, but we hope that the arrangement of the material, together with the appendices and the index, will help the reader to find information on specific points. The standard reference on Pascal is *Pascal User Manual and Report* by Kathleen Jensen and Niklaus Wirth (Springer-Verlag, New York–Heidelberg–Berlin, 1975). However, the present edition of this book has been updated to reflect the current state of the draft ISO standard for Pascal. The draft standard introduces only minor amendments to the Pascal language, apart from one major new feature (conformant array parameters), which has been omitted from this edition because its status is presently unclear.

For those wishing to study programming further we can wholeheartedly recommend *Algorithms +Data Structures = Programs* by Niklaus Wirth (Prentice-Hall, Englewood Cliffs, New Jersey, 1976).

Acknowledgments

Like all programmers, we owe a great debt to Professor Edsger Dijkstra, whose insights into the creative aspects of programming we have attempted to reflect. Equally, we wish to acknowledge the work of Professor Niklaus Wirth, whose programming language Pascal is by far the best tool available today for teaching the fundamental concepts of programming.

We wish to thank our colleagues in the Computing Science Department of Glasgow University for their encouragement and advice; in particular Dr John Jeacocke and Dr Jenifer Haselgrove whose perceptive comments were of great assistance. We gratefully acknowledge the comments and constructive criticisms made by readers of the first edition; they will find their comments reflected in improvements to this edition. Our gratitude goes to Professor D. C. Gilles for allowing us to prepare the manuscript on the Department's PDP 11/45 computer.

W. Findlay
D. A. Watt   May 1981

Contents

(Topics marked with an asterisk may be omitted on a first reading.)

Part I
First steps in programming

1
Computers and programming

1.1 Introduction

There can be few people, at least in the industrialized countries of the world, who have never had any contact with computers. Computers are now routinely used for mundane tasks such as producing bank statements, financial reports, electricity bills and payslips. Hotel and airline reservation systems have been made possible by computers. In industry, computers control machine tools and chemical plant. Scientists use computers to analyse experimental data, doctors generate 'cross-section' X-ray pictures, psychologists simulate mental processes. Manned and unmanned space exploration would hardly be possible without the assistance of computers. On the frivolous side, computers have been programmed to play games such as backgammon and chess. More ominously, military applications have a long history.

Computing has grown rapidly, from its origins before 1950 to its present position as one of the world's largest industries. There is no sign of this expansion slowing down. Indeed, the development of cheap integrated circuits means that domestic and personal computers are now becoming practical. These will more and more invade everyday life as domestic appliances, motor vehicles, communications systems and the like come increasingly to depend on them. This accelerating process has rightly been called the Second Industrial Revolution. Nobody can yet forsee with any certainty what the ultimate consequences for society may be, but it is already clear that vast changes lie ahead for us all.

Consider the impact of personal calculators on accepted ideas about education and numeracy. Computer technology will soon have a similar effect in all areas of clerical and skilled manual work. Many books are now edited and typeset by their authors, aided by computers. As a result they are much less expensive than would be possible with traditional printing technology. On the other hand the craft of the compositor is thereby made redundant, and the end product often lacks the elegance he might have given it. Concerns like these make it imperative that computers be understood as widely as possible.

One of the most common misconceptions is that computers are 'problem-solving' machines. Nothing could be further from the truth. In fact the successful application of computers is made possible only by finding solutions to problems which computers themselves have created. The most obvious of these is that a computer is useless without programs to control it. The writing of good computer programs is both a vital part of the modern economy and a fascinating intellectual exercise. Such is the topic of this book.

1.2 Hardware and software

Early computers filled large rooms with tall metal racks on which were fixed thousands of vacuum tubes, tanks of mercury and panels of flashing lights. The resemblance to an ironmonger's store was so compelling that the computer engineeers of the time wryly talked about their creations as 'hardware'. Nowadays a considerably more powerful computer fits easily in a briefcase, but the principles of its operation remain the same.

The hardware of every digital computer consists of a processor, a store and an assortment of peripheral devices. The *processor* is the unit which actually performs the calculations. It contains a *control unit* to direct operations, as well as an *arithmetic unit*. The latter is equivalent to an electronic calculator, but much faster, being capable of a million or more operations per second. To make use of this speed the processor must be able to access its data equally quickly. Retaining data for rapid access by the processor is the job of the computer's *store*. Some calculators have a handful of 'registers', or locations in which numbers can be kept. The store of a modest computer contains tens of thousands of locations. A calculator's numeric keys and display correspond to the *peripherals* or input/output devices of a computer. These allow data to be placed in the store and results to be taken out. Though very fast by human standards, peripherals are usually much slower than the processor and store.

A calculator is given instructions by pressing its function keys. However the great speed of a computer would be wasted if it could not be supplied with instructions as quickly as it obeys them. To make this possible the computer's instructions, encoded in numerical form, are held in store along with the data. The computer works in a cycle as follows.

(1) The control unit fetches the next instruction from store.
(2) The instruction is decoded into electronic signals by the control unit
(3) In response to these signals the arithmetic unit, the store, or a peripheral device carries out the instruction.
(4) The whole cycle repeats from step (1).

In this way long sequences of instructions can be obeyed automatically at the full speed of the processor. Such a sequence of instructions is called a *program*.

Individual computer instructions are very simple in their effect, the following examples being typical.

(a) Read an item of data into store from an input device.
(b) Copy an item of data from one location to another.
(c) Add the contents of two locations and place the sum in a third.
(d) If the content of a location represents a negative number, take the next instruction from a different part of the program; otherwise continue with the next instruction in sequence.
(e) Write an item of data from store to an output device.

An *algorithm* is a method for computing a result in a finite number of steps. It has been proved that anything which can be computed by an algorithm, can be computed by a program of elementary operations such as these. There are results which are not computable by any algorithm whatsoever. In these cases it may be possible to compute an approximation to the desired result. A method for doing this is called a *heuristic*. Heuristics are also useful when an algorithm exists but is impractically slow or needs too much store.

The collection of all the programs available in a computer system constitutes its *software*. This word was invented to emphasize that the programs are just as important as the hardware. It also contrasts them effectively. Hardware is visible, solid and substantial; software is somewhat intangible. The hardware of a computer system is not easily changed; the software is usually in a state of flux.

One of the most important parts of the software is the *operating system*, a set of control programs which are kept permanently in store. The operating system carries out many of the routine tasks needed to prepare and run a user's program; e.g. deciding which program to run next, making ready its input, bringing the program into store, allocating it some processor time, and so on.

1.3 Programming languages

The earliest computers were programmed in machine code: in other words, by giving them instructions directly in numerical form. However the drawbacks were soon recognized.

(a) Because of the very primitive nature of machine instructions, machine-code programming is both tedious and error-prone.

(b) For the same reason, machine-code programs are difficult to understand and to modify.
(c) Programming is a time-consuming and expensive business. It would be a great saving to be able to use the same program on different computers, but a machine-code program is specific to one model of computer and will not work on any other.

For these reasons machine-code is now seldom used.

Why not write programs in English? Computer programming is not unique in needing to describe sequences of actions precisely and in detail. The same requirement is often met in daily life. However, anyone who has struggled with the sometimes mystifying instructions in car maintenance handbooks, do-it-yourself manuals, or recipe books will agree that English is not ideally suited to the task. In fact the glories of English—its vast scope, its subtlety, its potential for ambiguity and metaphor—must be considered severe disadvantages when the aim is literalness, accuracy and completeness. A programming language must aim at the truth, the whole truth, and nothing but the truth.

English is at the opposite extreme from machine code and precisely for that reason must be rejected as a medium for practical computer programming. What is needed is a middle way: one which combines the readability and generality of English with the directness and precision of machine code. Languages of this sort are called *high-level programming languages*.

Knitting patterns offer an interesting example where a similar problem has been faced. A knitting pattern is comparable in complexity with a modest computer program, so it is understandable that a special 'knitting language' has evolved. It borrows many words from English, but these are used in stereotyped ways and with definite meanings. Another noteworthy feature of a knitting pattern is its division into two parts: a list of the materials and tools needed, followed by a list of instructions stating how to use them. The programming language used in this book, Pascal, shares both of these characteristics.

Any language can be studied from two points of view: that of its grammar, or *syntax*, and that of its meaning, or *semantics*. A good understanding of both is needed to use it properly. We will find that the semantics of Pascal can be described adequately in English. On the other hand a description of its syntax in English would be very tedious. Instead we will use a pictorial device, the *syntax diagram*. This is best explained by an example.

Stated in English, the Pascal definition of an integer number is the following. 'An integer number is a sequence of one or more decimal digits. A decimal digit is the character "0", or "1", or "2", or "3", or "4", or "5", or "6", or "7", or "8", or "9".' Exactly the same information is conveyed by Figure 1.1.

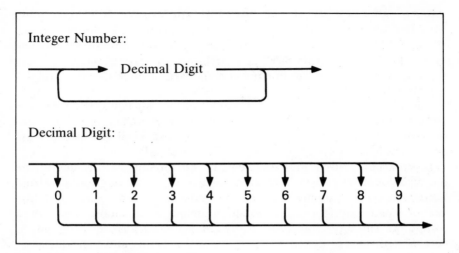

Figure 1.1. Syntax of Integer Numbers

This can be understood by following the arrows through the diagram, from entry to exit, and writing down a specimen of everything you pass. When you come to a fork, either path may be chosen. For instance, the integer number **365** is produced by going through Decimal Digit three times, choosing the fourth, seventh and sixth forks respectively. However the form **1,000** is *not* a valid integer number, according to Figure 1.1, because no path through the diagram includes a comma symbol.

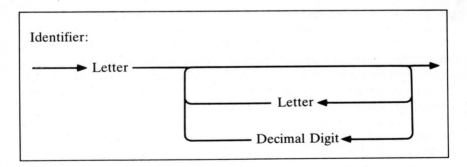

Figure 1.2. Syntax of Identifiers

As a slightly more complicated example, Figure 1.2 defines an identifier, widely used in Pascal for naming things. The English equivalent of this diagram is 'An identifier is a sequence of characters beginning with a letter and followed by zero or more letters or decimal digits.' The definition of letter is omitted; it is tedious in any form. For instance, X is an identifier produced by passing straight through Letter and out. In Letter, we choose the 24th fork! Similarly, A1D is produced by passing through Letter (and taking the first fork therein), then circling back through Decimal Digit (taking its second fork) and finally circling back through Letter (taking its fourth fork).

The identifiers A1D, A1d, a1D and a1d are all equivalent, because corresponding upper- and lower-case letters are interchangeable in identifiers and other Pascal words. In this book we shall consistently use upper-case to make the Pascal text stand out clearly.

A program written in Pascal cannot be directly performed by the hardware of a computer. To make it executable it must be translated from Pascal into an equivalent set of machine code instructions. This translation can be specified rigorously enough to make it a suitable task for a computer. Three programs are involved here: the translator program, or *compiler*; the user's Pascal text, or *source program*; and the equivalent machine code, or *object program*. Thus a Pascal program is run in two distinct stages.

(1) The Pascal compiler is brought into store and obeyed. It causes the computer to read the source program, check it for errors, and convert it into the corresponding object program.
(2) The object program is left in store as the result of stage (1). It is obeyed in turn and reads input, performs computations, and writes output, in exactly the manner specified by the Pascal source program.

Programs often contain errors in the use of the programming language and these are reported by the compiler during stage (1). The report usually takes the form of an error message or a number which refers to a list of error messages. These error messages are often helpful in finding the cause of the trouble. (However, the compiler may be misled by an error into taking later, perfectly correct, parts of a program as erroneous. Thus one genuine error can cause a whole group of messages to be output, many of which are spurious. Nothing more forcefully reminds a programmer that computers do not *understand* the programs which drive them.)

Exercises 1

1.1. Which of the following are valid identifiers, according to the syntax of Figure 1.2?

(a) SEVEN, (b) VII, (c) NMR7, (d) 7, (e) KERMIT, (f) JOE   90,
(g) ABCDEFGHIJKLMNOPQRSTUVWXYZ

1.2. Write down examples of sentences generated by the following syntax diagrams.

Sentence:

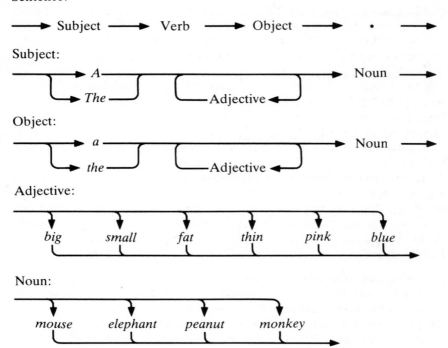

Subject:

Object:

Adjective:

Noun:

Verb:

1.3. Which of the following are valid sentences, according to the syntax of the previous exercise?

(a) *The big fat monkey ate a peanut.*
(b) *The pink elephant was killed.*
(c) *The monkey saw a pink elephant.*
(d) *The small, thin elephant killed a mouse.*
(e) *The mouse ate.*
(f) *A elephant was a elephant.*

1.4. Draw a syntax diagram which defines exactly, and solely, the Roman numerals from 1 to 10 (i.e. *I, II, III, IV, V, VI, VII, VIII, IX* and *X*). Your diagram should not consist merely of ten alternatives.

1.5*. Write down examples of chemical formulas generated by the following syntax diagrams.

Chemical Formula:

Component:

Element:

2
Data: types, constants and variables

2.1 Data and data types

The word 'data' means 'the things given'. We use the term to refer to the information which must be supplied to a program (or piece of program) before it can produce any results. Data may originate outside the computer, in which case it must be read from an input device, or it may already be available in the computer's store, having been placed there as a result of a previous computation.

An item of data represents some fact, observation or idea about the world. People can recognize data in speech, in pictures, in printed text and in many other forms. However, the input devices of a computer are much less adaptable than human sensory organs and almost all data presented to computers is in the form of a *text*, a sequence of characters from some character set. Such texts are usually punched on cards for input by means of a card reader, or typed directly into the computer at a terminal. There are devices which permit the input of sound and pictures to computers, but they are not common, and even these devices work by converting the data to what is basically a form of text.

Printed material has traditionally used a large set of symbols. The alphabet is often available in bold letters, in italics, and in many sizes and styles. There is also a huge assortment of symbols for use in mathematics and other specialized fields. For economic reasons computer input is much more restrictive. In fact most computers can process only a small, fixed set of characters. This will certainly include the capital letters, the decimal digits, the usual punctuation marks and a few of the mathematical signs.

Even this restricted set of characters allows a vast range of data to be input to the computer. With just two characters we can distinguish between true and false. The digits allow us to write integer numbers and these can represent a great variety of things, for example populations, votes, dates, sums of money, and so on. The digits together with the decimal point allow us to write numbers containing fractions (real numbers). Thus we can represent smoothly-varying quantities such as distances, times, weights, volumes and probabilities. Adding letters, punctuation marks and mathematical signs allows us to input human-language text: both 'natural' languages such as English and 'programming' languages such as Pascal.

A very important characteristic of a data item is its *type*, as this determines its meaning and constrains what can sensibly be done with it. In Pascal the values **TRUE** and **FALSE** constitute the **BOOLEAN** type; the whole numbers constitute the **INTEGER** type; the numbers with fractional parts constitute the **REAL** type; and the computer system's character set constitutes the **CHAR** type. Furthermore, the programmer can add to this list by defining his own types.

It is very easy to make a computer do totally meaningless calculations. One of the ways high-level languages help to avoid this is by *type checking*: that is, by ensuring that the types of the data involved in a computation are compatible with the operations to be performed.

In Pascal every item of data is considered to be of some specific type and there are rigid rules concerning how each type may be used. When a program is translated into machine code the compiler checks it to verify that these rules have been followed. For example, the compiler would reject a program which attempted to multiply a **CHAR** value (such as the ampersand symbol '&') by an **INTEGER** value (such as the number 7). Multiplication is simply not a meaningful operation on **CHAR** values.

In practice only radical differences of type are recognized. For instance, in Pascal all **INTEGER** values are treated alike. Adding an **INTEGER** value which represents a population and one which represents a sum of money would *not* be detected as an error by a Pascal compiler, even though the result would not represent any 'fact, observation or idea about the world'. (Pascal does, however, permit finer distinctions of type to be made than most other programming languages. This is a major factor contributing to its popularity.)

A consequence of this is that the data items processed by a program are imperfect representations of the world, because they lack many of the properties of the original information. At best they are more or less approximate *models*. Much of the interest of programming lies in choosing good models of the objects and processes the program is meant to represent, then seeing their behaviour when the program is run on a computer.

2.2 Constants and variables

Some of the data used in a program never change. For example, the ratio of the circumference of a circle to its diameter is approximately 3.14159 and this is an invariable fact. Such data are modelled in a program by *constants*, in other words by stating their values literally. It is often useful to give a symbolic name to a constant. The name can then be used throughout the program whenever the value of the constant is required. A suggestive name such as PI, rather than the obscure 3.14159, makes a program easier to read.

Other data are intrinsically subject to change. For example, in a program summing a list of numbers, the running total changes every time the next item from the list is added to it. Such data are modelled in a program by *variables.*

In programming a variable is best thought of as a *container* for a value. We will speak loosely about 'the value of a variable', but we should really say, in more precise language, 'the value contained in a variable'. Like a physical container a variable may be empty, in which case we will say that its value is *undefined*. Attempting to use an undefined value from an empty variable is one of the most common mistakes in programming. Variables can be both created and destroyed in a program: the value of a newly-created variable is undefined. Once a value has been placed in a variable it stays there until the program deliberately alters it, or until the variable itself is destroyed. Values of different types require variables of corresponding types to hold them. Again, we speak loosely of 'an INTEGER variable' when we really mean 'a variable capable of holding an INTEGER value'.

Like constants, the variables in our programs have names. This is essential, not a convenience as it was with constants. We must be able to refer to specific variables independently of their values, since their values may change. In a program a variable is created by a *declaration*. To declare a variable it is necessary to specify both its type and its name.

The instruction which alters the value of a variable is called an *assignment statement.* An assignment statement specifies a variable and an expression. When it is obeyed the expression is evaluated and the result is copied (assigned) to the variable. There are many other kinds of statement: some of them can be used to change variables, others use the existing values of variables.

More generally, definitions and declarations convey information about data types and data objects to the compiler; whereas statements specify actions to be taken by the computer when the program is obeyed. (The term 'statement' is rather misleading but unfortunately has become universal, for historical reasons. Statements would better be called 'commands' or 'instructions'.)

You may like to think of the various types of data as each having a characteristic shape. Variables would then be thought of as suitably-shaped boxes. We will often represent variables by boxes in this book. Unfortunately it is not practical to print boxes of several shapes, so all our boxes will be rectangular, regardless of type. When we picture a variable as a box, we will label the box with its identifier.

2.3 Definitions and declarations

A constant definition looks like an equation. On the left is the name to be defined, this is followed by the '=' sign, and this is followed in turn by the value to be ascribed to the constant. All of this can be summarized very concisely in pictorial form, by means of a syntax diagram: see Figure 2.1.

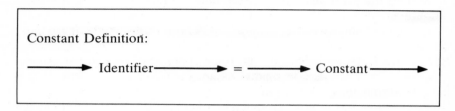

Figure 2.1. Syntax of Constant Definitions

This diagram does not give the syntax of a constant, as that would take us into other matters prematurely.

Several constant definitions may be given, or none. If there are any they must be separated from each other by semicolons, and the complete group must be introduced by the symbol **CONST**.

{The semicolon is widely used in Pascal to form lists of definitions, declarations and statements, so it is wise to be quite clear about its function. The Pascal semicolon does not 'terminate' things, unlike the full stop at the end of this paragraph. Rather, it separates them, more like the commas in this sentence; or the semicolon for that matter. Note that Example 2.1 does not end with a semicolon. Attention to this point will avoid much grief from trivial syntax errors in your programs.}

Example 2.1

```
CONST
  WORKINGDAYS = 5;
  WEEKSPERYEAR = 52;
  PI = 3.14159;
  SPEEDOFLIGHT = 299792.0;
  CMPERINCH = 2.54;
  AMPERSAND = '&';
  ASTERISK = '*'
```

These constant definitions establish two identifiers for integer constants (**WORKINGDAYS** and **WEEKSPERYEAR**), three identifiers for real constants (**PI**, **SPEEDOFLIGHT** and **CMPERINCH**) and two identifiers for character constants (**AMPERSAND** and **ASTERISK**).

There is no ambiguity about the type of a constant identifier. It is the same as the type of the value to the right of the '=' sign and Pascal has been designed so that this type is always obvious.

Variable declarations are a little more complicated than constant definitions and quite different in appearance. The variable declaration part of a program begins with the symbol **VAR**. This is followed by a group of one or more variable declarations, these being separated by semicolons. Each variable declaration consists of a list of identifiers, separated by commas, then a colon, and finally a type. See Figure 2.2 for the syntax

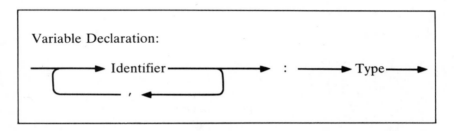

Figure 2.2. Syntax of Variable Declarations

diagram. Again, it would be premature to disclose the syntax of types, so take it on trust that **BOOLEAN, CHAR, INTEGER** and **REAL** are allowable.

{The following is a reliable general rule in Pascal: *within* definitions, declarations and statements, commas are used to separate the components of a list.}

Example 2.2

```
VAR
    WEEKLYPAY, YEARLYPAY : INTEGER;
    RADIUS, CIRCUMFERENCE, ORBIT : REAL;
    PUNCTUATION, INITIAL : CHAR;
    UNTAXED : BOOLEAN
```

Here we declare two **INTEGER** variables (**WEEKLYPAY** and **YEARLY-PAY**), three **REAL** variables (**RADIUS, CIRCUMFERENCE** and **ORBIT**), two **CHAR** variables (**PUNCTUATION** and **INITIAL**) and one **BOOLEAN** variable (**UNTAXED**). In terms of our 'boxes', we can picture the effect of these declarations as follows, where the question marks act as reminders that the values of newly-declared variables are undefined:

WEEKLYPAY ☐ ?   YEARLYPAY ☐ ?

CIRCUMFERENCE ☐ ?   RADIUS ☐ ?   ORBIT ☐ ?

PUNCTUATION ☐ ?   INITIAL ☐ ?

UNTAXED ☐ ?

2.4 Assignment statements

A value is copied into a variable when the computer obeys an assignment statement. Pascal assignment statements have a simple syntax. On the left is specified the variable whose contents are to be replaced, following this is the ':=' sign, and on the right is an expression whose value is to be assigned to the variable. This reads naturally if the ':=' sign is pronounced as 'becomes equal to'. Figure 2.3 contains the syntax diagram. (An expression is a formula by which a value is computed. Its syntax is defined fully in Appendix 1.3, but it is rather complicated, and it would be inadvisable to study that until more of the background has been covered. We begin by looking at **INTEGER** expressions in Chapter 3.)

Assignment Statement:

⟶ Variable ⟶ := ⟶ Expression ⟶

Figure 2.3. Syntax of Assignment Statements

Example 2.3

Using the constants and variables introduced in Examples 2.1 and 2.2, the assignment statements:

```
WEEKLYPAY := 100;
YEARLYPAY := WEEKLYPAY * WEEKSPERYEAR;
UNTAXED := FALSE;
INITIAL := 'W'
```

(where '*' is the multiplication sign of Pascal) will leave the values of the variables as follows:

WEEKLYPAY	100		YEARLYPAY	5200	

CIRCUMFERENCE	?	RADIUS	?	ORBIT	?

PUNCTUATION	?	INITIAL	'W'

UNTAXED	FALSE

Now consider the curious-looking assignment statement:

WEEKLYPAY := WEEKLYPAY + 5

This assignment statement takes the *current* value of **WEEKLYPAY**, adds 5, and finally assigns the result to **WEEKLYPAY**. Thus the effect of this assignment statement is to increase the value of **WEEKLYPAY** by 5:

WEEKLYPAY	105		YEARLYPAY	5200	

There are two important points to note here.

(a) When a value is assigned to a variable, its previous value (if any) is lost forever.

(b) The computer does *not* automatically change the value of **YEARLY-PAY** when we change the value of **WEEKLYPAY**. The computer will obey only *explicit* instructions. If we wish the value of **YEARLYPAY** to be changed accordingly, we must ensure that the assignment statement **YEARLYPAY := WEEKLYPAY * WEEKSPERYEAR** is obeyed *again*.

It is important not to be misled by the superficial similarity of assignment statements and constant definitions. The latter are static, giving a name to a fixed value (at 'compile time'), and have no effect when the program is obeyed by the computer. Assignment statements on the other hand are dynamic. Each time an assignment is performed by the computer (at 'run time') the value copied into the variable may be different. It is precisely to point out this crucial difference that the ':=' sign is used in assignments in place of the '=' sign.

Type checking is particularly effective at finding errors in assignments. The type-compatibility rule for assignments states: a value may be assigned only to a variable of the *same type*. Thus we are guaranteed that the value always 'fits' its container. For example, we can assign the value 100, but not **AMPERSAND** nor the contents of **UNTAXED**, to the **INTEGER** variable **WEEKLYPAY**. (The rule is actually more complicated than this. The simplified version above will be adequate for the present.)

Exercises 2

2.1. Many properties of a data item are either **TRUE** or **FALSE** (i.e. themselves values of type **BOOLEAN**). For example, the property 'is positive' is **TRUE** of the **REAL** value 1.2 but **FALSE** of the **REAL** values 0.0 and −1.2; the property 'has a non-zero fraction part' is **TRUE** when applied to the **REAL** value 1.414 but **FALSE** when applied to the **REAL** value 5.0. Write down at least three such properties (a) of **INTEGER** values; and (b) of **CHAR** values.

2.2. What is likely to be the most important type in a program (a) to compute spacecraft trajectories; (b) to edit an author's manuscript; and (c) to calculate bank balances?

2.3. If I is an **INTEGER** variable, C is a **CHAR** variable, R is a **REAL** variable, and B is a **BOOLEAN** variable, which of the following assignment statements are legal?

(a) I := 1
(b) I := R
(c) I := '&'
(d) C := 1
(e) C := I
(f) C := '&'
(g) B := FALSE
(h) B := C
(i) B := 1
(j) R := B
(k) R := '&'
(l) R := 1.0

3
The data type INTEGER

3.1 INTEGER values

The INTEGER type in Pascal allows us to represent, store and process integer (whole) numbers. In theory the set of integer numbers extends outward from zero to numbers with arbitrarily large positive or negative values. But this is a finite world, modelled by an even more finite computer, and infinite sets must be cut down to a practical size. Pascal recognizes this by providing, automatically, a constant identifier MAXINT, whose value is the largest number which can be held in an INTEGER variable. Typical values of MAXINT would be 32767 on a minicomputer and 2147483647 on a large computer. Indeed, the INTEGER type consists of all the integer values in the range:

$$-\text{MAXINT}, \ldots \ldots, -1, 0, +1, \ldots \ldots, +\text{MAXINT}$$

(MAXINT is an example of a *predefined constant*; you can use it without having to define it yourself.)

Arithmetic on INTEGER values will be performed correctly by the computer if all the operands, and all the intermediate results, lie in the range from −MAXINT to +MAXINT. If the allowable range is exceeded the result of the arithmetic is unpredictable. This is called *overflow* and the program must be considered to have failed. When an overflow occurs, on some computers, an error message is output and the program stops at once. Other computers do not detect overflow, so that the program may generate worthless results without any warning being given. Thus overflow is a serious matter, and it is the programmer's responsibility to try to avoid it.

INTEGER numbers are written as a sequence of decimal digits, optionally preceded by a sign: '−' indicates a negative number, '+' or no sign indicates a positive number. See Example 3.1.

Example 3.1

```
CONST
  POSITIVE = +1;
  NEGATIVE = −POSITIVE;
  BIGGEST = MAXINT;
  SMALLEST = −MAXINT;
  EMERGENCY = 999;
  DECREMENT = −15
```

Note that the value specified in a constant definition may itself be a previously-defined constant identifier, or its negative.

3.2 INTEGER expressions

From two INTEGER values we can calculate a new INTEGER value by addition, subtraction, multiplication or division. Pascal uses the conventional notation for arithmetic operators, modified to suit the computer's character set. Addition is denoted by '+', subtraction by '−', multiplication by '*' and division by the symbol DIV. It is also possible to obtain the remainder from a division, using the symbol MOD (short for 'modulo') in place of DIV.

Dividing one integer number by another does not always give an integral result: there may be a fractional part. To ensure that DIV always yields an integer any fractional part in the result is discarded. For example:

```
(+7) DIV (+2) =+3
(−7) DIV (+2) =−3
(+7) DIV (−2) =−3
(−7) DIV (−2) =+3
```

It is an error to attempt to divide any number by zero. It is also an error to attempt to compute a remainder using MOD, for a negative or zero divisor. The expression x MOD y, where y is greater than zero, yields a value for the remainder which is greater than or equal to zero and less than y. This is the smallest number which, subtracted from x, makes it an integral multiple of y. For example:

```
(+7) MOD 4 =+3
(−7) MOD 4 =+1
```

Multiplication and division by the same number do not always cancel out for INTEGER values, because DIV drops any fractional part. Thus the order in which they are done can affect the result. For example:

```
(7 DIV 2) * 2 = 3 * 2 = 6
(7 * 2) DIV 2 = 14 DIV 2 = 7
```

Similarly, it is not possible to cancel out common factors in multipliers and divisors:

(128 **DIV** 20) * 15 = 6   * 15 = 90
(128 **DIV**   4) *   3 = 32 *   3 = 96

The normal algebraic conventions apply in Pascal, so multiplications and divisions in an expression take priority over additions and subtractions. Thus in the expression A+B*C the multiplication of B and C is done first and A is added to the result. If this is not what is wanted then parentheses, '(' and ')', can be used to override the priority rules. For example in (A+B)*C the addition of A and B is done first and the result is multiplied by C.

It is allowable to prefix a sign to the first term of an expression. The '−' sign is the negation operator: the value of $-x$ is the negative of x. The '+' sign is the identity operator: the value of $+x$ is the same as the value of x, so the '+' may always be omitted. Multiplication and division take priority over identity and negation, which have the same priority as addition and subtraction. For example the expressions −X+4*Y and +4*Y−X are both equal to the expression (4*Y)−X.

Pascal has no operator for raising one number to the power of another, chiefly because it is difficult to specify such an operator in a way that is both simple and consistent with the type rules. In partial compensation SQR(x), a function which returns the square of x, is provided. It is often more efficient to evaluate SQR(x) than ($x*x$), particularly if x is a complicated expression.

One other useful function is ABS(x), which returns the absolute value of x. That is, if x is negative ABS(x) equals $-x$, otherwise ABS(x) equals x. For example, ABS(−5) and ABS(5) both give +5.

SQR and ABS are examples of *standard functions*, which are provided in Pascal to augment the more common operators.

Example 3.2

On each of the following lines is a group of three equivalent expressions. The first in each group is written in the simplest way possible, the rest show alternative formulations. As these examples illustrate, the sparing use of parentheses may clarify a complicated expression and overuse may have the opposite effect. Judicious spacing further improves readability.

−X	(−X)	(−(X))
X+Y	(X+Y)	((X)+(Y))
X*Y+Z	(X*Y)+Z	X*Y + Z
X MOD ABS(Y)*Z	X MOD ABS(Y) * Z	(X MOD ABS(Y)) * Z
SQR(SQR(X))	SQR(X*X)	X*X*X*X

Because of the danger of overflow, it is not always desirable to rearrange an expression into a mathematically equivalent form. For example, the expressions (A−B)*(A+B) and SQR(A)−SQR(B) are mathematically equal, but the latter is much more prone to overflow when A and B are large.

Exercises 3

3.1. Write constant definitions for the INTEGER constants DAYSIN-WEEK, INCHESPERFOOT (or CMPERMETRE) and YARDSPERMILE (or METRESPERKM).

3.2. Write declarations for INTEGER variables named GROSSPAY, TAX, UNIONDUES and NETTPAY.

3.3. What are the resulting values of these variables when the following assignment statements are obeyed in sequence? Draw suitable box diagrams.

UNIONDUES := 20; GROSSPAY := 4900; TAX := GROSSPAY DIV 3;
NETTPAY := GROSSPAY − TAX − UNIONDUES

3.4. Write assignment statements to calculate (a) UNIONDUES at £10 plus a hundredth of GROSSPAY, (b) TAX at a quarter of GROSSPAY, and (c) NETTPAY, for any value of GROSSPAY. Draw suitable box diagrams.

3.5. Write declarations and statements to calculate the minimum number of bank-notes and coins needed to pay out SUM in cash, assuming SUM is given as a multiple of the smallest unit of currency. Draw suitable box diagrams for each stage of the calculation.

3.6*. A non-negative number greater than MAXINT can be held in a computer as *two* INTEGER values. For example, if MAXINT is 32767 we can represent a number, n, with value up to 100 million, in the form of two INTEGER variables NM and NL, such that:

$$n = 10000*NM + NL$$

where NM = n DIV 10000 gives the most significant digits and NL = n MOD 10000 gives the least significant digits. Suppose two large numbers, x and y, are stored in this way in the INTEGER variables XM, XL and YM, YL. Write statements to place in ZM, ZL (a) the sum, (b) the difference and (c) the product of x and y. In what circumstances can overflow occur in your Pascal statements?

4
Towards the complete program

4.1 Input and output

So far we have seen how to write constant definitions, variable declarations and assignment statements. The latter can be used to compute new values from constants and from values which have been computed previously. These program elements allow us to specify computations of a restricted kind, but they provide no means to vary the data on which the computations are performed.

Example 4.1

The following statements, obeyed in sequence, compute the total number of seconds since midnight, given that the time of day is 9:12:30:

```
H :=   9;
M := 12;
S := 30;
TOTALSECS := 3600*H + 60*M + S
```

The fourth statement is quite general, but if we wish to repeat the computation for some other time of day, we have to modify the first three statements of the 'program' itself.

Now, the whole point of programming a computer is to be able to write a program *once*, and then make it work with *many* different sets of data. In our example, we would prefer the values assigned to H, M and S somehow to be supplied *on each occasion the program is run*, rather than being part of the program itself and therefore fixed. This would allow us to supply different values on each run.

Another limitation of our 'program' is that the computed value is simply placed in a store location (TOTALSECS), where it remains invisible. Thus we also need a means of getting results out of the computer.

The separation of a program and its data is a fundamental idea in computing. We should perceive a program as a general set of instructions for performing some computation. A program can be run many times, each time being supplied with different input data. The individual data items supplied in this way are read into the computer in response to explicit input instructions in the program; and results of the computation are written out, in some suitable form, in response to explicit output instructions. All computers are equipped with input devices which allow data to be read by a program, and with output devices which allow data to be written.

In some computer systems the input data is prepared in advance by the computer user, perhaps by punching the data on cards. These cards are read by a card-reader when the program is run on the computer. The program's output is printed on paper, by a line-printer, and the printed results are returned to the user after the program has completed its run. This is the *batch* mode of computing.

Alternatively the computer user might have a terminal connected to the computer. *While his program is running*, the user types the input data on the terminal's keyboard. This data is read by the program, and the program's output returns directly to the terminal, where it is either printed on paper or displayed on a screen. The terminal acts as a combination of an input device (the keyboard) and an output device (the printer or screen). This is the *interactive* mode of computing.

Whatever mode you use, your programs will contain input instructions which cause data to be read from some input device, and output instructions which cause data (results) to be written to some output device.

4.2 Input of integers

The role of an input instruction is to read an item of data and store it in a variable, so that subsequently it can be used in some computation. In Pascal this role is performed by the *READ statement*.

Example 4.1 (continued)

We can vary the data on which our 'program' works by replacing the first three assignment statements by READ statements:

```
READ (H);
READ (M);
READ (S);
TOTALSECS := 3600*H + 60*M + S
```

Suppose we supply the following input data:

12 25 0

The input data is read from left to right. The statement READ(H) causes the data item '12' to be read and the value 12 to be assigned to H; then the statement READ(M) causes the data item '25' to be read and the value 25 to be assigned to M; then the statement READ(S) causes the data item '0' to be read and the value 0 to be assigned to S. Thus in this case the 'program' computes the number of seconds from midnight to 12:25:0. We can make the 'program' deal with a different time of day simply by running it again with different input data.

In general, the effect of the READ statement READ(V), where V is an INTEGER variable, is to scan forwards through the input data, skipping any blank characters, until a data item is found; the value of this data item (which must be an integer *number*, possibly signed) is then assigned to V.

The three consecutive READ statements in Example 4.1 could be combined into a single READ statement with the same effect:

```
READ (H, M, S);
TOTALSECS := 3600*H + 60*M + S
```

H, M and S are *parameters* of the READ statement. A READ statement may have any number of parameters, all of which must be variables, and for each of these variables one data item is read.

4.3 Output of integers

The role of an output instruction is to get results out of the computer in some suitable form, e.g. printed on paper or displayed on a screen. In Pascal this role is performed by the *WRITE statement*.

Example 4.2

Continuing from Example 4.1, we could write out the total number of seconds since midnight by the following WRITE statement:

```
WRITE (TOTALSECS)
```

The following statements, executed in sequence, will read the number of hours, minutes and seconds since midnight, compute the total number of seconds since midnight, and write out all four numbers:

```
READ (H, M, S);
TOTALSECS := 3600*H + 60*M + S;
WRITE (H, M, S, TOTALSECS)
```

For example, if the input data is:

9 12 30

then the output would look like this:

   9   12   30 33150

Observe that a WRITE statement, like a READ statement, may have any number of parameters. However, each parameter of WRITE may be an *expression*, not necessarily a simple variable, and it is the value of this expression which is written.

Example 4.3

Assuming that M and N are INTEGER variables, the following statement writes the values of M and N followed by their sum, difference and product:

WRITE (M, N, M+N, M−N, M*N)

4.4 The complete program

To build a complete Pascal program, we must collect together all the necessary definitions, declarations and statements.

Example 4.4

Here is an example of a complete Pascal program which performs a simple tax calculation:

```
PROGRAM COMPUTETAX (INPUT, OUTPUT);

   (* This program computes a taxpayer's tax payment
      for a year, given as input the taxpayer's annual
      income and number of children. It is assumed
      that tax is calculated at one-third of income
      less tax allowances, where the allowances consist
      of a personal allowance of £5000 plus a child
      allowance of £1000 per child. *)

CONST
   PERSONALALLOWANCE = 5000;
   CHILDALLOWANCE    = 1000;
VAR
   NUMBEROFCHILDREN              : INTEGER;
   INCOME, TAXABLEINCOME, TAX: INTEGER;
```

```
BEGIN
READ (INCOME, NUMBEROFCHILDREN);
TAXABLEINCOME := INCOME - PERSONALALLOWANCE -
                NUMBEROFCHILDREN * CHILDALLOWANCE;
   (* ... taxable income is income less allowances *)
TAX := TAXABLEINCOME DIV 3;
   (* ... tax is calculated as a whole number of £ *)
WRITE (INCOME, TAXABLEINCOME, TAX, INCOME - TAX)
END.
```

This program first reads the taxpayer's income (in £) and number of children; then it computes the taxable income and tax; and finally it writes the income, taxable income, tax and nett income after tax. For example, if the input data is:

11000 4

then the written output from the program would look like this:

11000   2000   666 10334

This example illustrates all the parts of a complete program.

(1) 'PROGRAM COMPUTETAX' gives an identifier, COMPUTETAX, to the program.
(2) '(INPUT, OUTPUT)' specifies that this program performs both input and output. INPUT and OUTPUT are called *program parameters*. Program parameters will be treated fully in Chapter 17. Meanwhile, assume that INPUT must be present if the program reads any input, and that OUTPUT must be present if the program writes any output.
(3) The program parameters are followed by the program's *declarative part*. This consists of a group of constant definitions headed by CONST, followed by a group of variable declarations headed by VAR.
(4) The words BEGIN and END enclose the program's *statement part*. This contains a sequence of statements, separated by semicolons, and these statements are obeyed one after another in *exactly* their order of occurrence. The period following END marks the end of the program text.

Each piece of text enclosed between the special brackets '(*' and '*)' is called a *comment*. Although part of the program text, these comments are entirely ignored by the compiler and are included only to help explain the program to a human reader. A comment may be placed anywhere within a Pascal program text, except in the middle of a symbol such as a word or number.

The order of the program parts is summarized by the syntax diagrams of Figures 4.1, 4.2 and 4.3. Notice that CONST would be omitted in the

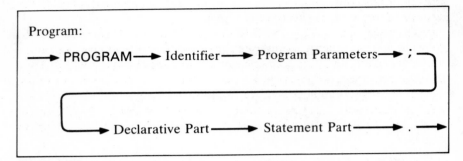

Figure 4.1. Syntax of Programs

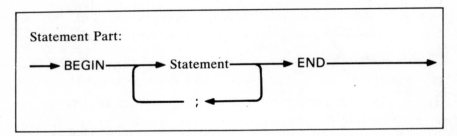

Figure 4.2. Syntax of Statement Parts

Figure 4.3. Syntax of Declarative Parts (simplified)

absence of any constant definitions, and that VAR would be omitted in the absence of any variable declarations.

PROGRAM, CONST, VAR, BEGIN and END are all *reserved words*. They are so called because, although they look like identifiers, they must not be chosen as identifiers for constants, variables or anything else. They have special, fixed, meanings in Pascal, implied by their occurrence in the syntax diagrams. Pascal has thirty-five reserved words in all, which are listed in Appendix 2.1; they include the operators DIV and MOD introduced in Chapter 3 (but not READ and WRITE, which are ordinary identifiers).

4.5 Programming style

You probably found the first complete program, in Example 4.4, easy to understand. Partly this was because the program was very short, with only four statements. (By comparison, some programs have been written which contain more than 100000 statements!) Another reason was that the program was deliberately written in a style intended to make it readable.

Here are the main features of good programming style, as illustrated by Example 4.4.

(a) The layout of the program text has been designed for easy reading. Each constant definition, each variable declaration and each statement is on a separate line. The symbols within each line are well spaced out. The constant definitions and variable declarations are indented to make the words CONST and VAR stand out. The program text is 'paragraphed' by blank lines separating its major parts.

(b) All the identifiers have been chosen to suggest the significance of the data they represent. For example, the variable NUMBEROFCHIL-DREN is clearly intended to hold a value which is the number of children.

(c) Comments are used in the program text to summarize the function of the program and to explain how it performs its function.

It must be emphasized that these stylistic features are intended solely for the benefit of the human reader. The layout of the program text is of no concern to the compiler (except that consecutive words and numbers must be spaced apart, just as in ordinary English: BEGIN A:=B END is interpreted very differently from BEGINA:=BEND). Comments also are entirely ignored by the compiler. Finally, any significance suggested to the human reader by an identifier like NUMBEROFCHILDREN is quite lost on the compiler (which understands no English); the compiler would accept the program just as well if another identifier such as N were used instead.

Example 4.5

As an illustration of *bad* programming style, let us rewrite the program of Example 4.4 without concern for layout, without comments, and with short meaningless identifiers.

```
PROGRAM COMPUTETAX(INPUT,OUTPUT);CONST
PA=5000;CA=1000;VAR N:
INTEGER;I,TI,T:INTEGER;BEGIN READ(I,N);TI:=I−PA−N*CA;T:=
TI DIV 3;WRITE(I,TI,T,I−T)END.
```

This version of the program is certainly much more concise than the original version, and moreover it will produce exactly the same results as the original when run on a computer. Its only drawback, but a major one, is that it is difficult and unpleasant for human readers.

Throughout this book a reasonably consistent programming style has been adopted. We do not suggest that you should imitate this style slavishly; feel free to develop your own style. What is important is that all your programs should be written in a style which makes them easily understood, by other programmers as well as by yourself.

4.6 Formatted input and output

Examine the sample output from the program of Example 4.4:

```
11000   2000    666 10334
```

What would you make of this output if you had never seen the program which produced it? It is just a line of numbers with no indication of their significance.

Since computer output is intended ultimately to be read by ordinary people (i.e. non-programmers), it is essential that the output should be self-explanatory, with appropriate headings, captions, etc. For this purpose we need a means of writing text as well as numbers. In Pascal we can cause a piece of text to be written by enclosing it in apostrophes and supplying it as a parameter in a **WRITE** statement. This text is written out, without the apostrophes, when the **WRITE** statement is obeyed.

Example 4.6

The statement:

```
WRITE ('TAX DUE IS £', TAX)
```

would produce output like this:

TAX DUE IS £   666

The text enclosed in apostrophes is called a *character string*, or simply a *string*. If the string itself is to contain an apostrophe, this apostrophe must be doubled to distinguish it from the apostrophe which ends the string. Thus the statement:

WRITE('THAT''S THE QUESTION')

would write the following output:

THAT'S THE QUESTION

The output in Example 4.6 still looks rather strange, because of the blank characters between the currency sign and the number. These are present because each number is written in a *field* of a certain width, and if the number has too few digits then the field is filled with blank characters to the left of the number. We can control the layout by specifying explicitly what field width we require for any parameter in a WRITE statement.

If no field width is specified explicitly, some default field width will be assumed. For an INTEGER parameter the default is typically 6 spaces (as above), but this default will vary from one compiler to another. For a string parameter the default field width is always just enough to accommodate the entire string.

Example 4.7

We could modify the WRITE statement of Example 4.6 as follows:

WRITE ('TAX DUE IS £', TAX : 4)

The suffix ':4' of the parameter 'TAX:4' specifies that the value of TAX is to be written in a field of 4 spaces. Now we can expect output like this:

TAX DUE IS £   666

If we replace the WRITE statement of Example 4.4 by the following:

WRITE 'INCOME: £',   INCOME:5,   '   TAXABLE: £',
          TAXABLEINCOME:5,   '   TAX: £',   TAX:5,   '   NETT: £',
          (INCOME−TAX):5)

then we can expect output like this:

INCOME: £11000   TAXABLE: £ 2000   TAX: £   666   NETT: £10334

Replacing each ':5' by ':1' makes the output look like this:

INCOME: £11000   TAXABLE: £2000   TAX: £666   NETT: £10334

since all the numbers are too large to fit into a field of only one space.

The last part of Example 4.7 shows that when you specify a field width too small for the number being written, the number is written in full but without any preceding blanks.

All data written by WRITE statements, whether numbers or strings or anything else, are written on a single line, as illustrated by Example 4.7. If we want to write output on *several* lines, we must use the *WRITELN statement* which forces subsequent output on to a new line.

Example 4.8

If we replace the WRITE statement of Example 4.4 by the following statements:

```
WRITE ('INCOME                    £', INCOME:5);
WRITELN;
WRITELN;
WRITE ('TAXABLE INCOME            £', TAXABLEINCOME:5);
WRITELN;
WRITE ('TAX DUE                   £', TAX:5);
WRITELN;
WRITE ('NETT INCOME               £', (INCOME−TAX):5);
WRITELN
```

then we can expect output like this:

```
INCOME                £11000

TAXABLE INCOME        £ 2000
TAX DUE               £  666
NETT INCOME           £10334
```

Note that the effect of two consecutive WRITELN statements is to leave a completely blank line.

We may also consider the input data to consist of a number of lines. (If the input data is punched on cards, then each card is considered to be a line of data.) This point is of no concern when using the READ statement to read numbers, since READ will automatically move on to a new line of input data if there is no more data on the current line. Thus program COMPUTETAX would happily accept its input data on two lines:

```
11000
4
```

For some purposes it is desirable to force the input data to be read a line at a time. For this purpose the *READLN statement* is useful: it causes the unread part of the current line of input data to be skipped, so any subsequent input will be taken from the next line.

Example 4.9

Consider the statements:

```
READ (NUMBEROFSHEEP); READLN;
READ (NUMBEROFGOATS); READLN
```

where **NUMBEROFSHEEP** and **NUMBEROFGOATS** are **INTEGER** variables. If the input data is:

```
10 SHEEP
 4 GOATS
```

then the values 10 and 4 will be read and assigned to the two variables; the textual data on both lines will be ignored. If the **READLN** statements were omitted, on the other hand, the second **READ** statement would fail, by attempting to interpret 'SHEEP' as an integer number.

A last word about input and output. The input data is always read from left to right within each line, and from one line to the next. Once a data item has been read, it cannot subsequently be re-read. {By comparison, a person reading a book can go back and re-read any passage he wishes.} Likewise, output data is written from left to right within each line, and from one line to the next, Once data has been written, it is not possible to go back and erase it, nor to write some more data above it. {By comparison, a person writing on paper can erase any part of his previous work, or write from the bottom of the page to the top, if he wishes.} These restrictions, which reflect the properties of the common computer input and output devices, have an important influence on many programs, as we shall see in later examples.

Exercises 4

4.1. Show what output you would expect from program **COMPUTETAX** if the following input data were supplied:

```
8000   6
```

4.2. Consider the following program:

```
PROGRAM BALANCEOFPAYMENTS (INPUT, OUTPUT);

(* This program computes a country's trading balance, given its
   import and export bills and its balance on 'invisible' trade. *)
```

```
VAR
  IMPORTS, EXPORTS, VISIBLEBALANCE,
    INVISIBLEBALANCE, TOTALBALANCE: INTEGER;
BEGIN
READ (IMPORTS, EXPORTS);
VISIBLEBALANCE := IMPORTS - EXPORTS;
READ (INVISIBLEBALANCE);
TOTALBALANCE := VISIBLEBALANCE + INVISIBLEBALANCE;
  (* ... positive for a surplus, negative for a deficit *)
WRITE (' IMPORTS EXPORTS VISIBLE INVISIBLE TOTAL');
WRITELN;
WRITE ('       £M      £M     £M       £M     £M');
WRITELN;
WRITELN;
WRITE (IMPORTS:10, EXPORTS:10,
  VISIBLEBALANCE:10, INVISIBLEBALANCE:10, TOTALBALANCE:10);
WRITELN
END.
```

Show exactly what output this program would produce, if the following input data were supplied:

(a)
    9120   9670   750
(b)
    555   405
      −12

4.3. Write down statements which output your name and address in the form you would print them on an envelope.

4.4. Write a program which reads a number and which outputs the number together with its square, cube and fourth power.

4.5. Write a program which reads three integers representing a date (day, month and year), and which outputs the date neatly in the form 'day/month/year' (writing only the last two digits of the year).

Programming exercises 4

4.6. Write a program which reads the number of seconds since midnight and outputs the time in the form 'hours:minutes:seconds', allowing two digits for each component of the time. Test your program by running it several times, with various numbers in the range 0 to 86399 as input data.

4.7. A business employs four grades of staff, of which grade A staff are paid monthly and grades B, C and D are paid weekly. Four lines of input data are supplied: the first line contains the number of grade A staff and their monthly pay rate; the remaining lines contain the number of staff and the weekly pay rate in each of grades B, C and D. Write a program which reads this data and outputs the total weekly pay bill, the total monthly pay bill and the total annual pay bill, with appropriate captions. Test your program by running it at least with the following input data:

```
 5  1500  A
10   150  B
20   200  C
50   125  D
```

5
The data type BOOLEAN

5.1 Conditions in programming

Valuable results can certainly be obtained with the simple statements introduced in the previous chapters: the assignment, reading and writing of **INTEGER** values. However these limited means effectively restrict the computer to the role of a calculator. For most applications the program being obeyed by the computer must be able to vary the course of the computation. It is sometimes necessary to select one of several alternative actions, depending on some stated conditions. At other times it is necessary to repeat an action over and over again, so long as some continuation condition is satisfied.

Take as an example a program which is processing a company's payroll file and printing each employee's payslip. The calculation of an employee's tax deduction illustrates the need for selective action, as the tax payable might depend on gross pay (with different rates of tax at different income levels), marital status, number of children, etc. To take account of these factors the program must be able to adapt its behaviour to the circumstances of the employee. Repetition is also needed: the program must be able to repeat the same calculation for every employee, stopping when all the payslips have been printed.

To make full use of the speed, reliability and flexibility of the computer in applications such as this we must have a way of expressing *in the program* conditions which the computer is to test.

Most of the conditions encountered in programming are very simple in nature: either they hold or they do not. If a condition holds it has the value **TRUE**. Otherwise it has the value **FALSE**. **TRUE** and **FALSE** are constant identifiers denoting the only two values of the **BOOLEAN** type.

The name **BOOLEAN** commemorates George Boole (1815–1864) who first placed the study of logic on a sound mathematical basis. His book *The Laws of Thought* described an algebra of logical values, now called Boolean Algebra, which underlies the manipulation of **BOOLEAN** values in the same way that the conventional algebra of arithmetic underlies the **INTEGER** type. To make progress in the study of programming a good understanding of the elements of Boolean Algebra is vital. Do not despair!

As you will discover in the following sections, Boolean Algebra is largely a formal restatement of common sense.

5.2 Comparisons

The most familiar way of computing a **BOOLEAN** value is by a *comparison*. In Pascal the values to be compared may be of any suitable type. It is not generally possible to compare values of different types, nor would it make any sense to do so. For example, it makes no sense to ask whether a **CHAR** value (such as the letter 'A') is equal to an **INTEGER** value (such as the number 9). For the present, take it that any two **INTEGER** values or any two **BOOLEAN** values can be compared.

The normal arithmetical rules for comparing signed numbers apply to **INTEGER** values, so that the comparisons −1<6, 100>99 and −23<−20 all have the value **TRUE**. Similarly, 7<3, −44>−37 and 13582<9 all have the value **FALSE**. The result of comparisons such as X=Y and A+B<C will, of course, depend on the values of X, Y, A, B and C.

Comparing **BOOLEAN** values is an unusual operation, but it can sometimes provide a very elegant formulation of a complicated condition. This is discussed in Section 5.5.

A full range of comparison operators is available in Pascal. Unfortunately several of the conventional mathematical symbols are absent from the character sets of most computers. To meet this problem the following notational conventions are used:

=	means 'is equal to'
<>	means 'is not equal to'
<	means 'is less than'
<=	means 'is less than or equal to'
>=	means 'is greater than or equal to'
>	means 'is greater than'

The expressions introduced in Chapter 3, and all expressions other than comparisons, are more correctly called simple expressions. An expression is either a simple expression or a comparison (see Figure 5.1). This syntax has two important consequences.

Firstly, comparison operators have the lowest priority of all operators in Pascal. Thus the expression 2*A<>B+C is entirely equivalent to the expression (2*A)<>(B+C).

Secondly, the convenient notations X<Y<Z, A>B>C, and so on, are not allowed in Pascal. We shall see in the next section how a double comparison such as **FREEZING<TEMPERATURE<BOILING** can be expressed properly.

It must be clearly understood that, in a program, a comparison makes the computer produce a TRUE or FALSE result. When we write a comparison such as TEMPERATURE>BOILING we are *not* stating a fact.

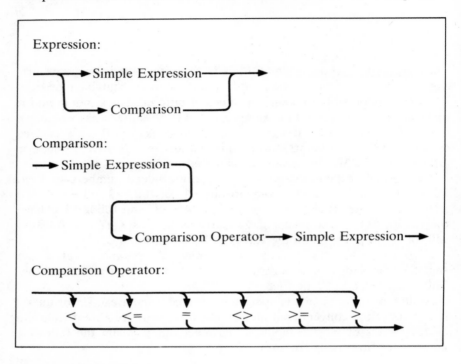

Figure 5.1. Syntax of Expressions

Rather, we are defining a condition which may or may not hold and which must be tested at that point in the program.

5.3 The BOOLEAN operators

It is often necessary to be able to construct BOOLEAN expressions which involve more than a single comparison. The operators AND, OR and NOT allow us to express a condition of any complexity, along lines similar to the construction of INTEGER expressions. (AND, OR and NOT are all reserved words.)

The operator AND takes two BOOLEAN operands and yields a BOOLEAN result which has the value TRUE if and only if both operands are TRUE. Definitions of BOOLEAN operators are most easily given in the form of a 'truth table' listing all possible operand values and the corresponding results. For the operator AND the truth table is:

x	y	x AND y
FALSE	FALSE	FALSE
FALSE	TRUE	FALSE
TRUE	FALSE	FALSE
TRUE	TRUE	TRUE

The word 'or' has two meanings in English. In the inclusive sense we have phrases such as 'These clothes are suitable for summer or winter wear.' In the exclusive sense we have 'Either the world is flat or it is round.' The inclusive meaning has been adopted in Boolean Algebra and hence in Pascal. The operator OR takes two BOOLEAN operands and yields a BOOLEAN result which has the value TRUE if at least one of the operands is TRUE:

x	y	x OR y
FALSE	FALSE	FALSE
FALSE	TRUE	TRUE
TRUE	FALSE	TRUE
TRUE	TRUE	TRUE

The operator NOT takes a single BOOLEAN operand and yields a BOOLEAN result which is the opposite of the operand. For NOT the truth table is particularly simple:

x	NOT x
FALSE	TRUE
TRUE	FALSE

Using AND we can recast the double comparison of the previous section in an acceptable form, as:

(FREEZING<TEMPERATURE) AND (TEMPERATURE<BOILING)

Note that the parentheses are necessary here, the reason being that the comparison operators are of lower priority than AND. Without parentheses we would have:

FREEZING < TEMPERATURE AND TEMPERATURE < BOILING

which is equivalent to:

FREEZING < (TEMPERATURE AND TEMPERATURE) < BOILING

This is meaningless, because the operands of AND must be BOOLEAN, and syntactically incorrect, because the double comparison has been inadvertently reintroduced. To avoid such errors, comparisons used as operands of AND, OR and NOT must always be parenthesized in Pascal.

5.4 Using BOOLEAN data

BOOLEAN data may be used in all the ways previously described for INTEGER data. BOOLEAN constants may be defined, for example:

FOREVER = FALSE

BOOLEAN variables may be declared, for example:

ISVOTER, ISPEER,
ISPRISONER, ISINSANE: BOOLEAN;

BOOLEAN expressions may be computed and their values assigned to BOOLEAN variables, for example:

ISVOTER := (AGE>18) AND
            NOT (ISPEER OR ISPRISONER OR ISINSANE)

and BOOLEAN values may be output by means of WRITE, for example:

WRITE (ISVOTER)

The effect of writing a BOOLEAN value is, naturally enough, to write either 'TRUE' or 'FALSE'.

We rely on the internal consistency of Pascal to avoid much tedious reworking of these ideas in the new context. Unfortunately, there is one minor restriction in Standard Pascal: READ cannot be used to read BOOLEAN values. Although a nuisance, this does not create insuperable difficulties.

Refer to the collected syntax diagrams of Appendix 1.3 to see how BOOLEAN operators fit into the syntax of expressions. The following are some of the most important consequences.

Firstly, AND has the same priority as '*', OR has the same priority as '+', and NOT has the highest priority of all operators in Pascal. Contrast the arithmetic expression $-A*B+C$, which is equivalent to $(-(A*B))+C$, with the BOOLEAN expression NOT A AND B OR C, which is equivalent to ((NOT A) AND B) OR C.

Secondly, parentheses may be included to override these priorities and to clarify complicated expressions. For example, A AND B OR C AND D is equivalent to (A AND B) OR (C AND D).

Thirdly, any of the following may stand by itself as a BOOLEAN expression: a BOOLEAN constant, a BOOLEAN variable, or a BOOLEAN function.

A useful standard function is ODD, which takes an INTEGER parameter, yielding **TRUE** if the parameter is an odd number and **FALSE** otherwise. In fact **ODD**(x) is equivalent to $((x)$ **MOD** $2<>0)$.

Example 5.1

The following program writes out the truth table for the **BOOLEAN** expression **A AND NOT B**.

```
PROGRAM TRUTHTABLE (OUTPUT);

VAR
   A, B: BOOLEAN;

BEGIN
WRITE ('A       B       A AND NOT B'); WRITELN;
WRITELN;
A := FALSE; B := FALSE;
WRITE (A, B, A AND NOT B); WRITELN;
B := TRUE;
WRITE (A, B, A AND NOT B); WRITELN;
A := TRUE; B := FALSE;
WRITE (A, B, A AND NOT B'; WRITELN;
B := TRUE;
WRITE (A, B, A AND NOT B); WRITELN
END (* TRUTHTABLE *).
```

5.5 The rules of Boolean Algebra

{This section may be omitted on a first reading.}

There are many rules, or 'laws', defining relationships between **NOT**, **AND** and **OR** which are of importance in formulating, simplifying and understanding **BOOLEAN** expressions. Several of these rules are closely analogous to rules in the algebra of arithmetic, which may be helpful in grasping their significance. Others have no helpful analogy.

The laws of Boolean Algebra are summarized below, the corresponding rules of arithmetic being given where possible. The symbol '$\equiv$' means 'is equivalent to'. In the cases which seem strange, it is a good idea to construct truth tables and so demonstrate their validity.

Redundancy laws

(R1) x **AND FALSE** $\equiv$ **FALSE** {c.f. $a \times 0 \equiv 0$}
(R2) x **AND TRUE** $\equiv x$ {c.f. $a \times 1 \equiv a$}

(R3) x OR FALSE $\equiv x$ {c.f. $a + 0 \equiv a$}
(R4) x OR TRUE $\equiv$ TRUE   {There is no analogy in arithmetic}
(R5) x AND $x \equiv x$ {No analogy}
(R6) x OR $x \equiv x$ {No analogy}
(R7) x AND NOT $x \equiv$ FALSE   {No analogy}
(R8) x OR NOT $x \equiv$ TRUE   {No analogy}

Commutative laws

(C1) x AND $y \equiv y$ AND x {c.f. $a \times b \equiv b \times a$}
(C2) x OR $y \equiv y$ OR x {c.f. $a + b \equiv b + a$}

Associative laws
(A1) $(x$ AND $y)$ AND $z \equiv x$ AND y AND $z \equiv x$ AND $(y$ AND $z)$
       {c.f. $(a \times b) \times c \equiv a \times b \times c \equiv a \times (b \times c)$}
(A2) $(x$ OR $y)$ OR $z \equiv x$ OR y OR $z \equiv x$ OR $(y$ OR $z)$}
       {c.f. $(a + b) + c \equiv a + b + c \equiv a +(b +c)$}

Distributive laws

(D1) $(x$ AND $y)$ OR $(x$ AND $z) \equiv x$ AND $(y$ OR $z)$
       {c.f. $(a \times b) + (a \times c) \equiv a \times (b + c)$}
E.g. (MARRIED AND (SALARY<=LIMIT)) OR
          (MARRIED AND (CHILDREN>1))
    $\equiv$ MARRIED AND ((SALARY<=LIMIT) OR (CHILDREN>1))
(D2) $(x$ OR $y)$ AND $(x$ OR $z) \equiv x$ OR $(y$ AND $z)$
       {There is no analogy in arithmetic}
E.g. (BRITISH OR SPEAKSGAELIC) AND (BRITISH OR SPEAKSIRISH)
    $\equiv$ BRITISH OR (SPEAKSGAELIC AND SPEAKSIRISH)

Involution law

(I1) NOT (NOT $x) \equiv x$ {c.f. $-(-a) \equiv a$}

E.g. NOT (NOT MARRIED) $\equiv$ MARRIED

De Morgan's laws

{Neither of these laws has an analogy in arithmetic}

(DeM1) NOT $(x$ AND $y) \equiv$ NOT x OR NOT y

E.g. NOT ((FREEZING<TEMPERATURE) AND
          (TEMPERATURE<BOILING))
    $\equiv$ NOT(FREEZING<TEMPERATURE) OR

NOT (TEMPERATURE<BOILING)
≡ (FREEZING>=TEMPERATURE) OR
(TEMPERATURE->=BOILING)

(DeM2) NOT (x OR y) ≡ NOT x AND NOT y

E.g. NOT ((SALARY<=LIMIT) OR (CHILDREN>1))
≡ NOT (SALARY<=LIMIT) AND NOT (CHILDREN>1)
≡ (SALARY>LIMIT) AND (CHILDREN<=1)

When BOOLEAN values are compared by an operator implying relative magnitude (i.e. '<=', '<', '>=' or '>'), the result follows from the fact that, in Pascal, FALSE is considered to be less than TRUE. Since the results of such comparisons are themselves BOOLEAN values, they can be defined by truth tables and have corresponding BOOLEAN expressions. The table for '<=' follows as an example:

x	y	$x <= y$
FALSE	FALSE	TRUE
FALSE	TRUE	TRUE
TRUE	FALSE	FALSE
TRUE	TRUE	TRUE

From any truth table we can derive an equivalent expression in terms of AND, OR and NOT. Then, using the rules of Boolean Algebra, this can be converted to its simplest equivalent form. For the example of '<=' we work as follows; $x<=y$ has the value TRUE if:

(a) x and y are both FALSE, i.e. (NOT x AND NOT y); or
(b) x is FALSE and y is TRUE, i.e. (NOT x AND y); or
(c) x and y are both TRUE, i.e. (x AND y).

Thus we can write:

$x <= y$ ≡ (NOT x AND NOT y) OR (NOT x AND y) OR (x AND y)

We can now simplify this expression:

$x <= y$ ≡ NOT x AND (NOT y OR y) OR (x AND y)   {D1}
≡ NOT x AND TRUE OR (x AND y)   {C2, R8}
≡ NOT x OR (x AND y)   {R2}
≡ (NOT x OR x) AND (NOT x OR y)   {D2}
≡ TRUE AND (NOT x OR y)   {C2, R8}
≡ NOT x OR y {C1, R2}

The laws applied at each step are indicated on the right.
More simply, we can use the single FALSE case: $x<=y$ is FALSE only

when x is **TRUE** and y is **FALSE**, i.e. only when (x **AND NOT** y). Thus we can write:

$$x <= y \equiv \text{NOT } (x \text{ AND NOT } y) \equiv \text{NOT } x \text{ OR } y \qquad \{\text{DeM1, I1}\}$$

Manipulations of expressions more complicated than this are unlikely to occur in practice. Indeed, complicated **BOOLEAN** expressions may be symptomatic of flaws in the design of a program.

Exercises 5

5.1. Let **NUMBER** be an **INTEGER** variable, and let **POSITIVE**, **ZERO** and **NEGATIVE** be **BOOLEAN** variables. Write statements which will assign to **POSITIVE**, **ZERO** and **NEGATIVE** values which are **TRUE** if the value of **NUMBER** is, respectively, greater than zero, equal to zero, and less than zero.

5.2. Let **LEFT** be a **BOOLEAN** variable and let **PAGENUMBER** be an **INTEGER** variable. Write a statement which will assign to **LEFT** a **BOOLEAN** value meaning 'the value of **PAGENUMBER** is even'.

5.3. Let **ENGLISH**, **FRENCH** and **MONOGLOT** be **BOOLEAN** variables, where **ENGLISH** means 'speaks English' and **FRENCH** means 'speaks French'. Write a statement which assigns to **MONOGLOT** a **BOOLEAN** value meaning 'speaks English or French, but not both'. Note that this is an example of the exclusive sense of the word 'or', as mentioned in Section 5.3.

5.4. Write a program which reads two **INTEGER** numbers, and outputs 'TRUE' if the first is a multiple of the second, and 'FALSE' otherwise.

5.5. Write a program which reads two integers representing a date (month and day of the month), and outputs 'TRUE' if that is the date of Christmas Day, and 'FALSE' otherwise.

5.6. Assuming that an **INTEGER** variable YEAR contains the number of a year, write a statement which assigns to a **BOOLEAN** variable LEAPYEAR a value meaning 'the year is a leap year'. (a) Assume that any year whose number is a multiple of 4 is a leap year. (b*) More accurately, take into account the fact that years whose numbers are multiples of 100, but not of 400, are *not* leap years. (Thus 2000 will be a leap year, but 1700, 1800 and 1900 were not.)

{The following exercises should not be attempted until Section 5.5 has been read.}

5.7. Construct **BOOLEAN** expressions for the other five comparison operators when applied to **BOOLEAN** operands, as was done in Section 5.5 for '<='.

5.8. Simplify the **BOOLEAN** expressions x=TRUE, x=FALSE, x<>TRUE, and $x<>$FALSE. What conclusions can be drawn about the advisability of writing such expressions in programs?

5.9. Simplify the following **BOOLEAN** expressions:

(a) $(a$ OR $x)$ AND $(b$ OR $x)$ AND $(c$ OR $x)$

(b) b OR NOT $(a$ AND $b)$

(c*) a AND x OR b AND x OR c AND x OR
     a AND y OR b AND y OR c AND y OR
     a AND c OR b AND c OR c

6
Fundamental control structures

6.1 Control structures

The programs in Chapters 4 and 5 had the simplest possible structure. Their statements were executed in textual order, so that every statement was obeyed once and only once. However, we have seen that selective and repetitive execution are necessary for practical use of a computer. We now turn to the language structures which allow this. They are called *control structures* because they control the order in which statements are obeyed.

In some programming languages (especially earlier ones such as FORTRAN and BASIC) it is necessary to describe selective and repetitive control structures in terms of very primitive statements, which are almost at the level of machine-code instructions. More modern languages, among them Pascal, have been designed to make life easier. They have notations—the WHILE and IF statements—that correspond exactly with repetitive and selective control structures.

6.2 Repetitive execution: the WHILE statement

The fundamental repetitive control structure in Pascal is the *WHILE statement*. Its syntax is given in Figure 6.1. Note that WHILE and DO are both reserved words.

The statement following DO is called the *component statement* and specifies the action to be repeated. The expression following WHILE gives the condition that must be satisfied if the statement is to be obeyed. In detail, the sequence of operations is as follows:

(1) Test the condition. If it is FALSE: continue from step (4).
(2) Obey the component statement, knowing the condition to be TRUE.
(3) Repeat from step (1).
(4) Knowing the condition to be FALSE, go on with the rest of the program.

Because of the link back from step (3) to step (1) repetitive control structures have come to be called *loops*. The component statement must be

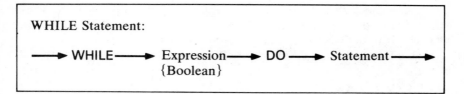

Figure 6.1. Syntax of the WHILE Statement

such that eventually (i.e. on the last repetition) it does something to make the condition **FALSE**. Failure to do this results in an *infinite loop* which is obeyed indefinitely, thus preventing further progress through the program.

The syntax of the WHILE statement requires the repeated action to be given by a *single* statement, but we often want to repeat a group of statements. This requirement is met by the *compound statement*, whose only significance is to cause a sequence of statements to be treated as a single statement for syntactic purposes. This is done by bracketing the statement sequence between the reserved words **BEGIN** and **END** (see Figure 6.2).

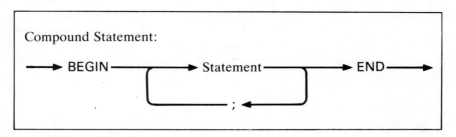

Figure 6.2. Syntax of the Compound Statement

Example 6.1

Pascal does not provide an operator to calculate powers of numbers. The following program fragment will calculate the B-th power of A for non-negative values of B (so that the result is an integer). A, B, I and POWER are INTEGER variables.

```
POWER := 1; I := 0;
WHILE I < B DO
  BEGIN
  POWER := POWER * A;
  I := I + 1
  END
```

We can check this solution by tracing through it with at least two test cases. Let us try B=0, and some B greater than 0, e.g. B=2. In either case POWER is initially set to 1 and I to 0. Suppose A contains 7.

If B is 0 the WHILE condition, I<B, already has the value FALSE, so that the body of the loop is not obeyed. Thus the final value of POWER is 1, which is correct.

If B is 2 the WHILE condition has the value TRUE and the body of the loop is obeyed. This alters POWER to 7 and I to 1. Again the condition is tested and found to be TRUE. The body of the loop then alters POWER to 49 and I to 2. On the third repetition the WHILE condition is found to be FALSE and the loop terminates. The final value of POWER is 49, which is also correct.

Study this program fragment carefully and convince yourself that the loop will always terminate and deliver the correct result, for any non-negative value of B. In particular, trace through it with A=3, B=1 and A=3, B=4.

It is usually more convenient to set down the results of tracing in a tabular form. A column is used to represent the successive values of each variable, the current value being that written lowest-down in the column. Each row shows the outcome of obeying a statement or testing a condition. The current statement or condition is shown in the first column, the second column being used for the value of the condition. If you feel it tedious to write and rewrite the same statements you may prefer to number them and record their numbers in the first column. Figure 6.3 repeats the checks on Example 6.1, in tabular form.

Example 6.2

The following program reads a list of numbers and writes their sum. To allow for varying amounts of data, the first data item is a number giving the size of the list which follows it; for example:

```
4
15   21   13   6
```

```
PROGRAM SUMBYCOUNT (INPUT, OUTPUT);

VAR
    SUM, SUMMAND, COUNT, SIZE : INTEGER;

BEGIN
SUM := 0;
COUNT := 0;

(* read the size of the list *)
READ (SIZE);
```

(a) A=7, B=0

Position	Condition	I	POWER
POWER := 1			1
I := 0		0	
{WHILE} I<B	FALSE		

(b) A=7, B=2

Position	Condition	I	POWER
POWER := 1			1
I := 0		0	
{WHILE} I<B	TRUE		
POWER := POWER*A			7
I := I+1		1	
{WHILE} I<B	TRUE		
POWER := POWER*A			49
I := I+1		2	
{WHILE} I<B	FALSE		

Figure 6.3. Checking Example 6.1

```
WHILE COUNT < SIZE DO
   (* read the next SUMMAND and add it to SUM *)
   BEGIN
   READ (SUMMAND);
   SUM := SUM + SUMMAND;
   COUNT := COUNT + 1
   END;

WRITE ('SUM OF INTEGERS READ IS ', SUM); WRITELN
END (* SUMBYCOUNT *).
```

The variable COUNT is used to keep track of how far through the data the program has reached. Just before the statements:

```
READ (SUMMAND);
SUM := SUM + SUMMAND
```

are executed, the value of COUNT is the number of entries in the list that have already been processed. After these statements, the program increases COUNT to correct it for the entry that has just been processed. Since COUNT starts at zero, and increases by one each time round the loop, it will become equal to SIZE after SIZE repetitions. Therefore COUNT<SIZE will be FALSE, and the loop will terminate, after having read and processed exactly SIZE entries.

The method of indicating the end of a list used in SUMBYCOUNT has the disadvantage that someone has to count the data. This is liable to error and may be impractical if there is a large quantity of data. An alternative approach is to mark the end of the list in some way the program can detect. If all the data are known to be positive numbers, a negative number could be used as an end-marker; for example:

15   21   13   6   −1

Example 6.3 illustrates the idea.

Example 6.3

```
PROGRAM SUMTOMARKER (INPUT, OUTPUT);

VAR
  SUM, SUMMAND: INTEGER;

BEGIN
SUM := 0;

(* read the first integer in the list *)
READ (SUMMAND);
WHILE SUMMAND >= 0 DO
  (* add a SUMMAND to SUM and read the next *)
  BEGIN
  SUM := SUM + SUMMAND;
  READ (SUMMAND)
  END;
WRITE ('SUM OF INTEGERS READ IS ', SUM); WRITELN
END (* SUMTOMARKER *).
```

SUMTOMARKER is simpler than SUMBYCOUNT: no auxiliary variables such as COUNT and SIZE are needed. However, in SUMTOMARKER the variable SUMMAND has two distinct meanings at different times. Usually it contains a data item to be added to SUM, but right at the end of the list it contains an end-marker which must *not* be added to SUM.

The logic of the WHILE statement takes care of this, although the repeated statement looks a little strange: it first adds SUMMAND to SUM and *then* reads a number into SUMMAND! This can work only if there is already a number in SUMMAND when the loop is first entered, as is the case here.

A deficiency of SUMTOMARKER is that it cannot process negative numbers, which it treats as end-markers. In general, it is difficult to find an end-marker that could never be confused with data. Fortunately, Pascal provides a way to detect the end of the input which is independent of the data itself: this is the standard BOOLEAN function EOF ('End Of File'). EOF(INPUT) has the value TRUE if and only if all the input data has been read. Its use is illustrated by Example 6.4.

Beware! SUMTOEOF, unlike SUMBYCOUNT and SUMTOMARKER, requires each number to be on a separate line of input. This is because, when reading numbers, the EOF test should be used only if the most recent input operation was READLN, rather than READ. This requirement will be explained in Section 8.2. Typical input to ADDTOEOF would be:

```
15
21
13
 6
```

Example 6.4

```
PROGRAM SUMTOEOF (INPUT, OUTPUT);

VAR
  SUM, SUMMAND: INTEGER;
BEGIN
SUM := 0;

WHILE NOT EOF(INPUT) DO
  (* read the next SUMMAND and add it to SUM *)
  BEGIN
  READ (SUMMAND);
  SUM := SUM + SUMMAND;
  READLN
  END;

WRITE ('SUM OF INTEGERS READ IS ', SUM); WRITELN
END (* SUMTOEOF *).
```

Note that SUMTOEOF combines the natural structure of SUMBY-COUNT and the simplicity of SUMTOMARKER.

Examples 6.2, 6.3 and 6.4 illustrate themes which appear in almost all programs. For this reason they are worth careful study. Hand-test them yourself, in the manner shown for Example 6.1. In particular, verify that they are correct: (a) when the list of numbers to be read is empty; (b) when there is just one number in the list; and (c) when there are several.

6.3 Selective execution: the IF statement

In Pascal, selective execution is programmed using the *IF statement*, which has the syntax given in Figure 6.4. IF, THEN and ELSE are all reserved words.

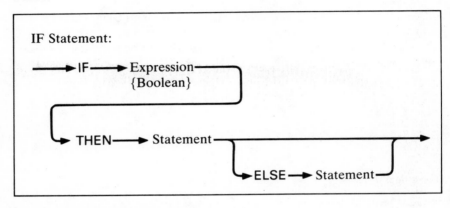

IF Statement:

Figure 6.4. Syntax of the IF Statement

The expression following IF represents the condition to be tested. The statement following THEN is executed only if the condition has the value TRUE; otherwise the statement following ELSE is executed (or none, if there is no ELSE part). In more detail the sequence of operations is as follows:

(1) Test the condition.
(2) If it is TRUE: obey the THEN part, and continue from step (4).
(3) If it is FALSE: obey the ELSE part, and continue from step (4).
(4) Go on with the rest of the program; nothing can be assumed about the value of the condition.

When the ELSE part is absent this simplifies to:

(1) Test the condition.
(2) If it is TRUE: obey the THEN part.
(3) Go on with the rest of the program; nothing can be assumed about the value of the condition.

The syntax, like that of Figure 6.1, forces the alternative actions to be specified by single statements. If either alternative action is required to consist of a number of statements, the remedy is the same: use **BEGIN** . . . **END** brackets to make a sequence of statements into a single (compound) statement.

Example 6.5

The following statement sets X to the larger of Y and Z:

```
IF Y>Z THEN
   X := Y
ELSE
   X := Z
```

Replacing Z by X throughout, we get a statement which sets X to the larger of Y and itself:

```
IF Y>X THEN
   X := Y
ELSE
   X := X
```

Since the **ELSE** part has no useful effect, it should be omitted:

```
IF Y>X THEN
   X := Y
```

Example 6.6

The following statements write suitable messages according to the value of SCORE:

```
IF SCORE>70 THEN
   WRITE ('EXCELLENT');
IF SCORE<30 THEN
   WRITE ('DISMAL');
IF (SCORE<=70) AND (SCORE>=30) THEN
   WRITE ('TYPICAL')
```

There is much redundancy in these statements. When SCORE exceeds 70 there is no point in making the two further tests of its value, both of which must give FALSE. Similarly, once SCORE is known to be less than 30 the test in the final IF statement is futile. This is an example of a very common situation: testing for one of several *mutually exclusive* conditions, with an appropriate action for each. It can be written more concisely using ELSE:

```
IF SCORE>70 THEN
  WRITE ('EXCELLENT')
ELSE
IF SCORE<30 THEN
  WRITE ('DISMAL')
ELSE
  WRITE ('TYPICAL')
```

In this form the expression **SCORE<30** is evaluated only if necessary and no test at all is required for the third alternative.

In Example 6.6 the use of separate IF statements with mutually exclusive conditions was clumsy rather than erroneous. Example 6.7 illustrates a situation in which separate IF statements *are* erroneous.

Example 6.7

The following statement increments A if it is negative and decrements A if it is positive or zero:

```
IF A<0 THEN
  A := A + 1
ELSE
  A := A - 1
```

Compare its effect with that of the following two sequences:

```
IF A<0 THEN                 IF A>=0 THEN
  A := A + 1;                 A := A - 1;
IF A>=0 THEN                IF A<0 THEN
  A := A - 1                  A := A + 1
```

when the value of A is initially (a) 0; and (b) −1. (The reason for the difference is that the component statements change the values of the variables being tested.)

Example 6.8

A common and quite subtle error is to try something along these lines:

```
IF (TALLY <> 0) AND (TOTAL DIV TALLY > THRESHOLD) THEN
  WRITE ('ACCEPTABLE AVERAGE')
ELSE
  WRITE ('UNACCEPTABLE AVERAGE')
```

The mistake is that, when TALLY is zero, TOTAL DIV TALLY causes an attempt to divide by zero (usually with disastrous results). In cases like this the two parts of the condition must be separated:

```
IF TALLY <> 0 THEN
  IF TOTAL DIV TALLY > THRESHOLD THEN
    WRITE ('ACCEPTABLE AVERAGE')
  ELSE
    WRITE ('UNACCEPTABLE AVERAGE')
```

An ambiguity lurking in the syntax of Figure 6.4 now comes to light! In a statement with the following structure:

```
IF . . . THEN IF . . . THEN . . . ELSE . . .
```

to which IF does the ELSE correspond? Pascal has the reasonable (though arbitrary) rule that in such a case the ELSE goes with the closest IF. We have anticipated this in the indentation of Example 6.8. Compare that with Example 6.9.

Example 6.9

```
IF TALLY <> 0 THEN
  BEGIN
  IF TOTAL DIV TALLY > THRESHOLD THEN
    WRITE ('ACCEPTABLE AVERAGE')
  END
ELSE
  WRITE ('NOTHING TO FIND THE AVERAGE OF')
```

It is advisable, in all doubtful cases, to make the meaning perfectly clear by liberal use of the statement brackets BEGIN and END.

6.4 Nested control structures

Very often a programming problem will demand both repetition and selection for its solution. There is no difficulty about this. Remember that the WHILE and IF constructs both *contain* statements and *are themselves* statements. Thus a WHILE can govern an IF or another WHILE and an IF can govern a WHILE or another IF (as we have already seen). Structures of any complexity can be built up in this way, each statement being *nested* within another. When it is necessary to govern a sequence of statements, rather than just one, the compound statement allows this to be done.

Example 6.10

Program DISPLAY is to read a sequence of integers, terminated by a negative end-marker. When a positive number is read, that many asterisks are to be written. Zeros are to be written numerically. {The effect is to display the data as a bar-chart, or histogram, thus making it easier for the user to assimilate.}

```
PROGRAM DISPLAY (INPUT, OUTPUT);

VAR
  STARCOUNT, WIDTHOFBAR : INTEGER;

BEGIN
(* read the first WIDTHOFBAR *)
READ (WIDTHOFBAR);
WHILE WIDTHOFBAR >= 0 DO
  BEGIN
  (* output a representation of WIDTHOFBAR *)
  IF WIDTHOFBAR = 0 THEN
    (* output WIDTHOFBAR in numerical form *)
    WRITE (WIDTHOFBAR : 1)
  ELSE
    (* output a row of WIDTHOFBAR asterisks *)
    BEGIN
    WRITE ('   ');
    STARCOUNT := 0;
    WHILE STARCOUNT < WIDTHOFBAR DO
      BEGIN
      WRITE ('*');
      STARCOUNT := STARCOUNT +1
      END
    END;
  (* start a new line of output *)
  WRITELN;
  (* read the next WIDTHOFBAR *)
  READ (WIDTHOFBAR)
  END
END (* DISPLAY *).
```

Note the layout of program DISPLAY. Here, as in the preceding examples, the repeated statements in loops have been indented relative to the WHILE symbol. Similarly, the alternative statements in selections have been indented relative to the IF and ELSE symbols. This convention shows clearly how much of the text is actually included in each construct and makes the program much easier to read.

It is essential to adopt a methodical approach when writing relatively complicated programs like **DISPLAY**. Methodical programming is the topic of the following chapter.

6.5 The REPEAT statement

{This section may be omitted on a first reading.}

We have already seen that with the **WHILE** construct it is possible for the number of repetitions to be zero. For example, in:

WHILE R >= N DO
  R := R−N

the statement R := R−N will not be executed at all if the condition R>=N is initially **FALSE**.

Usually this does exactly what we need. However, there are circumstances in which the degenerate case with no repetitions is known to be impossible, and it would be more natural to use a construct that guarantees at least one repetition. In Pascal this is the *REPEAT statement*.

The syntax of REPEAT statements is given in Figure 6.5. Note that several statements may be placed inside the loop, without **BEGIN** . . . **END**

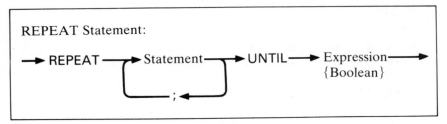

REPEAT Statement:

REPEAT ──→ Statement ──→ UNTIL ──→ Expression ──→
                                    {Boolean}
                ; ←──

Figure 6.5. Syntax of REPEAT Statements

brackets, since **REPEAT** and **UNTIL** themselves act as statement brackets. **REPEAT** and **UNTIL** are both reserved words.

The sequence of operations is as follows:

(1) Obey the statement(s) between **REPEAT** and **UNTIL**.
(2) Test the condition. If it is **FALSE**: repeat from step (1).
(3) Knowing the condition to be **TRUE**, go on with the rest of the program.

Compare this sequence of operations with that of the WHILE statement (see Section 6.2). The principal difference is this: in the WHILE statement the loop condition is tested *before* each repetition of the loop; in the REPEAT statement the loop condition is tested *after* each repetition of the loop. This distinction is emphasized by the position of the WHILE clause at the beginning of the WHILE statement and the position of the UNTIL clause at the end of the REPEAT statement. Note also that the REPEAT loop terminates when its condition is found to be TRUE, the opposite of the case with the WHILE statement.

Example 6.11

In program DISPLAY, Example 6.10, the inner loop outputs a row of asterisks. Each time the WHILE statement is obeyed the component statement is executed at least once, so the loop could be rewritten as a REPEAT statement:

```
REPEAT
  WRITE ('*');
  STARCOUNT := STARCOUNT + 1
UNTIL STARCOUNT>=WIDTHOFBAR
```

The advantage of this version is that it exhibits very clearly the fact that at least one asterisk will be output. Using WHILE, it is necessary to analyse almost the whole program to deduce the same fact.

Exercises 6

6.1. Work systematically through program DISPLAY from Example 6.10, tracing the actions of the computer as it reads data, changes variables, tests conditions and writes output. Show exactly what output is produced if the input data is:

5   17   9   6   0   1   −1

{Check your solutions to the following exercises by tracing through them with suitable input data.}

6.2. What does program DISPLAY do if a large number is included in the input data? Modify the program to make it write numerically any number which is too large. Choose as a limit a value which does not exceed the width of a line on whatever output device you use.

6.3. Write a program fragment which computes the factorial of N, given that the value of N is a positive integer. (The factorial of N is the product $1*2* \ldots *(N-1)*N$.)

6.4. Given that the value of N is a positive integer, write a program fragment which determines how many decimal digits are needed to write down the value of N. (For example, 99 needs two digits, and 100 needs three digits.)

6.5. Write a program fragment which outputs 'POSITIVE', 'NEGATIVE' or 'ZERO', depending on the value of N.

6.6. Write a program fragment which reads three integers representing today's date (day, month and year), followed by three integers representing a person's birth-date, and which outputs that person's age in years.

6.7. Write programs to read a list of positive integers and output the largest of them: (a) when the size of the list is given as the first datum; (b) when the list is terminated by a negative number; (c) using EOF.

6.8. If you have read Section 6.5, recast your answers to Exercise 6.7 so that the programs will output a suitable message if the list to be examined is empty.

Programming exercises 6

6.9. Modify your program of Exercise 4.6 to write the time in terms of the 12-hour clock rather than the 24-hour clock. (For example, write '10:50:30 P.M.' rather than '22:50:30'.)

6.10. (a) Write a program which reads an integer N and produces a table of the first N positive powers of 2. (b) Write a program which reads an integer N and produces a table of the positive powers of 2 which are less than or equal to N.

6.11. Details taken from an invoice are supplied as input data. Each line of input contains the number of units of one item invoiced, followed by the unit price of that item (in pence or cents). Write a program which will read this data, output the data in tabular form, and finally output the total amount invoiced. Use EOF(INPUT) to detect the end of the input data.

7
Programming methodically

This is a very important chapter. Read it carefully before going on to the rest of the book, and review it after reading Chapter 18.

7.1 Stepwise refinement

The objective of computer programming is the creation of correct, efficient and easily modified programs. *Correct*, because a program that gives the wrong results is useless. *Efficient*, because an inefficient program may be too costly to run. *Easily modified*, because a program may be changed many times during its life. Correctness is the primary criterion of a good program. Efficiency and modifiability, though important, are secondary. In certain circumstances it may be necessary to sacrifice efficiency for flexibility, or ease of modification for lower initial cost. We are not prepared to sacrifice correctness in any circumstances.

These may seem to be modest aims, but all the experience of the past indicates that achieving them is very difficult. Why is this so? The basic reason is the diversity of the skills a programmer must possess, and the complexity of their inter-relationships. The ideal programmer is versatile, creative, logical and persistent. He is capable of meticulous attention to detail, yet never loses sight of the overall picture.

Paragons such as this are few and far between. For the rest of us, in the face of such requirements, it seems wise to avoid difficulties of our own making. In particular, we can adopt a methodical habit of work. The method chosen perhaps matters less than its consistent application, but we advocate in this book a method which is both simple and effective: *stepwise refinement*.

The basic idea of stepwise refinement is this: given a complex problem, such as designing a program, split it up into several, more or less independent, *sub-problems*. If we can assume that these sub-problems are solvable we have an outline solution to the original problem. Call this the *Level 1 outline* of the solution. Now turn to the sub-problems and solve these separately. If a sub-problem is trivial, write down its final solution directly. If not, solve the sub-problem by applying stepwise refinement to it in turn. This generates a set of smaller sub-problems. Assuming that these are solvable they constitute a second, more detailed, solution of the original problem. This is the *Level 2 outline* of the solution. Go on in this way until all the remaining sub-problems are trivial. Combining all the final solutions of the sub-problems gives the final solution of the original problem, in the most convenient form: a complete design! Splitting up a problem into sub-problems is a *refinement step*; the successively more detailed outlines are the *levels of refinement*. We now bring this rather abstract idea to life with an example.

The stepwise refinement of program DISPLAY

The **DISPLAY** program from Example 6.10 was developed along the following lines. The program is to read and process a sequence of numbers, terminated by a negative end-marker. This at once suggests a loop, in fact the sort of loop used in Example 6.3. Each repetition of the loop processes a number, let us call it **WIDTHOFBAR** (remembering it will have to be declared as an **INTEGER** variable). The value of **WIDTHOFBAR** is to be represented by writing it out as a row of the histogram. To give the correct format each number should be represented on a separate line. Having output one number, the loop must read in the next. These considerations lead to the following sketch of the program.

Level 1 outline

```
PROGRAM DISPLAY (INPUT, OUTPUT);
declarations;
BEGIN
read the first WIDTHOFBAR;
WHILE not end of data DO
    BEGIN
    output a representation of WIDTHOFBAR;
    start of a new line of output;
    read the next WIDTHOFBAR
    END
END (* DISPLAY *).
```

This is intended to be a self-explanatory outline of the program. Material in upper case is already formalized in terms of Pascal. Material in lower case is informally descriptive of some action to be performed or some expression to be evaluated—the context should make clear which. For example, 'not end of data' must represent a **BOOLEAN** expression which we are to interpret in terms of the end-of-data condition. At the moment it does not matter how the condition is to be detected: any valid implementation will result in a correct program. In the same way, 'output a representation of WIDTHOFBAR' represents a statement which, we are to assume, will write out one row of the histogram.

The whole program can now be checked before any further refinements are made. This is done by tracing through it with sample data, just as we would do with the final program. Only when satisfied that the outline is correct do we continue with the refinement. Should any error be found it must be corrected in the Level 1 outline, *before* going on to produce Level 2. Program outlines should not be treated as provisional drafts of a solution, nor should refinements be thought of as amendments and corrections. Each outline of the program should be both correct and complete, given its level of detail. Check Level 1 now, using the data given in Exercise 6.1.

Refinements from Level 1

The most complex step in Level 1 is 'output a representation of WIDTH-OFBAR', so we shall refine that first. When WIDTHOFBAR is positive a row of that many asterisks is to be written; when it is zero its value is to be output numerically.

Refinement 1.1: output a representation of WIDTHOFBAR

```
IF WIDTHOFBAR = 0 THEN
   output WIDTHOFBAR in numerical form
ELSE
   output WIDTHOFBAR asterisks
```

Each of the remaining components of Level 1 can be trivially expanded into Pascal. They are then complete and need no further development.

Refinement 1.2: read the next WIDTHOFBAR

```
READ (WIDTHOFBAR)
```

Refinement 1.3: start a new line of output

```
WRITELN
```

Refinement 1.4: not end of data

```
WIDTHOFBAR >= 0
```

Refinement 1.5: read the first WIDTHOFBAR

```
READ (WIDTHOFBAR)
```

Replacing each of these components in the Level 1 outline by its refinement we get a more detailed outline of the program at Level 2. To show how it was derived we include appropriate comments.

Level 2 outline

```
PROGRAM DISPLAY (INPUT, OUTPUT);
declarations;
BEGIN
(* read the first WIDTHOFBAR *)
READ (WIDTHOFBAR);
WHILE WIDTHOFBAR >= 0 DO
  BEGIN
  (* output a representation of WIDTHOFBAR *)
  IF WIDTHOFBAR = 0 THEN
    output WIDTHOFBAR in numerical form
  ELSE
    output WIDTHOFBAR asterisks;
  (* start a new line of output *)
  WRITELN;
  (* read the next WIDTHOFBAR *)
  READ (WIDTHOFBAR)
  END
END (* DISPLAY *).
```

This must be checked before continuing the refinement. Try it now, using the same data as before.

Refinements from Level 2

Only two components of Level 2 can be refined at this point. Again, we start with the more complex: 'output **WIDTHOFBAR** asterisks'. A single asterisk is easily output by the statement WRITE('*'); to output several we must include this in a count-controlled loop (compare Example 6.2). This will require more than one statement, so it will all have to be enclosed in BEGIN and END brackets.

Refinement 2.1: output **WIDTHOFBAR** asterisks

```
  BEGIN
  prepare to output the row;
  WHILE WIDTHOFBAR asterisks have not yet been written DO
    output another asterisk
  END
```

Refinement 2.2: output **WIDTHOFBAR** in numerical form

```
  WRITE (WIDTHOFBAR:1)
```

Level 3 outline

```
PROGRAM DISPLAY (INPUT, OUTPUT);
declarations;
BEGIN
(* read the first WIDTHOFBAR *)
READ (WIDTHOFBAR);
WHILE WIDTHOFBAR >= 0 DO
  BEGIN
  (* output a representation of WIDTHOFBAR *)
  IF WIDTHOFBAR = 0 THEN
    (* output WIDTHOFBAR in numerical form *)
    WRITE (WIDTHOFBAR:1)
  ELSE
    BEGIN (* output WIDTHOFBAR asterisks *)
    prepare to output the row;
    WHILE WIDTHOFBAR asterisks have not yet been written DO
      output another asterisk
    END;
  (* start a new line of output *)
  WRITELN;
  (* read the next WIDTHOFBAR *)
  READ (WIDTHOFBAR)
  END
END (* DISPLAY *).
```

Once again, check this before we go on to Level 4.

Refinements from Level 3

To record the number of asterisks that have been output by the inner WHILE loop the program must keep a tally of them in a suitable variable. Thus we introduce the INTEGER variable STARCOUNT (remembering that it will have to be declared). Each time a row of asterisks is begun STARCOUNT will start off at zero; each time an asterisk is output it will be incremented by one. Thus the value of STARCOUNT represents the number of asterisks already output in the current row.

Refinement 3.1: WIDTHOFBAR asterisks have not yet been written

```
STARCOUNT < WIDTHOFBAR
```

Refinement 3.2: output another asterisk

```
BEGIN
WRITE ('*');
STARCOUNT := STARCOUNT + 1
END
```

The preparation for each row must include zeroizing **STARCOUNT**. Another point: zeros are output in a field of one column (see Refinement 2.2). To preserve the format of the bar-chart a blank should therefore be output before each row of asterisks.

Refinement 3.3: prepare to output the row

```
WRITE (' ');
STARCOUNT := 0
```

The whole program has now been converted to Pascal code, with the exception of the declarations. Since we know all the variables needed we can finally write:

Refinement 3.4: declarations

```
VAR
    STARCOUNT, WIDTHOFBAR : INTEGER
```

This completes the stepwise refinement of program **DISPLAY**. Checking the complete program has already been set as Exercise 6.1.

You may feel that writing a small program like **DISPLAY** in this manner is taking a sledgehammer to crack a nut. Rest assured that, for programs of a more realistic size and complexity, stepwise refinement is of immense help. In the meantime, while you are confined to small examples, the discipline it imposes may seem tedious. Persevere, gain experience with the technique, and you will reap the benefits later.

7.2 Case study I: The traffic survey problem

Problem specification

A traffic survey is conducted automatically by placing a vehicle detector at the roadside, connected by data link to a computer. A clock in the detector is started at the beginning of a survey. Every second thereafter the detector transmits a signal which the computer reads as the number 1. Whenever a vehicle passes, the detector transmits a signal which is read as the number 2. At the end of the survey the detector transmits a terminator signal which is read as the number 0. (Assume that no two signals exactly coincide.)

The following diagram illustrates a possible sequence of events, 'V' indicating the passage of a vehicle:

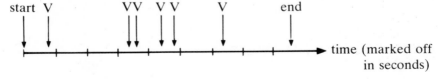

The corresponding sequence of signals sent to the computer would be:

2 1 1 1 2 2 1 2 2 1 1 2 1 1 0

Due to transmission errors a signal may occasionally be received as a number greater than 2.

The problem is to write a program which reads such a set of signals and outputs the following:

(a) The length of the survey period.
(b) The number of vehicles recorded.
(c) The length of the longest interval in which no vehicles pass. The length of a vehicle-free interval is to be taken simply as the number of timing signals received during this period. For example, the above data contains one 1-second interval, two 2-second intervals and one 3-second interval.
(d) The number of transmission errors. An error signal is to be taken as terminating a vehicle-free interval. (This prevents corrupted vehicle signals from exaggerating the length of vehicle-free intervals.)

Thus with the input data cited above, the expected results are:

(a) 8, (b) 6, (c) 3, and (d) 0.

If the third of the vehicle signals were corrupted, however, the expected results would be:

(a) 8, (b) 5, (c) 3, and (d) 1.

Solution

Perhaps the simplest way of looking at the data is to treat it as a random sequence of timing signals, vehicle signals and error signals: a simple list of positive numbers, terminated by a zero. This immediately suggests a WHILE loop of the form used in Example 6.3. The results to be produced must be accumulated over the whole list, so the Level 1 outline can be written as follows. (There is an alternative way of looking at the data, leading to a different program outline, so we shall call this version TRAFFIC(a) and the later version TRAFFIC(b).)

Level 1a outline

PROGRAM TRAFFIC (INPUT, OUTPUT);
declarations;
BEGIN
prepare to process signals;

WHILE not end of data **DO**
   process one signal and read the next;
output the results
END.

    As an exercise, devise some test data and use it to work through the Level 1a outline. What properties of the program can you check at this stage?

Refinements from Level 1a

Since the other elements seem to be quite simple, we tackle 'process one signal and read the next' first. The signal to be processed could be a timing signal, a vehicle signal or an error signal. This suggests that the refinement should be in terms of IF statements, with 'process a timing signal', 'process an error signal' and 'process a vehicle signal' as the components.

Refinement 1.1a: process one signal and read the next

BEGIN
IF it is a vehicle signal **THEN**
   process a vehicle signal
ELSE
IF it is an error signal **THEN**
   process an error signal
ELSE
   process a timing signal;
read the next signal
END

    Level 2a is derived by substituting this in Level 1a. As an exercise, write out the Level 2a outline in full, and check it with your test data.

Refinements from Level 2a

Remembering that one objective is to measure vehicle-free intervals, we see that 'process a vehicle signal', 'process an error signal' and 'process a timing signal' must interact in such a way that the start and end of each interval can be recognized. Define the *current interval* to be that which has elapsed since the most recent vehicle signal or error signal, and let INTERVAL be an INTEGER variable whose value is the length in seconds of the current interval. INTERVAL must be set to zero at the start of each vehicle-free interval (i.e. on receiving each vehicle or error signal), and 'process a timing signal' must increment it by one (as the timing signals come once a second). To count the vehicles and the errors, and to note the total elapsed time, we need three more INTEGER variables: VEHICLES, ERRORS and SECONDS.

Refinement 2.1a: process a timing signal

```
BEGIN
SECONDS := SECONDS + 1;
INTERVAL := INTERVAL + 1
END
```

A vehicle signal marks the end of one vehicle-free interval and the start of another. It is necessary to check the length of the interval just ended.

Refinement 2.2a: process a vehicle signal

```
BEGIN
VEHICLES := VEHICLES + 1;
check the length of the interval;
INTERVAL := 0
END
```

Processing an error signal is analogous to Refinement 2.2a.

Refinement 2.3a: process an error signal

```
BEGIN
ERRORS := ERRORS + 1;
check the length of the interval;
INTERVAL := 0
END
```

Substituting these refinements in Level 2a gives us Level 3a. As an exercise, write out Level 3a in full, and check it with your test data.

Refinements from Level 3a

The length of the current interval is held in INTERVAL. At the end of each interval we must check to see whether this is greater than the longest interval so far recorded. We introduce the INTEGER variable LONGEST to hold the latter.

Refinement 3.1a: check the length of the interval

```
IF INTERVAL>LONGEST THEN
    LONGEST := INTERVAL
```

We now introduce an INTEGER variable, SIGNAL, to hold the current signal number. To make the program more flexible, and easier to understand, we also introduce constants TERMINATOR (equal to 0), TIMINGSIGNAL (equal to 1) and VEHICLESIGNAL (equal to 2).

Refinement 3.2a: it is a vehicle signal

```
SIGNAL = VEHICLESIGNAL
```

Refinement 3.3a: it is an error signal

```
SIGNAL > VEHICLESIGNAL
```

Refinement 3.4a: not end of data

```
SIGNAL <> TERMINATOR
```

Refinement 3.5a: read the next signal

```
READ (SIGNAL)
```

Refinement 3.6a: output the results

The details depend entirely on the layout required, but this has not been specified. One possibility is shown in the complete program below.

Refinement 3.7a: prepare to process signals

```
VEHICLES := 0;
ERRORS := 0;
SECONDS := 0;
LONGEST := 0;
INTERVAL := 0;
READ (SIGNAL)
```

Refinement 3.8a: declarations

```
CONST
  TERMINATOR = 0;
  TIMINGSIGNAL = 1;
  VEHICLESIGNAL = 2;
VAR
  VEHICLES, ERRORS, SECONDS,
        LONGEST, INTERVAL, SIGNAL : INTEGER
```

Putting all of this together, we get a complete Pascal program.

Complete program for TRAFFIC(a)

```
PROGRAM TRAFFIC (INPUT, OUTPUT);
CONST
  TERMINATOR    = 0;
  TIMINGSIGNAL  = 1;
  VEHICLESIGNAL = 2;
VAR
  VEHICLES, ERRORS, SECONDS, LONGEST, INTERVAL, SIGNAL : INTEGER;
BEGIN
(* prepare to process signals *)
VEHICLES := 0;
ERRORS := 0;
```

```
SECONDS := 0;
LONGEST := 0;
INTERVAL := 0;
READ (SIGNAL);
WHILE SIGNAL<>TERMINATOR DO
  BEGIN (* process one signal and read the next *)
  IF SIGNAL=VEHICLESIGNAL THEN
    BEGIN (* process a vehicle signal *)
    VEHICLES := VEHICLES + 1;
    IF INTERVAL>LONGEST THEN
      LONGEST := INTERVAL;
    INTERVAL := 0
    END
  ELSE
  IF SIGNAL>VEHICLESIGNAL THEN
    BEGIN (* process an error signal *)
    ERRORS := ERRORS + 1;
    IF INTERVAL>LONGEST THEN
      LONGEST := INTERVAL;
    INTERVAL := 0
    END
  ELSE
    BEGIN (* process a timing signal *)
    SECONDS := SECONDS + 1;
    INTERVAL := INTERVAL + 1
    END;
  (* read the next signal *)
  READ (SIGNAL)
  END;
(* output the results *)
WRITE ('         NO. OF        NO. OF        ELAPSED        LONGEST');
WRITELN;
WRITE ('         VEHICLES        ERRORS        TIME        GAP');
WRITELN;
WRITE (VEHICLES:12, ERRORS:12, SECONDS:12, LONGEST:12);
WRITELN
END (* TRAFFIC(a) *).
```

An alternative solution

Another way of looking at the input data is to see it in terms of 'runs' of several consecutive signals of the same kind. This interpretation is a natural one, because we want to measure time *intervals* and each interval is defined by the start and end of a run of timing signals. Runs of vehicle and error signals have no significance in the problem posed, so those signals might as well be processed individually. Timing signals, on the other hand, should be processed in runs of as many consecutive occurrences as possible. For example, the following input data contains four runs of timing signals:

2   1   1   1   2   8   1   2   2   1   1   2   1   1   0

These ideas lead to the following alternative Level 1 outline, and its subsequent refinement. We shall call this version of the program TRAF-FIC(b).

Level 1b outline

PROGRAM TRAFFIC (INPUT, OUTPUT);
declarations;
BEGIN
prepare to process signals;
WHILE not end of data **DO**
    process a signal or interval and read the next signal;
output the results
END.

As an exercise, hand-test Level 1b with the same test data as before.

Refinements from Level 1b

If the signal on hand is a vehicle or an error signal, it is to be processed individually. If it is a timing signal, it is to be treated as the first of an interval, and the whole of the interval is to be processed. Since this will involve reading the next signal, the processing of vehicle and error signals must do likewise. Thus we do not have a separate step to read the next signal.

Refinement 1.1b: process a signal or interval and read the next signal

    BEGIN
    IF it is a vehicle signal **THEN**
        process a vehicle signal and read the next signal
    ELSE
    IF it is an error signal **THEN**
        process an error signal and read the next signal
    ELSE
        time a vehicle-free interval and read the next signal
    END

Level 2b is obtained by substituting this in Level 1b. As an exercise, write out Level 2b and hand-test it with your test data.

Refinements from Level 2b

There is explicit provision in this version of the program for timing the intervals, so processing a vehicle signal or an error signal involves no more than incrementing the appropriate tally. As before we use **INTEGER** variables **VEHICLES** and **ERRORS**.

Refinement 2.1b: process a vehicle signal and read the next signal

```
BEGIN
VEHICLES := VEHICLES + 1;
READ (SIGNAL)
END
```

Refinement 2.2b: process an error signal and read the next signal

```
BEGIN
ERRORS := ERRORS + 1;
READ (SIGNAL)
END
```

To time an interval we must note its beginning, process all the timing signals in the interval, and note its end.

Refinement 2.3b: time a vehicle-free interval and read the next signal

```
BEGIN
note the start of an interval;
WHILE it is a timing signal DO
   process a timing signal and read the next signal;
note the end of an interval
END
```

Inserting these refinements in Level 2b gives us Level 3b. As an exercise, write out Level 3b and hand-test it with your test data.

Refinements from Level 3b

We now introduce some **INTEGER** variables: **SECONDS**, to hold the elapsed time; **STARTTIME**, to hold the time at the beginning of an interval; and **LONGEST**, to hold the length of the longest recorded interval.

Refinement 3.1b: note the start of an interval

```
STARTTIME := SECONDS
```

Refinement 3.2b: process a timing signal and read the next signal

```
BEGIN
SECONDS := SECONDS + 1;
```

```
READ (SIGNAL)
END
```

Refinement 3.3b: note the end of an interval

```
IF SECONDS - STARTTIME > LONGEST THEN
    LONGEST := SECONDS - STARTTIME
```

The final Pascal program can now be constructed, using refinements 3.2a, 3.3a, 3.4a, 3.6a and slightly modified versions of 3.7a and 3.8a.

Complete program for TRAFFIC(b)

```
PROGRAM TRAFFIC (INPUT, OUTPUT);
CONST
    TERMINATOR    = 0;
    TIMINGSIGNAL  = 1;
    VEHICLESIGNAL = 2;
VAR
    VEHICLES,   ERRORS,
    SECONDS, STARTTIME, LONGEST, SIGNAL : INTEGER;
BEGIN
(* prepare to process signals *)
VEHICLES := 0;
ERRORS := 0;
SECONDS := 0;
LONGEST := 0;
READ (SIGNAL);
WHILE SIGNAL<>TERMINATOR DO
    BEGIN (* process a signal or interval and read the next signal *)
    IF SIGNAL=VEHICLESIGNAL THEN
        BEGIN (* process a vehicle signal and read the next signal *)
        VEHICLES := VEHICLES + 1;
        READ (SIGNAL)
        END
    ELSE
    IF SIGNAL>VEHICLESIGNAL THEN
        BEGIN (* process an error signal and read the next signal *)
        ERRORS := ERRORS + 1;
        READ (SIGNAL)
        END
    ELSE
        BEGIN (* time a vehicle-free interval and read the next signal *)
        (* note the start of an interval *)
        STARTTIME := SECONDS;
        WHILE SIGNAL=TIMINGSIGNAL DO
```

```
    BEGIN (* process a timing signal and read the next signal *)
    SECONDS := SECONDS + 1;
    READ (SIGNAL)
    END;
  (* note the end of an interval *)
  IF SECONDS − STARTTIME > LONGEST THEN
    LONGEST := SECONDS − STARTTIME
  END
 END;
(* output the results *)
WRITE ('          NO. OF      NO. OF      ELAPSED      LONGEST');
WRITELN;
WRITE ('        VEHICLES    ERRORS        TIME          GAP');
WRITELN;
WRITE (VEHICLES:12, ERRORS:12, SECONDS:12, LONGEST:12);
WRITELN
END (* TRAFFIC(b) *).
```

7.3 Making refinements

How do we choose a refinement? Part of the answer is that, like most things, it gets easier with practice. Many problems lead to similar program structures. The skilled programmer soon recognizes these structures in the specification, enabling him to write down suitable refinements very quickly. However there is a trap here. Quite small differences of specification can cause large differences of program structure, and parrotting a stock refinement then leads to difficulties. Habit should not be a substitute for thought.

A more adequate answer is that *every* action can be refined either as a sequence of actions, or as a loop, or as a selection. Anything which can be programmed, in any way at all, can be programmed using just these fundamental constructions. This is reassuring: we only have to choose one alternative from three. Although it is usually obvious which choice to make, the following points are worth noting.

Apparently the simplest kind of refinement is to split an action into several parts which are then performed in sequence. However, experience shows that many structural errors come from doing this wrongly, or when it is not appropriate. In particular, be sure that it is indeed possible to perform the component actions sequentially. For example, the sequence:

    read all data;
    calculate;
    write all results

implies that the data can all be stored until the calculation phase and that the results can all be stored until they are written. Often, however, it is necessary to incorporate data items into a calculation as they are read and to write results as soon as they are calculated. Be sure, too, that the components of a sequence are in the correct order. In the example:

    write all results;
    calculate;
    read all data

the error is clear, but in more complex situations mis-ordered sequences can be much less obvious.

A common sequence is of the form:

    preparation;
    WHILE continuation condition DO
        repeated action;
    finalization

where the 'preparation' or the 'finalization' may be absent. Here the loop does most of the work, but it may need to be started off properly and there may be some final tidying-up to do.

When refining a loop it is a good idea to tackle the 'continuation condition' first: this is usually easy. Then refine the 'repeated action', ensuring that it contains a statement which will eventually make the 'continuation condition' FALSE. If any 'finalization' is required refine that next. Lastly refine the 'preparation'. This has two things to do:

(a) It must establish an initial value for the 'continuation condition'. Sometimes this does not involve any action by the program; for example, EOF(INPUT) always has a value.

(b) It must initialize any variables whose values are used by the WHILE statement.

It may seem strange to leave 'preparation' to the end, but in stepwise refinement a good maxim is 'the first shall be last'. Until you know *what* you must prepare for, you cannot know *how* to prepare for it. Similarly, the declaration section of a program cannot be completed until all the variables have been introduced, and this is not known until all the statements have been fully refined.

When deciding between sequential, conditional and repetitive structures for a refinement, it is often helpful to take into account the structure of the input that must be accepted and the output that must be generated. Sometimes the structure of the input will determine the control structure to be used (for example Refinements 1.1a, 1.1b and 2.1b of program **TRAFFIC**, Section 7.2); sometimes the structure of the output is the important factor (for example Refinements 1.1, 2.1, etc., of program **DISPLAY**, Section 7.1).

Whatever its form, a good refinement usually has the following desirable properties:

(a) *Modularity*. A program is said to be modular if its various components are relatively independent of each other. Choose refinements whose components interact as little as possible. This reduces the complexity of the refinements to be made at the next level down. For example, **TRAFFIC**(a) is somewhat less modular than **TRAFFIC**(b). In TRAF-FIC(b) 'process a vehicle signal and read the next signal' and 'process an error signal and read the next signal' are quite independent of each other, and of the interval-timing (except for reading the next signal). In **TRAFFIC**(a), however, 'process a vehicle signal' and 'process an error signal' both use and change variables concerned purely with timing.

(b) *Localization*. A program displays good localization when related statements are written close to each other in the text. This improves readability by reducing the need to scan back and forth through a program to see how things connect together. In the **TRAFFIC** programs all of the output is written by a group of adjacent statements. It would have been possible to write the headings as part of 'prepare to process signals', but this would have made it more difficult to check that the headings and the numerical output correspond in position and layout. In the given versions this can be seen at a glance.

(c) *Consistency*. When you have to do the same sort of thing several times, do it the same way on each occasion (unless there is good reason to vary). In **TRAFFIC**(b) we refined 'process a vehicle signal and read the next signal' and 'process an error signal and read the next signal' into analogous Pascal statements. In either case it would have been correct to reverse the order of the assignment statement and the READ statement, but the effect would have been to confuse the reader. He would be left to wonder if some subtle reason for the difference had escaped him. When you *must* vary from a pattern, include a comment at that point to say why.

(d) *Delayed decisions*. Choose refinements which incorporate only those design decisions that cannot be postponed. This avoids committing the design prematurely to specific implementation ideas, increases the ease with which modifications can subsequently be made, and reduces the distracting effect of minutiae. Referring again to the **TRAFFIC** programs, the exact output format was a detail that could be post-poned to the very end of the development process.

(e) *Simplicity*. It is very difficult to keep in mind more than about half a dozen facts or inter-relationships. Avoid overloading yourself by choosing refinements with at most five or six components (two to four would be preferable). This reduces the likelihood of confusion and error.

From time to time every programmer finds that ideas stop flowing and a difficult problem blocks all further progress. When this happens, suspect that a design error at a higher level has set you an impossible task. However, if the design seems to be sound, there are a few things worth trying. First of all, look for a solution by someone else. This may be found in the literature of the subject, or there may be a ready-made program in a software library. Even if no solution of exactly the current problem turns up, you may still be able to find solutions to closely related problems. These are a fertile source of ideas. Failing that, try to simplify the problem, solve the simpler problem and then work back to the original.

When you find yourself staring blankly at the title of a refinement, bogged down with useless ideas, that is the time to put the problem aside. Relax, or work on something quite different. Unconscious mental processes will continue to grind away at the problem, free from conscious preconceptions. Often a solution will come to mind when you least expect it. Reading Robert Pirsig's novel *Zen and the Art of Motorcycle Maintenance* would be a profitable way to pass the time while you wait for inspiration. As well as being a good story, this book contains many insights into problem solving, most of which are directly relevant to programming by stepwise refinement.

It is important to use a consistent notation for stepwise refinement and to be thorough about writing down design decisions. In this way the written record of the design process acts as an extension of our limited memory, and allows more factors to be taken into account than would otherwise be possible.

Each program outline is written in terms of a set of actions and expressions whose implementation has not yet been determined. These actions and expressions should be given descriptive names that will suggest exactly what the program is doing, even to a casual reader of the program outline. Accuracy is much more important than conciseness, because a misleading or vague name is both a symptom and a cause of sloppy thinking. The aim in writing a program outline should be to make it so clear that it reads 'like a book'.

As a general rule, material to be refined into Pascal statements should be described in terms of an imperative verb or verb phrase (e.g. 'prepare . . .' or 'output . . .' or 'calculate . . .'). Similarly, material to be refined into an expression should be described in terms of a word or phrase defining an object (e.g. 'next summand') or a situation (e.g. 'at end of data').

In the search for clarity it is often tempting to name part of a program in terms of one possible implementation. Guard against this, for it biases all your later ideas and may blind you to an alternative, and better, implementation.

Our notation for refinement steps has been chosen with two points in mind. Firstly, a refinement expands an expression or action from the program outline at the level above and it should be made clear how it fits into that context. For this reason the refinements are numbered systematically, level by level. Secondly, a refinement introduces a new set of expressions and actions. These will form part of the program outline at the next level down and it should be made clear what they are implementing. For this reason each refinement is headed by its own descriptive name, given in full. By reading just the refinement step it is possible to see *what* is being done, *how* it is being done, and *where* it belongs in the overall structure. Omitting either the name or the number reduces this self-explanatory quality of the notation.

Using the numbers of the refinement steps we can draw a diagram which shows the structure of the complete program in a vivid way. The structure diagram of **TRAFFIC**(a), developed in Section 7.2, is shown in Figure 7.1.

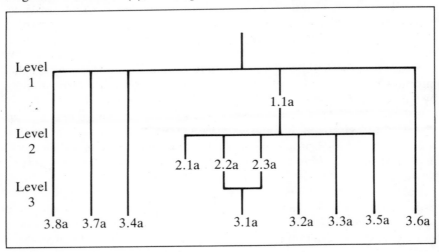

Figure 7.1. The structure of program **TRAFFIC**(a)

Each level of a program outline contains all the refinements of the previous level, as well as all the unrefined material, which is simply carried forward. Also, every refinement lies on a path down through the structure diagram, starting at Level 1. If no such path can be found for a refinement then it must be structurally invalid.

7.4 Testing and correcting

Newcomers to programming are usually surprised by how often they make mistakes. Many are reluctant to believe that the mistakes are their own fault and blame the computer instead. That is no way to become a good programmer. The only realistic attitude to this problem is a humble one: accept that mistakes will be made and try to minimize their effects.

Errors caused by misunderstanding the syntax and type rules of the programming language are 'trivial'. This may not be evident while you are struggling to master such a new and alien way of expressing yourself. However, the remark is supported by the fact that we can leave the detection of these errors to a compiler program. Of course it is desirable to avoid errors, so the syntax and semantics of the language should be learned thoroughly, and the language manual should be kept at hand for easy reference. If in doubt, look it up!

More serious are those errors of structure or logic which cause a program to fail when it is run. Some failures may be detected by the computer system, which should respond by supplying detailed and useful *diagnostic* information to help you discover the cause (although many systems are very unhelpful in this respect). Other failures only manifest themselves in erroneous output. Sometimes the failure is very obvious. Everyone has heard stories about computers terrorizing people with final demands for the payment of astronomical bills. Regrettably, these things do happen. Even more worrying is the thought that less extreme failures may completely escape attention. In fact the computer user has only two alternatives: either to trust a program, or not to use it. This places on the programmer the onus of convincing potential users that his program is trustworthy.

This is achieved by *testing*, a process which begins as soon as a Level 1 outline has been written. We have already seen how, by working through a program or a program outline with suitable data, its correct operation can be checked. The same technique may show up errors in processing that data, if such are present. Testing by hand can only be done on a small scale; more comprehensive tests are made by running the program on a computer with larger sets of data. This is indispensable, because people make as many mistakes during hand testing as they do when programming.

How can we devise good test data, whether for hand-testing or computer-testing? The best starting point is to consider all the control structures of the program, selecting test data to ensure that they are well exercised. It is necessary for proper testing that every statement in a program be obeyed at least once. But this is not sufficient. For example, a program fragment of the form:

```
statement 1;
IF condition THEN
    statement 2;
statement 3
```

gives rise to two different paths through the program. If the 'condition' is TRUE we get the path 'statement 1—statement 2—statement 3', but if it is FALSE the path followed is 'statement 1—statement 3'. Both possibilities must be tested. In other words, we also have to test the effect of *not* executing 'statement 2'. Similarly when testing a loop, we should ensure that it is tested: (a) when the body is not executed; and (b) when the body is executed several times.

We must also exercise the expressions in a program, to be sure that they represent the correct formulas. In arithmetic expressions large, small, positive, zero and negative data should be tried, as appropriate. An expression with BOOLEAN operators must be tested with every combination of TRUE and FALSE operands. If the expression is at all complicated this will require an enormous amount of test data, so here is another reason for keeping things simple.

To check the correct operation of the program, either by hand-testing or by computer testing, it will be necessary to compare the actual test results with the expected results for the same input data. Therefore it is sensible to choose test data for which the expected results can be determined easily by hand.

Take the example of program TRAFFIC(a), in Section 7.2.

(1) The outermost control structure is a loop controlled by the end-of-data condition. There are two cases: (a) when the body of the loop is not obeyed at all; and (b) the normal case in which the body is repeated once for each signal read. These cases will require separate test runs.
(2) The next structure to come out of the refinement was the chain of IF statements in 'process one signal and read the next'. To test this we need data in which only one kind of signal occurs (only timing signals, or only vehicle signals, or only error signals); data in which just two kinds of signal out of three occur (again, three cases); and data in which all three kinds of signal occur (one case).
(3) The last control structure to emerge was the IF statement in 'note the end of an interval'. This occurs in two places in the program. We must ensure that there are runs in which both, each, and neither of these are obeyed.

With these considerations in mind, we might select data sets for TRAFFIC(a) as follows:

(1a) 0
(1b) the following data sets cover this case.
(2a) 1 1 1 1 1 1 1 1 1 0
(2b) 2 2 2 2 2 2 2 2 0
(2c) 3 4 5 6 7 8 9 0
(2d) 2 1 2 1 2 1 2 1 0

(2e) 3 1 4 1 5 1 6 1 7 0
(2f) 2 3 2 4 2 5 2 6 2 0
(2g) 2 1 3 1 3 2 3 1 2 1 2 3 2 3 1 3 2 1 0
(3a) both IFs obeyed: data set (2g) covers this case.
(3b) one IF obeyed: data sets (2d) and (2e).
(3c) neither IF obeyed: data set (2a).
Although carefully constructed, these data sets by no means exhaust all the possibilities. Devise further test data sets yourself before reading on.

What do we expect the results to be for each case? By inspecting the problem specification, *not* the program, we can deduce that the output for each of these tests should be as follows:

	NO. OF VEHICLES	NO. OF ERRORS	ELAPSED TIME	LONGEST GAP
(1a)	0	0	0	0
(2a)	0	0	9	9
(2b)	8	0	0	0
(2c)	0	7	0	0
(2d)	4	0	4	1
(2e)	0	5	4	1
(2f)	5	4	0	0
(2g)	6	6	6	1

When we run the program we find that all cases give the expected output, except for case (2a), which gives:

NO. OF VEHICLES	NO. OF ERRORS	ELAPSED TIME	LONGEST GAP
0	0	9	0

Our careful choice of test data has paid off: we have discovered an error in TRAFFIC(a)! Trace through both TRAFFIC(a) and TRAFFIC(b) by hand, using test set (2a), before reading on. Can you see why the results are wrong for TRAFFIC (a)?

Any errors revealed during testing must be corrected as methodically as the program was originally constructed. Never make random changes to your program in the hope that the error will go away. You may succeed in masking the symptoms, but you will not cure the disease. Instead, work through the development of the program again, starting at Level 1, until you find the refinement where the error was introduced. Correct that refinement and carry the correction down to the Pascal coding, retesting each level as you go. Only then should you modify the program text. This approach ensures that the consequences of a change on other parts of the program are reviewed and keeps the program outlines accurate.

Let us correct TRAFFIC(a). The reason for its failure in case (2a) above is that it has not taken into account the vehicle-free interval at the end of the survey. Often this omission does not show up in the results, but in case (2a) the last (and only) interval happens to be the longest vehicle-free interval.

Careful study of Level 1a shows that it does not cater for this last interval. The wording of 'process one signal and read the next' implies that only one signal will be treated at a time, and its subsequent refinement confirms that checking the length of an interval takes place only when a vehicle or error signal is processed. To rectify this we insert 'check the length of the last interval' immediately after the loop in Level 1a. This is refined as Refinement 3.1a, so the amended program contains the statement:

```
IF INTERVAL>LONGEST THEN
   LONGEST := INTERVAL
```

immediately after the loop. Re-testing then shows that the program produces correct results for all the test cases listed above.

When can a program be assumed to be correct? Unfortunately the answer is: never! Like scientific theories, programs can never be *proved* correct by testing (although they can be proved to be incorrect, by demonstrating an error). A program which has always behaved perfectly may fail outright on the next set of data. Nonetheless, thorough testing is vital. If a program has performed according to specification on a variety of carefully-chosen and realistic sets of test data, confidence in it is justifiably increased.

7.5 Software development and documentation

{This section may be omitted on a first reading.}

Programming is not conducted in a vacuum. On the one hand, a program is written with some purpose in mind, whether serious or frivolous; and for some user or group of users, even if only for the programmer himself. On the other hand there is the computer: powerful but primitive. Developing a computer solution to the user's needs is a complex process, generally held to consist of the following six stages.

(1) First comes the job of discovering exactly what the user would like the computer to do. This may involve interviews, market surveys, or simple introspection (if you are your own user).
(2) The user requirement may need to be tempered with practicality, as there is no point in trying to provide a facility which is beyond the capacities of the computer system.
(3) The modified requirement is submitted to the user for approval. If approval is not forthcoming, steps (1) to (3) will have to be repeated

until a final and practical statement of the requirement is agreed upon (or until it is recognized that agreement cannot be reached).

(4) The user requirement has been stated in the user's terms and must now be expressed in terms of computer operations. In general a suite of programs will be needed, interacting with several sets of data. Usually the data is the heart of the matter. Once it is determined what data is initially available, and what must be generated by the system, each program can be specified by detailing its inputs and outputs. Such a specification is no more than a first refinement step, on a much larger scale than the refinements made *within* programs, but no different in principle.

(5) Given these specifications, each program is designed, written in a programming language, and tested.

(6) Since the user requirement is always subject to change, the programs may later need to be altered accordingly. If the required alterations are so extensive as to be impractical, the programs are obsolete, and the whole cycle begins again from step (1).

Steps (1) through (3) are known as *systems analysis,* step (4) is *system design,* step (5) is *implementation* and step (6) is *maintenance.* Taken together steps (5) and (6) constitute what we call *programming.* It is quite common for the implementation and maintenance phases to be the responsibility of different programmers.

This book is concerned almost exclusively with programming. Systems analysis and design are neglected here not because they are unimportant— quite the contrary—but because they depend on a mature understanding of the problems and possibilities of programming. A much longer book than this is required to do them justice.

The *documentation* of a program consists of those supporting specifications and descriptions which are needed by the user and by the maintenance programmer. It is of the utmost importance to document a program well. The user of a program is dependent on the documentation for his information about it and nothing is more annoying than discrepancies between what the documentation says and what the program actually does.

A 'User Guide' provides the information needed to exploit a program. It might contain some or all of the following sections.

(1) A brief description of the capabilities of the program. This is equivalent to the abstract of an article and its purpose is similar—to let the reader find out quickly whether the program is relevant to his needs.

(2) A detailed description. This contains a subsection for each facility of the program, giving precise descriptions of input and output requirements.

(3) Theoretical background. If the program is based on any mathematical

or scientific theory, a brief summary is given. In the case of work which has been published a reference is adequate.

(4) Resources used. The amount of store and time needed to run the program are stated, relating these factors to the amount of input. If this is not practical, the resources needed to run a 'typical' job are stated.

(5) Operational description. The instructions for the computer operator and/or the operating system control program are given, including the actions to be taken on the various kinds of failure.

The maintenance programmer can have his work greatly expedited by good documentation; bad documentation is useless. It may be necessary to scrap a poorly documented program and write a well-documented replacement which is cheaper to maintain. Even when maintaining a program which he wrote himself, the programmer often finds his own program difficult to understand after having set it aside for a few months to work on something else.

An 'Implementation Description' provides the information needed by the maintenance programmer. It might contain the following items.

(1) A complete program outline and refinement history, with discussion of the reasons for each design decision.

(2) A program structure diagram (e.g. Figure 7.1).

(3) The program text. Only the text of a program can lay claim to being a fully authoritative description. To assist the maintenance programmer, programs should be written with a view to readability. Consistent indentation, 'paragraphing' with additional blank lines, meaningful identifiers, informative comments—all these help the reader to understand a program.

Whatever its nature, documentation should be clearly written, complete, unambiguous, accurate, timely and up-to-date. Writing documentation to this standard is just as difficult as programming and should be undertaken with equal care. It is worth noting that many of the ideas that lead to readable programs also help in writing readable English. The principles of modularity, localization, consistency, and simplicity are particularly relevant.

Exercises 7

7.1. Systematically modify program DISPLAY to read one number per line of input. Negative numbers are to be accepted, and written numerically.

7.2. Which version of program **TRAFFIC** is the more efficient, in the sense of doing less work for the same result?

7.3. Systematically modify both versions of program **TRAFFIC** so that error signals are counted, but otherwise are ignored (i.e. do not end vehicle-free intervals).

7.4. Systematically modify both versions of program **TRAFFIC** so that error signals are counted, but otherwise are treated as if they were timing signals.

7.5. Systematically modify both versions of program **TRAFFIC** so that a warning message is output whenever eight consecutive error signals are received (indicating that there may be a fault in the data link). How is the modularity of the programs affected by these changes?

7.6*. Systematically modify both versions of program **TRAFFIC** so that the signals are read one per line of input and there is no terminator signal.

7.7. If you have read Section 6.5, systematically modify both versions of program **TRAFFIC** to use REPEAT statements, where appropriate, instead of WHILE statements.

7.8. Write a User Guide and an Implementation Description for program **TRAFFIC(b)**.

Programming exercises 7

7.9. Write a program which reads examination marks, one per line of input data, and outputs the number of passes (marks of 50 or over) and the number of failures (marks of under 50).

7.10. Write a program which reads details of transactions on a bank account and outputs a bank statement summarizing these transactions. The first line of the input data contains the initial balance (in £) of the bank account; the remaining lines of input data each contain a positive or negative number, a positive number indicating the amount (in £) of a credit transaction (deposit) and a negative number indicating the amount (in £) of a debit transaction (withdrawal). The bank statement should consist of the credits and debits, written in separate columns, followed by the initial and final balances of the account. An overdrawn (negative) balance should be indicated by writing the amount of the overdraft followed by the word 'OVERDRAWN'. For example, given the input data:

```
1000
+200
-500
+100
-1000
-100
```

your program should output a bank statement like this:

CREDITS (£)   DEBITS (£)

   200

             500

  100

           1000

            100

INITIAL BALANCE (£)   1000

FINAL   BALANCE (£)   300 OVERDRAWN

7.11. The takings from each turnstile of a stadium are available as data in the following form:

(a) the identification number of the turnstile;
(b) a series of positive integers, representing the income from the sale of tickets at that turnstile;
(c) a negative integer as terminator.

Write a program to read several such sets of data (one per line of input), calculate and output the total income for each turnstile separately, calculate and output the total income for the stadium, and report the number of the turnstile with the largest taking.

7.12. Air pollution counts (integer numbers in the range 0 to 100) have been measured for several consecutive days. This input data is terminated by a negative number. Write a program to find *peaks* in the pollution counts, that is, counts which are greater than those of the day before and the day after. For each peak the program should output the number of the day on which it occurred (counting from 1) and the pollution count on that day. The total number of peaks found, and the total number of measurements, are also to be output. How will you treat the first and last days in each set of data?

7.13. A cargo consisting of many separate items of differing weights is to be flown to its destination in a single aircraft, first-come first-served. In general, several trips will be required. Write a program to find out how many trips are necessary, and the total payload on each trip, given as input the maximum payload of the aircraft, followed by the weights of the items of cargo (all integer numbers rounded to the nearest kilogram, and all on separate lines). What will your program do (a) if no cargo weights are given; and (b) if a single item of cargo weighs more than the maximum payload?

Part II
Further simple data types

8
The data type CHAR

8.1 Using character data

Character data is the most common means of communication between people and computers: a program written in Pascal (or any other programming language), input data typed on a keyboard, and output printed on paper or displayed on a screen, are all expressed in characters.

For technical reasons computer character sets are restricted in size, and unfortunately not all computers use the same character set. The two most common are the ASCII (or ISO) character set, which consists of 128 characters, and the EBCDIC character set, which consists of 256 characters. They are listed in Appendix 5. All character sets include the upper-case letters, the digits, the blank character, some punctuation marks and some mathematical symbols.

To write programs which manipulate characters we need constants and variables whose values are characters. For this purpose Pascal provides the data type **CHAR**. A character constant is denoted in a program by enclosing the character between apostrophes, for example 'A' or '7' or '+' or ' ', the last of which denotes the blank character. An exceptional case is the apostrophe character itself, which is denoted by ' ' ' '.

Example 8.1

The following constant definitions make **BLANK** a synonym for the blank character and **QUERY** a synonym for the character '?':

  BLANK = ' '; QUERY = '?'

The following declares **CHARACTER** and **INITIAL** to be variables of type **CHAR**:

  CHARACTER, INITIAL : CHAR

We can now assign to these variables any character values from the character set in use on our computer, for example:

  CHARACTER := BLANK; INITIAL := 'W'

after which we can picture the variables as follows:

CHARACTER ⌈' '⌉   INITIAL ⌈'W'⌉

It is important to distinguish the latter assignment statement from

INITIAL := W

in which **W** is an *identifier* (denoting perhaps a constant or a variable), *not* the character 'W'.

Character values can be transmitted by reading and writing as well as by assignment. The statement READ(C), where C is a **CHAR** variable, reads a single character from the input data and stores that character in **C**. The statement WRITE(C) writes the character stored in **C**.

It must be emphasized that blank characters are *not* skipped by READ(C); the next character from the input data, whether blank or not, is the one which is stored in **C**. It must also be emphasized that a character to be read by READ(C) is *not* to be enclosed in apostrophes in the input data. Nor does WRITE(C) write apostrophes before and after the value of C. The convention of enclosing characters in apostrophes is used only within the text of a Pascal program, where it is needed to distinguish character values from the symbols of the program.

Example 8.2

The following program fragment reads a person's forename and surname (assuming that each name is followed by one or more blanks, and allowing for blanks preceding the forename as well). It writes the person's surname and initial. It uses the definition of **BLANK** and the declaration of **CHARACTER** and **INITIAL** from Example 8.1.

```
READ (CHARACTER);
(* skip any blanks preceding the forename *)
WHILE CHARACTER = BLANK DO
   READ (CHARACTER);
(* note the initial *)
INITIAL := CHARACTER;
(* skip the rest of the forename *)
WHILE CHARACTER <> BLANK DO
   READ (CHARACTER);
(* skip the blanks between the forename and the surname *)
WHILE CHARACTER = BLANK DO
   READ (CHARACTER);
(* read and write the surname *)
WHILE CHARACTER <> BLANK DO
   BEGIN
```

```
  WRITE (CHARACTER);
  READ (CHARACTER)
  END;
(* write the initial *)
WRITE (BLANK, INITIAL, '.')
```

For example, if the input contains:

EDSGER DIJKSTRA

then the output would be:

DIJKSTRA E.

Check this by hand-testing.

As illustrated by Example 8.2, character values may be compared using '=' or '<>'. They may also be compared using the other comparison operators '<', '<=', '>=' and '>'. You will be familiar with the alphabetic ordering of letters: 'A' comes before 'B', which in turn comes before 'C', etc. In Pascal, the comparisons 'A'<'B', 'B'<'C' and 'Z'>'A' all have the value TRUE, whereas the comparisons 'A'>'B' and 'Y'>'Z' have the value FALSE. The comparison INITIAL<='D' is TRUE if the value of INITIAL is one of the letters 'A', 'B', 'C' or 'D'; it is FALSE if the value of INITIAL is any other letter. In computers the alphabetic ordering is extended to the complete character set. Unfortunately, different character sets have different orderings, as you can see by comparing ASCII and EBCDIC (Appendix 5). For example, the digits come before the letters in ASCII, but the opposite is the case in EBCDIC. Nevertheless, all computer character sets respect the alphabetic ordering and also the numerical ordering for digits: '0'<'1', '1'<'2', and so on.

Example 8.3

The following program counts the letters and digits in the input data:

```
PROGRAM CHARACTERCOUNT (INPUT, OUTPUT);
VAR
  LETTERCOUNT, DIGITCOUNT : INTEGER;
  CHARACTER               : CHAR;
BEGIN
LETTERCOUNT := 0;
DIGITCOUNT   := 0;
WHILE NOT EOF(INPUT) DO
  BEGIN
  READ (CHARACTER);
  IF ('A' <= CHARACTER) AND (CHARACTER <= 'Z') THEN
    LETTERCOUNT := LETTERCOUNT+1
```

```
    ELSE IF ('0' <= CHARACTER) AND (CHARACTER <= '9') THEN
        DIGITCOUNT := DIGITCOUNT+1
    END;
  WRITE (LETTERCOUNT, ' LETTERS, ', DIGITCOUNT, ' DIGITS');
  WRITELN
  END.
```

This program assumes that, in the computer character set, every character between 'A' and 'Z' inclusive is a letter. This assumption is valid in most character sets including ASCII, but it is not strictly valid in EBCDIC where certain 'control characters' occur among the letters (see Appendix 5.2). These control characters are unlikely to appear in normal data, however, so the assumption is not a bad one. We shall continue to make this assumption in the examples.

If the program must allow for lower-case as well as upper-case letters, the first IF clause would be replaced by:

```
  IF ('A' <= CHARACTER) AND (CHARACTER <= 'Z') OR
     ('a' <= CHARACTER) AND (CHARACTER <= 'z') THEN
```

The program also assumes that every character between '0' and '9' inclusive is a digit. This assumption is in fact valid in every character set.

8.2 Text input and output in detail

We have now seen quite a variety of facilities for handling input and output: READ for reading integers and characters; WRITE for writing integers, characters and Boolean values; READLN; WRITELN; and EOF for testing whether all the input data has been read. These facilities have been introduced whenever convenient. It is now time to consolidate and extend our understanding of input and output in Pascal.

INPUT is the identifier of a set of data to be read by a Pascal program. OUTPUT is the identifier of a set of data which is written by a program. Both INPUT and OUTPUT may consist of several lines, with several characters on each line. This is the most convenient form of data for the human user of a computer, whether preparing input or examining output. Any set of input or output data with this structure is known as a *text file*.

To understand the input and output operations in detail, it is useful to visualize a text file as a sequence of characters and *end-of-line* markers, for example:

INPUT `P A R I S ▮ I N ▮ T H E ▮ S P R I N G - T I M E ▮`

The end-of-line markers serve to terminate the individual lines; they are indicated by ■ in the diagram above. If this text file were punched on cards, it would look like this:

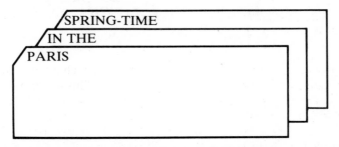

If the same text file were printed on paper, or displayed on a screen, it would look like this:

PARIS
IN THE
SPRING-TIME

Input and output of characters

When a program reads a text file, the reading position is initially at the very beginning of the text file, as indicated by the arrow:

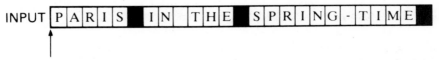

The statement **READ(C)**, where **C** is a **CHAR** variable, reads the character at the reading position, assigns it to **C**, and advances the reading position by one place:

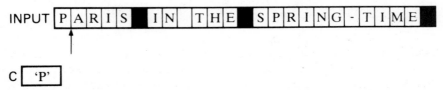

After reading four more characters, in this example, the program reaches the end of the first line:

If the program now obeys **READ(C)** again, a *blank* character is assigned to **C**, and the reading position advances to the start of the second line:

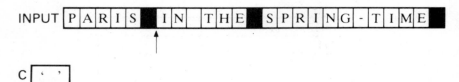

This is rather convenient when processing a text file, such as this one, containing words. The program can ignore any distinction between end-of-line markers and actual blank characters in the text file, both serving to separate words. The program of Example 8.3 also ignores the end-of-line markers, since it is concerned only with non-blank characters.

Sometimes, however, the program does need to know when the end of the current line of input has been reached. For this purpose Pascal provides the standard function **EOLN** ('End Of LiNe'), which is **TRUE** whenever the reading position is at an end-of-line marker. In our example text file there are three reading positions where **EOLN** will be **TRUE**:

In any of these positions, **READ(C)** assigns a blank to **C**.

Example 8.4

Using a **CHAR** variable **CHARACTER**, the following program fragment copies to **OUTPUT** the characters of a single line of **INPUT**:

```
WHILE NOT EOLN(INPUT) DO
  BEGIN
  READ (CHARACTER);
  WRITE (CHARACTER)
  END
```

As an exercise, trace the action of this program fragment given the above text file as input, assuming that the reading position starts: (a) at the beginning of the first line of input; (b) at the beginning of the last line of input; (c) at the third character of the last line.

The standard function **EOF** ('End Of File') is **TRUE** only when the reading position has passed the last end-of-line marker:

When **EOF** is **TRUE**, any further attempt to obey **READ** will fail, since there is no data left to be read.

The effect of **READLN** is to advance the reading position just past the end-of-line marker of the current line. If the reading position is *anywhere* in the second line, for example, **READLN** advances it just past the second end-of-line marker:

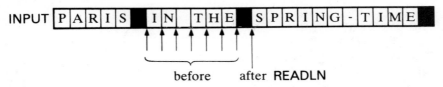

before   after **READLN**

If the reading position is anywhere in the *last* line, therefore, **READLN** makes **EOF** become **TRUE**.

Example 8.5

The following program exactly reproduces all its input data:

```
PROGRAM COPY (INPUT, OUTPUT);
VAR
  CHARACTER : CHAR;
BEGIN
WHILE NOT EOF(INPUT) DO
  BEGIN
  (* copy one line . . . *)
  WHILE NOT EOLN(INPUT) DO
    (* copy one character . . . *)
    BEGIN
    READ (CHARACTER);
    WRITE (CHARACTER)
    END;
  WRITELN;
  READLN
  END
END.
```

The inner loop is the same as Example 8.4 and is responsible for copying a single line of input. WRITELN terminates the current line of output. READLN skips to the start of the next line of input, or makes EOF become TRUE if the last line has just been copied. This is all repeated by the outer loop, which continues as long as EOF is FALSE, i.e. until the last line has been copied.

As an exercise, trace program COPY with the above text file as input. Trace it with different input to convince yourself that it works correctly (a) when supplied with input of no lines at all; and (b) when supplied with input containing an empty line.

As another exercise, trace the program with its statement part replaced by:

```
BEGIN
WHILE NOT EOF(INPUT) DO
  BEGIN
  READ (CHARACTER);
  WRITE (CHARACTER)
  END
END
```

and observe the different behaviour.

WRITE(C), where C is of type CHAR, writes a single character, the value of C. WRITE(C:W) writes the value of C at the right-hand end of a field of W spaces. The following diagrams show what characters are written in various cases:

Thus WRITE(' ':W) simply writes W blanks—a useful trick for spacing your output.

Input and output of numbers

You must understand clearly that when you write down '7' or '365', what you are writing is not itself a number but a *representation* of a number by a sequence of characters. There is nothing inherently meaningful about this representation. We could represent the number *seven* in many ways, for example '7' (decimal notation) or '111' (binary notation) or 'VII' (Roman notation). Decimal notation has been adopted as the standard representation for numbers read from and written to text files, but this was an arbitrary choice. There is nothing to prevent anyone from writing a program which, for example, reads and writes Roman numerals.

Numbers and other data require a representation inside the computer too, and this internal representation may well be different from the external representation. In particular, a binary representation is usually adopted for numbers inside the computer, since this is more efficient for computer arithmetic than decimal. Thus whenever a number is read from a text file it must be converted from character form into its internal representation; and whenever a number is written to a text file it must be converted from its internal representation into characters. These conversions are automatically performed by **READ** and **WRITE** respectively.

We can now describe precisely the effect of the statement **READ(I)**, where I is an **INTEGER** variable. The reading position is advanced first over any blanks and end-of-line markers, then over the characters which comprise the decimal representation of an integer number; finally this decimal representation is converted into the number's internal representation which is assigned to I. For example:

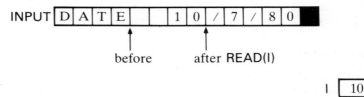

After '10' has been read, the character '/' immediately following it remains to be read subsequently. Instead of **READ(I)**, if we obeyed the statement **READ(D,C1,M,C2,Y)** where D, M and Y are **INTEGER** variables and C1 and C2 are **CHAR** variables, then we reach the following situation:

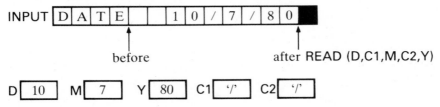

It is now possible to explain the point made in Section 6.2 about the interaction between **READLN** and **EOF**. Programs such as Example 6.4 which read one number per line of input data have the following outline structure:

```
WHILE NOT EOF(INPUT) DO
   BEGIN
   READ (NUMBER);
   process NUMBER;
   READLN
   END
```

In the following example, the arrows show the reading positions *after* each iteration of the loop, i.e. after **READLN** has been obeyed:

If the **READLN** statement were omitted, the reading position after each iteration would be immediately after the number just read:

After the sixth iteration, in this example, **EOF(INPUT)** would still be **FALSE**; so the program would then attempt to read a seventh number, causing it to fail. This is avoided by using **READLN**, which advances the reading position past the next end-of-line marker, thus making **EOF** become **TRUE** if the reading position was in the last line.

The use of **READLN** and **EOF** to detect the end of the input data is not restricted to input data containing one number per line. For example, the same idea could be used to read input data containing *two* numbers per line:

```
WHILE NOT EOF(INPUT) DO
  BEGIN
  READ (N1, N2);
  process N1 and N2;
  READLN
  END
```

The outer loop of program **COPY** (Example 8.5), which processes a *line of characters* at a time, has a similar structure. It is only when we process the input a *single character* at a time, as in Example 8.3, that we can dispense with **READLN** and still use **EOF** to detect the end of the input.

The precise effect of the statement WRITE(I:W), where I is **INTEGER**, is as follows. First, the value of I is converted from its internal representation to decimal. Then, if the decimal representation occupies fewer than **W** characters, blanks are added to the left to make up **W** characters exactly. Then all these characters are written on the current line of output. The following examples show what characters are written in various cases:

	W=5	W=3	W=1
I=+123	1 2 3	1 2 3	1 2 3
I=-9	- 9	- 9	- 9

Abbreviations

Frequently a **READ** statement is immediately followed by a **READLN** statement. Pascal allows the two to be combined into a single **READLN** statement with parameters. For example, the sequence:

READ (N1, N2); READLN

can be abbreviated to:

READLN (N1, N2)

Similarly, a **WRITE** statement can be combined with an immediately following **WRITELN**. For example, the sequence:

WRITE ('TOTAL IS ', SUM); WRITELN

can be abbreviated to:

WRITELN ('TOTAL IS ', SUM)

If you use these abbreviations, remember the order of operations carefully: with **READLN**, skipping past the end-of-line marker is always performed *last*; and with **WRITELN**, writing the end-of-line marker is always performed *last*.

Exercises 8

8.1. Modify program **CHARACTERCOUNT** (Example 8.3) to count periods, commas, semicolons and colons as well as letters and digits.

8.2. Write a program fragment which reads a line of text and outputs it with 'underlining', that is, with a hyphen under each character (on the following line).

8.3. Write a program fragment which reads a single line of characters and writes them out, replacing every sequence of consecutive blanks by a single blank. Then write a complete program which does the same for every line of input.

8.4. Modify program **COPY** (Example 8.5) to number each line of output, for example:

1 TO BE
2 OR NOT TO BE . . .
3 THAT IS THE QUESTION.

8.5. If you have read Section 6.5, recast Example 8.2 using REPEAT statements where appropriate.

Programming exercises 8

8.6. A mailing list is supplied as input data. Each line of the mailing list contains one person's name and address, divided up by obliques, e.g.:

HUGH MCSPORRAN/13 LOCH ROAD/TARBERT/SCOTLAND

Write a program which reads the mailing list and writes out the names and addresses, taking a new line at each oblique. Successive addresses are to be separated by two blank lines.

8.7. Write a program which mimics a simple calculator. The input is a series of integers separated by 'operations' ('+', '−' or '*') and terminated by '=', for example:

83+7*37=

The program is to compute the result of the calculation, 3330 in this case. The operations are to be performed from left to right: '*' has no priority over '+' or '−'.

8.8. Write a program which reads natural-language text (consisting of words separated by blanks and punctuation) and writes each word on a separate line. Treat each sequence of letters as a word, and ignore punctuation. (Note: you will not need to use the **EOLN** function in this program.)

8.9*. Write a program which reads natural-language text (as in the previous exercise), and which computes and writes the average number of letters per word and the average number of words per sentence in the text. These averages are quite good measures of the obscurity of a written text! For the purposes of this exercise, assume that every period ('.') marks the end of a sentence. Try your program on a substantial piece of text from a book.

9
Ordinal types

9.1 Enumeration types

So far we have looked in detail at three of Pascal's data types: INTEGER, whose values are whole numbers; BOOLEAN, whose values are FALSE and TRUE; and CHAR, whose values are the characters of some character set. Sometimes we need a wider choice than this; for example we might need a data type whose values are days of the week, or a data type whose values are months, or a data type whose values are primary colours. We could extend this list of useful data types indefinitely, and it would be unreasonable to expect Pascal to anticipate all possible needs. Instead Pascal provides a means for us to specifiy our own data types.

Suppose, for example, we wish to declare variables TODAY and TOMORROW whose values are days of the week. We *could* declare them as INTEGER variables, and write down statements like TODAY := 4 (where it is understood that 0 represents Sunday, 1 represents Monday, 2 represents Tuesday, and so on). This is rather artificial, and we must make an effort to remember which integers represent which days. An improvement is to introduce the constant definitions:

SUNDAY = 0; MONDAY = 1; TUESDAY = 2; WEDNESDAY = 3; THURSDAY = 4; FRIDAY = 5; SATURDAY = 6

which allow us to replace TODAY := 4 by the more natural TODAY := THURSDAY. Even now we can get into trouble: if TODAY's value is 6 and the program obeys the (perfectly legal) statement TOMMORROW := TODAY+1, what interpretation can be placed on TOMORROW's new value?

In fact, nearly all programming languages allow no better alternative to declaring TODAY and TOMORROW as INTEGER variables. Pascal is richer than most in that it allows us *explicitly* to declare variables whose values will model the days of the week, as follows:

TODAY, TOMMORROW : (SUNDAY,MONDAY,TUESDAY,
WEDNESDAY,THURSDAY,FRIDAY,
SATURDAY)

This declaration has three effects:

(a) it introduces a new data type (SUNDAY,MONDAY,TUESDAY, . . .);
(b) it implicitly defines **SUNDAY, MONDAY,** etc., to be constant identi-
    fiers which denote the values of this new data type (just as **FALSE** and
    TRUE denote the two values of the data type **BOOLEAN**);
(c) it declares **TODAY** and **TOMORROW** to be variables of this new
    data type.

The new data type is an example of an *enumeration type*, so called because
it is specified by enumeration of all its values.

Having declared these variables, we can write statements such as
TODAY := THURSDAY, after which we can picture the contents of
TODAY as follows:

TODAY | THURSDAY |

We *cannot* now write statements like **TODAY := 4**, since 4 is not a value of
the new data type; nor **TOMORROW := TODAY+1**, since the value of
TODAY is not a number and therefore cannot be added to anything.

The following are declarations of variables whose values will model
months and primary colours respectively:

MONTH: (JAN,FEB,MAR,APR,MAY,JUN,JUL,AUG,
            SEP,OCT,NOV,DEC);
COLOUR: (RED,YELLOW,BLUE)

These declarations allow us to write statements like **MONTH := MAY** and
COLOUR := YELLOW.

The syntax of enumeration types is summarized in Figure 9.1.

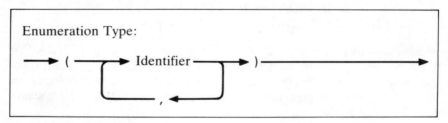

Figure 9.1. Syntax of Enumeration Types

Example 9.1

Assume the variable declaration:

DAY: (SUNDAY,MONDAY,TUESDAY,WEDNESDAY,THURSDAY,
            FRIDAY,SATURDAY)

In Pascal the constant identifier SUNDAY is unrelated to the string 'SUNDAY'. Indeed, no identifier in a Pascal program has any inherent significance. SUNDAY, MONDAY, etc. could be replaced by DIMANCHE, LUNDI, etc., or even by A, B, C, D, E, F and G, without affecting the meaning of the program. To emphasize this, Standard Pascal does not allow statements like WRITE(DAY), which you might expect to write one of the words 'SUNDAY', 'MONDAY', etc., depending on the value of DAY. If you wish to achieve this effect, therefore, you must program it explicitly:

```
IF      DAY = SUNDAY         THEN WRITE ('SUNDAY')
ELSE IF DAY = MONDAY         THEN WRITE ('MONDAY')
ELSE IF DAY = TUESDAY        THEN WRITE ('TUESDAY')
ELSE IF DAY = WEDNESDAY      THEN WRITE ('WEDNESDAY')
ELSE IF DAY = THURSDAY       THEN WRITE ('THURSDAY')
ELSE IF DAY = FRIDAY         THEN WRITE ('FRIDAY')
ELSE                              WRITE ('SATURDAY')
```

(We shall, however, find a better way to do the same thing in Section 9.7.)

The following program fragment reads a day of the week represented in the input data by 'S', 'M', 'T', 'W', 't', 'F' or 's', assuming that CHARACTER is a CHAR variable:

```
READ (CHARACTER);
IF      CHARACTER = 'S'      THEN DAY := SUNDAY
ELSE IF CHARACTER = 'M'      THEN DAY := MONDAY
ELSE IF CHARACTER = 'T'      THEN DAY := TUESDAY
ELSE IF CHARACTER = 'W'      THEN DAY := WEDNESDAY
ELSE IF CHARACTER = 't'      THEN DAY := THURSDAY
ELSE IF CHARACTER = 'F'      THEN DAY := FRIDAY
ELSE IF CHARACTER = 's'      THEN DAY := SATURDAY
ELSE
     WRITELN ('INVALID DAY-OF-THE-WEEK REPRESENTATION:',
          CHARACTER)
```

As illustrated by Example 9.1, values of the same enumeration type may be compared with one another. More operations applicable to enumeration types will be introduced in Section 9.4.

9.2 Subrange types

Suppose we wish to declare a variable NRDAYSINMONTH whose value will be the number of days in some month. We could declare NRDAYSIN-MONTH to be an INTEGER variable, but the trouble with this idea is that NRDAYSINMONTH can now be assigned values like 32 or −9999 which are meaningless in this context. In fact we know that the variable should take only values in the range from 28 to 31. Pascal allows us to incorporate this knowledge into the variable's type, as follows:

NRDAYSINMONTH : 28 . . 31

28 . . 31 is an example of a *subrange type*, specifically the subrange of INTEGER values from 28 to 31 inclusive. NRDAYSINMONTH can be used just like an ordinary INTEGER variable, with this exception: if inadvertently an out-of-range value such as 32 or −9999 is assigned to NRDAYSIN-MONTH, it can be detected automatically and a suitable error message can be issued by the computer. This error message will draw attention to a logical error in the program which might have remained undetected if NRDAYSINMONTH were an INTEGER variable.

We are not restricted to subranges of INTEGER. We can specify subranges also of CHAR or of any enumeration type, for example:

```
DIGIT          : '0' . . '9';
WEEKDAY        : MONDAY . . FRIDAY;
SUMMERMONTH : JUN . . AUG
```

The second and third declarations assume prior occurrences of the enumeration types (SUNDAY,MONDAY,TUESDAY, . . .) and (JAN,FEB, MAR, . . .) respectively. DIGIT can be used just like an ordinary CHAR variable, WEEKDAY just like a variable of type (SUNDAY,MON-DAY,TUESDAY, . . .), and so on, except that any attempt to assign an out-of-range value to one of these variables, for example by the statement WEEKDAY := SUNDAY, can be detected automatically.

Example 9.2

The following program, given as input the number of rainy days in each of the years 1900 to 1980, will write these numbers followed by a total for the whole period.

```
PROGRAM RAINYDAYS (INPUT, OUTPUT);
CONST
   FIRSTYEAR      = 1900;
   LASTYEARPLUS1  = 1981;
VAR
   YEAR                 : FIRSTYEAR . . LASTYEARPLUS1;
   NRRAINYDAYS          : 0 . . 366;
   TOTALRAINYDAYS       : 0 . . MAXINT;
BEGIN
TOTALRAINYDAYS: = 0;
YEAR := FIRSTYEAR;
WHILE YEAR < LASTYEARPLUS1 DO
```

```
  BEGIN
  READ (NRRAINYDAYS);
  WRITELN (YEAR:5, NRRAINYDAYS:8);
  TOTALRAINYDAYS := TOTALRAINYDAYS + NRRAINYDAYS;
  YEAR := YEAR+1
  END;
WRITELN ('TOTAL', TOTALRAINYDAYS:8)
END.
```

Observe that the variable **YEAR** is incremented in each iteration of the loop, and on the last iteration it will be incremented to 1981. That is why its declared type must be 1900 . . 1981, not just 1900 . . 1980.

The syntax of subrange types is summarized in Figure 9.2. The lower and upper bounds of the subrange must be *constants*, of the same type, and the lower bound must not exceed the upper bound.

Figure 9.2. Syntax of Subrange Types

The use of subrange types helps the programmer to find logical errors, since assigning an out-of-range value can be detected automatically and reported to the programmer when the program is run. Subrange types also help to make a program more understandable to the reader. A declaration like N: 1 . . 10 or N: 0 . . MAXINT, stating clearly the expected range of values of N, is much more informative than N: INTEGER. The latter declaration should preferably be used only when the range of possible values of N is not known.

9.3 Type definitions

We have already seen that constant definitions can help to make programs easier to write and to read. By giving a suitable identifier to a constant, as in the constant definition:

```
NRELEMENTS = 104
```

we can concentrate on the significance of the constant rather than its actual value.

For similar reasons Pascal provides the *type definition*, which is a means of giving an identifier to a type.

Example 9.3

The following are examples of type definitions:

```
DAYSOFTHEMONTH = 1 . . 31;
DAYSOFTHEWEEK =
  (SUNDAY,MONDAY,TUESDAY,WEDNESDAY,THURSDAY,FRIDAY,SATURDAY);
WEEKDAYS = MONDAY . . FRIDAY;
MONTHS    = (JAN,FEB,MAR,APR,MAY,JUN,JUL,AUG,SEP,OCT,NOV,DEC);
COLOURS   = (RED,YELLOW,BLUE);
LETTERS   = 'A' . . 'Z';
SEXES     = (MALE,FEMALE);
YEARSOFTHISCENTURY = 1900 . . 1999
```

DAYSOFTHEMONTH, DAYSOFTHEWEEK and so on, are thus defined to be *type identifiers*. We can now use these type identifiers in variable declarations such as:

```
DAY                 : DAYSOFTHEMONTH;
TODAY, TOMORROW     : DAYSOFTHEWEEK;
MONTH               : MONTHS;
WORKDAY             : WEEKDAYS;
COLOUR              : COLOURS;
INITIAL             : LETTERS;
YEAR                : YEARSOFTHISCENTURY
```

The above declaration of **DAY**, for example, amounts to the declaration:

```
DAY: 1 . . 31
```

but is clearer. Type identifiers like **DAYSOFTHEMONTH**, once defined, may be used in several declarations.

It may now be seen that **INTEGER**, **BOOLEAN** and **CHAR** are just predefined type identifiers. In fact, we can consider the definition of **BOOLEAN** to be:

```
BOOLEAN = (FALSE,TRUE)
```

The syntax of type definitions is summarized in Figure 9.3. In a program, any type definitions are grouped together and preceded by the reserved

Figure 9.3. Syntax of Type Definitions

word TYPE, exactly as constant definitions are grouped together and preceded by CONST. Type definitions (where present) must follow any constant definitions and precede any variable declarations.

9.4 Ordinal types in general

All the data types described so far—INTEGER, BOOLEAN, CHAR, enumeration types, and subranges thereof—are collectively called *ordinal types*. The ordinal types have certain properties in common which are not shared by the other data types of Pascal. (REAL is an example of a data type which is not ordinal. We shall meet others in the remainder of this book.)

Each value of a given ordinal type has a unique *predecessor* and a unique *successor*. For example:

(a) the predecessor of the INTEGER value 10 is 9, and its successor is 11;
(b) the predecessor of the CHAR value 'E' is 'D', and its successor is 'F' (at least in the ASCII and EBCDIC character sets);
(c) in the enumeration type MONTHS (Example 9.3), the predecessor of FEB is JAN, and its successor is MAR—since JAN and MAR immediately precede and succeed FEB in the enumeration (JAN,FEB, MAR,. . .).

However, one value of each type (e.g. JAN) has no predecessor, and one value of each type (e.g. DEC) has no successor.

Pascal provides two standard functions, PRED and SUCC, which take a single parameter of any ordinal type and return the predecessor and successor, respectively, of its value. Thus PRED(FEB) is JAN and SUCC (FEB) is MAR. In ASCII and EBCDIC, PRED('E') is 'D' and SUCC('E') is 'F'; SUCC('I') is 'J' in ASCII but something else in EBCDIC. If N is of type INTEGER, then PRED(N) is equivalent to N−1 and SUCC(N) to N+1.

Example 9.4

Assuming the declarations of TODAY and TOMORROW from Example 9.3, the following program fragment determines what day TOMORROW will be:

```
IF TODAY = SATURDAY THEN
   TOMORROW := SUNDAY
ELSE
   TOMORROW := SUCC(TODAY)
```

It would be an error to attempt to evaluate SUCC(TODAY) when TODAY's value is SATURDAY, since SATURDAY has no successor.

To every value of a given ordinal type there corresponds a unique INTEGER value, called its *ordinal number*. (Hence the terminology 'ordinal type'.) The standard function ORD accepts a parameter of any ordinal type and returns its ordinal number. The values of an enumeration type (including BOOLEAN) have ordinal numbers 0, 1, 2, etc. For example, the ordinal numbers of DAYSOFTHEWEEK values and BOOLEAN values are as follows:

```
(SUNDAY,MONDAY,TUESDAY,WEDNESDAY,THURSDAY,FRIDAY,SATURDAY)
    0       1       2         3          4       5        6

(FALSE,TRUE)
   0     1
```

The ordinal number of each INTEGER value is itself. CHAR values have ordinal numbers which depend on the particular character set in use; see Appendix 5.

These ordinal numbers imply an ordering on the values of every ordinal type. We have already seen, in Chapters 5 and 8, that we can compare two INTEGER values, or two BOOLEAN values, or two CHAR values, using any of the comparison operators '=', '<>', '<', '<=', '>=' or '>'. The same applies to all ordinal types. The value of the comparison A<B, where A and B are of the same ordinal type, is the same as the value of ORD(A)<ORD(B).

In the case of an enumeration type, the ordering of its values is the same as their order of enumeration. Thus, for the type DAYSOFTHEWEEK (Example 9.3), SUNDAY<MONDAY and FRIDAY>MONDAY are both TRUE; SATURDAY<SUNDAY and MONDAY>TUESDAY are both FALSE. The expression TODAY<TUESDAY has the value TRUE if and only if the value of TODAY is SUNDAY or MONDAY.

Example 9.5

The statement READ(NUMBER), where NUMBER is an INTEGER variable, reads an integer number in the conventional *decimal* notation. The following program fragment could be used to read an unsigned integer number represented in *octal* (base 8) notation. The number may be preceded by zero or more blanks.

```
READ (CHARACTER);
(* skip any blanks preceding the number *)
WHILE CHARACTER = ' '  DO
   READ (CHARACTER);
NUMBER := 0;
WHILE ('0' <= CHARACTER) AND (CHARACTER <= '7') DO
   BEGIN
```

```
NUMBER   :=   8*NUMBER   +   (ORD(CHARACTER)−ORD('0'));
READ (CHARACTER)
END
```
(* stops after reading a character which is not an octal digit *)

This uses a CHAR variable CHARACTER.

The expression ('0'<=CHARACTER) AND (CHARACTER<='7') is used to test whether the character stored in CHARACTER is an octal digit. To compute the value of the octal number we must determine the value *represented* by each octal digit. This value is *not* given simply by ORD(CHARACTER), since, for example, ORD('0') = 48 and ORD('7') = 55 in ASCII. However, in every character set the digits have consecutive ordinal numbers, so the value represented by any digit is given by the expression ORD(digit)−ORD('0').

For the type CHAR only, the inverse of ORD is also provided in Pascal. This is the standard function CHR, which accepts a single INTEGER parameter and returns the corresponding CHAR value (if such a CHAR value exists).

Example 9.6

Assume NUMBER contains an integer between 0 and 9999. Suppose we wish to write out its value as a 4-digit decimal number, for example the value 13 is to be written as '0013'. The statement WRITE(NUMBER:4) is not quite satisfactory, since it would replace leading zeros by blanks.

We can solve this problem by dividing successively by 1000, 100 and 10; at each step the quotient decides which digit is to be written, and the remainder is retained for the next division. Assuming the variable declarations:

```
QUOTIENT   : 0 . . 9;
REMAINDER : 0 . . 9999;
POWEROF10 : 0 . . 1000;
POS        : 0 . . 4
```

here is a solution:

```
POWEROF10 := 1000;
REMAINDER := NUMBER;
POS := 4;
WHILE POS > 0 DO
   BEGIN
   QUOTIENT := REMAINDER DIV POWEROF10;
   REMAINDER := REMAINDER MOD POWEROF10;
   WRITE (CHR(QUOTIENT + ORD('0')));
   POWEROF10 := POWEROF10 DIV 10;
```

```
POS := POS−1
END
```

The value of **QUOTIENT**, an integer in the range 0 to 9, is converted to the corresponding numeric character by adding **ORD('0')** and then applying **CHR** to the result. **CHR(QUOTIENT)** would be wrong, since **CHR(0)** to **CHR(9)** are *not* the digits '0' to '9' in general, certainly not in ASCII nor EBCDIC.

Verify the solution by hand-testing, assuming that the character set is (a) ASCII, (b) EBCDIC. (Refer to Appendix 5.)

This example is the basis for a number of special ways of formatting numbers for output: see Exercises 9.

When writing a program which manipulates characters, it is tempting to exploit the peculiarities of a particular character set. For example, if the character set is ASCII we might exploit this knowledge in Example 9.5 to write:

```
NUMBER := 8*NUMBER + (ORD(CHARACTER)−48)
```

A more subtle error is to assume that the character set has consecutive ordinal numbers for its letters, and use the expression **CHR(ORD('A')+I−1)** to yield the I-th letter of the alphabet. We might even get away with such errors—unless we tried to run our program on a different computer with a different character set, when the results would be ridiculous! A program which will run correctly on a variety of computers is much more useful than one which is tied to a particular computer. So, whenever possible, write programs that work for any choice of character set. If any part of a program is *unavoidably* dependent on a particular character set, it should be marked clearly by a suitable comment.

9.5 Type rules for ordinal types

The type rules of Pascal are designed to prevent meaningless operations like assigning a character to a **BOOLEAN** variable, or comparing a character with an integer. The Pascal compiler will detect all such errors, rather than allow the program to run and perhaps produce strange results.

Now that we have met a variety of ordinal types and operations, it is time to summarize the type rules associated with them.

Operands in expressions

In general, operators may not have operands of different types. Thus **DIV** must have two **INTEGER** operands, and **OR** must have two **BOOLEAN** operands. However, a variable of a subrange type may always be used as an operand as if it were declared without the range restriction. Functions like ORD and CHR must be used if it is required to convert values from one ordinal type to another.

Assignment compatibility

In general, the expression in an assignment statement must be *assignment-compatible* with the type of the variable on the left-hand side. Usually this requires the variable and the expression to be of the same type. However, the variable's type may be a subrange of the expression's type (provided that whenever the assignment is performed the expression's value is within the range of the variable's type), or vice versa. If these conditions are satisfied, the expression is said to be *assignment-compatible* with the variable's type.

9.6 Count-controlled repetition: the FOR statement

Refer back to Examples 6.2 and 6.3. There is a significant difference between the loops in these examples. In Example 6.3 the number of iterations of the loop cannot be predicted, since it depends on the data read by the loop itself. In Example 6.2, on the other hand, the number of iterations is known in advance of entering the loop: it is the value of SIZE.

Loops with a predetermined number of iterations are very common, and they all have the same characteristic feature: they use a *control variable* (COUNT in Example 6.2) to count the iterations. The control variable is first given an initial value; inside the loop it is incremented (or decremented); and the loop terminates when the control variable is found to have reached its final value.

Such loops occur so frequently that Pascal provides a special construct, the *FOR statement*, to simplify writing them.

Example 9.7

We can simplify the solution of Example 6.2, using a FOR statement, as follows:

```
PROGRAM SUMBYCOUNT (INPUT, OUTPUT);
VAR
   SUM, SUMMAND, COUNT, SIZE: INTEGER;
BEGIN
SUM := 0;
(* Read the size of the list *)
```

```
READ (SIZE);
FOR COUNT := 1 TO SIZE DO
  BEGIN
  READ (SUMMAND);
  SUM := SUM + SUMMAND
  END;
WRITELN ('SUM OF INTEGERS READ IS ', SUM)
END (* SUMBYCOUNT *).
```

The clause FOR COUNT := 1 TO SIZE DO means 'Repeatedly execute the following statement with the control variable COUNT taking consecutive values from 1 up to SIZE inclusive.' This clause replaces the clause WHILE COUNT < SIZE DO, *and* the statements COUNT := 0 and COUNT := COUNT+1, in Example 6.2.

What happens if the value of SIZE is 0? In Example 6.2, where COUNT is initialized to 0, the WHILE condition COUNT<SIZE is already FALSE, so no iterations at all are performed, therefore no more numbers are read and the sum is 0. Using the FOR statement also, no iterations are performed since the control variable's initial value, 1, is greater than its final value, 0. Thus this version of program SUMBYCOUNT also correctly computes the sum as 0 when SIZE is 0.

In Example 9.7 the control variable was used solely for counting. If desired, the repeated statement(s) may use the control variable's *value*. For example, we could insert the statement:

WRITE ('SUMMAND ', COUNT, ' WAS ', SUMMAND)

inside the loop of Example 9.7. However, the repeated statement(s) must not attempt to *alter* the control variable, for example by assigning a value to it. The FOR statement itself has the exclusive right to update the control variable, which it does 'behind the scenes' on every iteration.

There is one, rather subtle, difference between the programs of Examples 6.2 and 9.7. When we leave the WHILE statement in Example 6.2 the value of COUNT is equal to the value of SIZE, for example:

SIZE [8]   COUNT [8]

After leaving the FOR statement in Example 9.7, on the other hand, the value of the control variable COUNT would depend on the exact manner in which it is updated 'behind the scenes' by the FOR statement, and this might vary from one compiler to another. Consequently, we must assume that the control variable is *undefined* after leaving the FOR statement:

SIZE [8]   COUNT [?]

Example 9.8

The program of Example 9.2 can be rewritten more neatly using a FOR statement:

```
PROGRAM RAINYDAYS (INPUT, OUTPUT);
CONST
  FIRSTYEAR = 1900;
  LASTYEAR = 1980;
VAR
  YEAR               : FIRSTYEAR . . LASTYEAR;
  NRRAINYDAYS     : 0 . . 366;
  TOTALRAINYDAYS : 0 . . MAXINT;
BEGIN
TOTALRAINYDAYS := 0;
FOR YEAR := FIRSTYEAR TO LASTYEAR DO
  BEGIN
  READ (NRRAINYDAYS);
  WRITELN (YEAR:5, NRRAINYDAYS:8);
  TOTALRAINYDAYS := TOTALRAINYDAYS + NRRAINYDAYS
  END;
WRITELN ('TOTAL', TOTALRAINYDAYS:8)
END.
```

This solution avoids the problem mentioned in Example 9.2, since **YEAR** is no longer assigned the value 1981.

Example 9.9

Assuming the variable declarations:

```
MONTH               : MONTHS; (* see Example 9.3 *)
NRRAINYDAYS     : 0 . . 31;
TOTALRAINYDAYS : 0 . . 366
```

the following program fragment reads and totals 12 *monthly* rainy-day counts:

```
TOTALRAINYDAYS := 0;
FOR MONTH := JAN TO DEC DO
  BEGIN
  READ (NRRAINYDAYS);
  TOTALRAINYDAYS := TOTALRAINYDAYS + NRRAINYDAYS
  END
```

In this example the loop is repeated 12 times, with the control variable **MONTH** taking the values **JAN, FEB, . . ., DEC**.

Occasionally we need to write a FOR statement in which the control variable takes *decreasing* values. For this purpose we use DOWNTO instead of TO.

Example 9.10

The solution of Example 9.6 can be simplified using a FOR statement:

```
POWEROF10 := 1000;
REMAINDER := NUMBER;
FOR POS := 4 DOWN TO 1 DO
   BEGIN
   QUOTIENT := REMAINDER DIV POWEROF10;
   REMAINDER := REMAINDER MOD POWEROF10;
   WRITE (CHR(QUOTIENT + ORD('0')));
   POWEROF10 := POWEROF10 DIV 10
   END
```

Example 9.10 could have been written just as well with TO as with DOWNTO. Another example using DOWNTO will be found in Section 11.3.

The syntax of FOR statements is summarized in Figure 9.4. FOR, TO, DOWNTO and DO are all reserved words. The control variable must be declared just like any other variable, and its type must be *ordinal*. The

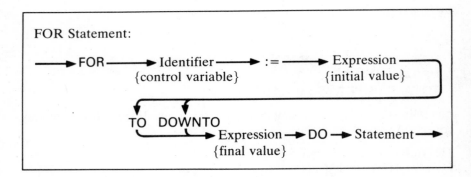

Figure 9.4. Syntax of FOR Statements

initial and final values of the control variable may be determined by any expressions assignment-compatible in type with the control variable. These expressions are evaluated just once, before entry to the loop.

9.7 Multi-way selection: the CASE statement

The IF statement allows a program to select one of *two* alternative courses of action—either the statement following THEN or the statement following ELSE—depending on the value of the BOOLEAN expression following IF. Frequently, however, we wish the program to select one of *several* different courses of action, as the following examples illustrate.

Example 9.11

Recall the first program fragment of Example 9.1, where we wished to select one of seven courses of action, depending on the value of DAY. The cascade of IF statements used in that example was clumsy and also rather inefficient, since the value of DAY could be inspected as many as six times. When there are more than seven courses of action, this style of programming is even less satisfactory.

What we need is a new construct in which the desired course of action is selected *immediately* after a single inspection of the value of DAY. For such a purpose Pascal provides the *CASE statement*:

```
CASE DAY OF
    SUNDAY:       WRITE ('SUNDAY');
    MONDAY:       WRITE ('MONDAY');
    TUESDAY:      WRITE ('TUESDAY');
    WEDNESDAY:    WRITE ('WEDNESDAY');
    THURSDAY:     WRITE ('THURSDAY');
    FRIDAY:       WRITE ('FRIDAY');
    SATURDAY:     WRITE ('SATURDAY')
END
```

Here DAY is the *case index* of the CASE statement. The constants SUNDAY, MONDAY, TUESDAY, etc., which are the potential values of the case index, are used as *case labels*, each placed in front of a component statement.

If the value of DAY is WEDNESDAY, for example, then the component statement WRITE('WEDNESDAY') is obeyed, and no other.

The effect of a CASE statement is as follows. The case index is evaluated, then *one* component statement is obeyed, namely that component statement which is labelled by the case index's value.

The syntax of CASE statements is summarized in Figure 9.5. CASE, OF and END are all reserved words. The case index may be any expression of any ordinal type, and the case labels must all be distinct constants of this same type. Notice that several case labels may be placed in front of the same component statement; this is useful when the same action is to be taken for several different case index values.

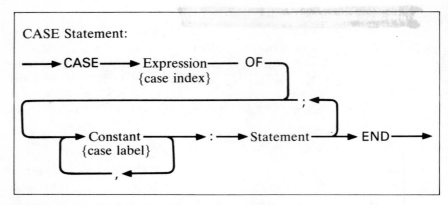

CASE Statement:

Figure 9.5. Syntax of CASE Statements (simplified)

Example 9.12

'Soundex' is a method of encoding names in such a way that slight spelling variations are unlikely to affect the code. The basis of the encoding is the following phonetic grouping of characters:

group 0: A, E, I, O, U, H, W, Y,
          all non-alphabetic characters;
group 1: B, F, P, V;
group 2: C, G, J, K, Q, S, X, Z;
group 3: D, T;
group 4: L;
group 5: M, N;
group 6: R.

{The characters of the name are first encoded as digits according to the grouping: thus 'SMITH' becomes '25030', and 'SCHMIDT' becomes '2205033'. Then consecutive similar digits are replaced by a single digit, and finally all zeros are removed: thus both 'SMITH' and 'SCHMIDT' become '253'.}

Given the variables:

```
CHARACTER : CHAR;
GROUP     : '0' . . '6'
```

Let us write a program fragment to store, in GROUP, the group into which CHARACTER falls.

We can solve this problem using a CASE statement with CHARACTER as the case index; the case labels will be character constants.

```
IF (CHARACTER<'A') OR (CHARACTER>'Z') THEN
  GROUP := '0' (* CHARACTER is non-alphabetic *)
ELSE
  CASE CHARACTER OF
    'A', 'E', 'I', 'O', 'U', 'H', 'W', 'Y':      GROUP := '0';
    'B', 'F', 'P', 'V':                          GROUP := '1';
    'C', 'G', 'J', 'K', 'Q', 'S', 'X', 'Z':      GROUP := '2';
    'D', 'T':                                    GROUP := '3';
    'L':                                         GROUP := '4';
    'M', 'N':                                    GROUP := '5';
    'R':                                         GROUP := '6'
  END
```

It is essential for every potential value of the case index to occur exactly once as a case label in a CASE statement. If the case index turns out to yield a value which is not present as a case label, the program will fail. In Example 9.12 only the letters were used as case labels, whereas **CHARAC-TER** could have any character value; hence the prior check which circumvents the CASE statement if the value of **CHARACTER** is definitely not a letter. (It is assumed, however, that the value of **CHARACTER** *is* a letter if it falls between 'A' and 'Z'.)

Example 9.13

The following program fragment updates the score in a table-tennis game. It uses the variables:

```
SERVERSCORE, OTHERSCORE : 0 . . MAXINT;
FINISHED : BOOLEAN;
POINT : (SERVERSPOINT,OTHERSPOINT,LET)
```

It assumes that the first three variables have been initialized, and that the result of the latest play has been recorded in the variable **POINT**.

```
CASE POINT OF
  SERVERSPOINT:
    BEGIN
    SERVERSCORE := SERVERSCORE+1;
    IF (SERVERSCORE>=21) AND
         (SERVERSCORE−OTHERSCORE>=2) THEN
      FINISHED := TRUE
    END;
  OTHERSPOINT:
    BEGIN
    OTHERSCORE := OTHERSCORE+1;
    IF (OTHERSCORE>=21) AND
```

```
            (OTHERSCORE—SERVERSCORE>=2) THEN
      FINISHED := TRUE
    END;
  LET:
END (* CASE *)
```

Example 9.13 illustrates nesting of compound statements and IF statements within a CASE statement. It also illustrates how we can arrange to do nothing at all in some cases (LET in the example): we use a *dummy statement* as the relevant component statement. A dummy statement consists of no symbols at all, and one can be 'seen' between 'LET:' and END in the example.

Exercises 9

9.1. Assuming the variable declarations:

  I : INTEGER; J : 1 .. 10; C : CHAR; S : (MALE,FEMALE)

which of the following are legal expressions?

(a) I+1   (b) I+J   (c) I=J   (d) I=C   (e) C=S
(f) C='*'   (g) S=MALE   (h) ORD(C)+I   (i) C=CHR(I)   (j) ORD(S)+1

Which of the following are legal statements?

(k) I := 1   (l) I := J   (m) J := I   (n) C := 'I'   (o) C := I
(p) C := CHR(I)   (q) I := C   (r) I := ORD(C)   (s) S := I   (t) S := SUCC(S)

Which of the following are legal FOR clauses?

(u)   FOR J := 1 TO I DO ...
(v)   FOR S := MALE TO FEMALE DO ...
(w)   FOR S := 0 TO 1 DO ...
(x)   FOR C := 'A' TO 'Z' DO ...

9.2. A university has faculties of Science, Medicine, Law and Arts. (a) Write a declaration of a variable FACULTY which can be used to indicate in which faculty a student is studying. (b) Write a program fragment to read a value for FACULTY, represented in the input data by a single character, 'S', 'M', 'L' or 'A'. (c) Write a program fragment which outputs, in full, the name of this faculty.

9.3. Assuming that today's date has been stored in the variables

  DAY: 1 .. 31; MONTH: MONTHS; YEAR: 0 .. 9999

(see Example 9.3 for the definition of MONTHS), write a program fragment which outputs today's date: (a) writing 1 for January, 2 for February, and so on; (b) writing the name of the month in full.

9.4. Continuing from the previous exercise, write a program fragment which updates the variables to tomorrow's date.

9.5. Recast Example 6.1 using a FOR statement.

9.6. Recast the inner loop of Example 6.10 using a FOR statement.

9.7. Modify Example 9.5 so that it reads a *decimal* number rather than an octal number. Further modify it so as to allow (but ignore) commas in the decimal number.

9.8. Modify Example 9.6 so that the output is preceded by a currency sign, e.g. '£0013'. Further modify it so that leading zeros are replaced by asterisks, e.g. '£**13'. (This idea is used in computer printing of cheques, rather than replacing the leading zeros by blanks, as a protection against fraud.)

9.9. Generalize Example 9.6 so that it writes a W-digit decimal number, where W is any positive integer. Then make it insert commas every three digits, e.g. '12,500,000'.

9.10. Assume that the charge for sending a parcel overseas is calculated as follows. First, its weight is rounded *up* to the nearest multiple of 15 grams. Then the charge is taken from the table:

Weight (grams)	Charge (pence)
15	12
30	22
45	31
60	36, plus 2 per *complete* 1000 km
75 and over	40, plus 3 per *complete* 1000 km

Given that its weight in grams and the distance in kilometres have been stored in the INTEGER variables WEIGHT and DISTANCE respectively, write a program fragment which assigns the charge in pence to the INTEGER variable CHARGE. Use a CASE statement.

Programming exercises 9

9.11. Write a program which reads an integer N, and outputs the squares and cubes of all the integers from 1 to N inclusive.

9.12. One of the earliest uses of computers was in cryptography. The simplest method of encoding a message is to encode each character by a unique integer (such as its ordinal number). This kind of code is broken rather easily, however, by an analysis based on the known relative frequencies of the characters. A better method is as follows: (a) encode the *first* character of the message by its ordinal number; (b) encode each *subsequent* character by adding its ordinal number to the *previous* character's encoding, and taking this sum modulo KEY (where KEY is a constant, which is supposed to be secret). For example, if KEY=300 and the first few characters of the message have ordinal numbers 100, 255, 35, 220, . . ., then the encoded message would start:

100
55 (= 255+100 modulo 300)
90 (= 35+55 modulo 300)
10 (= 220+90 modulo 300)

Write a program which, given a single-line message as input data, uses this method to encode the message as a sequence of integers, terminated by −1.

(b) Devise a method of *decoding* a message encoded as above. Write a program to perform this decoding, and test it with the output from your encoding program. Make sure that your decoding program successfully reconstructs the original message!

9.13. The population and GNP (gross national product, expressed in European Currency Units) for Belgium, Denmark, Eire, France, Germany, Holland, Italy, Luxembourg and the United Kingdom (in that order) are supplied as input data, in the form of two integers per line. Write a program which reads this data and outputs it as a table showing the name of each country, its population, its GNP and its *per capita* GNP. Include suitable headings, and a final line showing the total population, total GNP and average *per capita* GNP.

10
The data type REAL

10.1 Real numbers and real arithmetic

So far we have concerned ourselves only with *integer* arithmetic—the arithmetic of whole numbers. These numbers are useful for purposes of counting, but they are inadequate when we wish to deal with quantities that vary continuously, such as distances, time intervals, weights, probabilities and so on. For example, the distance between two points might be expressed as 14.65 metres, and the time interval between two events might be expressed as 9.2 seconds, both measurements involving a fraction. Such values are called *real numbers*.

Just as with integer numbers, the number of digits of a real number which can be stored in a digital computer is limited. As a consequence:

(a) there is a limit to the *magnitude* of real numbers which can be stored in the computer (typically about 10^{30} to 10^{70}); and
(b) there is a limit to the *precision* with which real numbers can be represented in the computer (this limit varies from about 6 to about 17 decimal digits on different systems).

The magnitude range is indeed enormous, and the precision may seem excellent. Nevertheless these limitations must be taken into account. In particular, the limited magnitude introduces the danger of overflow and the limited precision gives rise to a variety of subtle programming problems.

In order to exploit the available precision fully, only the most significant digits of a real number are stored. The position of the fractional point relative to the stored digits is held in a separate *scale factor*. Negative scale factors move the point to the left, positive scale factors move it to the right. For example, in a computer capable of storing a real number to 6 decimal digits:

0.0099	is stored as 9.90000 with a scale factor of -3
0.99	,, ,, ,, 9.90000 ,, ,, ,, ,, ,, -1
9.9	,, ,, ,, 9.90000 ,, ,, ,, ,, ,, 0
9900.0	,, ,, ,, 9.90000 ,, ,, ,, ,, ,, $+3$

8.7654321 ,,   ,,   ,, 8.76543 ,, ,, ,,   ,,   ,,   0
44530871.6 ,,   ,,   ,, 4.45309 ,, ,, ,,   ,,   ,, +7

This is the *floating-point* representation, so called because the number of stored digits is fixed and the point 'floats' relative to the stored digits. The computer automatically keeps track of the position of the point and takes this into account when performing arithmetic.

The limited precision of the floating-point representation forces numbers with too many significant digits to be *rounded,* as illustrated above. This can give surprising results.

Example 10.1

If we divide 1.0 by 3.0 and then multiply by 3.0, we might expect the result to be 1.0. The mathematical result of the division is 0.3333333333. . . ., but in our 6-digit computer this result must be rounded to 0.333333. Then when we multiply by 3.0, we end up with 0.999999!

Example 10.2

If we subtract 10000.0 from 10000.1 and then add 0.04, we expect the result to be 0.14, and in our 6-digit computer this will indeed be so. If we perform the calculation in a different order, however, we may get a different result. If we first add 0.04 to 10000.1, the mathematical result, 10000.14, is rounded to 10000.1; now when we subtract 10000.0, the result is 0.1!

In some computers, results of arithmetic operations are *truncated* rather than rounded, for example the value 0.66666666666 . . . . would be truncated to 0.666666 (with resulting error 0.00000066 . . . .) rather than rounded to 0.666667 (with resulting error 0.00000033 . . . .). Evidently, truncation causes even more inaccuracy than rounding.

In nearly every digital computer real numbers are stored in a binary base, rather than a decimal base. Nevertheless, the problems illustrated by these examples remain. The use of the binary base does create an additional problem for us, accustomed as we are to expressing numbers in decimal. Many numbers (such as 1/3) cannot be expressed exactly as decimal fractions. Similarly, there are many numbers (such as 0.9) which *can* be expressed exactly as decimal fractions, but which *cannot* be expressed exactly as binary fractions. Thus when we use a constant like '0.9' in a program, or in a set of data, we should be aware that the number actually stored in the computer will only be an approximation to 0.9.

Real numbers obtained by physical measurement can have only limited accuracy, which depends on the device used to measure them. This is the cause of *observational error*, and is important because we cannot expect a calculation to yield results which are more accurate than the original input data. For example, quoting the distance to the moon as '240000 miles, or 386473 kilometres' is just silly, since the original figure was accurate only to 2 significant digits.

Most real numbers, however accurately known or measured, cannot be represented exactly in a computer. This applies to all irrational numbers, to rational numbers which have no exact binary representation, and to numbers with too many significant digits. This phenomenon is called *representational error*, and it forces numbers input to the computer, and those resulting from arithmetic operations, to be rounded or truncated.

Arithmetic operations tend to compound any errors in their operands. For example, if we subtract 4.999996 (represented by 5.00000) from 6.00004 (represented by 6.00000), we get the result 1.00000, in spite of the fact that the mathematical result, 1.000008, rounded to 6 significant digits yields 1.00001. Thus results can be less accurate than the data from which they are derived. This phenomenon is called *computational error.*

Normally, representational errors will be smaller than observational errors; computer users should make sure of this by presenting their real data to a computer which can store more significant digits than their data actually possesses. We shall see, however, that representational errors can accumulate, especially in highly iterative programs, so it is unwise to neglect them.

10.2 REAL arithmetic in Pascal

Real numbers, within the limitations of magnitude and precision discussed in the previous section, are values of the Pascal data type **REAL**. We may declare variables whose type is **REAL**, and we may assign **REAL** values to such variables.

In Pascal, real numbers may be expressed either in the conventional notation for decimal fractions, or alternatively in the *scientific notation*, which is convenient for expressing very large and very small numbers, for example:

55E15	is equivalent to		55000000000000000.0
−3.8E3	,,	,,	,, −3800.0
1E−4	,,	,,	,, 0.0001
1.23E−20	,,	,,	,, 0.0000000000000000000123

Here E should be read as 'times ten to the power of'. The syntax of real numbers is summarized in Appendix 1.7.

REAL expressions may be composed in a similar manner to **INTEGER** expressions. The following operators may be used:

$$+ \quad - \quad * \quad /$$

The operator '/' denotes **REAL** division: the result of applying '/' to any two numbers is a **REAL** number as close as possible to the exact quotient of these numbers. Thus 7/3 yields the **REAL** result 2.33333 on a 6-digit computer (compare the expression 7 DIV 3, which yields the **INTEGER** result 2). The operator '/' has the same priority as '*'.

A **REAL** value may be assigned to a **REAL** variable by an assignment statement with a **REAL** expression to the right of ':='. Placing a **REAL** variable in a **READ** (or **READLN**) statement causes a real number to be read from the input data. Including a **REAL** expression in a **WRITE** (or **WRITELN**) statement causes a real number to be written.

Example 10.3

The following program reads the radius of a circle, computes its circumference and area, and outputs all three values:

```
PROGRAM CIRCLE (INPUT, OUTPUT);
CONST
  PI = 3.14159265;
VAR
  RADIUS, CIRCUMFERENCE, AREA : REAL;
BEGIN
READ (RADIUS);
CIRCUMFERENCE := 2 * PI * RADIUS;
AREA := PI * SQR(RADIUS);
WRITELN (RADIUS, CIRCUMFERENCE, AREA)
END (* CIRCLE *).
```

Given the input data:

    3.0

the output would look like this:

    3.000000E+00 1.884956E+01 2.827433E+01

Note that **REAL** values are by default written in scientific notation, with as many fraction digits as possible. Each number is preceded by '−' if negative, or by a blank otherwise. There is no extra spacing.

We can specify a field width explicitly in the usual way, for example:

WRITELN (RADIUS:8, CIRCUMFERENCE:10, AREA:10)

which simply decreases (or increases) the number of fraction digits written:

    3.0E+00 1.885E+01 2.827E+01

We can also request output in the conventional notation, by specifying the number of fraction digits required as well as the field width:

WRITELN (RADIUS:8:1, CIRCUMFERENCE:10:1, AREA:10:1)

would make the output look like this:

    3.0   18.8   28.3

Example 10.3 illustrates a use of the standard function **SQR** in a **REAL** expression. Pascal provides a variety of standard functions for performing useful, and sometimes complicated, calculations. Each of the following standard functions accepts a single **INTEGER** or **REAL** parameter, and returns a result of the same type:

ABS(x) computes the absolute value (magnitude) of x.
SQR(x)   ,,   ,, square of x.

Each of the following standard functions accepts a single **REAL** parameter and returns a **REAL** result:

SIN(x)   computes the sine of x.
COS(x)   ,,   ,, cosine of x.
ARCTAN(x)   ,,   ,, arctangent of x.
EXP(x)   ,,   ,, value of e raised to the power of x.
LN(x)   ,,   ,, logarithm of x to the base e.
SQRT(x)   ,,   ,, square root of x.

(The parameters of **SIN** and **COS**, and the result of **ARCTAN**, are angles expressed in *radians*.) Each of the following standard functions accepts a single **REAL** parameter and returns an **INTEGER** result:

ROUND(x) computes x rounded to the nearest integer.
TRUNC(x)   ,, x truncated to its integral part.

Thus **ROUND(2.6)** =3, but **TRUNC(2.6)** = 2; and **ROUND(−2.6)** = −3, but **TRUNC(−2.6)** = −2.

Finally, **REAL** expressions may be compared using any of the comparison operators '=', '<>', '<', '<=', '>=' or '>'.

Example 10.4

Given a rectangle with sides **SIDE1** and **SIDE2**, and a circle with radius **RADIUS**, where **SIDE1**, **SIDE2** and **RADIUS** are all **REAL** variables, the following program fragment determines which figure has the longer perimeter:

```
IF SIDE1 + SIDE2 > PI * RADIUS THEN
   WRITE ('RECTANGLE')
ELSE
   WRITE ('CIRCLE');
WRITELN (' HAS LONGER PERIMETER')
```

10.3 Type rules for REAL

Operands in expressions

Because there is a real number equivalent to every integer number, a REAL expression may contain INTEGER operands (which are converted automatically to REAL). This is illustrated by an expression from Example 10.3:

2 * PI * RADIUS

Assignment compatibility

It is legitimate to assign an INTEGER value to a REAL variable. Again an automatic conversion takes place. For example:

RADIUS := 3 has the same effect as RADIUS := 3.0

On the other hand, REAL operands may *not* be used in INTEGER expressions, nor may a REAL value be assigned to an INTEGER variable. If N is an INTEGER variable, the statement:

N := 3.14159

is invalid, because N may take only INTEGER values and there is no INTEGER value equal to 3.14159. Note that the statement:

N := 3.0

is also invalid. The constant '3.0' is of type REAL, even though its fraction part happens to be zero.

When reading a value into a REAL variable, the data item supplied may be either an INTEGER number or a REAL number.

10.4 Programming with REAL data

As a consequence of the inherent approximations in REAL arithmetic, 'obvious' equalities such as:

$$X / Y * Y = X$$

$$X + Y - Z = X - Z + Y$$

do not hold in REAL arithmetic. When writing programs which manipulate REAL data, we must always take arithmetic errors into account, as the following examples illustrate.

Example 10.5

Let us write a program fragment which determines whether a triangle is right-angled, given that the lengths of the sides of the triangle have been stored in **REAL** variables A, B and C, and assuming that side A is the longest.

Using a **BOOLEAN** variable **RIGHTANGLED**, we might be tempted to write down simply:

RIGHTANGLED := SQR(A) = SQR(B) + SQR(C)

which is a direct transcription of Pythagoras' Law.

Unfortunately, exact equality between two computed **REAL** values is extremely unlikely on a digital computer: representational and computational errors make it likely that the values being compared will be slightly different even when they would be expected to be equal.

The test is better expressed like this:

RIGHTANGLED := ABS((SQR(B) + SQR(C))/SQR(A) − 1) < 1.0E−4

This version checks whether SQR(A) and SQR(B)+SQR(C) are equal *to within 4 significant figures.* Observational and computation errors should be taken into account when selecting the tolerance figure (in this case 0.0001).

Example 10.6

Let us write a program which outputs a table of square roots of numbers from 1.0 to 1.1 inclusive, in steps of 0.001. There will be 101 lines of output, one for the starting value and one for each of 100 steps. We might be tempted to write down the following simple program:

```
PROGRAM SQUAREROOTS1 ( OUTPUT );
CONST
  FIRSTX = 1.0;
  LASTX = 1.1;
  STEPSIZE = 0.001;
VAR
  STEPNUMBER: 0 . . 101;
  X : REAL;
BEGIN
STEPNUMBER := 0;
X := FIRSTX;
WHILE X <= LASTX DO
  BEGIN
  WRITELN (STEPNUMBER:6, X:12:8, SQRT(X):12:8);
```

```
      STEPNUMBER := STEPNUMBER + 1;
      X := X + STEPSIZE
   END
END.
```

Here are the last few lines of output obtained by running this program on one computer:

```
      . . . . . .      . . . . . .
      . . . . . .      . . . . . .
95    1.09500444    1.04642463
96    1.09600449    1.04690242
97    1.09700453    1.04737985
98    1.09800458    1.04785717
99    1.09900463    1.04833424
```

The stored value of **STEPSIZE** was only an approximation to 0.001 (in fact it was slightly greater than 0.001) and it was this approximate value which was repeatedly added to **X**. The output shows that the value of **X** drifts further and further from what might naïvely be expected. Even worse, because **STEPSIZE** is too large, **X+STEPSIZE** is greater than **LASTX** in the 99th iteration, rather than the 100th. As a result the loop terminates one iteration too soon!

The following is an improved version of the program:

```
PROGRAM SQUAREROOTS2 ( OUTPUT );
CONST
   LASTSTEP = 100;
   FIRSTX = 1.0;
   STEPSIZE = 0.001;
VAR
   STEPNUMBER: 0..101;
   X : REAL;
BEGIN
STEPNUMBER := 0;
WHILE STEPNUMBER <= LASTSTEP DO
   BEGIN
   X := FIRSTX + STEPNUMBER*STEPSIZE;
   WRITELN (STEPNUMBER:6, X:12:8, SQRT(X):12:8);
   STEPNUMBER := STEPNUMBER + 1
   END
END.
```

The last few lines of output in this case were:

```
  . . . . .      . . . . . .
      . . . . . .    . . . . . .
 95  1.09500003  1.04642248
 96  1.09599996  1.04690015
 97  1.09700000  1.04737771
 98  1.09800005  1.04785502
 99  1.09899998  1.04833198
100  1.10000002  1.04880893
```

The reason for this improvement is that program SQUAREROOTS2 uses the INTEGER variable STEPNUMBER for counting, and computes X afresh in each iteration. This avoids the *cumulative* computational error observed with program SQUAREROOTS1, which uses the REAL variable X for counting. Even so, the computed values of X can be seen not to be exact.

Example 10.7

Write a program fragment which computes and outputs the roots of the quadratic equation:

$$Ax^2 + Bx + C = 0$$

given the REAL coefficients A, B and C. Assume that the roots are not complex.

The two roots are given by the formulas:

$$\frac{-B+S}{2A} \quad \text{and} \quad \frac{-B-S}{2A}$$

where S is the square root of $(B^2 - 4AC)$. We could transcribe these formulas directly:

```
S := SQRT(SQR(B)−4*A*C);
WRITELN ('ROOTS ARE :  ', (−B+S)/(2*A):12, ',', (−B−S)/(2*A):12)
```

But consider the case A=C=0.001, B=1.0; this gives S=0.999998 correct to 6 significant digits. Thus the first root will be computed as (−1.00000+0.999998)/0.002, that is −0.001 correct to only 1 significant digit. The problem here is *cancellation of significant digits*, caused by subtracting two nearly equal numbers 1.00000 and 0.999998. In general, addition and subtraction yield results which are accurate only to the same number of decimal places (not to the same number of significant digits) as their operands.

We can achieve greater accuracy by first computing the larger root (in magnitude), and then computing the other root using the fact that the product of the roots is C/A:

```
S := SQRT(SQR(B)−4*A*C);
```

```
IF B > 0 THEN
  LARGERROOT := (−B−S)/(2*A)
ELSE
  LARGERROOT := (−B+S)/(2*A);
WRITELN ('ROOTS ARE:  ',  C/A/LARGERROOT:12,  ',',
           LARGERROOT:12)
```

The following output was obtained by running each of the program fragments on one computer:

(1)
ROOTS ARE: −1.04308E−03, −9.99999E+02

(2)
ROOTS ARE: −1.00000E−03, −9.99999E+02

As you can see, the smaller root is very inaccurate in the first case.

Exercises 10

10.1. Express the following numbers in scientific notation, in such a way that each number's mantissa (the part of the left of E) lies between 0.1 and 1.0:

0.00000000001234   0.009   0.254   3.14159265   981.0   250000.0

10.2. Express the following numbers in ordinary fractional notation:

45.67E−10   981E−2   3.00E0   1.885E+1   2.82743E+3   93E6

10.3. Evaluate the following **REAL** expressions, working throughout to three significant decimal digits:

(A+B)+C   (B+C)+A   X*Y/Y   Z+Z+Z+Z+Z+Z+Z+Z+Z+Z   10*Z

assuming that A=0.004, B=1.00, C=−1.00, X=3.88, Y=3.88 and Z=0.333. Comment on the results.

10.4. Write down Pascal expressions which will compute the following: (a) the volume of a sphere whose radius is R; (b) the surface area of a rectangular block whose sides have lengths A, B and C; (c) the polar coordinates of a point whose rectangular coordinates are X and Y; and (d) the power dissipated in an electrical component whose resistance is R and whose rated voltage is V.

10.5. Given the lengths A, B and C of the sides of a triangle, write a program fragment which outputs the area of the triangle. (If S is half the perimeter of the triangle, the area is equal to the square root of $S(S−A)(S−B)(S−C)$. No triangle with sides A, B and C exists if $S(S−A)(S−B)(S−C)$ is negative.)

Programming exercises 10

10.6. Write a program which reads real numbers AMOUNT and RATE, and an integer N, and which outputs a table showing the simple interest and the compound interest which will have accrued after 1, 2, . . ., N years to the sum of money AMOUNT at the annual rate of interest RATE. Sums of money should be written in the conventional format for your national currency. (Simple interest is calculated on AMOUNT only. Compound interest is calculated each year on AMOUNT plus all the interest accumulated in previous years.)

10.7. A rough graph of a suitable function can be plotted on a line-printer, like this:

```
GRAPH OF X*X*X − 6*X*X + 11*X       SCALE FACTOR =2.0

0.0 *
0.5 |        *
1.0 |           *
1.5 |          *
2.0 |           *
2.5 |         *
3.0 |         *
3.5 |            *
4.0 |               *
4.5 |                    *
5.0 |
```

The position of the plotted point in each line is obtained by multiplying the function value by a suitable scale factor (2.0 above) and then rounding to the nearest integer. Write a program which plots $SIN(X)$ for values of X from 0 to 180 *degrees*, in intervals of 5 degrees. Use a scale factor of 50.0. Then modify the program to handle negative function values, and extend the plot of $SIN(X)$ to 360 degrees.

10.8. Write a program which reads positive real numbers and computes their square roots, *without* using the standard function SQRT. Use *Newton's method*: if E is an estimate of the square root of X, then a better estimate is $(E+X/E)/2$. Initialize E to 1, then repeatedly replace E by a better estimate using the formula above, stopping when two successive estimates are equal to within 4 significant digits.

Part III
Arrays and strings

11
Arrays

11.1 The need for arrays

So far we have met only *simple* variables. These are variables whose values are single numbers, truth values, characters or such like. Much of programming, however, is concerned with collections of data, such as *arrays*, which we now introduce by means of an example.

Example 11.1

Consider an election contested by four candidates. Let us write a program fragment to read the ballots and count the votes cast for each candidate. Assume that the candidates are numbered 1 to 4, and that each ballot is presented as a line of input containing one of these candidate numbers.

The following is a skeleton solution:

```
initialize all vote-counts to 0;
WHILE not all ballots have been read DO
    BEGIN
    read a ballot;
    increment the chosen candidate's vote-count
    END;
write all vote-counts
```

To hold the vote-counts, we could use four INTEGER variables COUNT1, COUNT2, COUNT3, and COUNT4. If the candidate number on each ballot is read into an INTEGER variable BALLOT, we could refine as follows:

```
(* increment the chosen candidate's vote-count *)
IF BALLOT = 1 THEN
    COUNT1 := COUNT1 + 1
ELSE IF BALLOT = 2 THEN
    COUNT2 := COUNT2 + 1
ELSE IF BALLOT = 3 THEN
    COUNT3 := COUNT3 + 1
```

```
ELSE IF BALLOT = 4 THEN
    COUNT4 := COUNT4 + 1
```

You might feel that this solution is rather clumsy. Imagine how much worse it would be if the program were modified to handle ten or fifty candidates!

If we observe that the variables COUNT1, COUNT2, COUNT3 and COUNT4 are all used in exactly the same way, however, we have a clue to a better solution. Let us rename the variables COUNT[1], COUNT[2], COUNT[3], and COUNT[4]. The variables now form an *array*, with a single identifier COUNT. We distinguish the variables from one another by writing an *index* between square brackets after COUNT. {Indices in programming are in many respects similar to subscripts in mathematics. In conventional mathematical notation the subscripts are written below the line without brackets; Pascal uses brackets because of the limitations of most computer input devices.} COUNT[2] is one *component* of the array COUNT, namely the component whose index is 2.

We have made no real progress if we can use only constants as indices. The power of the index notation, however, is such that we can use any suitable *expression* as an index. For example, we can use COUNT [BALLOT] to refer to the component of COUNT whose index is the value of BALLOT. Thus we can recast our refinement as follows:

```
(* increment the chosen candidate's vote-count *)
COUNT[BALLOT] := COUNT[BALLOT] + 1
```

This is much more elegant and, moreover, requires no modification if the number of candidates is changed.

Arrays occur outside computer programming, in the guise of *tables*. For example:

(a) A table of the atomic weights of the chemical elements is an array. If we call the array ATOMICWEIGHT, we can for example denote the atomic weight of silicon by ATOMICWEIGHT[SI].

(b) A table of the number of days in each month is an array. If we call the array DAYSINMONTH, we can for example denote by DAYSIN-MONTH[MAY] the number of days in May.

(c) A substitution cipher is a table which maps each letter on to another letter. If we call the table CIPHER, we can for example denote the encipherment of 'A' by CIPHER['A'].

11.2 Arrays in Pascal

In Pascal an array is declared just like any other variable, but its type will be an *array type* which specifies:

(a) the range of indices of the array, and

(b) the type of its components.

It is an important property of an array that every component has the same type.

Example 11.1 (continued)

The array variable COUNT would be declared in Pascal as follows:

COUNT: ARRAY [1. .4] OF 0. .MAXINT

This declaration specifies that the variable COUNT's type is an array:

(a) whose *index type* is 1. .4, i.e. its indices are 1, 2, 3 and 4; and

(b) whose *component type* is 0. .MAXINT, i.e. each component of the array is of type 0. .MAXINT.

We can picture COUNT as a row of 'boxes', or store locations, one for each index value, for example:

	1	2	3	4
COUNT	27	36	0	9

Here the current value of the component COUNT[1] is 27, the current value of COUNT[2] is 36, the current value of COUNT[3] is 0, and the current value of COUNT[4] is 9.

COUNT[BALLOT] is an example of an *indexed variable*. The component of COUNT for which it stands depends on the *current* value of BALLOT. It is most important that this value is indeed a value of the index type, 1. .4. Suppose that the value of BALLOT is 0. Then COUNT[BALLOT] in this case stands for COUNT[0], which does not exist. This is a common and serious programming error ('index out of range') which must always be avoided, since it will cause the program to fail.

In this example, it is quite possible that one of the numbers read may be outside the range 1 to 4, and our program, as it stands, might indeed fail. We should modify the program to avoid this possibility of failure. We might reasonably treat a number outside the range 1 to 4 as a 'spoilt ballot', and make the program count the spoilt ballots separately. Here is a complete program for the election problem which does this:

```
PROGRAM ELECTION (INPUT, OUTPUT);
CONST
  NRCANDIDATES = 4;
VAR
  COUNT       : ARRAY [1. .NRCANDIDATES] OF 0. .MAXINT;
  SPOILT      : 0. .MAXINT;
  CANDIDATE : 1. .NRCANDIDATES;
  BALLOT      : INTEGER;
```

```
BEGIN
(* initialize all vote-counts to 0 *)
FOR CANDIDATE := 1 TO NRCANDIDATES DO
   COUNT[CANDIDATE] := 0;
SPOILT := 0;
WHILE NOT EOF(INPUT) DO        (* not all ballots have been read *)
   BEGIN
   (* read a ballot *)
   READLN (BALLOT);
   (* increment the chosen candidate's vote-count,
          unless the ballot was spoilt *)
   IF (BALLOT >= 1) AND (BALLOT <= NRCANDIDATES) THEN
      COUNT[BALLOT] := COUNT[BALLOT] + 1
   ELSE
      SPOILT := SPOILT + 1
   END;
(* write all vote-counts *)
WRITELN ('CANDIDATE': 10, 'VOTES': 10);
FOR CANDIDATE := 1 TO NRCANDIDATES DO
   WRITELN (CANDIDATE: 10, COUNT[CANDIDATE]: 10);
WRITELN ('THERE WERE', SPOILT: 5, 'SPOILT BALLOTS.')
END.
```

The refinement of 'initialize all vote-counts to 0' includes a loop which assigns 0 to each component of COUNT in turn; and the refinement of 'write all vote-counts' includes a loop which writes the value of each component in turn.

As an exercise, devise some test data (including some 'spoilt ballots') and hand-test program ELECTION.

The use of the constant identifier NRCANDIDATES makes the program more flexible: if the program had to be modified to handle more candidates, then only the constant definition would need to be altered.

The syntax of array types is summarized in Figure 11.1. ARRAY and OF are both reserved words. Array types may be used, like other types, in type definitions as well as in variable declarations.

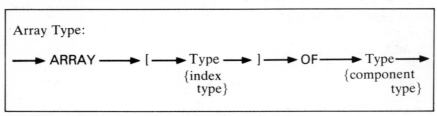

Figure 11.1 Syntax of Array Types (simplified)

The syntax of indexed variables is summarized in Figure 11.2. Any expression can be used as an index; we are not restricted to constants or simple variables. In every case, however, the index expression must yield a value of the array's index type. An indexed variable may be used anywhere a simple variable can, as illustrated by Example 11.1.

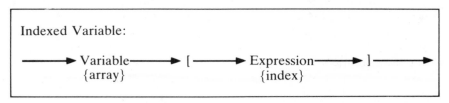

Figure 11.2. Syntax of Indexed Variables (simplified)

Within reason, any *ordinal* type may be chosen as the *index type* of an array: BOOLEAN, CHAR, any enumeration type, or any subrange type.

Example 11.2

Assuming the type definition:

```
MONTHS = (JAN,FEB,MAR,APR,MAY,JUN,JUL,AUG,SEP,
          OCT,NOV,DEC)
```

the following are legitimate array variable declarations:

```
CHARCOUNT        : ARRAY [CHAR] OF 0. .MAXINT;
LETTERCOUNT      : ARRAY ['A'. .'Z'] OF 0. .MAXINT;
DAYSINMONTH      : ARRAY [MONTHS] OF 28. .31;
MONTHLYRAINFALL  : ARRAY [MONTHS] OF REAL;
SUMMERRAINFALL   : ARRAY [JUN. .AUG] OF REAL;
YEARLYRAINFALL   : ARRAY [1900. .1999] OF REAL
```

DAYSINMONTH might be used to store the number of days in each month. After initialization it might look like this:

| | FEB | | APR | | JUN | | AUG | | OCT | | DEC |
JAN		MAR		MAY		JUL		SEP		NOV	
DAYSINMONTH	31	28	31	30	31	30	31	31	30	31	30	31

here showing the current value of DAYSINMONTH[JAN] to be 31, and so on.

The index type determines the number of components of an array; for example, YEARLYRAINFALL above will have 100 components, and MONTHLYRAINFALL will have 12.

Although the stores of some computers are very large, they are not unlimited and a declaration of an array with index type **1. .100000** or **INTEGER**, for example:

PRIME : ARRAY [INTEGER] OF BOOLEAN

is very unlikely to be acceptable to a compiler! Most programming problems, certainly those you will meet in this book, can be solved without using very large arrays; if you find yourself declaring an array with thousands of components, ask yourself whether you have missed a more economical solution.

There is no restriction at all on the *component type* of any array.

Example 11.3

The following is a legitimate array type definition:

LINES = ARRAY [1 . . 120] OF CHAR

The following are legitimate array variable declarations:

WETTESTMONTH : ARRAY [1900. .1999] OF MONTHS;
DAYSINMONTH : ARRAY [MONTHS] OF 28. .31;
PAGEIMAGE   : ARRAY [1 . . 64] OF LINES;
PRIME   : ARRAY [1 . . N] OF BOOLEAN

provided **N** is a constant identifier. (**N** must not be a variable.)

Arrays of characters are of special interest because they can be used for storing and manipulating legible data, i.e. words and text. This important topic will be discussed in Chapter 12.

11.3 Component-by-component processing of arrays

The most common manipulation of arrays is component-by-component processing, whereby we perform similar operations on some or all components of the array, one component at a time. We have already seen some simple examples of component-by-component processing: the initialization of the vote-counts, and the writing of the vote-counts, in Example 11.1.

Since several components are to be processed, component-by-component processing is performed by a loop. We need a variable to index the array. If we know in advance which components are going to be processed, we can use a FOR statement whose control variable will range over the indices of these components. Otherwise we use a WHILE (or REPEAT) statement; in this case the variable used for indexing the array must be explicitly initialized, and incremented or decremented inside the loop.

Example 11.4

Assuming the type identifier MONTHS is defined as in Example 11.2, and given a table of monthly rainfall readings stored in the array:

RAINFALL : ARRAY [MONTHS] OF REAL

let us write a program fragment to determine the total rainfall for the whole year. We declare the following variables:

MONTH : MONTHS;
TOTAL : REAL

and we use MONTH as the indexing variable. Here we can use a FOR statement:

```
(* Determine total rainfall for the whole year *)
TOTAL := 0;
FOR MONTH := JAN TO DEC DO
  TOTAL := TOTAL + RAINFALL[MONTH]
```

The solution can easily be adapted to process only some of the array components, for example:

```
(* Determine total rainfall from April to September *)
TOTAL := 0;
FOR MONTH := APR TO SEP DO
  TOTAL := TOTAL + RAINFALL[MONTH]
```

Verify these solutions by hand-testing.

Example 11.5

Continuing Example 11.4, let us write a program fragment to determine the maximum rainfall in any one month of the year.

This problem amounts to finding the value of the largest of RAINFALL [JAN], ..., RAINFALL[DEC]. We need the variables:

MONTH   : MONTHS;
MAXRAINFALL : REAL

This problem can be solved by initializing MAXRAINFALL to the first component of the array, then comparing MAXRAINFALL in turn with each of the remaining components, updating MAXRAINFALL to any component which is found to be greater. This can be done with a FOR statement:

```
(* Determine maximum monthly rainfall *)
MAXRAINFALL := RAINFALL[JAN];
FOR MONTH := FEB TO DEC DO
  IF RAINFALL[MONTH] > MAXRAINFALL THEN
    MAXRAINFALL := RAINFALL[MONTH]
```

Example 11.6

We return to the election problem (Example 11.1). Let us modify program ELECTION to determine the winner of the election, i.e. the candidate with the greatest number of votes (neglecting the possibility of a tie).

This amounts to finding the *index* of the maximum component of the array COUNT. Note the difference from Example 11.5, where the problem was to find the *value* of the maximum component.

We insert the variable declaration:

WINNER : 1. .NRCANDIDATES

and add the following at the end of the program:

```
(* determine the election winner, neglecting ties *)
WINNER := 1;
FOR CANDIDATE := 2 TO NRCANDIDATES DO
    IF COUNT[CANDIDATE] > COUNT[WINNER] THEN
        WINNER := CANDIDATE
```

Another common theme is *linear search*, whereby the components of an array are examined one by one to find which component, if any, satisfies some specified condition.

Example 11.7

Assume the variable declarations:

```
LIST    : ARRAY [1. .N] OF INTEGER;
TARGET : INTEGER
```

Let us develop a program fragment which will search LIST for a component which equals the value of TARGET. For example, in the following situation (assuming N = 10):

	1	2	3	4	5	6	7	8	9	10
LIST	13	7	45	0	99	13	21	77	37	19

TARGET 99

we should find that LIST[5] matches TARGET. On the other hand, if the value of TARGET is 22, we should find that no component of LIST matches TARGET.

The program must examine LIST[1], LIST[2], etc., in turn until *either* it finds a component which matches TARGET *or* it has examined all the components without success. This observation leads to the following outline solution:

initialize the search;
WHILE the search is incomplete DO
   try to match TARGET to the next component of LIST;
IF the search was successful THEN
   report which component of LIST matches TARGET
ELSE
   report lack of success

We will need a variable, say LOC, to index the array. The outline also suggests introducing a BOOLEAN variable, MATCHED, to use in the WHILE and IF conditions. Completing the refinement:

```
LOC := 0; MATCHED := FALSE;
WHILE NOT MATCHED AND (LOC < N) DO
   BEGIN
   LOC := SUCC(LOC);
   IF LIST[LOC] = TARGET THEN
      MATCHED := TRUE
   END;
IF MATCHED THEN
   WRITE ('TARGET MATCHED AT INDEX', LOC)
ELSE
   WRITE ('TARGET NOT MATCHED')
```

The comparison LOC<N is essential in the WHILE condition, otherwise when TARGET is not matched by any component of LIST the program would fail by attempting to inspect LIST[N+1]. Check your understanding of the solution by hand-testing using the data cited above, with the value of TARGET being (a) 99, and (b) 22.

This solution forces us to declare LOC with type 0. .N. It would be preferable to declare LOC with type 1. .N, since it is used to index LIST. In fact, there is an alternative solution which does allow LOC to be declared with type 1. .N. This is based on the observation that, during the search, there are *three* possible states: (a) a match has been found; (b) there is definitely no match; and (c) it is not yet known whether there is a match or not. We can represent these states by introducing the variable:

```
MATCH : (UNKNOWN, YES, NO)
```

to replace MATCHED, and refining the outline solution as follows:

```
LOC := 1; MATCH := UNKNOWN;
WHILE MATCH = UNKNOWN DO
   IF LIST[LOC] = TARGET THEN
      MATCH := YES
   ELSE IF LOC = N THEN
      MATCH := NO
```

```
    ELSE
        LOC := SUCC(LOC);
    IF MATCH = YES THEN
        WRITE ('TARGET MATCHED AT INDEX', LOC)
    ELSE
        WRITE ('TARGET NOT MATCHED')
```

This time **LOC** is initialized to 1, but it never exceeds **N** because if **LOC** equals **N** and **LIST[LOC]** does not match **TARGET** then **MATCH** is set to **NO** and **LOC** is *not* incremented. Verify this solution by hand-testing using the same data as before.

It should be obvious to you that the WHILE condition in the second solution will always be **TRUE** the first time it is tested, so the loop must be repeated at least once. If you have read Section 6.5, improve this solution further using a REPEAT statement.

Example 11.8

Returning once more to the election problem, let us modify program **ELECTION** to determine which candidate, if any, received a clear majority of the votes cast.

First we must modify the program to accumulate the total number of unspoilt ballots, and hence the required majority. We add:

```
(* determine required majority *)
VOTES := 0;
FOR CANDIDATE := 1 TO NRCANDIDATES DO
    VOTES := VOTES + COUNT[CANDIDATE];
MAJORITY := VOTES DIV 2 + 1
```

together with the necessary variable declaration:

```
VOTES, MAJORITY : 0. .MAXINT
```

The rest of the solution is analogous to Example 11.7:

```
(* determine which candidate, if any,
            received at least MAJORITY votes *)
CANDIDATE := 1;
CLEAR := UNKNOWN;
WHILE CLEAR = UNKNOWN DO
    IF COUNT[CANDIDATE] >= MAJORITY THEN
        CLEAR := YES
    ELSE IF CANDIDATE = NRCANDIDATES THEN
        CLEAR := NO
    ELSE
        CANDIDATE := SUCC(CANDIDATE);
```

```
IF CLEAR = YES THEN
    WRITE ('CLEAR MAJORITY FOR CANDIDATE', CANDIDATE)
ELSE
    WRITE ('NO CLEAR MAJORITY')
```

This assumes the variable declaration:

CLEAR : (UNKNOWN, YES, NO)

Check this program fragment by hand-testing in the following three cases:

(a)   COUNT | 27 | 36 | 0 | 8 | MAJORITY | 36 |

(b)   COUNT | 10 | 20 | 30 | 70 | MAJORITY | 66 |

(c)   COUNT | 27 | 36 | 0 | 9 | MAJORITY | 37 |

All the previous examples have illustrated problems where we know exactly the size of the array required to store the data. The following example illustrates a situation where this is not the case.

Example 11.9

Let us write a program which reads a single line of characters and outputs them in reverse order. (This might be the first step in constructing a rhyming dictionary.)

Clearly the program must read and store all the characters before writing them. A natural place to store all the characters is in an array, but we do not know how many characters will be supplied as input, so how big should the array be? In situations like this it is necessary to declare an array big enough to hold the largest number of characters likely ever to be supplied, and to use another variable to count the *actual* number of characters supplied as input. In this example, 80 would be a reasonable upper limit, since input data on cards and on many terminals is in fact limited to 80 characters per line. Here is a solution:

```
PROGRAM REVERSELINE (INPUT, OUTPUT);
CONST
    MAXLINELENGTH = 80;
VAR
    LINE    : ARRAY [1. .MAXLINELENGTH] OF CHAR;
    COUNT : 0. .MAXLINELENGTH;
    POS     : 1. .MAXLINELENGTH;
```

```
BEGIN
(* read and store a line of characters *)
COUNT := 0;
WHILE NOT EOLN(INPUT) DO
  BEGIN
  COUNT := COUNT+1;
  READ (LINE[COUNT])
  END;
(* write the line of characters in reverse *)
FOR POS := COUNT DOWNTO 1 DO
  WRITE (LINE[POS]);
WRITELN
END.
```

For example, given the following input data:

THE QUICK BROWN FOX JUMPED OVER THE LAZY DOG.

after reading all the characters up to the period we have:

COUNT [45]

LINE: with positions 1 2 3 ... 42 43 44 45 46 ... 80, containing 'T' 'H' 'E' ... 'D' 'O' 'G' '.' ? ... ?

The components LINE[46] to LINE[80] remain undefined, but the rest of the program does not attempt to inspect them.

What will happen if a line of more than 80 characters is supplied after all? The program will fail when it attempts to increment COUNT to 81. Since the limit of 80 is arbitrary, it is good programming practice to allow for this limit being exceeded. Here we need only change the WHILE condition to:

(COUNT < MAXLINELENGTH) AND NOT EOLN(INPUT)

to ensure that no more than MAXLINELENGTH characters are read and stored in LINE.

This program illustrates the use of DOWNTO in a FOR statement. The control variable POS is made to take *decreasing* values COUNT, COUNT−1, . . ., 2, 1, so that the characters are written out in reverse order. Given the input data cited above, the output would be:

.GOD YZAL EHT REVO DEPMUJ XOF NWORB KCIUQ EHT

Check your understanding of program REVERSELINE by hand-testing. (Hint: choose a smaller value for MAXLINELENGTH, say 10. Include a test with more than 10 characters as input.)

11.4 Multi-dimensional arrays

As we have seen, the components of an array may be of any type we choose. In particular, the components may themselves be arrays. An array whose components are simple (i.e. single numbers, truth values, characters or such like) is called a *one-dimensional array*. An array whose components are themselves one-dimensional arrays is called a *two-dimensional array*. Likewise, we can define three-dimensional arrays, and so on.

All the arrays in previous examples have been one-dimensional, except for **PAGEIMAGE** in Example 11.3 which is a two-dimensional array of characters.

Example 11.10

Consider a table containing the marks scored by a class of students in each of several papers of an examination. Assume the number of papers and the number of students are given by the constant identifiers **NRPAPERS** and **NRSTUDENTS** respectively. The marks of one student could be stored in a one-dimensional array of type:

ARRAY [1. .NRPAPERS] OF 0. .100

The whole marks table could be stored in an array of such arrays, i.e. a two-dimensional array:

MARK : ARRAY [1. .NRSTUDENTS] OF
           ARRAY [1. .NRPAPERS] OF 0. .100

Assume the variable declarations:

STUDENT : 1. .NRSTUDENTS;
PAPER   : 1. .NRPAPERS

The indexed variable **MARK[STUDENT]** selects one component of the array **MARK**. This component is itself an array with **NRPAPERS** components; in fact it is an array containing all the marks of the student numbered **STUDENT**. Thus we can apply an index to it: **MARK [STUDENT][PAPER]** is the mark obtained by the same student in paper **PAPER**.

We can think of a two-dimensional array as having rows and columns. The array **MARK** would have one row for each student and one column for each paper. Assuming **NRSTUDENTS**=10 and **NRPAPERS**=4, it might look like this:

MARK

33	51	27	20
83	90	66	85
100	88	82	75
44	32	0	21
32	50	49	52
65	49	62	56
29	46	52	39
77	68	80	63
55	52	65	60
72	49	66	54

{Compare the mathematical notation for matrices.} Then MARK[2], the set of marks scored by student 2, is row 2 of MARK:

83	90	66	85

Finally, MARK[2][4], the mark scored by student 2 in paper 4, is component 4 of row 2. Here the value of MARK[2][4] is 85.

Multi-dimensional arrays are so common that Pascal allows multi-dimensional array types to be abbreviated. For example, the declaration of MARK in Example 11.10 could be abbreviated to:

MARK : ARRAY [1. .NRSTUDENTS, 1. .NRPAPERS] OF 0. .100

Likewise, the indexed variable MARK[STUDENT][PAPER] may be abbreviated to MARK[STUDENT,PAPER].

The simplest examples of manipulation of multi-dimensional arrays are row and column processing.

Example 11.11

Given the array MARK of Example 11.10, let us write a program fragment to output the total mark of each student.

The best way to attack this problem is to consider it as an example of component-by-component processing of MARK, forgetting for the moment that the components of MARK are themselves arrays. We declare:

STUDENT : 1. .NRSTUDENTS

and write:

FOR STUDENT := 1 TO NRSTUDENTS DO
    calculate and write the total mark of student STUDENT

Now the refinement of 'calculate and write the total mark of student STUDENT' will itself be an example of component-by-component processing, this time of the array MARK[STUDENT]. We further declare:

PAPER : 1. .NRPAPERS;
TOTAL : 0. .MAXINT

(We know that TOTAL cannot exceed 100*NRPAPERS, but unfortunately 0. .100*NRPAPERS is not a legal subrange type in Pascal.) The refined solution is:

```
FOR STUDENT := 1 TO NRSTUDENTS DO
   (* calculate and write the total mark of student STUDENT *)
   BEGIN
   TOTAL := 0;
   FOR PAPER := 1 TO NRPAPERS DO
     TOTAL := TOTAL + MARK[STUDENT,PAPER];
   WRITELN (STUDENT, TOTAL)
   END
```

Verify this solution by hand-testing.

This example illustrates a typical situation: a two-dimensional array being processed by two nested loops, using two indexing variables.

Example 11.12

Vectors in mathematics are one-dimensional arrays, and matrices are two-dimensional arrays. The following declare V to hold an N-element vector, and A, B and S to hold M×N matrices (where M and N are suitably defined constants):

```
V       : ARRAY [1. .N] OF REAL;
A, B, S : ARRAY [1. .M, 1. .N] OF REAL
```

11.5 Type rules for arrays

Indexing

An index expression must be assignment compatible with the array variable's index type.

Assignment compatibility

A complete array may be assigned to an array variable provided the two arrays are of *identical* type. This is the case only if both variables are declared at the same place, or are declared with the same type identifier. For example, if we declare:

```
MARK        : ARRAY [1. .NRSTUDENTS] OF
                     ARRAY [1. .NRPAPERS] OF 0. .100;
ONESTUDENT : ARRAY [1. .NRPAPERS] OF 0. .100
```

the assignment statement

```
ONESTUDENT := MARK[STUDENT]
```

would be illegal since the two array variables are declared separately. On the other hand, if we introduce the type definition:

```
STUDENTSMARKS = ARRAY [1. .NRPAPERS] OF 0. .100
```

and rewrite the variable declarations as follows:

```
MARK        : ARRAY [1. .NRSTUDENTS] OF STUDENTSMARKS;
ONESTUDENT : STUDENTSMARKS
```

then the above assignment statement *would* be allowed, since both arrays are now of type **STUDENTSMARKS**. Its effect would be to copy a complete row of **MARK** into the array **ONESTUDENT**.

Exercises 11

11.1. Assume the number of rooms in a hotel is given by a constant **NRROOMS**. (a) Write a declaration of an array variable suitable for keeping track of which rooms are free. (b) Write a program fragment which counts how many hotel rooms are free, given that appropriate values have been stored in the array.

11.2. Write a program fragment which reverses the order of the integers in an array A of type **ARRAY [1. .100] OF INTEGER**.

11.3. Write a program fragment which determines the *range* of the elements, i.e. the maximum difference between any two elements, of the array **YEARLYRAINFALL** of Example 11.2.

11.4. Modify program **ELECTION** (Example 11.1) so that it writes the vote counts in the form of a histogram with one asterisk for each vote, for example:

```
CANDIDATE 1 *************************
CANDIDATE 2 ***********************************
CANDIDATE 3
CANDIDATE 4 *********
```

11.5. Modify program **ELECTION** (Example 11.1) so that it handles *any* number of candidates up to a *maximum* of 10. The actual number of candidates is provided as the first line of the input data.

11.6. Write a program fragment which normalizes the vector V of Example 11.12, i.e. divides each component by the maximum of the components' absolute values.

11.7. Write a program fragment, using the matrices A, B and S of Example 11.12, which sets S to the matrix sum of A and B.

11.8*. Given a square matrix:

MATRIX : ARRAY [1. .N, 1. .N] OF INTEGER

write program fragments which determine: (a) whether MATRIX is symmetrical about the main diagonal; and (b) whether MATRIX is lower-triangular, i.e. every element above the main diagonal is zero. (The main diagonal is the one which runs from MATRIX[1,1] to MATRIX[N,N].)

Programming exercises 11

11.9. Write a program which accumulates the frequency of occurrence of each of the letters of the alphabet in its input data, and which outputs the frequency of each letter as a percentage of the total number of letters read. Run the program with some text from a book as input data.

11.10. The heights of a group of people are provided as input, one per line. Write a program which computes and outputs the mean and standard deviation of these measurements, the number of measurements which are within one standard deviation of the mean, the number which are between one and two standard deviations from the mean, and the number outside this range. Note that it will be necessary to store all the measurements; you may assume that there are not more than (say) 100 of them.

The standard deviation of a group of N measurements is given by the formula SQRT(SUMOFSQUARES/N−SQR(MEAN)), where MEAN is their mean and SUMOFSQUARES is the sum of their squares.

11.11. *Pascal's triangle* is the following pattern:

```
                1
              1   1
            1   2   1
          1   3   3   1
        1   4   6   4   1
      1   5   10  10   5   1
    1   6   15  20  15   6   1
                etc.
```

in which each integer inside the triangle is the sum of the two integers above it. {Mathematicians should recognize that the integers in Pascal's triangle are the binomial coefficients. Both the triangle and the programming language are named after the great Frenchman Blaise Pascal (1623–1662).}

Write a program to generate the first ten rows (say) of Pascal's triangle.

11.12. Write a program which reads and writes a table **MARK** (declared as in Example 11.11). Assume that the table elements are supplied paper by paper, i.e. all the marks for paper 1, followed by all the marks for paper 2, and so on. The table is to be written with one row for each student and one column for each paper. On the right of each row write the student's total mark. At the foot of each column write the average mark (rounded to the nearest integer) for the paper. Also write the average total mark at the foot of the totals column.

11.13. Write a program which reads a representation of a bridge hand of 13 cards, and which outputs (a) the contents of the hand, with the cards arranged in descending order by rank within each suit, and (b) the points value of the hand (counting 4 for an Ace, 3 for a King, 2 for a Queen and 1 for a Jack), e.g.:

```
CLUBS        K   10   9
DIAMONDS  J    9   4   3
HEARTS       A   Q   10   8   2
SPADES       7
```

POINTS VALUE = 10

On input, each card is to be represented by a pair of integers, the first representing its suit (1 for Clubs, 2 for Diamonds, 3 for Hearts, 4 for Spades), and the second representing its rank (14 for Ace, 13 for King, 12 for Queen, 11 for Jack, 2–10 for other ranks). The cards are supplied in random order. (Hint: use a two-dimensional **BOOLEAN** array, with one element for every card of the pack.)

12
Packed arrays and strings

12.1 Packed arrays

Up to now we have pictured simple items of data (e.g. numbers, characters and truth values) as occupying one 'box' or store location each. This is the natural or *unpacked* arrangement for storing such data.

When we are dealing with bulky arrays, however, it may be expedient to consider more economical use of storage. In certain circumstances, this can be achieved by squeezing several items of data into each store location. Since it is not the purpose of this book to explain exactly how numbers, characters and so on are represented in computer storage, we shall illustrate this idea by analogy.

Consider the example of an array of ten two-digit integers. Normally this would occupy ten store locations, e.g.:

51	27	20	44	32	0	21	4	99	18

If our computer can accommodate a four-digit integer in each store location, however, we can squeeze two components of this array into each store location, so the whole array will fit in only five store locations:

5127	2044	3200	2104	9918

If our computer can accommodate six-digit integers, we need only four store locations (with part of one location unoccupied):

512720	443200	210499	18????

In each case, we say that the array is *packed*. It is still possible to access the individual components of a packed array, but such access is more difficult since it will require the stored data to be broken down into its constituent digits. Thus the saving of space has been bought at the expense of slowing down access to individual components.

In Pascal, any array may be specified as packed simply by prefixing **ARRAY** by the reserved word **PACKED**.

Example 12.1

In a hotel room reservation system, it might be convenient to use a BOOLEAN array FREE, such that FREE[ROOM] indicates whether room ROOM is free or not. If the number of rooms to be controlled is large, it would make sense to store this array in packed form:

FREE : PACKED ARRAY [1 . . NRROOMS] OF BOOLEAN

Typically, packing might reduce the storage required for this array by a factor between 4 and 32.

Notice that there is no way in Pascal to specify exactly how the data is to be packed. The Pascal compiler will *automatically* choose a suitable arrangement, which will depend on the size of the items to be packed and on the capacity of the computer's store locations.

Using the attribute PACKED generally makes no difference to the meaning of a program, in the sense that the program will produce the same results whether PACKED is present or absent. The only difference PACKED makes is to the efficiency of the program: less space will be required to store its data, but access to individual components may be slower and require a longer machine-code program.

Generally speaking, you should not concern yourself at this stage with the problems of balancing storage space against execution time. The main reason for mentioning the PACKED attribute here is to introduce the important topic of the next section.

12.2 Strings

A *string* is just a packed character array with a lower bound of 1. We have used strings already, as parameters in WRITE statements such as:

WRITE ('TOTAL')

Here the string 'TOTAL' is just a constant of the *string type*:

PACKED ARRAY [1 . . 5] OF CHAR

5 being the *length* of the string, i.e. the number of characters in it. We can also define string constants, define string types, and declare string variables, as illustrated by Example 12.2.

Example 12.2

CONST
  THISBOOK = 'PASCAL   ';
  MAXTITLELENGTH = 10;

TYPE
  NAMES = PACKED ARRAY [1 .. 12] OF CHAR;
VAR
  TITLE : PACKED ARRAY [1 .. MAXTITLELENGTH] OF CHAR;
  AUTHOR1, AUTHOR2 : NAMES

Using these we may write statements like:

TITLE := THISBOOK;
AUTHOR1 := 'B I LL F I NDLAY'
AUTHOR2 := 'DAVI D WATT   '

Note that a string must always be *exactly* the same length as the string variable to which it is being assigned. For example, we may assign any 10-character string to TITLE, but not any shorter or longer string.

String variables are useful for storing and manipulating legible data, i.e. words and text. For example, given the declarations of Example 12.2, we can store in AUTHOR1 and AUTHOR2 names up to 12 characters long:

AUTHOR1 | 'B' | 'I' | 'L' | 'L' | ' ' | 'F' | 'I' | 'N' | 'D' | 'L' | 'A' | 'Y' |

AUTHOR2 | 'D' | 'A' | 'V' | 'I' | 'D' | ' ' | 'W' | 'A' | 'T' | 'T' | ' ' | ' ' |

These diagrams emphasize that AUTHOR1 and AUTHOR2 are arrays of characters. Alternatively we may picture string variables like this:

AUTHOR1 | 'BILL FINDLAY' |

AUTHOR2 | 'DAVID WATT   ' |

Note that AUTHOR2 has been assigned a name with fewer than 12 significant characters; the number of characters has been made up to 12 by adding blanks. This common practice is known as *padding* or *filling out* with blanks. Notice also that the name itself has been placed as far to the left as possible; the extra blanks have been added on the right. We say that the name has been stored *left-justified*. Analogously, the name could be stored *right-justified* in the string, but left-justification is the more usual convention for words and text. (Right-justification is the convention for output of numbers to a text file, however: see Section 8.2.)

Example 12.3

Assume that a title has been stored, left-justified, in the string variable TITLE of Example 12.2, for example:

TITLE | 'C' | 'A' | 'T' | 'C' | 'H' | ' ' | '2' | '2' | ' ' | ' ' |

Let us write a program fragment to output the title centred on the line, assuming for this purpose that the line width is **LINEWIDTH**=60 columns.

This can be done quite simply once we know the actual length of the title, i.e. excluding padding blanks:

> determine the actual length of the title, **LENGTH**;
> write the title, preceded by **((LINEWIDTH−LENGTH) DIV 2)** blanks

We can determine the length of the title by searching *backwards*, i.e. from right to left, to find the rightmost non-blank character. This is just an example of linear search. We define the constant:

BLANK = ' '

and declare the variables:

> **LENGTH: 0 . . MAXTITLELENGTH;**
> **PADDING: BOOLEAN**

We can now refine the program fragment thus:

```
(* determine the length of the title *)
LENGTH := MAXTITLELENGTH;
PADDING := TRUE;
WHILE PADDING AND (LENGTH > 0) DO
  IF TITLE[LENGTH] <> BLANK THEN
    PADDING := FALSE
  ELSE
    LENGTH := LENGTH−1;
(* write the title preceded by necessary blanks *)
WRITELN (BLANK: (LINEWIDTH−LENGTH) DIV 2, TITLE)
```

Assuming the contents of **TITLE** shown above, the output from this program fragment would be:

> CATCH 22

in which the title is indented by 26 spaces.

As Example 12.3 illustrates, a statement like **WRITE(TITLE)** may be used to write a complete string. On the other hand, Standard Pascal does *not* allow a statement like **READ(TITLE)** to be used to read a complete string, since it would be unclear how many characters were to be read. Instead we must program string input ourselves. The following example illustrates one way to do so.

Example 12.4

Write a program fragment to read characters into the string variable

STRING : PACKED ARRAY [1 . . L] OF CHAR

Exactly **L** characters are to be read, unless the end of the current line of input is reached, in which case **STRING** is to be filled out with blanks.

Since every component of **STRING** is to be assigned a character—either a character read from input or a padding blank—this problem can be solved most neatly using a FOR statement:

```
FOR POS := 1 TO L DO
   IF EOLN(INPUT) THEN
      STRING[POS] := BLANK
   ELSE
      READ (STRING[POS])
```

which uses the variable **POS: 1 . . L.**

Verify the following cases (with **L**=10) by hand-testing:

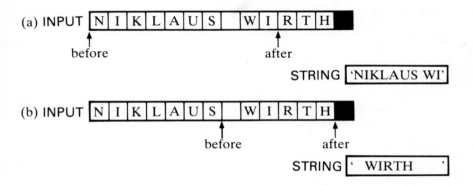

Example 12.4 illustrates why you must program string input yourself: you might wish to read **L** characters exactly; or in different circumstances you might prefer to stop reading characters at an end-of-line, or at a blank, or at a non-alphabetic character. Moreover, you might wish to skip preceding blanks before storing any characters in the string (see Exercises 12).

You will be familiar with the ordinary *alphabetical ordering* of words. For example, names in a telephone directory would be ordered as follows:

Dahl
Dijkstra
Hoare
Knuth
Wilkes
Wirth

The names are ordered on their first letters; names which have the same first letters are ordered on their second letters; and so on. In computers an ordering is defined for all characters (not just letters) so we can generalize this to the *lexicographic ordering* of strings.

As you know already, individual characters may be compared using the comparison operators '=', '<>', '<', '<=', '>=' and '>'. We may also compare complete strings (of the same length) using these same operators. For example, if the value of NAME is 'WIRTH   ', then the expressions

NAME = 'WIRTH   '   NAME <> 'DIJKSTRA'
NAME > 'WILKES '   NAME >= 'DAHL   '
NAME < 'WULF   '   NAME <= 'WIRTH   '

all have the value TRUE.

Example 12.5

Let us develop a program which reads a sequence of names, one per line, and checks whether the names are in lexicographic order or not. Assume that no name is longer than MAXLENGTH characters.

The program can read the names one at a time, and compare each name (except the first) with the name immediately before it in the sequence. Thus we need to declare two string variables, to hold the current name and the previous name. With the variable declaration:

THISNAME, LASTNAME :
  PACKED ARRAY [1 . . MAXLENGTH] OF CHAR

here is an outline solution:

read a name into LASTNAME;
WHILE more names remain to be read DO
  BEGIN
  read a name into THISNAME;
  check that LASTNAME precedes THISNAME in lexicographic order;
  LASTNAME := THISNAME
  END

The commands 'read a name into . . .' can be refined along the lines of Example 12.4, adding READLN in each case so that the condition 'more names remain to be read' can be refined simply to NOT EOF(INPUT). The remaining refinement is straightforward using a comparison operator on the two string variables:

(* check that LASTNAME precedes THISNAME in
  lexicographic order *)
  IF LASTNAME > THISNAME THEN
    WRITELN (LASTNAME, ' SHOULD FOLLOW ', THISNAME)

Check the solution by hand-testing: (a) using the sequence of names cited above; and (b) having interchanged two of the names.

As a rule of thumb, character arrays should always be packed, to take advantage of the ability in Pascal to use string constants and to compare strings directly. Typically, packing compresses character arrays by a factor of 4, and assignment and comparison of strings are speeded up by a similar factor.

12.3 Type rules for strings

Assignment compatibility

A string must be exactly the same length as the string variable to which it is to be assigned. (This rule is slightly less restrictive than the assignment-compatibility rule for other arrays: see Section 11.5.)

Comparisons

Strings to be compared must be exactly the same length.

Exercises 12

12.1. Modify the program fragment of Example 12.3 so that it 'underlines' the title in the following style, as well as centring it.

12.2. Assume that some text has been stored, but *not* left-justified, in the array STRING of Example 12.4. Write a program fragment which will left-justify this text within STRING.

12.3. (a) Rewrite Example 12.4 to read characters up to a blank or end-of-line. If fewer than L non-blank characters are read, STRING is to be padded with blanks. If more than L non-blanks are read, the excess characters are to be discarded. (b) Modify your solution to skip blanks before storing any characters in STRING.

12.4. Modify Example 11.7 so that LIST and TARGET contain 10-character strings rather than integers.

12.5. (a) A string variable TIMESTRING contains the time of day in the format '17:14', i.e. the hours and minutes parts are each exactly two digits. Write a program fragment which uses TIMESTRING to compute the number of minutes since midnight. (b) Write a program fragment which, given the number of minutes since midnight as an integer, reconstructs the time in the same string format.

Programming exercises 12

12.6. Write a program which reads English-language text and counts all occurrences of the words 'HE' and 'SHE'.

12.7. A car dealer keeps a record of all his sales in the form of a text file, with each line having the fixed format:

characters 1–8:   registration number;
characters 9–17:   make;
characters 18–20: sale date.

Each item is left-justified within its character field. The sale date is coded as the last two digits of the year followed by a single letter for the month ('A' for January, 'B' for February, and so on). For example:

```
T KY123 P   DATSUN      75A
L DN614 R   TRI UMP H   76H
WDC11N      CHEVROLET74L
P RS 975 W  RENAULT     80G
B ON919 V   AUDI        79B
```

Write a program which will read such data and output the details of all Renaults sold from August 1977 (77H) to July 1978 (78G) inclusive. *Hint*: treat the dates as 3-character strings, and use string comparisons on them.

12.8. Each line of input data contains a person's full name, with the surname marked by an asterisk, for example:

ABU JA'FAR MOHAMMED IBN MUSA *AL-KHOWARIZMI
*HALAYUDHA
*CHU SHIH-CHIEH
BLAISE *PASCAL

Write a program which reads the names and outputs each person's name with the surname first, followed by a comma and all the other names, for example:

AL-KHOWARIZMI, ABU JA'FAR MOHAMMED IBN MUSA
HALAYUDHA
CHU, SHIH-CHIEH
PASCAL, BLAISE

12.9*. Sometimes it is useful to be able to output 'banner headlines', in larger than normal characters. For examples, 'PASCAL' might be output as:

```
PPP    AA    SSS   CCC   AA    L
P  P   A   A  S     C      A    A  L
PPP    AAAA  SS    C      AAAA  L
P      A   A    S  C      A    A  L
P      A   A  SSS   CCC   A    A  LLLL
```

Design a complete set of letters for banner headlines, and write a program which outputs each line of input data as a banner headline. *Hint*: for each letter initialize and use an array of perhaps five four-character strings, for example:

' AA '
'A   A'
'AAAA'
'A   A'
'A   A'

Part IV
Subprograms

13
Functions

13.1 The need for functions

Suppose we are writing a program in which we want to determine whether the INTEGER variables CHECKSUM and PARITY have odd values. We could include in our program expressions such as (CHECKSUM MOD 2 <> 0) and (PARITY MOD 2 <> 0). A better way to achieve the same effect, however, would be to use the standard function ODD. The program would then contain the expressions ODD(CHECKSUM) and ODD(PARITY). These expressions are more readable, partly because they are shorter, but more importantly because the identifier ODD concentrates attention on the *meaning* of the expressions rather than the way they are computed. They are also more pleasant to write. The tedium of reworking similar expressions several times is avoided, and with it the risk of making a mistake.

When we consider functions such as SIN and EXP which are defined by complicated algorithms containing many statements, these advantages are strongly emphasized.

Although programming languages like Pascal provide a fair selection of such standard functions, this selection is necessarily limited. For example, Pascal does not provide standard functions to compute the tangent of a given angle, nor to determine whether a given number is prime, nor to determine whether a given character is a letter, although such functions might sometimes be just as useful as ODD, SIN and EXP. Since we cannot expect a programming language to anticipate every conceivable need for a function, we need a facility by which we ourselves can provide functions to our own specification. In Pascal this facility is called the *function declaration*.

13.2 Functions in Pascal

ODD(CHECKSUM) and SIN(2*PI*X) are examples of *function designators*, and in these examples CHECKSUM and 2*PI*X are called *actual parameters*. Each actual parameter is an expression of a type appropriate to the function.

The syntax of function designators is summarized in Figure 13.1. This shows that, in general, a function designator may have several actual parameters (although none of the standard functions has more than one).

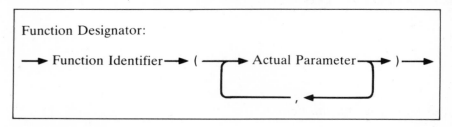

Function Designator:

Figure 13.1 Syntax of Function Designators (simplified)

To write our own function declaration, we must specify the identifier of the function, the type(s) of its parameter(s), and the type of the result to be computed. This information decides the way in which the function may be invoked. The function declaration must also contain statements which specify how the function result is computed from the values of the actual parameters.

A function may be invoked from several different places, possibly with different actual parameters. For example, if we declare a function TAN to compute the tangent of an angle, we might wish in different places to evaluate TAN(A) or TAN(B+C). This implies that the declaration of TAN cannot refer directly to any actual parameter. The problem is solved by introducing into the declaration of TAN an identifier, say X, which will stand for the value of the actual parameter. Thus X will stand for the value of A during the computation of TAN(A), and it will stand for the value of B+C during the computation of TAN(B+C). We call X a *formal parameter*, and it is available for use only *inside the declaration of* TAN. In general, each function declaration must specify an identifier for each of its formal parameters.

Example 13.1

We might declare the tangent function as follows:

```
FUNCTION TAN ( X : REAL ) : REAL;
  BEGIN
  TAN := SIN(X) / COS(X)
  END
```

This example illustrates the features of a function declaration.

(a) 'FUNCTION TAN' defines the function identifier to be TAN.

(b) '(X : REAL)' is the function's *formal parameter part*. This says that the function has a single formal parameter whose identifier is X and whose type is REAL.
(c) ': REAL' following the formal parameter part defines the function's *result type* to be REAL.
(d) BEGIN and END enclose the *statement part* of the function declaration.
(e) Within the statement part, the special assignment statement TAN := SIN(X)/COS(X) assigns a value to the function itself. It is this value which is returned when the function is invoked.

Since TAN has a single REAL formal parameter, it must be invoked by a function designator containing a single REAL expression as actual parameter. This function designator is itself a REAL operand (since the result type of TAN is REAL), and as such it may be used in REAL expressions, for example:

```
HEIGHT := RANGE * TAN(ELEVATION)
WRITE (TAN(DEGREES*PI/180))
```

In the first of these statements, the function designator TAN(ELEVA-TION) is evaluated as follows: first the current value of the actual parameter ELEVATION is assigned to the formal parameter X of TAN; then the statement part of TAN is executed, and the value assigned to TAN is treated as the value of the function designator. The value of the function designator in this statement is multiplied by RANGE and the product assigned to HEIGHT.

In the second statement, the function designator TAN(DEGREES*PI/180) is evaluated similarly, except that the value of the actual parameter DEGREES*PI/180 is assigned to X. The value of the function designator in this statement is written out.

The following complete program, incorporating the function TAN, writes a table of tangents of angles 0, 10, 20, . . ., 360 degrees. Note that the function declaration is inserted between the program's variable declarations and statement part.

```
PROGRAM TABLEOFTANS ( OUTPUT );

CONST
  PI = 3.1415926536;
VAR
  DEGREES : 0. .360;
  LINE      : 0. .36;

FUNCTION TAN ( X : REAL ) : REAL;
  BEGIN
  TAN := SIN(X)/COS(X)
  END (*TAN*);
```

```
BEGIN (*TABLEOFTANS*)
WRITELN ('ANGLE':5, 'TANGENT':15); WRITELN;
FOR LINE := 0 TO 36 DO
  BEGIN
  DEGREES := 10*LINE;
  WRITE (DEGREES:5);
  IF DEGREES MOD 180 = 90 THEN
    WRITELN ('INFINITY':15)
  ELSE
    WRITELN (TAN(DEGREES*PI/180):15)
  END
END (*TABLEOFTANS*).
```

Example 13.2

Given the type definitions:

```
YEARS         = 1753. .9999;
MONTHS        = (JAN,FEB,MAR,APR,MAY,JUN,
                 JUL,AUG,SEP,OCT,NOV,DEC);
MONTHLENGTHS = 28. .31
```

the following function determines whether a given year is a leap year:

```
FUNCTION ISLEAP ( YEAR : YEARS ) : BOOLEAN;
  BEGIN
  ISLEAP := (YEAR MOD 4 = 0) AND (YEAR MOD 100 <> 0)
            OR (YEAR MOD 400 = 0)
  END (*ISLEAP*)
```

and the following function invokes ISLEAP to determine the number of days in a given month and year:

```
FUNCTION NRDAYSIN ( MONTH : MONTHS;
                    YEAR : YEARS ): MONTHLENGTHS;
  BEGIN
  CASE MONTH OF
    JAN, MAR, MAY, JUL, AUG, OCT, DEC:
      NRDAYSIN := 31;
    APR, JUN, SEP, NOV:
      NRDAYSIN := 30;
    FEB:
      IF ISLEAP(YEAR) THEN
        NRDAYSIN := 29
      ELSE
        NRDAYSIN := 28
```

END
END (*NRDAYSIN*)

ISLEAP has one formal parameter, of type YEARS, and its result type is BOOLEAN. Therefore a function designator invoking ISLEAP must have a single actual parameter of type YEARS, and it is itself a BOOLEAN operand. For example, see how the function designator ISLEAP(YEAR) is used as an IF condition within function NRDAYSIN.

NRDAYSIN has two formal parameters—the first of type MONTHS and the second of type YEARS—and its result type is MONTHLENGTHS. Therefore a function designator invoking NRDAYSIN must have two actual parameters—the first an expression of type MONTHS and the second an expression of type YEARS—and it is itself an operand of type MONTHLENGTHS. An example of such a function designator would be NRDAYSIN(FEB,1984), which would yield the value 29.

A function designator must supply one actual parameter for each formal parameter of the function it invokes. Whenever the function designator is to be evaluated, the value of each actual parameter is assigned to the corresponding formal parameter, as illustrated below.

FUNCTION TAN (X : REAL): REAL;

BEGIN

. . . .

END

TAN (DEGREES*PI/180)

FUNCTION NRDAYSIN (MONTH: MONTHS; YEAR: YEARS):
MONTHLENGTHS;

BEGIN

. . . .

END

NRDAYSIN (FEB, 1984)

The syntax of function declarations is summarized in Figures 13.2 and 13.3. FUNCTION is a reserved word.

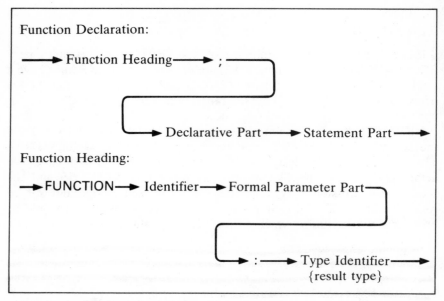

Figure 13.2 Syntax of Function Declarations

Note that the result type of a function, and the types of its formal parameters, must all be specified by *type identifiers*. These may be standard type identifiers, such as **REAL** or **BOOLEAN**; otherwise they must be defined outside the function, like **YEARS**, **MONTHS** or **MONTH-LENGTHS** above.

Every function must yield a result which is a single value. This means that the result type may be any ordinal type or **REAL**, but not an array type

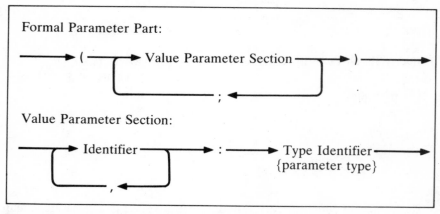

Figure 13.3 Syntax of Formal Parameter Parts (simplified)

nor a string type. There is no such restriction, however, on the types of the parameters; Example 13.3 demonstrates a function with an array parameter.

13.3 Declarations within functions

The examples in the previous section illustrate functions whose results can be computed essentially by obeying a single statement involving the formal parameters. More usually, several statements are needed to work out the result and these statements may require variables of their own, variables which are of no concern to the rest of the program. Such variables could be declared in the program's declarative part, as *global variables*. However, doing this would make the working of the function dependent on something outside of itself; it would no longer be self-contained. To avoid this, Pascal allows a function to have its own internal declarative part, as we can see in Figure 13.2. As well as variables, we can declare constants, types, and even further functions, inside the function declaration, and these will be available for use only within the function. Thus the function resembles a complete program in miniature—it is an example of a *subprogram*.

Example 13.3

Assuming the type definitions:

```
MONTHS = (JAN,FEB,MAR,APR,MAY,JUN,
          JUL,AUG,SEP,OCT,NOV,DEC);
MONTHLYSTATS = ARRAY [MONTHS] OF REAL
```

the following function returns the value of the largest component of a given array of type MONTHLYSTATS.

```
FUNCTION MAXIMUM ( STATS : MONTHLYSTATS ) : REAL;
  VAR
    MAX    : REAL;
    MONTH : MONTHS;
  BEGIN
  MAX := STATS[JAN];
  FOR MONTH := FEB TO DEC DO
    IF STATS[MONTH]>MAX THEN
      MAX := STATS[MONTH];
  MAXIMUM := MAX
  END (*MAXIMUM*)
```

Note that the auxiliary variable MAX is necessary, since MAXIMUM is *not* a variable and cannot be used as such in an expression. Within a function's statement part the function identifier normally may appear only to the left of ':=' in assignment statements.

The function could be incorporated into a complete program as follows.

```
PROGRAM YEARLYMAXIMA ( INPUT, OUTPUT );

TYPE
  MONTHS = (JAN,FEB,MAR,APR,MAY,JUN,
              JUL,AUG,SEP,OCT,NOV,DEC);
  MONTHLYSTATS = ARRAY [MONTHS] OF REAL;

VAR
  RAINFALL, TEMPERATURE : MONTHLYSTATS;
  MONTH                 : MONTHS;

FUNCTION MAXIMUM ( STATS : MONTHLYSTATS ) : REAL;
  VAR
    MAX    : REAL;
    MONTH : MONTHS;
  BEGIN
  MAX := STATS[JAN];
  FOR MONTH := FEB TO DEC DO
    IF STATS[MONTH]>MAX THEN
      MAX := STATS[MONTH];
  MAXIMUM := MAX
  END (*MAXIMUM*);

BEGIN (*YEARLYMAXIMA*)
FOR MONTH := JAN TO DEC DO
  READ (RAINFALL[MONTH], TEMPERATURE[MONTH]);
WRITELN ('MAXIMUM MONTHLY RAINFALL:',
        MAXIMUM(RAINFALL):4:1);
WRITELN ('MAXIMUM MEAN TEMPERATURE:',
        MAXIMUM(TEMPERATURE):4:1)
END (*YEARLYMAXIMA*).
```

(Observe the indentation of the internal declarative and statement parts of the function declaration relative to the word FUNCTION. This indentation helps to set them apart from the declarative and statement parts of the main program.)

Note that the *global variable* MONTH, declared and used in the main program, is quite distinct from the *local variable* MONTH declared and used inside the function.

Let us see exactly what happens when the function is invoked by the function designator MAXIMUM(RAINFALL) in the first WRITELN statement. Before this statement is obeyed, the store picture will look like this:

RAINFALL | 8.0 | 8.9 | 8.4 | 7.7 | 6.5 | 3.3 | 3.4 | 3.0 | 4.8 | 6.8 | 7.5 | 8.1 |

TEMPERATURE | | | | | | | | | | | | |

MONTH | ? |

(The contents of TEMPERATURE are not shown because they are irrelevant to the following discussion.) When we enter the function to evaluate MAXIMUM(RAINFALL), we require additional storage for the function result, for the formal parameter STATS, and for the local variables MAX and MONTH. The formal parameter STATS is assigned the value of the corresponding actual parameter, RAINFALL, but the function result and local variables are initially undefined:

MAXIMUM | ? |

STATS | 8.0 | 8.9 | 8.4 | 7.7 | 6.5 | 3.3 | 3.4 | 3.0 | 4.8 | 6.8 | 7.5 | 8.1 |

MAX | ? | MONTH | ? |

- -

RAINFALL | 8.0 | 8.9 | 8.4 | 7.7 | 6.5 | 3.3 | 3.4 | 3.0 | 4.8 | 6.8 | 7.5 | 8.1 |

TEMPERATURE | | | | | | | | | | | | |

MONTH | ? |

After the statement part of MAXIMUM has been obeyed, the store picture will look like this:

MAXIMUM | 8.9 |

STATS | 8.0 | 8.9 | 8.4 | 7.7 | 6.5 | 3.3 | 3.4 | 3.0 | 4.8 | 6.8 | 7.5 | 8.1 |

MAX | 8.9 | MONTH | ? |

- -

RAINFALL | 8.0 | 8.9 | 8.4 | 7.7 | 6.5 | 3.3 | 3.4 | 3.0 | 4.8 | 6.8 | 7.5 | 8.1 |

TEMPERATURE | | | | | | | | | | | | |

MONTH | ? |

All the storage above the broken line is now discarded, since it was needed only for the evaluation of the function designator, and thus we return to the original picture:

RAINFALL

8.0	8.9	8.4	7.7	6.5	3.3	3.4	3.0	4.8	6.8	7.5	8.1

TEMPERATURE

MONTH

?

Although the function result location (MAXIMUM) is discarded, its *value*—in this case 8.9—is retained as the value of the function designator MAXIMUM(RAINFALL). In this example the value of the function designator is immediately used in a WRITELN statement. Thus the output from this WRITELN statement will be:

MAXIMUM MONTHLY RAINFALL: 8.9

Example 13.4

The following function attempts to compute the number of syllables in a word, given the spelling and length of the word. It assumes a suitable definition of the constant MAXWORDLENGTH, and the type definitions:

```
TYPE
  WORDLENGTHS   = 0. .MAXWORDLENGTH;
  WORDSPELLINGS = PACKED ARRAY
                             [1. .MAXWORDLENGTH] OF CHAR;

FUNCTION NRSYLLABLES (WORD: WORDSPELLINGS;
                      LENGTH: WORDLENGTHS )
          : WORDLENGTHS;
VAR
  FOLLOWSVOWEL, ISVOWEL: BOOLEAN;
  SYLLABLECOUNT         : WORDLENGTHS;
  INDEX                 : 1. .MAXWORDLENGTH;
  CH                    : CHAR;
BEGIN
(* simply counts sequences of consecutive vowels *)
SYLLABLECOUNT := 0; FOLLOWSVOWEL := FALSE;
FOR INDEX := 1 TO LENGTH DO
  BEGIN
  CH := WORD[INDEX];
  ISVOWEL := (CH='A') OR (CH='E') OR (CH='I') OR
             (CH='O') OR (CH='U') OR (CH='Y');
```

```
IF ISVOWEL AND NOT FOLLOWSVOWEL THEN
    SYLLABLECOUNT := SYLLABLECOUNT+1;
FOLLOWSVOWEL := ISVOWEL
END;
NRSYLLABLES := SYLLABLECOUNT
END (*NRSYLLABLES*)
```

This function could be incorporated in a textual analysis program. As you can see, the method used by the function is rather naïve. Once incorporated in the program, however, the function could be improved to take into account the detailed syllabization rules of the natural language. (You could attempt this as an exercise.) It would be necessary only to modify the function's internal declarative and statement parts. Provided that the function *heading* remains unaltered, the function designators invoking **NRSYLLABLES** need not be altered at all. This is very important because these function designators might be numerous and scattered all over a large program, so changing them all would be a tedious and error-prone task.

As Example 13.4 illustrates, a subprogram is a very convenient way of gathering together in one place the declarations and statements needed to perform some routine task, isolating its messy details from the rest of the program. The subprogram is a powerful tool for achieving the ideals of localization and modularity recommended in Chapter 7.

Let us conclude by summarizing the manner in which a function designator is evaluated.

(1) A store location is created for the function result. Its initial value is undefined.
(2) The actual parameters of the function designator are paired off, from left to right, with the formal parameters of the function. (It follows that for each formal parameter exactly one actual parameter must be supplied.)
(3) A store location is created for each formal parameter of the function, to which is assigned the value of the corresponding actual parameter. (It follows that each actual parameter must be an expression assignment-compatible with the type of the corresponding formal parameter.)
(4) A store location is created for each local variable of the function. Its initial value is undefined.
(5) The function's statement part is obeyed.
(6) Finally, all store locations created for the function result, for the formal parameters and for the local variables are discarded. The *value* from the function result location is retained as the value of the function designator.

Exercises 13

13.1. Given that today's month and year have been stored in variables
THISMONTH and THISYEAR, write a statement, invoking the function
NRDAYSIN (Example 13.2), which assigns to an INTEGER variable N the
number of days in this month next year.
13.2. Modify function MAXIMUM (Example 13.3) by making it determine
the maximum component of STATS over the months MONTH1 to
MONTH2 (instead of over the whole year), where MONTH1 and
MONTH2 are additional formal parameters.
13.3. (a) Write a function which returns the fourth power of a given REAL
value. (b) Write a statement which outputs the fourth power of the sum of
A and B.
13.4. Write a function which decides whether a given character is a letter
or not, and a function which decides whether a given character is a digit or
not. Use your functions to rewrite program CHARACTERCOUNT of
Example 8.3.
13.5. Modify Example 12.3 by introducing a function which computes the
actual length of a title supplied as a parameter.
13.6. (a) Write a function which determines whether a given integer is
prime, i.e. has no factors other than itself and 1. (b) Write a program
fragment which reads an integer and outputs it together with the appropriate message 'PRIME' or 'NON-PRIME'.
13.7. Make your answers to Exercise 11.8 into functions, with MATRIX as
the formal parameter of each function.
13.8. Write a function which accepts a person's full name (one or more
forenames followed by a surname) supplied as a string parameter, and
returns the initial letter of the surname.

Programming exercises 13

13.9. The integer logarithm of a positive integer N to the base B is the
largest integer L such that the L-th power of B does not exceed N. Write a
function which computes the integer logarithm of N to the base B. Write a
program, incorporating your function, which outputs a table of integer
logarithms, to the bases 2, 3 and 10, of all the integers from 1 to (say) 50.
13.10. The total interest payable on a bank loan is calculated as the
product of the amount of the loan, the loan period in months, and the
monthly interest rate. The capital and interest are paid off in equal
monthly instalments over the period of the loan. Write a function which
computes the monthly repayment, given as parameters the amount of the
loan, the loan period and the monthly interest rate. Include your function

in a program which reads the monthly interest rate, and outputs a table showing the monthly repayment for loans of £100, £200, . . ., £1000, and for loan periods of 3, 6, . . ., 24 months.

13.11*. Write a function which, given a Roman numeral stored left-justified in a string, returns its integer value. (Take into account combinations like IV, whose value is 4, not 6.) Make sure your function deals sensibly with incorrectly formed Roman numerals. Write a program which reads Roman numerals and outputs them together with their values.

14
Procedures

14.1 The need for procedures

In Chapter 13 we have viewed a function as a self-contained piece of program, or subprogram, which takes one or more parameter values and returns a single result. This result is used immediately on return from the function, for example as an operand in an expression. {This view of a function subprogram corresponds quite closely to the mathematical concept of a function.}

By 'self-contained' we mean that the declaration of a subprogram may contain many details which are of no concern outside the subprogram. These include the statements which compute the subprogram's result(s), and the constants, variables and so on, declared inside the subprogram and used in these statements. Once the subprogram has been written and we are confident of its correctness, we are interested only in the results it can provide.

Frequently we need subprograms which avoid the restrictions of functions, for example a subprogram with several results, or no results at all, or a subprogram whose result is an array or string. In Pascal such subprograms can be written as *procedures*. Unlike a function designator, a procedure invocation does not itself have a value. Instead, a procedure is invoked by a new form of statement, called a *procedure statement*

All our examples of functions have shown parameters being used in a particular way: to supply values for use by the functions. Parameters can be used in this way with procedures too. There is also a second, very different, way of using parameters: to get results *out* of a procedure and stored in variables, where they can be retained for later use. By such means a procedure can have as many results as desired. Thus there are two major parameter mechanisms in Pascal, which are discussed in detail in Section 14.3.

We have used some procedures already, namely the standard procedures READ, WRITE and so on. In fact, READ and WRITE statements are special forms of procedure statements. They are, however, rather irregular in that they accept actual parameters of varying numbers and types. These procedures are rather like irregular verbs: each is a special case unto itself! An ordinary procedure has a fixed number of parameters, with fixed types.

14.2 Procedures in Pascal

A procedure is unlike a function in that it does not itself have a value; therefore a procedure has no result type. Apart from this, and the replacement of FUNCTION by the reserved word PROCEDURE, the syntax of a procedure declaration is similar to that of a function declaration; see Figure 14.1.

Procedure declarations, like function declarations, are inserted between the program's variable declarations and its statement part. For a complete summary of the positioning of constant definitions, type definitions, variable declarations and procedure and function declarations, see the Declarative Part syntax diagram in Appendix 1.2.

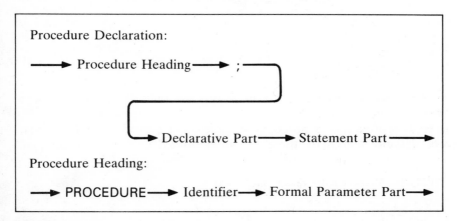

Figure 14.1. Syntax of Procedure Declarations

We invoke a procedure by means of a *procedure statement.* Like a function designator this specifies the identifier of the procedure to be invoked, together with some actual parameters; see Figure 14.2.

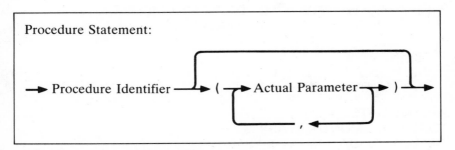

Figure 14.2. Syntax of Procedure Statements

Apart from the treatment of actual parameters (described in Section 14.3), the effect of obeying a procedure statement is simply to obey the procedure's statement part.

Example 14.1

The following little procedure writes out a date in the form 'day/month/ year' (with only the last two digits of the year written), given the day of the month, the month and the year. We assume appropriate definitions of the type identifiers DAYSOFTHEMONTH, MONTHS and YEARS (see below).

```
PROCEDURE WRITEDATE ( D : DAYSOFTHEMONTH;
                      M : MONTHS;
                      Y : YEARS            );
   BEGIN
   WRITE (D:2, '/', M:2, '/', (Y MOD 100):2)
   END (*WRITEDATE*)
```

This procedure will pass back no results when invoked; its only effect is to write some output.

Here is a complete program, incorporating procedure WRITEDATE, which simply reads in the three components of a date, writes that date, and writes the date exactly nine months thereafter:

```
PROGRAM DATES ( INPUT, OUTPUT );

TYPE
   DAYSOFTHEMONTH = 1..31;
   MONTHS         = 1..12;
   YEARS          = 0..9999;
VAR
   DAY     : DAYSOFTHEMONTH;
   MONTH : MONTHS;
   YEAR    : YEARS;

PROCEDURE WRITEDATE ( D : DAYSOFTHEMONTH;
                      M : MONTHS;
                      Y : YEARS            );
   BEGIN
   WRITE (D:2, '/', M:2, '/', (Y MOD 100):2)
   END (*WRITEDATE*);

BEGIN (*DATES*)
READ (DAY, MONTH, YEAR);
WRITEDATE (DAY, MONTH, YEAR);
WRITELN;
```

```
IF MONTH > 3 THEN
   WRITEDATE (DAY, MONTH–3, YEAR+1)
ELSE
   WRITEDATE (DAY, MONTH+9, YEAR);
WRITELN
END (*DATES*).
```

Given the input:

5 10 1979

this program will output:

5/10/79
5/ 7/80

Here is an alternative version of procedure **WRITEDATE**, which writes the *name* of the month and also writes the year in full.

```
PROCEDURE WRITEDATE ( D : DAYSOFTHEMONTH;
                      M : MONTHS;
                      Y : YEARS            );
   BEGIN
   WRITE (D:1, '   ');
   CASE M OF
       1: WRITE ('JANUARY');
       2: WRITE ('FEBRUARY');
       3: WRITE ('MARCH');
       4: WRITE ('APRIL');
       5: WRITE ('MAY');
       6: WRITE ('JUNE');
       7: WRITE ('JULY');
       8: WRITE ('AUGUST');
       9: WRITE ('SEPTEMBER');
      10: WRITE ('OCTOBER');
      11: WRITE ('NOVEMBER');
      12: WRITE ('DECEMBER')
      END;
   WRITE (YEAR :5)
   END (*WRITEDATE*)
```

This illustrates the flexibility of procedures: the new version of procedure **WRITEDATE** can easily be slotted into the program in place of the old version, and the procedure statements invoking it need not be changed at all, since the procedure's heading remains unchanged. Given the input cited above, the program with this modified procedure would output:

5 OCTOBER 1979
5 JULY 1980

14.3 Value parameters and variable parameters

So far we have seen formal parameters used only to supply *values* for use by a function or procedure. Such formal parameters are called *value parameters*, and their mechanism is very simple: on entry to the function or procedure, each value parameter is assigned the value of the corresponding actual parameter.

In Example 14.1, the formal parameters of procedure WRITEDATE—D, M and Y—were all value parameters. Thus the effect of the procedure statement WRITEDATE(DAY,MONTH−3,YEAR+1) is to obey the statement part of WRITEDATE having assigned the value of DAY to D, the value of MONTH−3 to M, and the value of YEAR+1 to Y. Once the value parameters have been assigned the values of the actual parameters, there is no further interaction between the actual parameters and the formal parameters. If a procedure assigns a new value to a value parameter, this assignment has no effect whatsoever on the corresponding actual parameter.

A procedure, therefore, cannot use value parameters to pass back any results. For this purpose a new kind of formal parameter is needed, one which allows a procedure to *change* the value of the corresponding actual parameter. Since the actual parameter must be capable of receiving a new value, it follows that the actual parameter must be a *variable*. Hence formal parameters of this kind are called *variable parameters*. A variable parameter merely represents the variable which is placed in the corresponding actual-parameter position.

A variable parameter is specified by placing the word VAR in front of it in the formal parameter part of the procedure declaration.

Example 14.2

The following procedure will determine the minimum of three given INTEGER values, and pass back this minimum through the variable parameter MIN.

```
PROCEDURE FINDMINIMUM ( A, B, C : INTEGER;
                        VAR MIN : INTEGER );
  BEGIN
  IF A < B THEN
    MIN := A
  ELSE
    MIN := B;
  IF C < MIN THEN
    MIN := C
  END (*FINDMINIMUM*)
```

Assuming the variable declaration:

WEEKS, CONTRIBUTIONS, BENEFIT : INTEGER

an example of a procedure statement invoking FINDMINIMUM would be:

FINDMINIMUM (600, 5*CONTRIBUTIONS, 25*WEEKS, BENEFIT)

which would have the effect of storing in BENEFIT the minimum of 600, 5*CONTRIBUTIONS and 25*WEEKS. Let us see exactly how this works. Immediately before obeying the procedure statement, suppose we have the following situation:

WEEKS [4] CONTRIBUTIONS [150] BENEFIT [?]

Now we enter procedure FINDMINIMUM. A, B and C are value parameters, so we create store locations for them and assign them the values of the corresponding actual parameters, namely the values of 600, 5*CONTRIBUTIONS and 25*WEEKS respectively. On the other hand, MIN is a variable parameter. Instead of receiving the current value of BENEFIT, MIN will represent the variable BENEFIT itself. We illustrate this by drawing an arrow between MIN and the location of BENEFIT:

Now we start to obey the statement part of procedure FINDMINIMUM. The expression A<B evaluates to TRUE, so we obey the statement MIN:=A. Since MIN is a variable parameter, we assign the value of A, not to MIN itself, but to *the variable represented by* MIN, i.e. BENEFIT:

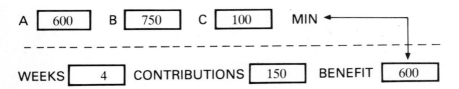

Now to evaluate the expression C<MIN, we compare the current value of C with the current value of *the variable represented by* MIN, i.e. BENEFIT;

thus the expression evaluates to TRUE. We obey the statement MIN:=C, whose effect is to assign the value of C to BENEFIT:

Finally we leave the procedure, and discard all the store locations above the broken line. Thus obeying the procedure statement has had the following nett effect:

| WEEKS | 4 | CONTRIBUTIONS | 150 | BENEFIT | 100 |

Since procedure FINDMINIMUM passes back only one result, of type INTEGER, we might prefer to replace it by an INTEGER function with only A, B and C as formal parameters:

```
FUNCTION MINIMUM ( A, B, C : INTEGER ) : INTEGER;
  VAR
    MIN : INTEGER;
  BEGIN
  IF A < B THEN
    MIN := A
  ELSE
    MIN := B;
  IF C < MIN THEN
    MIN := C;
  MINIMUM := MIN
  END (*MINIMUM*)
```

In this version, MIN is an ordinary local variable. The same effect as our procedure statement could now be achieved by the assignment statement:

BENEFIT := MINIMUM(600,5*CONTRIBUTIONS,25*WEEKS)

When a choice is available, a function is often more convenient to use than a procedure. In the following example, however, we require a subprogram with *three* results, one of which moreover is an array. For this purpose a procedure is the more appropriate choice.

Example 14.3

Suppose that we are supplied with input data in the form of natural-language text, which consists of 'words' separated by blanks (and end-of-lines). We are to treat any sequence of non-blank characters as a word, and assume that no word is longer than **MAXWORDLENGTH** characters.

When writing a program which processes such textual data, it is a good idea to include a procedure whose task is to read a single word and to pass back the word itself and its length.

The procedure must take into account the possibility that the next word in the input data may be preceded by several blanks, so two steps will be necessary, the first to scan (and ignore) blanks, the second to scan (and store) the non-blank characters which comprise the word itself. The procedure must also take into account the possibility that the unread input data consists entirely of blanks, implying that all the words have already been read.

At this stage it is unnecessary to commit ourselves on how to store the word. Let us just agree that the word's spelling will be assigned to a variable parameter of type **WORDSPELLINGS**, and that its length will be assigned to a second variable parameter of type **WORDLENGTHS**; we shall define these types later. A third variable parameter, of type **BOOLEAN**, is also needed to indicate whether a word is actually read.

```
PROCEDURE READWORD ( VAR INWORD : WORDSPELLINGS;
                     VAR INLENGTH : WORDLENGTHS;
                     VAR SUCCESS : BOOLEAN );
   local declarations;
   BEGIN
   skip any blanks up to the next word or end of input data;
   SUCCESS := not end of data;
   IF SUCCESS THEN
      read a word into INWORD, storing its length in INLENGTH
   END (*READWORD*)
```

'Skip any blanks . . .' will be refined into a loop which continues until either a non-blank character is read or EOF becomes TRUE. 'Read a word . . .' will be refined into a loop which continues until a blank following the word is read. (Even the last word on the last line must be followed at least by an end-of-line marker, which is read as a blank.)

We must now commit ourselves to a definition of the types **WORD-SPELLINGS** and **WORDLENGTHS**. Let us choose the type definitions:

```
WORDSPELLINGS = PACKED ARRAY
                        [1. .MAXWORDLENGTH] OF CHAR;
WORDLENGTHS   = 1. .MAXWORDLENGTH
```

which will allow us to store words up to **MAXWORDLENGTH** characters in length; and let us decide to store each word left-justified in **INWORD**.

After further refinements, we may arrive at the following solution:

```
PROCEDURE READWORD ( VAR INWORD : WORDSPELLINGS;
                     VAR INLENGTH : WORDLENGTHS;
                     VAR SUCCESS : BOOLEAN);
  CONST
    BLANK = ' ';
  VAR
    CHARACTER: CHAR;
    I: 0. .MAXWORDLENGTH;
BEGIN
(* skip any blanks up to the next word or end of input data *)
CHARACTER := BLANK;
WHILE NOT EOF(INPUT) AND (CHARACTER = BLANK) DO
  READ (CHARACTER);
SUCCESS := NOT EOF(INPUT);
IF SUCCESS THEN
  (* read a word into INWORD, storing its length in INLENGTH *)
  BEGIN
  I := 0;
  WHILE CHARACTER <> BLANK DO
    BEGIN
    (* store CHARACTER unless INWORD is already full *)
    IF I < MAXWORDLENGTH THEN
      BEGIN
      I := I+1;
      INWORD[I] := CHARACTER
      END;
    READ (CHARACTER)
    END;
  INLENGTH := I;
  (* fill out with blanks *)
  FOR I := INLENGTH+1 TO MAXWORDLENGTH DO
    INWORD[I] := BLANK
  END
END (*READWORD*)
```

Here is a complete program, incorporating READWORD and another procedure, which simply reads words and writes them one per line:

```
PROGRAM COPYWORDS ( INPUT, OUTPUT );
CONST
  MAXWORDLENGTH = 16;
TYPE
  WORDSPELLINGS = PACKED ARRAY
                         [1. .MAXWORDLENGTH] OF CHAR;
```

```
   WORDLENGTHS   = 1..MAXWORDLENGTH;
VAR
   WORD : WORDSPELLINGS;
   LENGTH : WORDLENGTHS;
   WORDFOUND : BOOLEAN;

PROCEDURE READWORD ( VAR INWORD : WORDSPELLINGS;
                     VAR INLENGTH : WORDLENGTHS;
                     VAR SUCCESS : BOOLEAN);

   . . . . . . . . . . . . . . . . . . . .
   . . . . . . . . . . . . . . . . . .   (* as above *)
   . . . . . . . . . . . . . . . . . .

PROCEDURE WRITEWORD ( OUTWORD : WORDSPELLINGS;
                      OUTLENGTH : WORDLENGTHS);
   VAR
     1 : WORDLENGTHS;
   BEGIN
   FOR I := 1 TO OUTLENGTH DO
     WRITE (OUTWORD[I]);
   WRITELN
   END (*WRITEWORD*);

BEGIN (*COPYWORDS*)
READWORD (WORD, LENGTH, WORDFOUND);
WHILE WORDFOUND DO
   BEGIN
   WRITEWORD (WORD, LENGTH);
   READWORD (WORD, LENGTH, WORDFOUND)
   END
END (*COPYWORDS*).
```

Suppose the input data is:

PARIS
IN THE
SPRING-TIME

When we obey the statement READWORD(WORD,LENGTH,WORD-
FOUND), the variable parameters INWORD, INLENGTH and SUCCESS
represent the variables WORD, LENGTH and WORDFOUND respectively;
in particular, INWORD represents the *whole* of the array WORD. On the
first entry to READWORD we have:

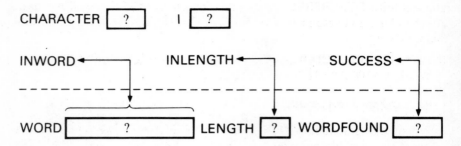

Assignment of characters to INWORD[1], INWORD[2] and so on, will actually result in these characters being stored in WORD[1], WORD[2] and so on. Thus after the first invocation of READWORD we have:

WORD `'PARIS            '` LENGTH `5` WORDFOUND `TRUE`

and after the fourth invocation:

WORD `'SPRING-TIME   '` LENGTH `11` WORDFOUND `TRUE`

On the fifth invocation, WORDFOUND is set to FALSE but WORD and LENGTH are unaltered.

As an exercise, work through program COPYWORDS with the input data given above, verify the effects of procedure READWORD, and show what output is produced.

The following example illustrates a slightly different usage of a variable parameter. The actual parameter's value is both used and changed.

Example 14.4

The following little procedure can be invoked with any INTEGER variable as actual parameter. The effect is to increment its value by one.

```
PROCEDURE INCREMENT ( VAR COUNT : INTEGER );
  BEGIN
  COUNT := COUNT+1
  END (*INCREMENT*)
```

Suppose we wished to count the frequencies of individual upper-case letters, and the total frequency of all other characters, in a piece of text. Let us declare the variables:

```
LETTERFREQ : ARRAY ['A' . .'Z'] OF INTEGER;
OTHERFREQ  : INTEGER;
CHARACTER  : CHAR
```

and initialize **OTHERFREQ**, and each component of **LETTERFREQ**, to 0. After storing a character in **CHARACTER** we can update the appropriate frequency by:

```
IF ('A' <= CHARACTER) AND (CHARACTER <= 'Z') THEN
   INCREMENT (LETTERFREQ[CHARACTER])
ELSE
   INCREMENT (OTHERFREQ)
```

When the statement **INCREMENT(LETTERFREQ[CHARACTER])** is obeyed, the variable parameter **COUNT** represents the variable **LETTERFREQ[CHARACTER]**, i.e. a *single* component of the array **LETTERFREQ**. For example, when **CHARACTER** has the value 'C', **COUNT** represents **LETTERFREQ['C']**:

The effect of the procedure statement will then be to change the value of **LETTERFREQ['C']** from 4 to 5; the remaining components of **LETTERFREQ** will not be disturbed.

The syntax of formal parameter parts, including value parameters and variable parameters, is summarized in Figure 14.3. A variable parameter section is distinguished from a value parameter section (see Figure 13.3) by the reserved word **VAR**.

Let us summarize the effect of obeying a procedure statement.

(1) The actual parameters of the procedure statement are paired off, from left to right, with the formal parameters of the named procedure. (It follows that for each formal parameter exactly one actual parameter must be supplied.)

(2) For each *value parameter* of the procedure a store location is created, to which is assigned the value of the corresponding actual parameter. (It follows that the actual parameter must be an expression assignment-compatible with the type of the value parameter.)

(3) Each *variable parameter* of the procedure is made to represent the corresponding actual parameter (which must be a variable of identically the same type as the variable parameter).

(4) For each local variable of the procedure a store location is created whose initial value is undefined.

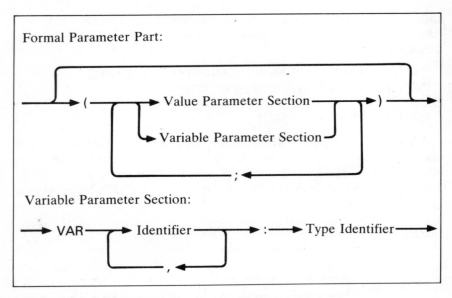

Figure 14.3. Syntax of Formal Parameter Parts (simplified)

(5) The procedure's statement part is obeyed. At this stage value parameters behave exactly like ordinary local variables, but each reference
to a variable parameter is effectively a reference to the actual
parameter it represents. In particular, assigning a value to variable
parameter effectively changes the value of the actual parameter.

(6) Finally, all store locations created for formal parameters and local
variables of the procedure are discarded.

Thus the effect of obeying a procedure statement is similar to the
evaluation of a function designator, except for the absence of a function
result. Compare the summary above with the summary at the end of
Chapter 13. (The latter summary, however, took only value parameters
into account.)

Although it is not illegal in Pascal for a function to have variable
parameters, you will find no such examples in this book. It is more natural
to use functions with only value parameters, since this corresponds more
closely to the mathematical concept of functions. If a function, when
invoked, changes the value of any non-local variable, either through a
variable parameter or by any other means, or performs any input or
output, this phenomenon is known as a *side-effect.* Side-effects are
generally considered to be bad programming practice, since they tend to
make programs more difficult to understand.

14.4 The scope rules of Pascal

Declarations of identifiers inside a subprogram have no meaning outside that subprogram; we say that such identifiers are *local* to the subprogram. On the other hand, identifiers declared outside a subprogram can generally be used inside the subprogram; the constant identifier **MAXWORD-LENGTH** was used in this way in Example 14.3.

It is time that we clarified these issues by stating what are known as the *scope rules* of Pascal. We shall use the program of Figure 14.4 for illustration.

In Figure 14.4 we have boxed in the declarative part and statement part of the program, and the declarative part and statement part of each of the two procedures. Each of these boxes is called a *block*.

Observe that the blocks are *nested*, that is a block may lie entirely within another block, but blocks do not overlap in any other way. This nesting is a consequence of the syntax of Pascal.

In general, there will be one block for each procedure declaration, one block for each function declaration, and one block for the program as a whole. Any formal parameters in a procedure or function heading are included in the corresponding block. Let us name each block after the corresponding procedure, function or program identifier. Thus, in Figure 14.4 we have an outer block, **LABELS**, and two inner blocks, **READLABEL** and **WRITELINE**.

Scope Rule 1. No identifier may be declared more than once in the same block.

The reason for this rule is simple: if we could declare an identifier, say I, twice in the same block, then each occurrence of I in a statement of the block would be ambiguous.

Nevertheless, Pascal allows the same identifier to be declared in different blocks. In Example 14.5, L is declared in two of the blocks: in block **LABELS** as a constant identifier, and in block **WRITELINE** as a value parameter. These are two distinct entities. Also, J is declared in two of the blocks, in both cases as a variable identifier, coincidentally having the same type in both declarations. Despite this coincidence, these two declarations introduce *two distinct variables*.

How can we tell, in general, when we use an identifier which has several declarations, to which of these declarations we are referring?

Scope Rule 2. If any identifier I is used in a statement S, find the smallest block which encloses both S and a declaration of I; then the occurrence of I in S corresponds to that declaration.

PROGRAM LABELS (INPUT, OUTPUT);

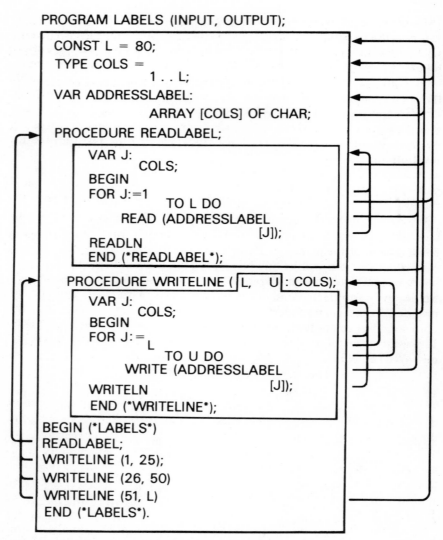

CONST L = 80;
TYPE COLS =
        1 . . L;
VAR ADDRESSLABEL:
        ARRAY [COLS] OF CHAR;
PROCEDURE READLABEL;

VAR J:
      COLS;
BEGIN
FOR J:=1
        TO L DO
    READ (ADDRESSLABEL
            [J]);
READLN
END (*READLABEL*);

PROCEDURE WRITELINE (L,   U : COLS);

VAR J:
      COLS;
BEGIN
FOR J: =
      L
        TO U DO
    WRITE (ADDRESSLABEL
            [J]);
WRITELN
END (*WRITELINE*);

BEGIN (*LABELS*)
READLABEL;
WRITELINE (1, 25);
WRITELINE (26, 50)
WRITELINE (51, L)
END (*LABELS*).

Figure 14.4. A Program with Nested Blocks

Consider the statement WRITELINE(51,L) in block LABELS. The smallest block enclosing both this statement and a declaration of L is block LABELS itself, where L is defined to be a constant with value 80. The same applies to the occurrence of L in the FOR clause in block READLABEL. But now consider the occurrence of L in the FOR clause in block WRITELINE. The smallest block enclosing both this statement and a declaration of L is block WRITELINE, where L is declared as a value parameter. On different occasions this L will have the values 1, 26 and 51.

Likewise, each occurrence of J in the statement part of READLABEL refers to the variable J declared within READLABEL, and each occurrence of J in the statement part of WRITELINE refers to the variable J declared within WRITELINE.

In Figure 14.4 arrows have been drawn from all identifier occurrences to the corresponding declarations.

What happens if, when applying Scope Rule 2, no block can be found containing both the statement and a declaration of the identifier? This is simply a programming error—the identifier has not been declared (at least not in the correct place).

Scope Rule 3. An identifier may be used only within a block where it is declared.

In Example 14.5, U cannot be used in block LABELS nor in block READLABEL; it can be used only in block WRITELINE, where it is declared.

These three scope rules apply equally to all identifiers: constant identifiers, type identifiers, variable identifiers, formal parameters, and even procedure and function identifiers.

Identifiers declared in a given block are described as *local* to that block. Identifiers used in a given block but declared in an enclosing block are described as *non-local* to the inner block. Identifiers declared in the outermost block (the main program) are described as *global*, since potentially they can be used anywhere.

We can now clarify the status of the standard constant, type, procedure and function identifiers. Imagine these to be declared in an invisible block enclosing every program: see Figure 14.5. In terms of the scope rules, the standard constant, type, function and procedure identifiers are not really special. We can, if we wish, redeclare any of their identifiers for our own purposes. Normally that would not be wise, however, since it would make their original declarations in the invisible outer block inaccessible; but see Example 14.6.

We have already seen some examples illustrating how the scope rules can be exploited in practical programming. In program COPYWORDS of Example 14.3, local variables named I were declared inside each of the two procedures. In Example 13.2 YEAR was used as a formal parameter in two different functions. In program YEARLYMAXIMA of Example 13.3, MONTH was used both as a local variable within a function and as a global variable. As these examples illustrate, the scope rules allow identifiers for formal parameters, local variables and so on, to be chosen freely within each subprogram. If they happen to be the same as identifiers declared in outer blocks, the coincidence does not affect the meaning of the program. This facility should be used with restraint, since using one identifier

```
CONST
    MAXINT = . . . .;

TYPE
    INTEGER = . . . .;
    BOOLEAN = ( FALSE, TRUE);
    . . . . . . . . . . . . . . .


PROCEDURE READ . . . .;
    . . . . . . . . . . . .
    . . . . . . . . . . .;


FUNCTION EOF;
    . . . . . . . . . . .
    . . . . . . . . . . .;


    . . . . . . . . . . . . . . . . . . . . . . . .

    . . . . . . . . . . . . . . . . . . . . . . . .


PROGRAM . . . .;
    . . . . . . . . . . .
    BEGIN
    . . . . . . . . . . .

    . . . . . . . . . . .
    END.
```

Figure 14.5. The Invisible Outer Block

indiscriminately for a variety of purposes in different places will make a program difficult to understand.

Here is another example of the usefulness of the scope rules.

Example 14.6

Suppose that someone has written a program which outputs a series of tables, one table per page (for example, tables of mathematical functions, or tables of students' examination marks grouped by subject). In skeleton form, the program might look like this:

PROGRAM TABLES (INPUT, OUTPUT);

. . . .

. . . .

BEGIN
PAGE;
write the first table;
PAGE;
write the second table;

. . . .

. . . .

END.

PAGE is a standard procedure, whose effect is to force subsequent output on to a fresh page.

Now suppose that most of the tables being written turn out to occupy only a few lines. Moreover computer paper is becoming very expensive; so, in order to economize on paper, we decide to separate the tables by lines across the page, instead of taking separate pages.

We could modify the program by replacing each invocation of PAGE by appropriate WRITELN statements. A much neater solution is to insert our own declaration of the procedure PAGE:

PROGRAM TABLES (INPUT, OUTPUT);

. . . .

. . . .

PROCEDURE PAGE;
  BEGIN (* paper-saving version *)
  WRITELN; WRITELN;
  WRITELN ('– – – – – – – – – – – – – – – – – – –');
  WRITELN; WRITELN
  END (*PAGE*);

BEGIN (*TABLES*)
PAGE;
write the first table;
PAGE;
write the second table;

. . . .

. . . .

END (*TABLES*).

The scope rules ensure that each procedure statement invoking PAGE uses our own procedure and not the standard version in the invisible outer block.

This solution is very flexible; if desired, we could go back to writing one table per page simply by removing the procedure declaration. No change to the rest of the program is necessary.

Example 14.6 also illustrates the use of a parameterless procedure. Compare the declaration of **PAGE** with the syntax diagrams of Figures 14.1 and 14.3, and compare the procedure statements invoking it with the syntax diagram of Figure 14.2.

Exercises 14

14.1. Write a procedure which outputs N blank lines, where N is its formal parameter. Write a statement which invokes your procedure to output four blank lines.

14.2. Write a procedure which interchanges the values of its two parameters (both of type **T**, which you may assume to be defined elsewhere).

14.3. The Pascal **READ** statement cannot be used to read a **BOOLEAN** value. Write a procedure which reads a **BOOLEAN** value, represented in the input data by one of the characters 'F' or 'T', and passes it back through a parameter. The procedure should skip any blanks and end-of-lines preceding the 'F' or 'T'.

14.4. Make the program fragments of Examples 9.1 and 9.11 into procedures.

14.5. Write a procedure **READLINE** which reads one line of characters and passes it back through a string parameter of type **PACKED ARRAY [1. .L] OF CHAR** (see Example 12.4). You will find this procedure useful for many subsequent programming exercises.

14.6*. Assume the type definitions:

```
CENTRES      = (FRANKFURT,LONDON,NEWYORK,PARIS,
                TOKYO,ZURICH);
PROFILES     = ARRAY [CENTRES] OF REAL;
CURRENCIES = (DEUTSCHMARK,FFRANC,SFRANC,STERLING,
                USDOLLAR,YEN)
```

(a) Write a procedure which locates the maximum and minimum components of a parameter of type **PROFILES**. The *indices* of the maximum and minimum components are to be passed back through parameters. (Assume that no two components are exactly equal.)

(b) Assume that each component of the two-dimensional array:

CURRENCYVALUE : ARRAY [CURRENCIES] OF PROFILES

contains the value (relative to gold, say) of one currency at one trading centre. Write a program fragment, invoking your procedure, to determine at which centres a dealer could most profitably buy Sterling and sell Sterling, and to compute his percentage profit on the deal.

Programming exercises 14

14.7. Modify procedure WRITEWORD of Example 14.3 so that OUT-WORD is written on the same line as the previous word, unless that would make the output line longer than (say) 40 characters, in which case OUTWORD is to be written on a new line. Adjacent words are to be separated by a single blank.

Test program COPYWORDS with your amended procedure. Only minimal changes to the rest of the program should be necessary.

14.8. Assume the type definitions:

INDEXRANGE = 1. .N;
LISTS   = ARRAY [INDEXRANGE] OF ITEMS

(a) Write a procedure SEARCH which searches LIST (a parameter of type LISTS) for a component which equals TARGET (a parameter of type ITEMS). If the search is successful, the index of the matched component is to be assigned to LOCATION (a parameter of type INDEXRANGE). FOUND (a BOOLEAN parameter) is to be set appropriately. (See Example 11.7.)

(b) Incorporate your procedure in a program which defines ITEMS = INTEGER. The program should first read N integers into an array. Then it should read further integer targets, one per line. For each target it should invoke the procedure to search the array, and output a message indicating whether and where the target was located.

(c) Modify your program to handle 10-character names, rather than integers. You will need to change the type definition of ITEMS, but your search procedure should not need to be changed at all. The only other change to your program should be to the statements which read the input data. Adapt procedure READLINE (see Exercise 14.5) and use it in your program.

14.9. Write a program which reads the number of a year and the day of the week on which 1 January falls, and which outputs a complete calendar for that year. Include in your program a procedure which, given the name of a month, the number of days in that month, and the day of the week on which the first day of that month falls, outputs a calendar for that month, and passes back the day of the week on which the month ends.

15
Methodical programming with subprograms

15.1 The virtues of subprograms

All the example programs in Chapter 13 and 14 could have been written without using any procedures or functions. You might well ask, then, why take the trouble to learn how to use them? There are several very good reasons why this effort is worthwhile, reasons which should become more and more convincing as you go on to write larger and larger programs.

(a) Procedures and functions can be used to build a program from small self-contained pieces, which we have called subprograms. Each subprogram can be written and tested separately, which facilitates the task of writing and testing a large program. Equally important, each subprogram can be read and understood separately, and this makes the program as a whole easier to understand.

(b) Subprograms give names (identifiers) to pieces of program. By the judicious choice of identifiers for subprograms, as well as for constants, types and variables, we can make a program read almost like prose.

(c) Once declared, a subprogram may be invoked at several places, with different actual parameters if required. This makes it unnecessary to write similar pieces of program several times, which would be a tedious and error-prone task. Note that the use of parameters provides valuable flexibility in this respect.

(d) Another source of flexibility is the ease with which one version of a subprogram can be replaced by another (see Example 14.1). This flexibility is a consequence of the self-contained nature of subprograms.

(e) As we have seen, variables declared inside a subprogram occupy storage only while that subprogram is being obeyed. At other times this storage can be used for other purposes. On the other hand, global variables—those declared in the main program—occupy storage for the entire duration of the program. Thus we can economize on storage space by declaring each variable only in the subprogram where it is actually needed.

We can illustrate some of these points by comparing two versions of the same program, one being monolithic, the other being conveniently broken down into procedures.

Example 15.1

Let us develop a program which reads two $N \times N$ integer matrices, computes and writes their matrix product.

The problem specification suggests the following program outline:

```
PROGRAM MATRIXPRODUCT ( INPUT, OUTPUT );
    global declarations;
    BEGIN
    read matrix A;
    read matrix B;
    make P the matrix product of A and B;
    write matrix P
    END.
```

Now we refine 'read matrix A', 'read matrix B', and so on. If we simply substitute these refinements into the program outline, we obtain a mono-lithic program like the following:

```
PROGRAM MATRIXPRODUCT ( INPUT, OUTPUT ); (* version (a) *)
CONST
    N = 10;   (* say *)
TYPE
    MATRIX = ARRAY [1 .. N, 1 .. N] OF INTEGER;
VAR
    A, B, P: MATRIX;
    I, J, K: 1 .. N;
    SCALARPRODUCT: INTEGER;
BEGIN (MATRIXPRODUCT(a)*)
(* read matrix A *)
FOR I := 1 TO N DO
    FOR J := 1 TO N DO
        READ (A[I,J]);
(* read matrix B *)
FOR I := 1 TO N DO
    FOR J := 1 TO N DO
        READ (B[I,J]);
(* make P the matrix product of A and B *)
FOR I := 1 TO N DO
    FOR J := 1 TO N DO
        BEGIN
        SCALARPRODUCT := 0;
```

```
      FOR K := 1 TO N DO
         SCALARPRODUCT := SCALARPRODUCT + A[I,K]*B[K,J];
      P[I,J] := SCALARPRODUCT
      END;
   (* write matrix P *)
   FOR I := 1 TO N DO
      BEGIN
      WRITE ('[');
      FOR J := 1 TO N DO
         WRITE (P[I,J]);
      WRITELN ('   ]')
      END
   END (*MATRIXPRODUCT(a)*).
```

In refining this program, we should observe that each refinement introduces details irrelevant to the rest of the program. Therefore it is a good idea to package each refinement as a separate procedure, with the relevant matrix or matrices as parameter(s). Indeed, 'read matrix A' and 'read matrix B' are sufficiently similar to be refined into statements invoking the same procedure. Each command in the program outline now becomes a single procedure statement.

```
PROGRAM MATRIXPRODUCT ( INPUT, OUTPUT ); (* version (b) *)
CONST
   N = 10;   (* say *)
TYPE
   MATRIX = ARRAY [1 .. N, 1 .. N] OF INTEGER;
VAR
   A, B, P : MATRIX;

PROCEDURE READMATRIX ( VAR M: MATRIX );
   VAR
      I, J : 1 .. N;
   BEGIN
   FOR I := 1 TO N DO
      FOR J := 1 TO N DO
         READ (M[I,J]);
   END (*READMATRIX*);

PROCEDURE WRITEMATRIX ( M: MATRIX );
   VAR
      I, J : 1 .. N;
   BEGIN
   FOR I := 1 TO N DO
      BEGIN
```

```
      WRITE ('[');
      FOR J := 1 TO N DO
        WRITE (M[I,J]);
      WRITELN ('   ]')
      END
  END (*WRITEMATRIX*);

PROCEDURE MULTIPLYMATRICES (M1, M2 : MATRIX;
                               VAR PRODUCT : MATRIX );
  VAR
    I, J, K: 1 .. N;
    SCALARPRODUCT: INTEGER;
  BEGIN
  FOR I := 1 TO N DO
    FOR J := 1 TO N DO
      BEGIN
      SCALARPRODUCT := 0;
      FOR K := 1 TO N DO
        SCALARPRODUCT := SCALARPRODUCT +
                            M1[I,K]*M2[K,J];
      PRODUCT[I,J] := SCALARPRODUCT
      END
  END (*MULTIPLYMATRICES*);

BEGIN (*MATRIXPRODUCT(b)*)
READMATRIX (A);
READMATRIX (B);
MULTIPLYMATRICES (A, B, P);
WRITEMATRIX (P)
END (*MATRIXPRODUCT(b)*).
```

MATRIXPRODUCT(a) cannot be read without at once plunging into a morass of nested loops. Compare the statement part of program **MATRIXPRODUCT**(b), which is much easier to read and understand because of its brevity and its well-chosen procedure identifiers. It is simply a formalization in Pascal syntax of the original program outline. The messy details of matrix manipulation have been relegated to procedures, which can be read separately if desired.

Compare also the variable declarations in each program. In **MATRIXPRODUCT**(a) these declarations are rather cluttered, with the important **MATRIX** variables placed on an equal footing with others which are merely auxiliary variables. In **MATRIXPRODUCT**(b) only the important **MATRIX** variables are declared at the head of the program, where they stand out clearly; the declarations of auxiliary variables have been relegated to the procedures where they are needed.

MATRIXPRODUCT(a) contains two similar pieces of program, one for reading the matrix A, one for reading the matrix B. MATRIXPRODUCT(b) avoids this duplication by substituting two procedure statements invoking the same procedure, READMATRIX, with actual parameters A and B respectively.

Although these two pieces of program are very short, it would be annoying if they had to be changed consistently (for example, if the matrix components were to be read in column by column, instead of row by row). In MATRIXPRODUCT(a) changes would be necessary in two places. In MATRIXPRODUCT(b) the change could be made in a single place, in the declaration of READMATRIX; consequently the chance of error would be reduced.

The flexibility inherent in the use of procedures would become even more apparent if the programs were to be changed to write the matrices A and B as well as their product. The following would be inserted in the program outline:

write matrix A;
write matrix B

In MATRIXPRODUCT(a) these would be refined into yet more nested loops, making the program even less clear. In MATRIXPRODUCT(b) they would be refined immediately into the procedure statements:

WRITEMATRIX (A);
WRITEMATRIX (B)

which would not reduce the program's clarity at all.

A good, methodical approach to implementing a program such as MATRIXPRODUCT(b) would be to write and test the procedures one at a time.

(1) We could first write WRITEMATRIX and try it in a test program of the form:

```
BEGIN (* test WRITEMATRIX *)
assign arbitrary values to the components of A;
WRITEMATRIX (A)
END.
```

(2) Then we could write READMATRIX and test it using the following test program:

```
BEGIN (* test READMATRIX *)
READMATRIX (A);
WRITEMATRIX (A);
END.
```

(3) Finally we could write **MULTIPLYMATRICES** and test it in the completed program **MATRIXPRODUCT**.

This approach to testing is called 'bottom-up' testing, because we test the procedures on the bottom level of the program's structure diagram before testing the higher level(s) up to the main program (see Figure 15.1). Bottom-up testing uses temporary test programs which serve only to invoke the procedures under test.

MATRIXPRODUCT

READMATRIX   WRITEMATRIX   MULTIPLYMATRICES

Figure 15.1. Structure diagram of program **MATRIXPRODUCT** (b)

An alternative approach is 'top-down' testing, whereby we write and test the top-level main program before writing and testing the lower-level subprograms. Top-down testing makes use of temporary, dummy versions of the subprograms.

(1) The main program of **MATRIXPRODUCT** is written *first*, in its final form.
(2) Then we write **WRITEMATRIX**, and test it using the main program and temporary versions of **READMATRIX** and **MULTIPLYMATRICES**. The temporary **READMATRIX** could, for example, simply assign arbitrary values to the components of its formal parameter **M**. The temporary **MULTIPLYMATRICES** could simply make **PRODUCT** a copy of **M1**.
(3) Then we replace the temporary **READMATRIX** by its final version and repeat the test, still using the temporary **MULTIPLYMATRICES**.
(4) Finally we replace the temporary **MULTIPLYMATRICES** by its final version, and test what is now the complete program.

Observe that the same version of the main program is used at all stages of top-down testing.

We have stressed how subprograms can be exploited to structure even quite small programs written by a single programmer. In the development of large programs they are absolutely essential. Professional programmers often work in teams, collaborating in the construction of very large programs (up to 100000 statements or more). A convenient method of splitting up such a task is to have each programmer independently write and test a single *module*—either a single subprogram or a related group of subprograms. This exploits the self-contained nature of subprograms. Later, the modules are combined to form a complete program.

Another common practice of experienced programmers is to write and test subprograms of general utility, and then to deposit them in 'libraries' where they become accessible to others. This avoids duplication of effort, and makes sophisticated algorithms available even to inexperienced programmers. The standard procedures and functions of Pascal form such a library, which is available to every Pascal programmer (see Appendix 3).

A programmer wishing to use subprograms written by another need not be concerned with *how* each subprogram performs its computation. The user needs to know only *what* each subprogram computes, and how it should be invoked (i.e. the number and types of its parameters, and its result type in the case of a function). The former information should be provided by an accurate abstract; the latter information is provided simply by the procedure or function heading.

15.2 Case study II: sorting

Problem specification

A list of names is supplied as input data, one name per line. The names are in no particular order. Write a program which will read all the names and output them in lexicographic order. Assume that there are no more than 100 names, and that each name is at most 20 characters in length.

Solution

This is an example of *sorting*, a recurrent theme in computer programming. A bewildering variety of sorting techniques have been devised. Here we shall illustrate one of the simplest, called *insertion sorting*.

We can keep the names in a list. Let us arrange to read the names one at a time, and to insert each name immediately in its correct place in the list. For example, if the list already contains the names:

'Dijkstra', 'Knuth', 'Wirth'

and the next name is 'Hoare', this name will be inserted between 'Dijkstra' and 'Knuth', so now the list will consist of:

'Dijkstra', 'Hoare', Knuth', 'Wirth'.

In this way the names in the list will always be in correct order. This analysis leads to our level 1 outline.

Level 1 outline

```
PROGRAM SORTNAMES ( INPUT, OUTPUT );
global declarations;
BEGIN
make the list empty;
WHILE not end of input data DO
  BEGIN
  read a name;
  insert the new name in its correct position in the list
  END;
write all the names in listed order
END.
```

As an exercise, hand-test the Level 1 outline using suitable test data.

Refinements from Level 1

We must decide how to store the list. Since we are to assume that no more than 100 names will be input, we can store the list in an array with space for 100 names. We also need a variable to keep track of the actual number of names in the list. So we shall introduce the global declarations:

```
CONST
  MAXNAMES = 100;
  . . .
VAR
  SIZE : 0 . . MAXNAMES;
  LIST : ARRAY [1 . . MAXNAMES] OF NAMES;
  . . .
```

where the type **NAMES** can be defined later. These decisions lead to the following refinements.

Refinement 1.1: make the list empty

```
SIZE := 0
```

Refinement 1.2: insert the new name in its correct position in the list

In general, the new name will be inserted in some intermediate position. This will require the names already stored in the array **LIST** in this and subsequent positions to be shifted along to make room for the new name. For example, in the following situation:

	1	2	3	4		
LIST	"Dijkstra"	"Knuth"	"Wirth"	?		SIZE 3

if the name to be inserted is 'Hoare', the names in positions 2–3 of LIST must be shifted into positions 3–4 before storing the new name in position 2:

Since LIST has room for only MAXNAMES names, we ought to test whether LIST is already full before attempting to insert a new name. This leads to the following refinement:

```
IF SIZE < MAXNAMES THEN
  BEGIN
  find the position, NEWPOSITION, where the new name will be
      inserted;
  shift up the names in positions NEWPOSITION to SIZE inclusive;
  place the new name in position NEWPOSITION;
  SIZE := SIZE+1
  END
ELSE
  issue a warning that the new name cannot be sorted
```

Since this program fragment involves details, and variables such as NEWPOSITION, which are of purely local interest, it is a good candidate for a procedure. The name to be inserted should be a parameter. Thus Refinement 1.2 becomes:

```
INSERTNAME (name just read)
```

and we must introduce the global procedure declaration:

```
PROCEDURE INSERTNAME ( NEWNAME : NAMES );
  VAR
    NEWPOSITION : 1 . . MAXNAMES;
  BEGIN
  IF SIZE < MAXNAMES THEN
    BEGIN
    find the position, NEWPOSITION, where NEWNAME will be
        inserted;
    shift up the names in positions NEWPOSITION to SIZE inclusive;
    place NEWNAME in position NEWPOSITION;
    SIZE := SIZE + 1
    END
  ELSE
    issue a warning that NEWNAME cannot be sorted
  END (*INSERTNAME*)
```

Refinement 1.3: write all the names in listed order

Using a variable, POSITION, this can easily be refined directly into Pascal:

```
FOR POSITION := 1 TO SIZE DO
    WRITELN (LIST[POSITION])
```

This is another candidate for a procedure, with POSITION as a local variable. So Refinement 1.3 becomes:

WRITEALLNAMES

and we introduce the global procedure declaration:

```
PROCEDURE WRITEALLNAMES;
    VAR
        POSITION : 1 .. MAXNAMES;
    BEGIN
    FOR POSITION := 1 TO SIZE DO
        WRITELN (LIST[POSITION])
    END (*WRITEALLNAMES*)
```

Nearly all the operations on the list (represented by the variables LIST and SIZE) have now been wrapped up tidily in the procedures INSERT-NAME and WRITEALLNAMES. The only exception is Refinement 1.1. To be consistent we shall make that also into a procedure statement:

MAKELISTEMPTY

and introduce the following global procedure declaration:

```
PROCEDURE MAKELISTEMPTY;
    BEGIN
    SIZE := 0
    END (*MAKELISTEMPTY*)
```

The advantages of this way of using procedures are:

(a) The main program now contains no direct references to LIST and SIZE; all these references are collected together in three procedures which will be adjacent to one another. This improves the localization of the program.
(b) The main program is expressed largely in terms of procedure statements like MAKELISTEMPTY and INSERTNAMES (name just read), which concentrate attention on *what* is being done rather than *how* it is being done.
(c) It is fairly easy to modify the program to use a different representation of the list of names. (This will be done in Example 20.3.) Only the global declarations (including the procedures) need to be altered. If

procedures are not used in this way, the whole program would have to be scanned for possible alterations.

Level 2 outline

```
PROGRAM SORTNAMES ( INPUT, OUTPUT );
global declarations;
BEGIN (*SORTNAMES*)
MAKELISTEMPTY;
WHILE not end of input data DO
  BEGIN
  read a name;
  INSERTNAME (name just read)
  END;
WRITEALLNAMES
END (*SORTNAMES*).
```

Let us hand-test the outline of procedure **INSERTNAME** with several test cases.

(1)

NEWNAME ["Knuth"]   NEWPOSITION [?]

	1	2	3	4	
LIST	?	?	?	?		SIZE [0]

In this situation, **SIZE<MAXNAMES** has the value **TRUE**; 'find the position . . .' should set **NEWPOSITION** to 1; 'shift up the names . . .' should do nothing, since there are no names in positions 1 to 0 inclusive; 'place **NEWNAME** . . .' should place 'Knuth' in **LIST[1]**; and SIZE:=SIZE+1 will increment **SIZE** to 1.

(2)

NEWNAME ["Dijkstra"]   NEWPOSITION [?]

	1	2	3	4	
LIST	"Knuth"	?	?	?		SIZE [1]

In this situation, **SIZE<MAXNAMES** has the value **TRUE**; 'find the position . . .' should set **NEWPOSITION** to 1; 'shift up the names . . .'

should shift 'Knuth' into LIST[2]; 'place NEWNAME . . .' should place 'Dijkstra' in LIST[1]; and SIZE:=SIZE+1 will increment SIZE to 2.

(3)

NEWNAME "Wirth"   NEWPOSITION ?

- -

| 1 | 2 | 3 | 4 | | |
LIST "Dijkstra" "Knuth" ? ?] SIZE 2

In this situation, SIZE<MAXNAMES has the value TRUE; 'find the position . . .' should set NEWPOSITION to 3; 'shift up the names . . .' should do nothing, since there are no names in positions 3 to 2 inclusive; 'place NEWNAME . . .' should place 'Wirth' in LIST[3]; and SIZE:=SIZE+1 will increment SIZE to 3.

(4)

NEWNAME "Hoare"   NEWPOSITION ?

- -

| 1 | 2 | 3 | 4 | | |
LIST "Dijkstra" "Knuth" "Wirth" ?] SIZE 3

In this situation, SIZE<MAXNAMES has the value TRUE; 'find the position . . .' should set NEWPOSITION to 2; 'shift up the names . . .' should shift 'Knuth' and 'Wirth' into LIST[3] and LIST[4]; 'place NEW-NAME . . .' should place 'Hoare' in LIST[2]; and SIZE:=SIZE+1 will increment SIZE to 4. Thus we reach the situation illustrated above (at Refinement 1.2).

(5) When the value of SIZE is 100, SIZE<MAXNAMES has the value FALSE, so INSERTNAME will do nothing except issue a warning message.

As an exercise, hand-test the Level 2 outline of the main program, and the completed procedure WRITEALLNAMES.

Refinements from Level 2

First we can complete the refinement of procedure INSERTNAME.

Refinement 2.1: find the position, NEWPOSITION, where NEWNAME will be inserted

This can be done by linear search, comparing NEWNAME in turn with LIST[1], LIST[2], and so on, until we find a name in the list which should *follow* NEWNAME in lexicographic order. We must set NEWPOSITION to the position of this name in the list. If no such name is found, we must set NEWPOSITION to SUCC(SIZE), indicating that the new name will be inserted at the end of the list. The details are shown below, in the completed program.

Refinement 2.2: shift up the names in positions NEWPOSITION to SIZE inclusive

```
FOR POSITION := SIZE DOWNTO NEWPOSITION DO
  LIST[SUCC(POSITION)] := LIST[POSITION]
```

If NEWPOSITION equals SUCC(SIZE), this loop shifts no names at all, which is precisely what we want.

(Note the use of DOWNTO to ensure that the last name in the list is shifted first. Can you see what will happen if we use:

```
FOR POSITION := NEWPOSITION TO SIZE DO
  LIST[SUCC(POSITION)] := LIST[POSITION]
```

instead?)

Refinement 2.3: place NEWNAME in position NEWPOSITION

```
LIST[NEWPOSITION] := NEWNAME
```

As an exercise, hand-test the completed procedure INSERTNAME with the test data used for testing its Level 2 outline. Alternatively, you could test Refinements 2.1–2.3 individually.

Refinement 2.4: read a name

We must now decide how to represent a name, that is how to define the type NAMES. Given the assumption in the problem specification, we can introduce the global declarations:

```
CONST
  NAMELENGTH = 20;
  . . .
TYPE
  NAMES = PACKED ARRAY [1 . . NAMELENGTH] OF CHAR;
  . . .
```

Now 'read a name' can be refined along the lines of Example 12.4. Again, this is a good candidate for a procedure, especially as it is the only part of this program which manipulates a name character by character. The details are shown below, in the completed program. The refinement includes a READLN to allow the following refinement.

Refinement 2.5: not end of input data

```
NOT EOF(INPUT)
```

Completed program

```
PROGRAM SORTNAMES ( INPUT, OUTPUT );

CONST
  MAXNAMES   = 100;
  NAMELENGTH =  20;
TYPE
  NAMES = PACKED ARRAY [1 .. NAMELENGTH] OF CHAR;
VAR
  SIZE            : 0 .. MAXNAMES;
  LIST            : ARRAY [1 .. MAXNAMES] OF NAMES;
  CURRENTNAME : NAMES;

PROCEDURE READNAME ( VAR NAME: NAMES );
  VAR
    COL : 1 .. NAMELENGTH;
  BEGIN
  FOR COL := 1 TO NAMELENGTH DO
    IF EOLN(INPUT) THEN
      NAME[COL] := ' '
    ELSE
      READ (NAME[COL]);
  READLN
  END (*READNAME*);

PROCEDURE WRITEALLNAMES;
  VAR
    POSITION : 1 .. MAXNAMES;
  BEGIN
  FOR POSITION := 1 TO SIZE DO
    WRITELN (LIST[POSITION])
  END (*WRITEALLNAMES*);

PROCEDURE MAKELISTEMPTY;
  BEGIN
  SIZE := 0
  END (*MAKELISTEMPTY*);

PROCEDURE INSERTNAME ( NEWNAME : NAMES );
  VAR
    POSITION, NEWPOSITION : 1 .. MAXNAMES;
    LOCATED               : BOOLEAN;
  BEGIN
  IF SIZE < MAXNAMES THEN
```

```
      BEGIN
      (* find the position where NEWNAME will be inserted *)
      NEWPOSITION := 1;
      LOCATED := FALSE;
      WHILE NOT LOCATED AND (NEWPOSITION <= SIZE) DO
        IF NEWNAME <= LIST[NEWPOSITION] THEN
          LOCATED := TRUE
        ELSE
          NEWPOSITION := SUCC(NEWPOSITION);
      (* shift up the names in succeeding positions *)
      FOR POSITION := SIZE DOWNTO NEWPOSITION DO
        LIST[SUCC(POSITION)] := LIST[POSITION];
      (* place NEWNAME in position *)
      LIST[NEWPOSITION] := NEWNAME;
      SIZE := SIZE+1
      END
    ELSE
      WRITELN (NEWNAME,
               ' CANNOT BE SORTED: TOO MANY NAMES.')
    END (*INSERTNAME*);

BEGIN (*SORTNAMES*)
MAKELISTEMPTY;
WHILE NOT EOF(INPUT) DO
  BEGIN
  READNAME (CURRENTNAME);
  INSERTNAME (CURRENTNAME)
  END;
WRITEALLNAMES
END (*SORTNAMES*).
```

As an exercise, hand-test procedure READNAME, and the completed program.

Program SORTNAMES has an interesting property. As it stands it serves to sort 20-character strings, but it can easily be adapted to sort single characters, integer numbers, real numbers, months, or any other items which can be ordered! It is necessary only to change the definition of the type identifier NAMES, the refinement of 'read a name', and possibly the WRITELN statement in procedure WRITEALLNAMES. It can even be adapted to sort more complex items like dates or telephone directory entries, although that would force us to replace the simple comparison NEWNAME<=LIST[POSITION] in procedure INSERTNAME by something more complex (see Exercises 15 and 16).

Exercises 15

15.1. Systematically modify both versions of program **MATRIXPRODUCT** (Example 15.1) to compute and write the sum as well as the product of the two input matrices.

15.2. Systematically modify both versions of program **MATRIXPRODUCT** (Example 15.1) to handle *lower-triangular* matrices, i.e. matrices where every component above the main diagonal is zero, for example ($N=4$):

$$\begin{bmatrix} 9 & 0 & 0 & 0 \\ 1 & 3 & 0 & 0 \\ 2 & 5 & 1 & 0 \\ 8 & 5 & 7 & 4 \end{bmatrix}$$

The components above the diagonal are omitted from the input data, so each matrix is input as one component value for row 1, followed by two component values for row 2, and so on.

15.3. Systematically modify program **SORTNAMES** so that it sorts integers rather than names.

15.4*. Surnames beginning with 'Mc' or 'Mac' are very common in Scotland (for example 'McKay' or 'MacKay'). It is conventional in directories to sort names beginning with 'Mc' as if they began with 'Mac'. Systematically modify program **SORTNAMES** so that it sorts names beginning with 'Mc' in conventional directory order.

Programming exercises 15

15.5. Write a program which reads 12-character names, one per line, and outputs the names together with their Soundex codes. For an explanation of the Soundex system, see Example 9.12. The Soundex code is to be a 4-character string. If the code would be too long, it is to be truncated to four characters; if it would be too short, it is to be padded out with '0' characters (*not* blanks).

15.6*. Write a procedure which reads a molecular formula, enclosed in parentheses, such as (Na2SO4), and passes back the molecular weight of the compound it represents. Assume that the molecular formula itself contains no parentheses.

Write a program which uses your procedure to read a number of molecular formulas, one per line of input, and which writes their molecular weights. Your program should declare and initialize tables of atomic symbols and atomic weights to be used by your procedure:

```
TYPE
    ELEMENTS = (HYDROGEN,HELIUM, . . .);
```

```
VAR
   SYMBOL : ARRAY [ELEMENTS] OF
                     PACKED ARRAY [1 . . 2] OF CHAR;
   ATOMICWEIGHT: ARRAY [ELEMENTS] OF REAL
```

For the purposes of this exercise, you need take only a few of the more common elements into account.

Part V
Further data structures

16
Records

16.1 The need for records

The concept of a *record* is familiar in everyday life. Examples include the information about a student held by a university records office, or the information about a book contained in a library catalogue. Such records might be kept as entries in a loose-leaf folder, on index cards, or stored in a computer system.

The concept of a record is very useful in programming, too. When we talk about records in everyday life there is a connotation of long-term storage. This connotation is not necessarily present in programming. Here we shall view a record simply as a fixed collection of information relating to a single object, where sometimes we wish to refer to the information as a whole, and at other times we wish to refer, by name, to the individual items of information. The latter are known as *fields*.

Example 16.1

A *date* consists of three components: the day of the month, the month, and the year. Sometimes we are interested in individual components, for answering queries such as 'What month is it?' At other times we are interested in the date as a whole, as a single piece of information, for answering queries such as 'What is today's date?' A date may be described by a record with three fields.

Example 16.2

A population registry office would be interested in the following information about people in its area:
(a) surname,
(b) forename,
(c) date of birth,
(d) sex, and
(e) marital status.

This information about one person can be considered to comprise a record with five fields.

The concept of a record is most fruitful when we consider similar records relating to several similar objects. For example, the registry office will have records for many different people, such as 'my record' or 'David's record'. Each of these records will contain the same fields, so we can talk about 'my surname', or 'David's date of birth'. In each case we combine a possessive ('my' or 'David's'), indicating *which record* we are talking about, with a noun ('surname' or 'date of birth'), indicating *which field* of that record we are talking about. Similarly we can talk about different dates, such as 'today' or 'the date of the next eclipse', and about individual fields of these dates, such as 'the year of the next eclipse'.

It is most important to understand the distinction between records and arrays. First, the fields of a record may have different types, whereas the components of an array must all have the same type. Second (a consequence of this), the fields of a record must be selected by name, whereas the components of an array are selected by indices, which may be variable. It makes sense to talk about the I-th component of an array, but not about the I-th field of a record, since we could not be sure what its type was.

16.2 Records in Pascal

A *record type* in Pascal is specified by writing down the identifiers and types of its fields (using syntax similar to that of variable declarations), enclosed between the reserved words **RECORD** and **END**. There is no restriction on the types of the fields.

To refer to an individual field of a record we use a *field designator*, in which the record variable is suffixed by a period and the field identifier.

Example 16.1 (continued)

The type definition:

```
DATES = RECORD
            DAY: 1 . . 31;
            MONTH: 1 . . 12;
            YEAR: 0 . . 9999
         END
```

could be used to declare variables whose values are dates:

TODAY, MANANA, NEXTECLIPSE: DATES

Each of these record variables can be visualized as a box divided into three compartments, named DAY, MONTH, and YEAR:

```
            MONTH                              MONTH
     DAY          YEAR                  DAY          YEAR
TODAY │  3  │  8  │ 1980 │   NEXTECLIPSE │  1  │  4  │ 1984 │
```

An example of a field designator is TODAY.MONTH, which designates the field MONTH of the record variable TODAY. In the diagram, the current value of the field TODAY.DAY is 3, TODAY.MONTH is 8, and TODAY.YEAR is 1980.

Example 16.2 (continued)

The structure of our registry office records could be specified by the type definition:

```
PERSONALDETAILS =
  RECORD
    SURNAME,
          FORENAME   : PACKED ARRAY [1 . . 12] OF CHAR;
    BIRTHDATE         : DATES;
    SEX               : (MALE,FEMALE);
    MARITALSTATUS : (SINGLE,MARRIED,DIVORCED,WIDOWED)
  END
```

The variable declaration:

```
MYDETAILS, YOURDETAILS: PERSONALDETAILS
```

declares two variables of this type.

The following program fragment will output some data from the record YOURDETAILS:

```
WRITE (YOURDETAILS.FORENAME, '  ',
       YOURDETAILS.SURNAME, ' IS ');
CASE YOURDETAILS.SEX OF
  MALE:   WRITE ('MALE');
  FEMALE: WRITE ('FEMALE')
END
```

The following statement updates one field of MYDETAILS:

```
MYDETAILS.MARITALSTATUS := MARRIED
```

The syntax of record types is summarized in Figure 16.1. A record type may be used, like any other type, in type definitions and in variable declarations.

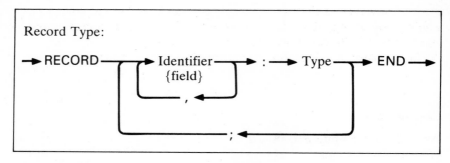

Figure 16.1. Syntax of Record Types (simplified)

The syntax of field designators is summarized in Figure 16.2. A field designator may be used anywhere an ordinary variable may be used, as illustrated in Example 16.2.

Figure 16.2. Syntax of Field Designators

In a field designator such as **YOURDETAILS.SURNAME**, we say that the field identifier **SURNAME** is *qualified* by the record variable **YOUR-DETAILS**. A field identifier used in a statement normally must be qualified. For example:

WRITE (SURNAME)

would be ambiguous, since we do not know whether **SURNAME** here designates **MYDETAILS.SURNAME** or **YOURDETAILS.SURNAME** or something else altogether.

Within each record type, every field must have a distinct identifier. However, field identifiers may be the same as identifiers given to constants, types, variables, procedures, functions and fields of other record types. The requirement to qualify the field identifiers ensures that no ambiguity arises.

16.3 Operations on complete records

We have seen that the individual fields of a record may be used just like ordinary variables. A major advantage of collecting data together in records, however, is that we may choose sometimes to treat a record as a whole, without regard to its individual fields. Thus we are interested in the operations that Pascal allows on complete records.

The simplest is assignment, which copies one record into another.

Example 16.3

Assume the definition of types **DATES** from Example 16.1, and the variable declarations:

TODAY, LETTERDATE : DATES

The single assignment statement:

LETTERDATE := TODAY

copies the *whole* of the record **TODAY** into the variable **LETTERDATE**. It is equivalent to the three assignments of individual fields:

```
LETTERDATE.DAY    := TODAY.DAY;
LETTERDATE.MONTH := TODAY.MONTH;
LETTERDATE.YEAR   := TODAY.YEAR
```

but it is both clearer and more concise than the latter.

Assume the definition of type **PERSONALDETAILS** from Example 16.2, and the variable declaration:

NEWBORN : PERSONALDETAILS

Since the field **NEWBORN.BIRTHDATE** is itself a record of type **DATES**, we can use the assignment statement:

NEWBORN.BIRTHDATE := TODAY

Whole records may be used as actual parameters of subprograms—both as value parameters and as variable parameters.

Example 16.4

Let us write a procedure which will inspect the registry office records of a man and a woman to determine whether they may legally marry, and if so to update their records accordingly. The procedure will take the two records as parameters. Since it may update these records, they must be variable parameters.

{Marriage laws vary considerably from state to state. The following is based on the current law of Scotland.}

```
PROCEDURE MARRY ( VAR HUSBAND, WIFE: PERSONALDETAILS;
                        VAR LEGAL: BOOLEAN );
  BEGIN
  LEGAL := (HUSBAND.SEX = MALE) AND
           (WIFE.SEX = FEMALE) AND
           (HUSBAND.MARITALSTATUS <> MARRIED) AND
           (WIFE.MARITALSTATUS <> MARRIED);
  IF LEGAL THEN
    (* update the records *)
    BEGIN
    HUSBAND.MARITALSTATUS := MARRIED;
    WIFE.MARITALSTATUS := MARRIED
    END
  END (* MARRY *)
```

The actual parameters corresponding to HUSBAND and WIFE must be record variables of the same type as the formal parameters. For example, given the variable declarations:

```
NAPOLEON, JOSEPHINE : PERSONALDETAILS;
PERMIS              : BOOLEAN
```

we may use the procedure statement:

```
MARRY (NAPOLEON, JOSEPHINE, PERMIS)
```

We can make procedure MARRY more elaborate by checking in addition that both partners have reached the age of majority. For this purpose it will be convenient to introduce a function which, given a person's details, computes that person's age in years. The PERSONAL-DETAILS record will be a value parameter to this function. (Let us assume that today's date is available in a *global* variable TODAY.)

```
PROCEDURE MARRY ( VAR HUSBAND, WIFE: PERSONALDETAILS;
                        VAR LEGAL: BOOLEAN );
  CONST
    AGEOFMAJORITY = 16;

  FUNCTION AGE ( PERSON: PERSONALDETAILS ): INTEGER;
    BEGIN
    IF (TODAY.MONTH > PERSON.BIRTHDATE.MONTH) OR
       (TODAY.MONTH = PERSON.BIRTHDATE.MONTH) AND
          (TODAY.DAY >= PERSON.BIRTHDATE.DAY) THEN
      AGE := TODAY,YEAR − PERSON.BIRTHDATE.YEAR
    ELSE
      AGE := TODAY.YEAR − PERSON.BIRTHDATE.YEAR − 1
    END (* AGE *);
```

```
BEGIN (* MARRY *)
LEGAL := (HUSBAND.SEX = MALE) AND
         (WIFE.SEX = FEMALE) AND
         (HUSBAND.MARITALSTATUS <> MARRIED) AND
         (WIFE.MARITALSTATUS <> MARRIED) AND
         (AGE(HUSBAND) >= AGEOFMAJORITY) AND
         (AGE(WIFE) >= AGEOFMAJORITY);
IF LEGAL THEN
   (* update the records *)
   BEGIN
   HUSBAND.MARITALSTATUS := MARRIED;
   WIFE.MARITALSTATUS := MARRIED
   END
END (* MARRY *)
```

16.4 The WITH statement

When writing statements to process a single record, we tend to find ourselves using the same record variable time and time again to qualify field identifiers. Since this can become rather tedious, Pascal provides a convenient shorthand, in the form of the *WITH statement*.

Example 16.5

The program fragment in Example 16.2 could be abbreviated as follows:

```
WITH YOURDETAILS DO
  BEGIN
  WRITE (FORENAME, '  ', SURNAME, ' IS ');
  CASE SEX OF
    MALE:   WRITE ('MALE');
    FEMALE: WRITE ('FEMALE')
    END (*CASE*)
END (* WITH *)
```

We simply write the name of the record variable (YOURDETAILS) between WITH and DO, and inside the WITH statement there is no need to qualify the field identifiers of that particular record.

The syntax of WITH statements is summarized in Figure 16.3. WITH and DO are both reserved words.

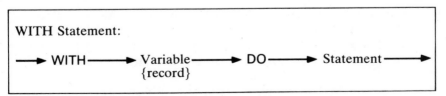

WITH Statement:

Figure 16.3. Syntax of WITH Statements (simplified)

Inside a WITH statement, any unqualified identifier which is a field identifier of the record variable actually designates that field. So, inside the WITH statement of Example 16.5, the unqualified identifier SURNAME, which is a field identifier of the record variable YOURDETAILS, actually designates the field YOURDETAILS.SURNAME.

A WITH statement is the only place where a field identifier may be used without qualification.

When we are processing more than one record of the same type, we can abbreviate the field designators of only one of these records.

Example 16.6

The function AGE of Example 16.4 may be recast as follows:

```
FUNCTION AGE ( PERSON : PERSONALDETAILS ) : INTEGER;
  BEGIN
  WITH PERSON.BIRTHDATE DO
    IF (TODAY.MONTH > MONTH) OR
       (TODAY.MONTH = MONTH) AND
          (TODAY.DAY >= DAY) THEN
      AGE := TODAY.YEAR — YEAR
    ELSE
      AGE := TODAY.YEAR — YEAR — 1
  END (* AGE *)
```

Here DAY, MONTH and YEAR, where unqualified, refer to the fields of PERSON.BIRTHDATE. There is no ambiguity, as the corresponding fields of TODAY are still qualified.

WITH statements play a part in the scope rules of Pascal (Section 14.4). The component statement of a WITH statement acts as a block in which the field identifiers of the record variable may be imagined to have been declared as ordinary variables. The behaviour of WITH statements can now be understood by applying the normal scope rules of Pascal.

16.5 Data structures

A *data structure* is just an organized collection of data. Arrays and records are different kinds of data structures, with their own particular properties. An array is a data structure whose components are homogeneous and are selected by (variable) indices. A record is a data structure whose components are non-homogeneous and are selected by (fixed) names. The fact that the components of arrays and records may themselves be structured allows us to build up data structures of some complexity.

Data structures form a subject of study in their own right, a subject whose proper treatment is well beyond the scope of this book. We shall confine ourselves here to examples illustrating some simple structures.

A record with fields which are themselves records is sometimes called a *hierarchical record*.

Example 16.7

The record type **PERSONALDETAILS** of Example 16.2 contains a field, **BIRTHDATE**, which is itself a record, of type **DATES**. Thus records of type **PERSONALDETAILS** have a hierarchical structure, which can be pictured in a diagram such as Figure 16.4.

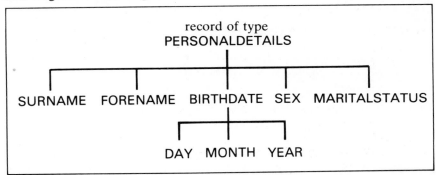

Figure 16.4. Hierarchical Structure of Type **PERSONALDETAILS**

The field **MYDETAILS.BIRTHDATE** is itself a record variable, so we may select a field from it, such as **MYDETAILS.BIRTHDATE.YEAR**. The following statements are all equivalent:

```
WRITE (MYDETAILS.BIRTHDATE.YEAR)

WITH MYDETAILS DO
  WRITE (BIRTHDATE.YEAR)

WITH MYDETAILS.BIRTHDATE DO
  WRITE (YEAR)
```

Hierarchical records are often processed by nested **WITH** statements, for example:

```
WITH MYDETAILS DO
  BEGIN
  SEX := MALE;
  MARITALSTATUS := SINGLE;
  WITH BIRTHDATE DO
    BEGIN
```

```
      DAY := 24; MONTH := 11; YEAR := 1947
      END
   END
```

Tables are very useful data structures, of which we have already seen some rather simple examples (Chapter 11). In general, a table may have several items of data in each entry; that is, each table entry may itself be a record.

Example 16.8

A table of the names and populations of a number of cities might be defined as follows:

```
CITY : ARRAY [1 . . MAXCITIES] OF
         RECORD
            NAME : PACKED ARRAY [1 . .10] OF CHAR;
            POPULATION : INTEGER
         END
```

whence the population of the N-th city would be designated:

```
CITY[N].POPULATION
```

Example 16.9

A personal telephone directory might be stored as an array of records, each holding a name, trunk dialling code and (local) number. The array would have to be big enough for the maximum number of directory entries, and we would also need to know how many were actually being used. Using the type definitions:

```
NAMES    = PACKED ARRAY [1 . . 16] OF CHAR;
CODES    = PACKED ARRAY [1 . . 4] OF CHAR;
NUMBERS = PACKED ARRAY [1 . . 8] OF CHAR
```

we can represent the directory as follows:

```
DIRECTORY : RECORD
               NRENTRIES : 0 . . MAXENTRIES;
               ENTRY : ARRAY [1 . . MAXENTRIES] OF
                          RECORD
                             NAME : NAMES;
                             CODE : CODES;
                             NUMBER : NUMBERS
                          END
            END
```

(CODE has been defined as a string rather than an integer because it is necessary to represent leading zeros. NUMBER has been defined as a string because many computers would not be able to cope with seven-digit integers.)

DIRECTORY might be visualized as follows, assuming that MAXENTRIES=8:

DIRECTORY

	NAME		CODE	NUMBER
NRENTRIES	6			
ENTRY	'ADDYMAN, A.	'	' 061'	'273 7121'
	'ELDER, J.	'	'0232'	' 4 5133'
	'FINDLAY, W.	'	' 041'	'339 8855'
	'WATT, D.	'	' 041'	'339 8855'
	'WELSH, J.	'	' 061'	'236 3311'
	'WILSON, I.	'	' 061'	'273 7121'
	?		?	?
	?		?	?

Let us write a procedure which outputs the number and dialling code of a person whose name is given, or a suitable message if there is no such name in DIRECTORY. This is an example of linear search.

```
PROCEDURE WRITETELEPHONENUMBER ( GIVENNAME: NAMES );
  VAR
    INDEX: 1 .. MAXENTRIES;
    STATUS: (UNKNOWN, PRESENT, ABSENT);
  BEGIN
  WITH DIRECTORY DO
    IF NRENTRIES = 0 THEN
      WRITELN ('THE DIRECTORY IS EMPTY')
    ELSE
      BEGIN
      STATUS := UNKNOWN;
      INDEX := 1;
      WHILE STATUS=UNKNOWN DO
        WITH ENTRY[INDEX] DO
          IF NAME = GIVENNAME THEN
            BEGIN
            STATUS := PRESENT;
            WRITELN (GIVENNAME, ' (', CODE, ')', NUMBER)
            END
```

```
                ELSE
                IF INDEX=NRENTRIES THEN
                    STATUS := ABSENT
                ELSE
                    INDEX := SUCC(INDEX);
            IF STATUS=ABSENT THEN
                WRITELN ('THERE IS NO ENTRY FOR ', GIVENNAME)
            END
    END (* WRITETELEPHONENUMBER *)
```

Inside the outer WITH statement we have access to the fields of **DIREC-TORY**, for example **NRENTRIES**, without qualification. Inside the loop we examine one directory entry, namely **ENTRY[INDEX]**. Since each entry is itself a record variable, we conveniently make use of a further WITH statement to access its component fields without qualification. Thus, for example:

WRITELN (GIVENNAME, ' (', CODE, ')', NUMBER)

is equivalent to the much less concise:

WRITELN (GIVENNAME,
            ' (', DIRECTORY.ENTRY[INDEX].CODE, ')',
            DIRECTORY.ENTRY[INDEX].NUMBER)

The directory could alternatively have been stored in four separate variables:

```
NRENTRIES : 0 .. MAXENTRIES;
NAME      : ARRAY [1 .. MAXENTRIES] OF NAMES;
CODE      : ARRAY [1 .. MAXENTRIES] OF CODES;
NUMBER    : ARRAY [1 .. MAXENTRIES] OF NUMBERS
```

But these declarations do not reflect the logical structure of the directory. They are more cumbersome than the original declaration, and so too would be the procedure which searches the directory. (Convince yourself of this by rewriting it accordingly.)

16.6 Variant records

{This section may be omitted on a first reading.}

All the records we have seen so far have been completely rigid in their structure, in that all records of one type have had the same number of fields, with the same names and the same types.

Sometimes it is convenient to use records with a more flexible structure. Pascal allows for *variant records*, in which the number and types of the fields may vary to some extent.

Example 16.10

A lending library might keep the following information in its catalogue about each item in stock:

(a) reference number,
(b) title,
(c) name of author/composer,
(d) name of publisher,
(e) class of item—book or recording,
(f) number of edition (books only),
(g) year of publication (books only),
(h) name of performer (recordings only).

We could represent this information by a record with eight fields, but that would be wasteful, since only six or seven fields will be used in any one case.

With a variant record, the class of the library item determines the fields that actually are present in each record:

```
ITEMCLASSES = (BOOK,RECORDING);

LIBRARYITEMS =
  RECORD
    REF : 0 . . 999999;
    TITLE : PACKED ARRAY [1 . . 30] OF CHAR;
    AUTHOR : PACKED ARRAY [1 . . 16] OF CHAR;
    PUBLISHER : PACKED ARRAY [1 . . 20] OF CHAR;
    CASE CLASS : ITEMCLASSES OF
      BOOK :
        ( EDITION : 1 . . 50;
          YEAR: −2000 . . 1999 );
      RECORDING :
        ( PERFORMER : PACKED ARRAY [1 . . 20] OF CHAR )
  END
```

Up to CASE the fields are defined normally. The clause 'CASE CLASS: ITEMCLASSES OF' defines a special field, called a *tag field*, of type ITEMCLASSES. This gives each record of type LIBRARYITEMS the following special property: the number and types of the fields *following* the tag field will depend upon the tag field's *current value*. Specifically, when the tag field's current value is BOOK, the tag field is assumed to be followed by two fields, EDITION and YEAR; when its current value is RECORDING, on the other hand, it is assumed to be followed by a single field, PERFORMER. Thus the internal structure of the record variable:

ITEM : LIBRARYITEMS

will depend upon the current value of ITEM.CLASS:

	REF	TITLE	AUTHOR	PUBLISHER	CLASS	EDITION	YEAR
ITEM					BOOK		

or:

	REF	TITLE	AUTHOR	PUBLISHER	CLASS	PERFORMER
ITEM					RECORDING	

Suppose the library catalogue has been stored as a table as follows:

```
CATALOGUE :
    RECORD
        NRITEMS : 0 . . MAXITEMS;
        ACCESSION : ARRAY [1 . . MAXITEMS] OF LIBRARYITEMS
    END
```

where the number of items actually held is kept in the NRITEMS field. The following procedure will output the contents of CATALOGUE:

```
PROCEDURE WRITECATALOGUE;
    VAR
        INDEX : 1 . . MAXITEMS;
    BEGIN
    WRITELN ('REF.':6, 'TITLE':34, 'AUTHOR':20, 'PUBLISHER':24,
            ' ':4, 'OTHER DETAILS');
    WRITELN;
    WITH CATALOGUE DO
        FOR INDEX := 1 TO NRITEMS DO
            WITH ACCESSION [INDEX] DO
            BEGIN
            WRITE (REF:6, TITLE:34, AUTHOR:20, PUBLISHER:24, ' ':4);
            CASE CLASS OF
                BOOK:
                    WRITELN ('EDITION ', EDITION:2, YEAR:8);
                RECORDING:
                    WRITELN ('PERFORMED BY ', PERFORMER)
                END (*CASE*)
            END
    END (* WRITECATALOGUE *)
```

It would be a serious error to attempt to access the field PERFORMER when the tag field's value is not RECORDING, for then the field PERFORMER does not exist. Similarly, it would be wrong to attempt to access the fields EDITION and PUBLISHER when the tag field's value is not BOOK (see the diagram above). That is why the procedure inspects the tag field of each record (using a **CASE** statement), in order to deduce which further fields are available for examination.

The complete syntax of record types (including variant records) is given in Appendix 1.7. A tag field may be of any *ordinal* type, but note that its type must be specified by a type *identifier*.

A variant must be specified for *every* value of the tag field's type, if necessary using empty variants for values that have no additional fields associated with them.

Example 16.11

Given that the input data consists of English-language text, let us write a procedure to read and store a single 'token', where a token is a word, a period, a comma, a semicolon, a colon, or an end-of-data indication. Assume that a word is a sequence of consecutive letters. All other characters are to be ignored.

On reading a token the procedure should note what kind of token it is. When the token is a word, the procedure should in addition store its spelling. In the other cases, however, no further information is needed. The natural way to represent a token, therefore, is by a variant record:

```
TOKENKINDS = (WORD,PERIOD,COMMA,SEMICOLON,
              COLON,ENDMARKER);
TOKENS =
  RECORD
    CASE KIND : TOKENKINDS OF
      WORD:
        ( SPELLING : PACKED ARRAY [1 .. MAXLENGTH] OF CHAR);
      PERIOD, COMMA, SEMICOLON, COLON, ENDMARKER:
        ( )
  END
```

This illustrates three points:

(a) the tag field may be the first field of a record;
(b) the tag field may be the last field of the record for some values of the tag field—this is specified simply by putting nothing between the parentheses, thus defining an empty variant;
(c) several values of the tag field may share the same variant.

Given this definition of type **TOKENS**, we can write the procedure as follows:

```
PROCEDURE READTOKEN ( VAR TOKEN : TOKENS );
  VAR
    LENGTH: 0 .. MAXLENGTH;
    FILL : 1 .. MAXLENGTH;

  FUNCTION ISLETTER ( CH : CHAR ) : BOOLEAN;
    BEGIN
    ISLETTER := ('A' <= CH) AND (CH <= 'Z')
    END (* ISLETTER *);

  BEGIN (* READTOKEN *)
  (* skip characters up to the beginning of a token,
     or end of input, whichever comes sooner . . . *)
  WHILE NOT ( EOF(INPUT) OR ISLETTER(CURRENTCHAR) OR
               (CURRENTCHAR='.') OR (CURRENTCHAR=',') OR
               (CURRENTCHAR=';') OR (CURRENTCHAR=':') ) DO
    READ (CURRENTCHAR);
  WITH TOKEN DO
    IF EOF(INPUT) THEN
      KIND := ENDMARKER
    ELSE
    IF ISLETTER (CURRENTCHAR) THEN
      BEGIN
      KIND := WORD;
      (* store the spelling of the word *)
      LENGTH := 0;
      REPEAT
        IF LENGTH < MAXLENGTH THEN
          BEGIN
          LENGTH := LENGTH + 1;
          SPELLING[LENGTH] := CURRENTCHAR;
          END;
        READ (CURRENTCHAR)
      UNTIL NOT ISLETTER(CURRENTCHAR);
      (* pad out the spelling with blanks *)
      FOR FILL := LENGTH+1 TO MAXLENGTH DO
        SPELLING[FILL] := ' '
      END
    ELSE
      BEGIN
      CASE CURRENTCHAR OF
        '.': KIND := PERIOD;
        ',': KIND := COMMA;
        ';': KIND := SEMICOLON;
        ':': KIND := COLON
        END (*CASE*);
```

```
    READ (CURRENTCHAR)
    END
END (* READTOKEN*)
```

Assignment of the value **WORD** to the tag field **TOKEN.KIND** brings the field **TOKEN.SPELLING** into existence. Only thereafter is assignment to (components of) **TOKEN.SPELLING** legitimate.

This procedure assumes the existence of a *non-local* variable **CURRENT-CHAR** which has been suitably initialized, either to the first character of the input or (harmlessly) to a blank. The procedure would not work properly if **CURRENTCHAR** were a local variable. For example, if the input starts:

I, CLAUDIUS

then on the first invocation of **READTOKEN**, after the word 'I' has been read and stored, the value of **CURRENTCHAR** is ','. On the next invocation of **READTOKEN**, however, the value of **CURRENTCHAR** would be *undefined* (since local variables are always initially undefined on entry to a subprogram), so the comma would have been lost. Therefore, **CURRENTCHAR** must be a non-local variable to ensure that it preserves its value between successive invocations of **READTOKEN**. {This paragraph has no connection with variant records, but it is important nevertheless!}

16.7 Packed records

{This section may be omitted on a first reading.}

A record type may be prefixed with the reserved word **PACKED**. This asks the compiler to economize on storage space for records of that type, even if access to the fields is thereby made more difficult for the computer (recall Section 12.1).

Example 16.12

Variables of the type **DATES**, defined in Example 16.1, normally would occupy three store locations, thus:

12	8	1980

Observe, however, that the day and the month each need only two (decimal) digits, and that the year needs only four digits. Thus it may be desirable to amend the definition of DATES as follows:

DATES = PACKED RECORD
                    DAY : 1 . . 31;
                    MONTH : 1 . . 12;
                    YEAR : 0 . . 9999
           END

If our computer is able to accommodate eight-digit integers, all three components of the date can be combined into one eight-digit integer which needs just one store location:

12081980

Even if our computer can accommodate only six-digit integers (say), space can be saved by combining the day and the month:

1208	1980

In any event, the degree of packing used (if any) is determined by the compiler and not by the programmer.

16.8 Type rules for records

Assignment compatibility

A record may be assigned only to a record variable of the same type.

Example 16.13

Consider the variable declarations:

COMPLEXNUMBER : RECORD
                    REALPART, IMAGPART : REAL
           END;
ROOT1, ROOT2 : RECORD
             REALPART, IMAGPART : REAL
       END

ROOT1 and ROOT2 are considered to be of the same type, because they are declared together. COMPLEXNUMBER is considered to be of a different type, because it is declared separately. Thus the assignment statements:

ROOT1 := ROOT2
ROOT2 := ROOT1

are both valid; but the statements:

COMPLEXNUMBER := ROOT1
ROOT1 := COMPLEXNUMBER
ROOT2 := COMPLEXNUMBER
COMPLEXNUMBER := ROOT2

are all invalid.

Exercises 16

16.1 (a) Write a definition of a record variable suitable for storing payroll details of an employee, namely the employee's name, number, grade (manual, skilled, clerical or managerial) and rate of pay. (b) Write a procedure which outputs these details in a suitable format.

16.2. (a) Rewrite procedure **WRITEDATE** of Example 14.1 to accept a single parameter of type **DATES** (see Example 16.1), rather than three separate parameters. (b) Rewrite program **DATES** of Example 14.1 correspondingly.

16.3. (a) Write a definition of a record type suitable for describing the position (latitude and longitude, in degrees) of a place on the Earth's surface. (b) Write a function which returns the solar time difference between two given places on the Earth's surface (1 hour for each 15 degrees difference in longitude). (c) Write a procedure which reads the position of a place, presented as two signed real numbers. (d) Write a procedure which outputs the position of a given place in degrees and minutes, using conventional notation (e.g. the latitudes +45.5 and −45.5 should be written as 45:30N and 45:30S respectively). (e) Write a program fragment which reads the positions of two places, and which outputs these positions together with the solar time difference between them.

16.4. Modify program **SORTNAMES** of Section 15.2 to read, sort by name and output the personal telephone directory of Example 16.9.

{Attempt the following exercise only after reading Section 16.6.}

16.5. (a) Write a definition of a record type suitable for describing a plane figure, namely its shape plus the following: (i) for a circle, its radius, (ii) for a rectangle, the two lengths of its sides, or (iii) for a triangle, the lengths of all its sides. (b) Write a function which returns the area of a given plane figure.

Programming exercise 16

16.6. Write a procedure which outputs a single line containing the personal details from a record parameter of type **PERSONALDETAILS**

(Example 16.2). Write a procedure which reads personal details from a single line of input data in the same format and stores them in a parameter of type **PERSONALDETAILS**. Assume that a person's sex is represented externally by a single character 'M' or 'F', and marital status by a single character 'S', 'M', 'D' or 'W'. Write a program to test these procedures and procedure **MARRY** (Example 16.4).

16.7. Write a program which reads the x- and y-coordinates of the vertices of a polygon (given in clockwise order) and outputs the number of sides and the perimeter of the figure. (Hint: use a record to represent the position of a vertex.)

16.8. An entry in a city telephone directory consists of a name, an address and a telephone number. A name is a string of at most 20 characters and an address is a string of at most 30 characters. A telephone number consists of a three-digit exchange code and a four-digit line number. Write a program which reads directory entries (supplied in any format you choose) and outputs them in two columns on each page. You may assume that the entries are supplied in alphabetical order. On output, the entries must be arranged in order *down* the columns and under suitable column headings. On the last page the two columns should be as equal as possible.

17
Files

17.1 Files and file structures

All the programs that have appeared so far have had one thing in common: they have used at most one stream of input data, INPUT, and one stream of results, OUTPUT. This is quite unrepresentative of many computer applications which require programs to read and write several sets of data at once.

Much of the data handled by computer systems is never seen by humans. Instead, results generated by one program are often intended to be read subsequently by another program, or even by the program that produced them. When this is the case, computer time and storage space can be saved by keeping data on machine-readable media (such as magnetic tapes and disks) in their *internal* representations, thus avoiding the effort of converting data between internal and external forms on reading and writing.

It is helpful to take a somewhat abstract view of the sets of data read and written by programs. We call such sets of data *files*, regardless of whether they are stored on magnetic tape or disk, keyed in at a terminal, punched on a deck of cards, printed on paper, or whatever; and regardless of whether the data is in internal or external form. From this point of view, a deck of cards prepared at a key-punch is an example of a file capable only of being read, and a set of printed results is an example of a file capable only of being written. Other kinds of file are capable of being both written and read.

The following are some typical applications of files.

Example 17.1

A bank might maintain a file containing details of each account, including the account number, the customer's name and address and the current balance.

This file would be processed at the end of each day to update the balances as a result of the day's debit and credit transactions, and to

produce bank statements for the customers. The program which does this would therefore read two files:
(a) details of the transactions, possibly punched on cards; and
(b) a file containing details of all accounts as they stood at the start of the day.
The program would write two files:
(c) printed bank statements for those customers whose monthly statements were due; and
(d) an updated copy of (b) with amended balances.
The file (d) would then be kept for reading by the same program on the following day.

Other programs might make use of the same accounts file, for example to open new accounts, to close old accounts, and to note changes of address.

Example 17.2

A reference library might run a computer system to help borrowers find books containing information of interest to them. The user of such a system would type, on the keyboard of a computer terminal, queries such as 'List all books about computer programming'. This is an example of *information retrieval*.

The information retrieval program would read two files:

(a) a file containing relevant details of all books in stock; and
(b) the queries typed at the keyboard.
It would write one file:
(c) the information requested by the user, perhaps displayed on a screen, or typed on paper so that it can be taken away.

Again, it would be necessary for other programs to manipulate the same file of book details, for example to add details of newly acquired books.

These examples illustrate the fact that data may have an existence in its own right, independently of any program. Data is not always generated for the benefit of specific programs—programs are often written to manipulate data which already exists!

Many different file structures are possible, of which the simplest is the *serial file*. A serial file consists simply of a sequence of *components*, all of the same type. The accounts file of Example 17.1 might be a serial file whose components are records. INPUT and OUTPUT are serial files whose components are single characters and end-of-line markers. Serial files have the property that their components must be read (or written) in strict sequence, starting from the first. So, for example, it is not possible to read the 100th component until the preceding 99 have been read.

Such a file structure would not be appropriate for the information retrieval system of Example 17.2. It would be very inefficient to have to scan through the whole file to find details about a few books. A different file structure, one which permits *direct* access to a specified component, is required in this and similar applications. We shall not consider such file structures here.

We shall picture a serial file, which currently is being read, as follows:

The reading position, shown by the arrow, indicates how far the program has progressed in reading the file; here four components have been read. If all components of the file have been read, we describe the situation as *end-of-file*:

Any attempt to read a component at end-of-file will cause the program to fail.

We shall picture a serial file, which currently is being written, as follows:

Writing a component to this file makes it longer:

While a serial file is being written, the writing position is always at end-of-file. Consequently writing to a serial file always *appends* a component to it.

A serial file is similar to an array in that all its components have the same type. There the similarity ends. It is important to understand the distinctions between arrays and serial files. First, the size of an array is fixed, whereas the size of a serial file varies as it is written, starting at zero components and expanding (virtually) without limit. Second, the components of an array may be accessed at random, whereas only one component of a serial file is accessible at any time (the component at the reading or writing position).

17.2 Files in Pascal

Pascal concerns itself only with serial files, so henceforth we shall use the terms 'file' and 'serial file' synonymously.

As it appears to a Pascal program, a file is an ordinary variable: it has an identifier and it is declared in a variable declaration. Its type specifies that it is a file, and also specifies the type of its components.

Example 17.3

Recall the bank accounts file of Example 17.1. Given a type declaration such as:

```
ACCOUNTS =
  RECORD
    NAME     : PACKED ARRAY [1 .. NAMELENGTH]
                           OF CHAR;
    ADDRESS : PACKED ARRAY [1 .. ADDRESSLENGTH]
                           OF CHAR;
    BALANCE : INTEGER
  END
```

We could declare a bank accounts file as follows:

```
ACCOUNTSFILE: FILE OF ACCOUNTS
```

The syntax of file types is summarized in Figure 17.1. **FILE** and **OF** are both reserved words. The only restriction on the choice of component type

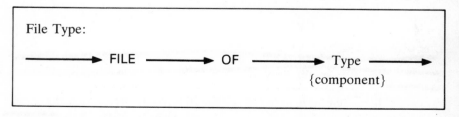

Figure 17.1. Syntax of File Types

is that it may not itself be a file type, nor may it contain any file type. (Note that the component type need not be a record type.)

A file is generated by writing components to it, one at a time. This is achieved using the following standard procedures:

REWRITE(F)   makes the file F ready for writing, by emptying it of all components and establishing the initial writing position.

WRITE(F,*x*)   appends to the file F a component whose value is that of the expression *x*, and moves the writing position to the new end-of-file. The expression *x* must be assignment compatible with the component type of F.

The effect of WRITE(F,*x*) is illustrated below:

It is not possible to write to any file until it has been prepared for writing by REWRITE. The only exception to this rule is the file OUTPUT: the statement REWRITE(OUTPUT) is performed automatically at the start of any program which has OUTPUT among its program parameters.

Once a file has been generated it may be read by the program which wrote it, or by some other program. This is achieved using the following standard procedures:

RESET(F)   makes the file F ready for reading, by moving the reading position to the start of the file.

READ(F,V)   copies the next component of the file F into the variable V, then advances the reading position past this component. The components of F must be assignment compatible with the type of V.

After obeying RESET(F), F looks like this:

The effect of READ(F,V) is illustrated below:

It is not possible to read from any file until it has been prepared for reading by RESET. The only exception to this rule is the file INPUT: the statement RESET(INPUT) is performed automatically at the start of any program which has INPUT among its program parameters.

READ(F,V) will fail if F is already at end-of-file. In order to prevent this we must be able to test the end-of-file condition, and for this purpose the BOOLEAN standard function EOF(F) is provided. In the last diagram, EOF(F) is FALSE, but it will become TRUE after a further two components have been read.

File variables can be used as actual parameters to these, and other, standard procedures. We can also pass files as variable parameters to subprograms we have written ourselves. Pascal does not, however, allow whole file variables to be used in any other way. In particular, assignment of files is forbidden and files cannot be used as value parameters.

Example 17.4

A company might keep a payroll file containing the following details for each of its employees: name, employee number, grade (manual, skilled, clerical, or managerial), pay rate, tax allowance, and number of weeks (or months) of service. This file would be used for printing out payslips, for supplying data to the tax authorities, for calculating pension entitlement, and so on.

The following program calculates the week's pay of all weekly-paid employees (that is, all except managers). Tax is to be deducted automatically according to the formula *(pay rate − tax allowance) * 33%*. The program outputs a table showing the name, number, gross pay, tax deduction and nett pay of each employee. It also generates an updated file taking account of the past week's service.

```
PROGRAM  WEEKLYPAY(OLDPAYROLL,NEWPAYROLL,OUTPUT);
CONST
   TAXRATE = 0.33;
```

```
TYPE
  GRADES = (MANUAL,SKILLED,CLERICAL,MANAGERIAL   );
  MONEY = INTEGER;
  EMPLOYEERECORDS =
    RECORD
      NAME : PACKED ARRAY [1 . . 16] OF CHAR;
      NUMBER : 0 . . 9999;
      GRADE : GRADES;
      PAYRATE : MONEY;
      TAXALLOWANCE : MONEY;
      SERVICE : 0 . . MAXINT
    END;
VAR
  OLDPAYROLL, NEWPAYROLL: FILE OF EMPLOYEERECORDS;
  ONEEMPLOYEE : EMPLOYEERECORDS;

PROCEDURE PROCESS ( VAR EMPLOYEE: EMPLOYEERECORDS );
  VAR
    NETTPAY, TAXDEDUCTION: MONEY;
  BEGIN
  WITH EMPLOYEE DO
    IF GRADE <> MANAGERIAL THEN
      BEGIN
      TAXDEDUCTION := ROUND (TAXRATE *
                            (PAYRATE—TAXALLOWANCE));
      NETTPAY := PAYRATE — TAXDEDUCTION;
      WRITELN (NAME, NUMBER:8, PAYRATE/100:12:2,
              TAXDEDUCTION/100:12:2, NETTPAY/100:12:2);
      SERVICE := SERVICE + 1
      END
  END (* PROCESS *);

BEGIN (* WEEKLYPAY *)
RESET (OLDPAYROLL);
REWRITE (NEWPAYROLL);
WRITELN ('NAME': 16, 'NUMBER': 8, 'GROSS PAY': 12,
        'TAX': 12, 'NETT PAY': 12);
WRITELN;
WHILE NOT EOF(OLDPAYROLL) DO
  BEGIN
  READ (OLDPAYROLL, ONEEMPLOYEE);
  PROCESS (ONEEMPLOYEE);
  WRITE (NEWPAYROLL, ONEEMPLOYEE)
  END
END (* WEEKLYPAY *).
```

This example illustrates the purpose of the program parameters: they are the identifiers of files used by the program. However, only files which are assumed to exist before the program is run (such as **OLDPAYROLL**), or which are to be kept after the program is run (such as **NEWPAYROLL**), should be listed as program parameters. Some programs use files for *temporary* storage of large quantities of data, taking advantage of the (virtually) unlimited size of files: such files should not be listed as program parameters. This applies particularly to files declared inside subprograms.

Program parameters may stand for different files in different runs of the program. Consider program **WEEKLYPAY**, for example: the actual file represented by **NEWPAYROLL** in one week's run would be the same file as that represented by **OLDPAYROLL** in the following week's run.

All file variables, whether program parameters or not, must be declared in the usual way. Again, **INPUT** and **OUTPUT** are exceptions to this rule: they must *not* be declared even if they are used.

The syntax of program parameters is summarized in Appendix 1.1.

17.3 Text files

Text files, that is, files whose components are characters and end-of-line markers, are of special interest because they are the normal means of communication between humans and computers. Pascal provides a standard file type, **TEXT**, which is used to declare text files. The standard file variables **INPUT** and **OUTPUT** are of type **TEXT**.

Everything said in Section 17.2 applies to text files in particular, as well as to files of other types. Recall, however, that **INPUT** and **OUTPUT** must not be initialized by **RESET** or **REWRITE** and must not be declared.

The standard procedures we have used with **INPUT** and **OUTPUT** may be used with any text file by giving the name of the file as the (optional) first parameter. Furthermore:

(a) **READ, READLN, EOF** and **EOLN** may be invoked without a text file parameter, in which case they operate on **INPUT**. Similarly, **WRITE, WRITELN** and **PAGE** may be invoked without a text file parameter, in which case they operate on **OUTPUT**.

(b) **READ, READLN, WRITE** and **WRITELN** may be invoked with parameters of various types, in addition to the optional text file parameter. This is because, for many purposes, reading and writing one character at a time is too primitive. For example, we want to be able to read and write numbers, with automatic tranformations between their internal and external forms. Here is a list of all the allowable parameter types:

READ, READLN	WRITE, WRITELN
CHAR	CHAR
INTEGER	INTEGER
REAL	REAL
	BOOLEAN
	string

(c) READ, READLN, WRITE and WRITELN may be invoked with *several* parameters of these types.
(d) READLN and WRITELN may be invoked with just a text file parameter, if only the effect on the end-of-line marker is required.

Example 17.5

The following program makes an exact copy of a text file, without using the standard files INPUT and OUTPUT. Compare it with Example 8.5.

```
PROGRAM COPY (ORIGINAL, DUPLICATE);
VAR
  ORIGINAL, DUPLICATE : TEXT;
  CHARACTER : CHAR;
BEGIN
RESET (ORIGINAL);
REWRITE (DUPLICATE);
WHILE NOT EOF(ORIGINAL) DO
  BEGIN
  WHILE NOT EOLN(ORIGINAL) DO
    BEGIN
    READ (ORIGINAL, CHARACTER);
    WRITE (DUPLICATE, CHARACTER)
    END;
  WRITELN (DUPLICATE);
  READLN (ORIGINAL)
  END
END (* COPY *).
```

17.4 File buffers

{This section may be omitted on a first reading.}

We have seen, in Section 17.2, that the statement READ(F,V) has *two* effects: it copies the next component of F into the variable V, then it advances the reading position of F. In certain applications it is convenient to be able to separate the second step from the first. For such purposes, the concept of the *file buffer* is useful.

Consider a file **F** which is being read; the file buffer of **F**, which is designated **F** ↑ , is a copy of the component of **F** at the current reading position:

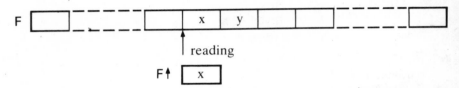

The file buffer can be used like any variable. In particular its value may be inspected directly without having to copy it into another variable.

The reading position may be advanced, *automatically* updating the file buffer, by means of the standard procedure GET(F), whose effect on **F** (above) is as follows:

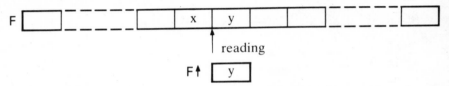

It may now be seen that the statement **READ(F,V)** is equivalent to:

   BEGIN V := F ↑; GET(F) END

RESET(F) copies the *first* component of F into F ↑ :

Example 17.6

Recall the payroll file described in Example 17.4. It is required to update the payroll file to include details of new employees. To this end a second file has been generated, consisting of records of the same type as those of the payroll file, and containing details of the new employees. All employees are assumed to have distinct employee numbers, and in both files the records are assumed to be arranged in ascending order by employee number. Write a program to generate an updated payroll file, also ordered by employee number.

For example, if the employee numbers in the two input files are as follows:

Old payroll: 3, 7, 8, 9, 11, 12, 15, 19
New employees: 1, 2, 5, 6, 10, 14

then the new payroll file should contain records for the following employees, in order:

New payroll: 1, 2, 3, 5, 6, 7, 8, 9, 10, 11, 12, 14, 15, 19

This is an example of *merging*, an important operation in commercial data processing.

At each step of the merge, we wish to compare the next record of the updates file, UPDATES, with the next record of the old payroll file, OLDPAYROLL. The record which contains the smaller employee number is to be appended to the new employee file, and only the file from which that record was fetched is to have its reading position advanced. The records to be compared are available in the file buffers UPDATES ↑ and OLDPAYROLL ↑, which can be inspected without advancing the reading position of either UPDATES or OLDPAYROLL. If we find that UPDATES ↑ contains the smaller employee number, for example, we append UPDATES ↑ to the new payroll file and then obey GET(UPDATES), leaving OLDPAYROLL ↑ undisturbed for comparison with the following record of UPDATES.

```
PROGRAM MERGE ( UPDATES, OLDPAYROLL, NEWPAYROLL );

TYPE
   GRADES = (MANUAL,SKILLED,CLERICAL,MANAGERIAL);
   MONEY = INTEGER;
   EMPLOYEES =
      RECORD
         NAME : PACKED ARRAY [1 .. 16] OF CHAR;
         NUMBER : 0 .. 9999;
         GRADE : GRADES;
         PAYRATE : MONEY;
         TAXALLOWANCE : MONEY;
         SERVICE : 0 .. MAXINT

      END;
VAR
   UPDATES, OLDPAYROLL, NEWPAYROLL: FILE OF EMPLOYEES;

BEGIN
RESET (UPDATES);
RESET (OLDPAYROLL);
```

```
REWRITE (NEWPAYROLL);
(* merge until one file is exhausted *)
WHILE NOT (EOF(UPDATES) OR EOF(OLDPAYROLL)) DO
  IF UPDATES ↑ . NUMBER < OLDPAYROLL ↑ . NUMBER THEN
    BEGIN
    WRITE (NEWPAYROLL, UPDATES ↑ );
    GET (UPDATES)
    END
  ELSE
    BEGIN
    WRITE (NEWPAYROLL, OLDPAYROLL ↑ );
    GET (OLDPAYROLL)
    END;
(* copy any records left in either file *)
WHILE NOT EOF(OLDPAYROLL) DO
  BEGIN
  WRITE (NEWPAYROLL, OLDPAYROLL ↑ );
  GET (OLDPAYROLL)
  END;
WHILE NOT EOF(UPDATES) DO
  BEGIN
  WRITE (NEWPAYROLL, UPDATES ↑ );
  GET (UPDATES)
  END
END (* MERGE *).
```

This program serves to illustrate the use of file buffers and **GET**. It must be admitted, however, that it would *not* be acceptable in the real world of commercial data processing, since it depends on all the assumptions about the two input files. In practice, files are generated by programs which may be incorrect, they are recorded on media which are not completely reliable, and they are read and written by peripheral devices which sometimes fail. A realistic file-processing program must, therefore, check that the assumptions about its input files do indeed hold, taking appropriate action if they do not (see Exercises 17).

A file which is being written also has associated with it a file buffer, in which the value of each new component is stored until the writing position is advanced:

The file buffer may be used like any variable, so we may store a value in it, then examine or update it later if we wish.

The writing position is advanced by means of the standard procedure PUT(F). This appends the contents of the file buffer to the file itself, and leaves the file buffer *undefined*:

It may now be seen that the statement WRITE(F,*x*) is equivalent to:

BEGIN F ↑ := *x*; PUT(F) END

17.5 Interactive programs

{Section 17.4 must be read before this section.}

Most computer systems allow a user to 'converse' with a running program. Using a terminal it is possible to type data directly into the computer and receive results immediately, either on a display screen or printed on paper for future reference. This is *interactive computing*. It has been made economically possible by the development of *multi-access operating systems* which share a large computer among many users working concurrently and by small, cheap computers for individual use—*personal computers*.

A Pascal program written for non-interactive systems should work without change on an interactive system. The user would start the program, type in all the data, and finally out would come the results to the terminal. Apart from getting output sooner, no advantage is gained from using an interactive system in this way. What is really wanted is for the user and the program to converse, the program perhaps asking questions and the user replying with the necessary data. In this way the program can guide the user through a complex job. Applications of this kind include airline reservation systems, computer-assisted instruction and computer games.

Let us take a very simple example—a program to read integer numbers, one per line of input, and output their squares. A typical conversation with this program might look as follows, where the material in italics is typed by the program and the rest by the user:

NUMBER? **19**
  THE SQUARE OF 19 IS 361

NUMBER? **7**
THE SQUARE OF 7 IS 49
NUMBER? ********

To end the conversation, the user types something to indicate the end of the input. This will depend on the operating system being used; we have given ******** above as an example.

A program to this specification follows:

```
PROGRAM SQUARES (KEYBOARD, DISPLAY);
CONST
  PROMPT = 'NUMBER? ';
VAR
  KEYBOARD, DISPLAY : TEXT;
  NUMBER : INTEGER;
BEGIN
REWRITE (DISPLAY);
WRITE (DISPLAY, PROMPT);
RESET (KEYBOARD);
WHILE NOT EOF(KEYBOARD) DO
  BEGIN
  READ (KEYBOARD, NUMBER);
  WRITELN (DISPLAY, '   THE SQUARE OF ', NUMBER:1,
                    ' IS ', SQR(NUMBER):1);
  WRITE (DISPLAY, PROMPT);
  READLN (KEYBOARD)
  END
END (* SQUARES *).
```

When this program is run with the data shown above, the following sequence of events takes place:

(1) The program prepares the file variable **DISPLAY** for writing and outputs the *prompt*, a message inviting the user to type the first number. It then prepares the file variable **KEYBOARD** for reading. Recall that **RESET(KEYBOARD)** places the first character of the text file **KEYBOARD** in **KEYBOARD** ↑ , the buffer variable. Accordingly, the system sets up an input operation to read data from **KEYBOARD**, *even though the Pascal program has not yet obeyed any READ statement*. The program waits for the user to finish typing.

(2) The user sees the prompt and responds by typing '19' and some end-of-line indication, the details of which depend on the operating system.

(3) The program resumes execution. **KEYBOARD** ↑ is equal to '1' and **EOF(KEYBOARD)** is **FALSE**. The loop is entered, the **READ** statement scans the data line, converts the integer number to internal form, and

assigns it to **NUMBER**. The **WRITELN** statement then outputs the result (which appears on a fresh line because of the end-of-line marker just typed by the user) and takes a new line. The **WRITE** statement outputs the next prompt. Finally, to ensure that **EOF(KEYBOARD)** will have a useful value, the loop performs a **READLN** statement. This skips past the end-of-line marker which the user typed after the '19' and places the first character of the next line in **KEYBOARD ↑** . Again the system sets up an input operation and the program waits for the user.

(4) The user now types '7' and an end-of-line marker.
(5) The program continues as in step (3), until it once more waits at the **READLN** statement.
(6) This time the user types an end-of-file indication.
(7) The program resumes. **EOF(KEYBOARD)** is now **TRUE** and **KEYBOARD ↑** is undefined. The loop terminates, and so does the program.

Observe that we have to be very careful about the relative positions of the input and output statements in this program. If the **RESET (KEYBOARD)** statement had been any earlier, the program would have waited for input *before* giving the user the first prompt. Similarly, if the **READLN(KEYBOARD)** statement had been placed before any of the other statements in the body of the loop, reading the next datum and writing the results or the prompt would have gone out of sequence.

As an exercise, work out exactly what would happen, from the user's point of view: (a) if the **READLN** were placed before the second **WRITE**; (b) if the **READLN** were placed before the **WRITELN**; and (c) if the **RESET** were placed before the first **WRITE**.

So far so good. Now, however, a problem arises. Some operating systems require that data typed by an interactive user must be read from the standard file **INPUT** and that results for the terminal must be written to the standard file **OUTPUT**. Let us amend the program in accordance with these requirements. We get the following:

```
PROGRAM SQUARES (* second version *) (INPUT, OUTPUT);
CONST
  PROMPT = 'NUMBER? ';
VAR
  NUMBER: INTEGER;
BEGIN
(* implicit REWRITE(OUTPUT) and RESET(INPUT) here *)
WRITE (OUTPUT, PROMPT);
WHILE NOT EOF(INPUT) DO
  BEGIN
  READ (INPUT, NUMBER);
```

```
    WRITELN (OUTPUT, ' THE SQUARE OF ', NUMBER:1,
                     ' IS ', SQR(NUMBER):1);
    WRITE (OUTPUT, PROMPT);
    READLN (INPUT)
    END
END (* SQUARES *).
```

Trace through this version of the program with the data used above. The problem should quickly become apparent: although the loop would work well enough, the initialization goes wrong. Before the program can output the first prompt, an *automatic* RESET(INPUT) is performed, and the program waits for the user to type a line of data. Unfortunately, the user will also be waiting—for a prompt which will never appear! Thus the prompts and responses are forced out of sequence from the start.

In reaching this conclusion we have assumed that the statement RE-SET(INPUT) causes an input transfer to be set up immediately. In practice this is not necessary. No transfer need be performed until: (a) INPUT ↑ is inspected (either explicitly, or implicitly by means of READ or READLN); or (b) EOLN(INPUT) is tested; or (c) EOF(INPUT) is tested. By delaying the transfer to one of these points, the difficulty with RESET disappears and an interactive program can use INPUT as its interactive input file. The input transfer set up by READLN can be delayed similarly. This removes the constraints on the order of the statements inside the loop. The result of these implementation features (which are in complete conformity with Standard Pascal) is that writing interactive programs need differ from writing non-interactive programs only in the use of prompts.

Exercises 17

17.1. Write a procedure which counts the components in a given file, a parameter of type FILE OF ITEMS. (The definition of type ITEMS is irrelevant here.)

17.2. (a) Write a procedure which copies a given file, of type FILE OF ITEMS, to a second file of the same type. Assume that the second file has already been prepared for writing. (b) Using this procedure, write a program which copies to a file of type FILE OF ITEMS the concatenation of two other files of the same type.

17.3. Write a procedure, with a parameter of type FILE OF INTEGER, which searches this file for a component equal to a given target value, setting a BOOLEAN parameter accordingly.

{The following exercises should not be attempted until Section 17.4 has been read.}

17.4. Modify program MERGE (Example 17.6) so that it writes an error message every time it finds an employee record out of sequence in either input file.

17.5*. Modify the procedure **READTOKEN** of Example 16.11 so that it uses **INPUT** ↑ instead of the non-local variable **CURRENTCHAR** to look ahead in the data.

17.6*. The Drinkers' Club maintains a file containing the names and other details of all its members, ordered by name. The Temperance Society maintains a similar file containing details of *its* members. Write a program which reads both files and outputs details of everyone who is a member of both groups.

Programming exercises 17

{To run the following programs, you will have to find out how to create and access files on the computer you use.}

17.7. Write a program with three text file parameters: **INPUT**, **OLDTEXT** and **NEWTEXT**. **NEWTEXT** is to be made a copy of **OLDTEXT**, except for certain one-to-one character transliterations. Each line of **INPUT** contains exactly two characters, xy, specifying that all occurrences of x in **OLDTEXT** are to be converted to y in **NEWTEXT**.

17.8. The personal telephone directory of Example 16.9 may be stored as a file of entries, say **DIRECTORYFILE**, rather than as an array of entries. (a) Write a program which reads names, dialling codes and numbers from **INPUT** and writes them as records to **DIRECTORYFILE**. (b) Write a program which reads names from **INPUT** and searches **DIRECTORYFILE** to determine the corresponding telephone numbers (where known).

17.9*. (a) A bank accounts file (as in Example 17.3) is to be created from scratch. The first **NAMELENGTH** characters of each line of **INPUT** contain a customer's name (left-justified), the next **ADDRESSLENGTH** characters contain the customer's address, and the remainder of the line contains the customer's account number. Every customer starts with a balance of zero. Write a program which reads this data and generates the bank accounts file. (b) Write a program to update a bank accounts file and produce printed bank statements, as described in Example 17.1. Details of each transaction are supplied as a single line of **INPUT** containing the customer's account number followed by the amount of the transaction (positive for a credit transaction, negative for a debit transaction). Each bank statement must contain the customer's name, address and account number, original balance, list of transactions, and updated balance. A bank statement is to be printed for every customer, even where there are no transactions. Both the accounts file and the set of transactions are supposed to be ordered on the customer's account number; your program must print an error message every time an account number is found to be out of sequence, and take some appropriate recovery action.

17.10. If you have read Section 17.5, modify the program of Exercise 8.7 to work as an interactive calculator facility.

18
Methodical programming with data structures

18.1 Programming by stepwise refinement: a review

In Chapter 7 we stressed the advantages of programming methodically. By systematically developing a program from its specification we aim to arrive at a program which is easy to understand and relatively free from errors. In Chapter 15 we showed how subprograms can be exploited during methodical program development. The example programs in the intervening chapters have been developed by the methods introduced in Chapters 7 and 15. However, these examples were intended primarily to illustrate the features of the programming language Pascal, rather than to illustrate the process of program development itself. By now you will be acquainted with the principal features of Pascal, but your experience of program development is probably limited to rather small programs. Now that we have all the necessary programming tools at our disposal, it is time to see how programming problems of a more realistic size can be tackled methodically.

Let us recap on the technique of *programming by stepwise refinement*. We start by devising and writing down an outline solution, a 'program' which contains commands expressed in English, in addition to Pascal statements and control structures. We call this the Level 1 outline. Having completed Level 1, we *refine* some of these commands, by breaking them down into program fragments which may themselves be expressed partly in Pascal and partly in English. (We must of course ensure that the old commands are broken down into commands which are in some sense simpler, so that we have taken a step nearer to a complete solution.) By substituting these refinements into Level 1, we obtain a more detailed 'program', which we call Level 2. We continue in this way, filling detail in our outline solution, until we finally arrive at a program expressed entirely in Pascal.

The point of writing commands in English is that for the time being we concern ourselves only with *what* these commands will do, and only at a later stage decide *how* they will perform their tasks. Thus the fundamental advantage of programming by stepwise refinement is that it enables a programming problem to be solved in small, manageable steps. The task of testing the solution is also broken down into manageable sub-tasks. We can hand-test the refinements individually, and if we are satisfied that they are individually correct, we can be reasonably sure that the complete solution is also correct (provided of course that the refinements have been combined correctly).

If you have tended to ignore this advice while doing the programming exercise, preferring a haphazard approach to a systematic one, you will probably have learned your lesson the hard way! It is likely that your programs contained a lot of errors, which were detected only by exhaustive testing on a computer (or, still worse, remain undetected) and that correcting these errors was a tedious affair. Even if you have been able to solve small programming problems intuitively, you will find that intuition alone is not adequate for solving larger problems; a systematic approach becomes absolutely essential.

In this chapter we present two case studies, each describing the solution of a problem which is complex enough to illustrate the practical difficulties of program development. We shall see that these relate as often to the judicious choice of data structures as to the organization of control. The lessons to be learned from these case studies are summarized and generalized in the last section of the chapter.

To derive the maximum benefit from each case study, we recommend that you first read and thoroughly understand the problem specification; then attempt to solve the problem yourself; and only finally, read the solution. These are not unrealistic 'model' solutions; they are fully worked through, and they illustrate the errors and indecisions that are more or less inevitable in program development.

18.2 Case study III: text formatting

Problem specification

Write a program which will read natural language from a text file, RAWTEXT, and write it to the standard text file OUTPUT in paragraphs, with each line justified on both the left and the right margins. The text is supplied in free format, with successive words being separated by one or more blanks and/or end-of-lines. Each punctuation mark, such as a period or a comma, may be assumed to follow the preceding word *immediately*, that is without intervening blanks. A new paragraph is indicated by the special 'word' /PAR/, but the text does not necessarily start with a new paragraph.

The number of characters to be written on each line of output is to be read from the standard text file INPUT.

On output, as many words as possible are to be written on each line, with successive words on the same line separated by one or more blanks. Each punctuation mark must follow the preceding word immediately and must be on the same line. Each line is to be right-adjusted, if necessary, by writing extra blanks between words, the extra blanks being distributed as evenly as possible. No word may be split between two lines. The first line of each paragraph must be indented six spaces on the left, and must be preceded by a blank line. The last line of each paragraph, and the last line of the whole text, are *not* to be right-adjusted.

Assume that no word is longer than twenty characters. The program should ensure that the specified line width is sufficient to accommodate the longest possible word.

For example, if the input text is:

```
THE PRINCIPLES OF NEWSPEAK
/PAR/
NEWSPEAK WAS THE OFFICIAL LANGUAGE OF OCEANIA
AND HAD BEEN DESIGNED TO MEET THE IDEOLOGICAL
NEEDS
OF INGSOC.
/PAR/
IN THE YEAR 1984
THERE WAS NOT AS YET ANYONE
WHO USED NEWSPEAK AS HIS SOLE MEANS
OF COMMUNICATION,
EITHER IN SPEECH OR IN WRITING.
IT WAS EXPECTED THAT NEWSPEAK WOULD HAVE FINALLY
SUPERSEDED OLDSPEAK
(OR STANDARD ENGLISH, AS WE SHOULD CALL IT)
BY ABOUT THE YEAR 2050.
```

then the written text on lines of 30 spaces should look like this:

```
THE PRINCIPLES OF NEWSPEAK

      NEWSPEAK      WAS      THE
OFFICIAL  LANGUAGE  OF  OCEANIA
AND HAD BEEN DESIGNED TO MEET
THE     IDEOLOGICAL    NEEDS    OF
INGSOC.
      IN    THE    YEAR    1984    THERE
WAS NOT AS YET ANYONE WHO USED
NEWSPEAK  AS  HIS  SOLE  MEANS  OF
COMMUNICATION,      EITHER      IN
SPEECH   OR   IN   WRITING.   IT   WAS
```

EXPECTED THAT NEWSPEAK WOULD
HAVE FINALLY SUPERSEDED
OLDSPEAK (OR STANDARD ENGLISH,
AS WE SHOULD CALL IT) BY ABOUT
THE YEAR 2050.

Solution

This is one of those problems in which close inspection of the specification reveals possibilities for simplification. A little thought should convince you that there is nothing special about the treatment of punctuation. If we combine each punctuation mark with the preceding word as a single string, then our program will meet the output specification without taking any special account of punctuation. Therefore, we shall treat any sequence of non-blank characters in the input text as a single 'word'.

The nature of the problem suggests that the heart of Level 1 will be some sort of loop. As always, the first question we must answer is 'What should be done during each repetition of the loop?' A number of answers are possible:

(a) deal with a single character;
(b) deal with a single word;
(c) generate a complete line of output;
(d) deal with a complete paragraph.

Surely option (a) can be rejected immediately, since the action to be taken on each character read will vary wildly according to circumstances, such as whether the character is blank or non-blank.

Option (b) is quite attractive. The input text can be viewed as a sequence of words (treating /PAR/ as a word), so it is natural to use a loop which processes one word per repetition.

Option (c) is less attractive. Although the output text may be viewed as a sequence of lines, this sub-division is not at all apparent in the input text.

Option (d) is also quite attractive, for both the input and the output texts may equally naturally be viewed as sequences of paragraphs. As each paragraph in turn contains a number of words, a nested loop will be necessary to deal with individual words.

A good guiding principle in such circumstances is to opt for the solution which most accurately reflects the structure of both the input and the output data. Here it is not immediately clear whether option (b) or option (d) is better.

An experienced programmer might be able to choose between the alternatives by thinking ahead, mentally making one or two further refinements in each case, and judging which alternative will lead to the better solution. {This is much the same mental process as that adopted by a chess player, who must choose between alternative moves by thinking ahead a few moves and judging which alternative will lead to the better position.} Until we learn such foresight, we are forced to try both alternatives in turn and compare the results. {This, at least, is a strategy denied to chess players!}

In both versions it seems better to view the raw text as a sequence of 'tokens', rather than as a sequence of words, a token being either a word, or a paragraph mark, or an end-of-data mark. Both versions may need to initialize the processing of these tokens. Version (b) will need to initialize the processing of lines, at the least to read and validate the requested line width. Version (d) may additionally need to initialize the processing of paragraphs. These thoughts lead to the following Level 1 outlines.

Level 1b outline

```
PROGRAM TEXTFORMATTER (* version b *)
                      ( INPUT, RAWTEXT, OUTPUT );
global declarations;
BEGIN
prepare the processing of lines;
prepare the processing of tokens;
read a token;
WHILE there is data to process DO
  BEGIN
  IF the token is a word THEN
     append the word followed by a blank to the current line,
        right-adjust the line and start a new line if necessary
  ELSE (* the token is a paragraph mark *)
     start a new paragraph;
  read a token
  END
END.
```

Level 1d outline

```
PROGRAM TEXTFORMATTER (* version d *)
                      ( INPUT, RAWTEXT, OUTPUT );
global declarations;
BEGIN
prepare the processing of paragraphs;
prepare the processing of lines;
prepare the processing of tokens;
read a token;
WHILE there is data to process DO
```

```
BEGIN
IF the token is a paragraph mark THEN
  BEGIN
  start a new paragraph;
  read a token
  END;
  process a paragraph
END
END .
```

Since 'process a paragraph' in Level 1d is more complex than anything in Level 1b, we shall refine it first.

Refinement 1d.1: process a paragraph

This involves processing a number of words (possibly none) up to the end of the raw text or the start of the next paragraph, whichever comes sooner.

```
WHILE the token is a word DO
  BEGIN
  append the word followed by a blank to the current line,
    right-adjust the line and start a new line if necessary;
  read a token
  END
```

Level 2d outline

This is obtained by substituting Refinement 1d.1 into Level 1d:

```
PROGRAM TEXTFORMATTER (* version d *)
                          ( INPUT, RAWTEXT, OUTPUT );
global declarations;
BEGIN
prepare the processing of paragraphs;
prepare the processing of lines;
prepare the processing of tokens;
read a token;
WHILE there is data to process DO
  BEGIN
  IF the token is a paragraph mark THEN
    BEGIN
    start a new paragraph;
    read a token
    END;
```

```
(* process a paragraph *)
WHILE the token is a word DO
    BEGIN
        append the word followed by a blank to the current line,
            right-adjust the line and start a new line if necessary;
        read a token
    END
END
END .
```

The elements in Level 2d which remain to be refined are similar to those in Level 1b, but it is clear that the latter is a more concise solution, and it is Level 1b (henceforth labelled simply Level 1) which we shall adopt.

Testing Level 1

Let us hand-test Level 1 with the example data. Assume a line width of 30 columns. The following table shows each token read followed by the current line of output after dealing with that token. We use ƀ to represent a single blank.

Token	Current line of output
THE	THEƀ
PRINCIPLES	THEƀPRINCIPLESƀ
OF	THEƀPRINCIPLESƀOFƀ
NEWSPEAK	THEƀPRINCIPLESƀOFƀNEWSPEAKƀ
/PAR/	ƀƀƀƀƀƀ

{This is the start of a new paragraph.}

NEWSPEAK	ƀƀƀƀƀƀNEWSPEAKƀ
WAS	ƀƀƀƀƀƀNEWSPEAKƀWASƀ
THE	ƀƀƀƀƀƀNEWSPEAKƀWASƀTHEƀ
OFFICIAL	OFFICIALƀ

{The previous line, already 23 characters long, cannot accommodate the word 'OFFICIAL', so it will have been right-adjusted in some way, and a new line started.}

LANGUAGE	OFFICIALƀLANGUAGEƀ
. . .	
. . .	
. . .	
YEAR	THEƀYEARƀ
2050.	THEƀYEARƀ2050.ƀ
(end-of-data)	THEƀYEARƀ2050.ƀ

{The program terminates.}

Refinements from Level 1

Refinement 1.1: append the word followed by a blank to the current line, right-adjust the line and start a new line if necessary

```
BEGIN
IF the word will not fit into the current line THEN
   right-adjust and output the current line;
append the word to the current line;
IF a blank will fit into the current line THEN
   append a blank to the current line
END
```

Notice that there is no need to take immediate action if there is no room for the blank: the next word (if there is one) will certainly start a new line.

Testing refinement 1.1

Assume that the line width is 30 and that the current line contains 24 characters. The following table shows the contents of the current line after dealing with each of several words of varying size.

Word	Current line of output	Size
THE	?????????????????????????THEƀ	28
MEANS	????????????????????????MEANSƀ	30

{The next word, if any, will force this line to be right-adjusted.}

| ANYONE | ???????????????????????ANYONE | 30 |

{There was no room for the blank. Again, the next word, if any, will force this line out.}

| WRITING | WRITINGƀ | 8 |

{The word is too long to fit into the current line. The current line is right-adjusted, and a new line is started before appending the word.}

Level 2 outline

This is obtained by substituting Refinement 1.1 into Level 1:

```
PROGRAM TEXTFORMATTER ( INPUT, RAWTEXT, OUTPUT );
global declarations;
BEGIN
prepare the processing of lines;
prepare the processing of tokens;
read a token;
```

```
WHILE there is data to process DO
  BEGIN
  IF the token is a word THEN
     (* append the word followed by a blank to the current line,
        right-adjust the line and start a new line if necessary *)
     BEGIN
     IF the word will not fit into the current line THEN
        right-adjust and output the current line;
     append the word to the current line;
     IF a blank will fit into the current line THEN
        append a blank to the current line
     END
  ELSE (* the token is a paragraph mark *)
     start a new paragraph;
  read a token
  END
END .
```

Refinements from Level 2

A noteworthy characteristic of the Level 2 outline is the frequent recurrence of 'line' and 'token'. This strongly suggests that a data structure to represent a line, and another to represent a token, will be central to the development of **TEXTFORMATTER**. We could proceed by designing these data structures and then refining the component steps of Level 2 accordingly.

For example, we might decide to represent a token by a string variable, say S, to hold its spelling, and an **INTEGER** variable, say W, to hold its width. The refinement of 'read a token' would place the characters of the word left-justified in S and padded on the right with blanks, setting W appropriately. If there were no words left in the input data, W would be set to zero and S to all blanks. We could then make refinements such as the following.

Refinement 2.1': there is data to process

$W > 0$

Refinement 2.2': the token is a word

$S <> '/PAR/$

Going on in this way, and making similar refinements for the 'line' data structure, we might develop a workable program.

But this would be to ignore one of the main criteria guiding our choice of refinements: the importance of delaying decisions as long as possible, including those relating to data structures. By fixing on a representation for tokens and lines too early, we force the rest of the development to fit into that mould. If we have made a poor choice it will prove very difficult to change, as the entire program will be dependent on the details of the structure we have chosen. In short, the program will have very little modularity.

Let us decide, then, *not* to fix on detailed representations of 'line' and 'token' at the moment. Instead we will assume that each can be represented by a record variable of appropriate type, say LINE of type LINES and TOKEN of type TOKENS.

We can, however, make some declarations which are independent of the details of LINES and WORDS and which we can anticipate being useful.

```
CONST
   BLANK = ' ';
   . . .
TYPE
   STYLES = (ADJUSTED, UNADJUSTED);
   . . .
```

Further progress can be made by refining the steps of Level 2 in terms of two clusters of subprograms, one cluster concerned with LINE and another concerned with TOKEN. Since there is only one variable of type TOKENS and only one of type LINES it will be sufficient for these subprograms to access their data structures as non-local variables. The variable and its associated subprograms form a module, which 'packages' the details of the representation. Should it later turn out that several variables of type TOKENS or type LINES are needed, it will be a simple matter to amend the subprograms to use parameters instead.

We will declare a procedure, READTOKEN, to read the next word or paragraph mark or end-of-data mark and place it in TOKEN.

Refinement 2.1: read a token

   READTOKEN

Refinement 2.2: there is data to process

   TOKEN is not an end-of-data mark

Refinement 2.3: the token is a word

   TOKEN is a word

We will declare a BOOLEAN function, LINEHASROOMFOR, which will return TRUE if there is enough room on the current line for as many more characters as are specified by its parameter.

Refinement 2.4: the word will not fit into the current line

NOT LINEHASROOMFOR (the size of the word)

We will declare a procedure, WRITELINE, which will output the current line, leaving LINE clear to accept the first word of a new line. WRITELINE will have a parameter of type STYLES which specifies whether the line is to be right-adjusted or not.

Refinement 2.5: right-adjust and output the current line

WRITELINE (ADJUSTED)

We will declare a procedure, APPENDWORDTOLINE, to add a word at the end of the current line. At the moment it is not clear whether this procedure is best considered as part of the TOKEN cluster, as part of the LINE cluster, or as a separate cluster on its own.

Refinement 2.6: append the word to the current line

APPENDWORDTOLINE

Refinement 2.7: a blank will fit into the current line

LINEHASROOMFOR (1)

We will declare a procedure, APPENDBLANKTOLINE, to add a blank to the end of the current line. This will only be called if there is in fact room for the blank.

Refinement 2.8: append a blank to the current line

APPENDBLANKTOLINE

To start a new paragraph it is necessary to output the current line, unadjusted, output an extra blank line, and start a new line with an indentation. We will declare a procedure, INDENTLINE, to do the latter.

Refinement 2.9: start a new paragraph

```
BEGIN
WRITELINE (UNADJUSTED);
WRITELN;
INDENTLINE
END
```

We will declare procedures, SETUPLINE and SETUPTOKEN, to initialize the LINE and TOKEN clusters respectively.

Refinement 2.10: prepare the processing of lines

SETUPLINE

Refinement 2.11: prepare the processing of tokens

SETUPTOKEN

Inserting these refinements in Level 2 gives us Level 3.

Level 3 outline

```
PROGRAM TEXTFORMATTER ( INPUT, RAWTEXT, OUTPUT );
global declarations;
BEGIN
SETUPLINE;
SETUPTOKEN;
READTOKEN;
WHILE TOKEN is not an end-of-data mark DO
  BEGIN
  IF TOKEN is a word THEN
    (* append the word followed by a blank to the current line,
       right-adjust the line and start a new line if necessary *)
    BEGIN
    IF NOT LINEHASROOMFOR (the size of the word) THEN
      WRITELINE (ADJUSTED);
    APPENDWORDTOLINE;
    IF LINEHASROOMFOR(1) THEN
      APPENDBLANKTOLINE
    END
  ELSE (* the token is a paragraph mark *)
    (* start a new paragraph *)
    BEGIN
    WRITELINE (UNADJUSTED);
    WRITELN;
    INDENTLINE
    END;
  READTOKEN
  END
END .
```

Testing Level 3

Refinements 2.1 to 2.11 being so short, there is little point in testing them individually. Instead we should test the whole of Level 3. Do that now as an exercise.

If you tested Level 3 exhaustively, then you will have discovered an error. The very last line of the output text is not written! Go back and make appropriate changes to Levels 1, 2 and 3, and add the new refinement step needed.

Refinements from Level 3

We have almost completely converted the statement part of **TEXTFOR-MATTER** into Pascal. To make any further progress we will have to start refining the subprograms that have been introduced, but before we can do that it is necessary to decide on representations for **TOKEN** and **LINE**.

In the case of type **TOKENS** there are three things to represent: words, paragraph marks and end-of-data marks. The appropriate structure for this is a variant record (see Section 16.6) whose tag field defines which kind of token it is. For the word variant we must hold its spelling and its size. The spelling can be stored left-justified in a string, padded with blanks. Neither the paragraph mark nor the end-of-data mark requires any further information to be stored, so these variants are empty. Accordingly, the following must be included among the global declarations.

```
CONST
    MAXWORDSIZE = 20;
    . . .
TYPE
    WORDSIZES = 1 . . MAXWORDSIZE;
    TOKENKINDS = (AWORD, APARAGRAPHMARK, ANENDMARK);
    TOKENS = RECORD
                CASE KIND : TOKENKINDS OF
                    AWORD :
                        ( SPELLING :
                            PACKED ARRAY [WORDSIZES] OF CHAR;
                        SIZE : WORDSIZES );
                    APARAGRAPHMARK, ANENDMARK:
                        (  )
             END;
    . . .
VAR
    TOKEN : TOKENS;
    . . .
```

We can now make the following trivial refinements which complete the statement part of **TEXTFORMATTER**.

Refinement 3.1: **TOKEN** is not an end-of-data mark

```
TOKEN.KIND <> ANENDMARK
```

Refinement 3.2: **TOKEN** is a word

```
TOKEN.KIND = AWORD
```

Refinement 3.3: the size of the word

    TOKEN.SIZE

Refinement of READTOKEN

We have already seen a similar procedure in Example 14.3. Using that as a source of ideas, we can write down the present version directly. Test this refinement yourself.

```
PROCEDURE READTOKEN;
  VAR
    CHARACTER : CHAR;
    I: 0 . . MAXWORDSIZE;
  BEGIN
  CHARACTER := BLANK;
  WHILE NOT EOF(RAWTEXT) AND (CHARACTER = BLANK) DO
    READ (RAWTEXT, CHARACTER);
  WITH TOKEN DO
    BEGIN
    IF EOF(RAWTEXT) THEN
      KIND := ANENDMARK
    ELSE
      BEGIN
      I := 0;
      KIND := AWORD;
      WHILE CHARACTER <> BLANK DO
        BEGIN
        IF I < MAXWORDSIZE THEN
          BEGIN
          I := I + 1;
          SPELLING[I] := CHARACTER
          END;
        READ (RAWTEXT, CHARACTER)
        END;
      SIZE := I;
      FOR I := SIZE+1 TO MAXWORDSIZE DO
        SPELLING[I] := BLANK;
      IF SPELLING = '/PAR/              ' THEN
        KIND := APARAGRAPHMARK
      END
    END
  END (* READTOKEN *)
```

We now decide how to represent the current line. The most important point to observe is that we must *not* write out individual words immediately they are appended to the line, because that would make it impossible to go back and insert extra blanks between them when it is necessary to right-adjust the line. Therefore we must keep the current line in store until we are ready to right-adjust it. The most natural representation for a line, as for a word, is a string. This forces us to choose an upper limit on the line width, but the paper on which we are writing will have a limited width anyway. We need a field, WIDTH, to hold the line width specified by the user. The width chosen must be great enough for the widest possible word, preceded by an indentation. Finally, we must be able to tell whether a word will fit into the current line, so we need a field, SIZE, to keep track of the number of characters already placed in the line. The following must therefore be added to the global declarations.

```
CONST
   INDENT = 6;
   MINLINEWIDTH = 26; (* = INDENT + MAXWORDSIZE *)
   MAXLINEWIDTH = 80; (* assumed width of the paper *)
   . . .
TYPE
   LINEPOSITIONS = 1 . . MAXLINEWIDTH;
   LINESIZES = 0 . . MAXLINEWIDTH;
   LINES = RECORD
              WIDTH : MINLINEWIDTH . . MAXLINEWIDTH;
              SIZE : LINESIZES;
              COLUMN : PACKED ARRAY [LINEPOSITIONS] OF
              CHAR
           END;
   . . .
VAR
   LINE: LINES;
   . . .
```

We now refine the remaining subprograms. Test each of these refinements yourself.

Refinement of LINEHASROOMFOR

This is straightforward.

```
FUNCTION LINEHASROOMFOR
                  (SPACENEEDED : WORDSIZES): BOOLEAN;
         BEGIN
         WITH LINE DO
           LINEHASROOMFOR :=
                   SPACENEEDED <= (WIDTH − SIZE)
         END (* LINEHASROOMFOR *)
```

Refinement of WRITELINE

WRITELINE must output the line which has just been built up, either right-adjusted or otherwise, according to its parameter. It must also start a fresh line of output and make the LINE data structure empty, ready for the first word of the next line.

Level 1 outline of WRITELINE

```
PROCEDURE WRITELINE (STYLE: STYLES);
   local declarations;
   BEGIN
   WITH LINE DO
     BEGIN
     CASE STYLE OF
       ADJUSTED:
         write LINE with right-adjustment;
       UNADJUSTED:
         write LINE verbatim
     END;
     WRITELN;
     make LINE empty
     END
   END (* WRITELINE *)
```

The following two refinements are dependent on their position inside the WITH statement.

Refinement 1.1 of WRITELINE: make LINE empty

```
SIZE := 0
```

Refinement 1.2 of WRITELINE: write LINE verbatim

```
FOR I := 1 TO SIZE DO
  WRITE (COLUMN[I])
```

Writing adjusted lines seems quite complicated, so we introduce a local procedure, WRITEADJUSTEDLINE, to package up the details.

Refinement 1.3 of WRITELINE: write LINE with right-adjustment

```
WRITEADJUSTEDLINE
```

Refinement 1.4 of WRITELINE: local declarations

```
VAR
  I : LINEPOSITIONS;
declaration of WRITEADJUSTEDLINE
```

Level 2 of WRITELINE is obtained by incorporating these refinements in Level 1. Only the declaration of WRITEADJUSTEDLINE remains to be refined.

Refinement of APPENDBLANKTOLINE

This is simple.

```
PROCEDURE APPENDBLANKTOLINE;
  BEGIN
  WITH LINE DO
    BEGIN
    SIZE := SIZE + 1;
    COLUMN[SIZE] := BLANK
    END
  END (* APPENDBLANKTOLINE *)
```

Refinement of INDENTLINE

There are two requirements here: (a) LINE.COLUMN[1] through LINE.COLUMN[INDENT] must be made blank; (b) LINE.SIZE must be left equal to INDENT. We can assume that LINE.SIZE initially has the value 0, as assigned to it by WRITELINE. Therefore, all that is needed is to append a blank to the line, INDENT times. The Pascal code follows directly from this.

```
PROCEDURE INDENTLINE;
  VAR
    I : 1 .. INDENT;
  BEGIN
  FOR I := 1 TO INDENT DO
    APPENDBLANKTOLINE
  END (* INDENTLINE *)
```

Refinement of APPENDWORDTOLINE

The issue here is whether APPENDWORDTOLINE is best considered as an operation on TOKEN, on LINE, or on both. At stake are the modularity and efficiency of the program. The most efficient approach, but the least modular, is for APPENDWORDTOLINE to have full access to the details of both data structures and to manipulate them directly (as do READTOKEN and APPENDBLANKTOLINE). This we reject, as it would bind together two otherwise separate clusters.

The least efficient approach, but the most modular, is for APPEND-WORDTOLINE to form a separate cluster of its own. It would access

TOKEN and LINE entirely by means of subprograms in those clusters. Since that would require two procedure calls for every character copied from the word to the line, it might be too slow. Moreover, it seems difficult to give a natural definition of a subprogram that obtains successive characters of a word, at any rate with the present definition of type TOKENS.

A third alternative is to consider APPENDWORDTOLINE as part of the LINE cluster. This also requires an operation to fetch successive characters of a word. Another difficulty is that it seems somewhat artificial to hide the details of just one data structure from a subprogram which uses both of them equally.

The same remark applies to the idea of placing APPENDWORDTOLINE in the TOKEN cluster. However, in this case it would need to use a procedure, APPENDCHARTOLINE to the LINE cluster, which is very similar to APPENDBLANKTOLINE and implements a natural operation on lines. We will therefore take this approach as a compromise.

```
PROCEDURE APPENDWORDTOLINE;
  VAR
   I : WORDSIZES;
  BEGIN
  WITH TOKEN DO
    FOR I := 1 TO SIZE DO
      APPENDCHARTOLINE (SPELLING[I])
  END (* APPENDWORDTOLINE *)
```

We could make APPENDCHARTOLINE a local subprogram of APPENDWORDTOLINE. Alternatively, if we make it global, we can alter APPENDBLANKTOLINE so that it simply does APPENDCHARTO-LINE(BLANK). This costs one more procedure call for each blank appended to the line—a negligible penalty. A more important effect is to confine to a single subprogram the details of appending characters to lines—a very significant increase in modularity. This is much the better choice: go back and alter the refinement of APPENDBLANKTOLINE accordingly. (It turns out to be even simpler than we thought!)

Refinement of APPENDCHARTOLINE

This is analogous to our original version of APPENDBLANKTOLINE.

```
PROCEDURE APPENDCHARTOLINE (CHARACTER: CHAR);
  BEGIN
  WITH LINE DO
    BEGIN
    SIZE := SIZE + 1;
```

```
        COLUMN[SIZE] := CHARACTER
        END
      END (* APPENDCHARTOLINE *)
```

Refinement of SETUPTOKEN

The **TOKEN** data structure needs no initialization, but we must **RESET** the **RAWTEXT** file before reading any tokens from it.

```
  PROCEDURE SETUPTOKEN;
    BEGIN
    RESET (RAWTEXT)
    END (* SETUPTOKEN *)
```

Refinement of SETUPLINE

The **WIDTH** and **SIZE** fields of **LINE** must be initialized.

```
  PROCEDURE SETUPLINE;
    VAR
      WIDTHWANTED : INTEGER;
    BEGIN
    READ (INPUT, WIDTHWANTED);
    WITH LINE DO
      BEGIN
      IF WIDTHWANTED < MINLINEWIDTH THEN
        WIDTH := MINLINEWIDTH
      ELSE
      IF WIDTHWANTED > MAXLINEWIDTH THEN
        WIDTH := MAXLINEWIDTH
      ELSE
        WIDTH := WIDTHWANTED;
      SIZE := 0
      END
    END (* SETUPLINE *)
```

Refinement of WRITEADJUSTEDLINE

We have a line of characters which is to be expanded to a width of **LINE.WIDTH** characters exactly. This is achieved by distributing extra blanks as evenly as possible among the inter-word gaps on the line. The specification is vague about this distribution, so we are free to choose a strategy which is easy to implement.

Let us consider each gap in turn: if **NRGAPS** is the number of gaps not yet widened, and **EXTRABLANKS** is the number of blanks remaining to be distributed, then we can widen the gap under consideration by (**EXTRA-BLANKS DIV NRGAPS**) blanks and then decrease **EXTRABLANKS** accordingly. It is easy to prove that this distribution expands the line to exactly **LINE.WIDTH** characters.

If, moreover, we scan the line (and its gaps) from left to right, then we can write the words and the widened gaps as we deal with them, so there is no need to shift characters within **LINE** itself.

There will be a blank at the end of the current line if **APPENDBLANK** was obeyed more recently than **APPENDWORD**. If so, this blank is to be discarded. There will also be some blanks at the beginning of the current line if the line is the first of a paragraph. If so, these blanks are *not* to be considered as a gap to be widened. We shall find it convenient to introduce two variables, **LEFTMOST** and **RIGHTMOST**, and make them indicate the first and last non-blank characters of the line.

Level 1 outline of WRITEADJUSTEDLINE

```
PROCEDURE WRITEADJUSTEDLINE;
  VAR
    EXTRABLANKS, NRGAPS, WIDENING: LINESIZES;
    LEFTMOST, RIGHTMOST, POS: LINEPOSITIONS;
  BEGIN
  WITH LINE DO
    BEGIN
    make LEFTMOST the position of the leftmost non-blank;
    make RIGHTMOST the position of the rightmost non-blank;
    make NRGAPS the number of inter-word gaps;
    EXTRABLANKS := WIDTH − RIGHTMOST;
    FOR POS := 1 TO RIGHTMOST DO
      IF there is an inter-word gap at position POS THEN
        BEGIN
        WIDENING := EXTRABLANKS DIV NRGAPS;
        WRITE (BLANK : (WIDENING+1));
        EXTRABLANKS := EXTRABLANKS − WIDENING;
        NRGAPS := NRGAPS − 1
        END
      ELSE
        WRITE (COLUMN[POS])
    END
  END (* WRITEADJUSTEDLINE *)
```

Testing Level 1 of WRITEADJUSTEDLINE

The test cases to be considered are:

(a) a line which is the first line of a paragraph;
(b) a line which is not the first of a paragraph;
(c) a line which is already completely filled;
(d) a line which requires extra blanks between words;
(e) a line with only one word.

Test case (a) is considered here. The rest are left to you as an exercise. Test case (e) is of particular interest; does WRITEADJUSTEDLINE deal with this case satisfactorily?

Suppose that WIDTH has the value 30, that SIZE has the value 29, and that the first 29 characters of COLUMN are:

ƀƀƀƀƀƀINƀTHEƀYEARƀ1984ƀTHEREƀ

Then LEFTMOST should be set to 7 and RIGHTMOST to 28. Thus EXTRABLANKS is set to 2. Counting the inter-word gaps should set NRGAPS to 4 (since the leading blanks do not count as a gap). As we go round the loop, we write 'ƀƀƀƀƀƀIN' before coming to the first gap. We calculate WIDENING=0, so we write 1 blank, EXTRABLANKS remains at 2, and NRGAPS is decremented to 3. After further writing 'THE' we come to the second gap. We calculate WIDENING=0, so we write 1 blank, EXTRABLANKS remains at 2, and NRGAPS is decremented to 2. After further writing 'YEAR' we come to the third gap. This time we calculate WIDENING=1, so we write 2 blanks, EXTRABLANKS is reduced to 1, and NRGAPS is decremented to 1. After further writing '1984' we come to the fourth gap. We calculate WIDENING=1, so we write 2 blanks, and EXTRABLANKS and NRGAPS are reduced to 0. After further writing 'THERE' the loop terminates. So the written line is:

ƀƀƀƀƀƀƀINƀTHEƀYEARƀƀ1984ƀƀTHERE

Refinement 1.1 of WRITEADJUSTEDLINE:
    make LEFTMOST the position of the leftmost non-blank

    LEFTMOST := 1;
    WHILE COLUMN[LEFTMOST] = BLANK DO
        LEFTMOST := SUCC(LEFTMOST)

Refinement 1.2 of WRITEADJUSTEDLINE:
    make RIGHTMOST the position of the rightmost non-blank

    RIGHTMOST := SIZE;
    WHILE COLUMN[RIGHTMOST] = BLANK DO
        RIGHTMOST := PRED(RIGHTMOST)

Refinement 1.3 of WRITEADJUSTEDLINE:
make **NRGAPS** the number of inter-word gaps

Since exactly one blank has been placed between consecutive words in
COLUMN, this can be done simply by counting the blank characters
between the first and last words:

```
NRGAPS := 0;
FOR POS := LEFTMOST TO RIGHTMOST DO
  IF COLUMN[POS] = BLANK THEN
    NRGAPS := NRGAPS + 1
```

Refinement 1.4 of WRITEADJUSTEDLINE:
there is an inter-word gap at position **POS**

```
(POS > LEFTMOST) AND (COLUMN[POS] = BLANK)
```

The latter part of this condition is based on the same observation as
Refinement 1.3. The first part ensures that we are looking at an *inter-word*
gap rather than a blank introduced at the start of a paragaph.

Testing Refinements 1.1 to 1.4 of WRITEADJUSTEDLINE

Test these refinements as an exercise.

Level 4 of TEXTFORMATTER

Putting together all these refinements, we have the final program. Test it
yourself with some text from a book.

```
PROGRAM TEXTFORMATTER ( INPUT, RAWTEXT, OUTPUT );

CONST
  BLANK = ' ';
  MAXWORDSIZE = 20;
  INDENT = 6;
  MINLINEWIDTH = 26; (* = INDENT + MAXWORDSIZE *)
  MAXLINEWIDTH = 80; (* assumed width of the paper *)

TYPE

  (* - - - - Types for the LINE data structure - - - - *)

  STYLES = (ADJUSTED, UNADJUSTED);
  LINEPOSITIONS = 1 .. MAXLINEWIDTH;
  LINESIZES = 0 .. MAXLINEWIDTH;
```

```
LINES = RECORD
            WIDTH : MINLINEWIDTH . . MAXLINEWIDTH;
            SIZE : LINESIZES;
            COLUMN :
                PACKED ARRAY [LINEPOSITIONS] OF CHAR
        END;

(* - - - - Types for the TOKEN data structure - - - - *)

WORDSIZES = 1 . . MAXWORDSIZE;
TOKENKINDS = (AWORD, APARAGRAPHMARK, ANENDMARK);
TOKENS = RECORD
            CASE KIND : TOKENKINDS OF
            AWORD :
              ( SPELLING :
                    PACKED ARRAY [WORDSIZES] OF CHAR;
                SIZE : WORDSIZES );
              APARAGRAPHMARK, ANENDMARK:
                ( )
        END;

VAR
TOKEN : TOKENS;
LINE : LINES;
RAWTEXT : TEXT;

(* - - - - The LINE cluster of subprograms - - - - *)

PROCEDURE SETUPLINE;
  VAR
    WIDTHWANTED: INTEGER;
  BEGIN
  READ (INPUT, WIDTHWANTED);
  WITH LINE DO
    BEGIN
    IF WIDTHWANTED < MINLINEWIDTH THEN
      WIDTH := MAXLINEWIDTH
    ELSE
    IF WIDTHWANTED > MAXLINEWIDTH THEN
      WIDTH := MAXLINEWIDTH
    ELSE
      WIDTH := WIDTHWANTED;
    SIZE := 0
    END
  END (* SETUPLINE *);
```

```
PROCEDURE APPENDCHARTOLINE (CHARACTER: CHAR);

  BEGIN
  WITH LINE DO
    BEGIN
    SIZE := SIZE + 1;
    COLUMN[SIZE] := CHARACTER
    END
  END (* APPENDCHARTOLINE *);

PROCEDURE APPENDBLANKTOLINE;
  BEGIN
  APPENDCHARTOLINE (BLANK)
  END (* APPENDBLANKTOLINE *);

PROCEDURE INDENTLINE;
  VAR
    I: 1 .. INDENT;
  BEGIN
  FOR I := 1 TO INDENT DO
    APPENDBLANKTOLINE
  END (* INDENTLINE *);

FUNCTION LINEHASROOMFOR
            ( SPACENEEDED: WORDSIZES ): BOOLEAN;
  BEGIN
  WITH LINE DO
    LINEHASROOMFOR := SPACENEEDED <= (WIDTH - SIZE)
  END (* LINEHASROOMFOR *);

PROCEDURE WRITELINE (STYLE: STYLES);

  VAR
    I: LINEPOSITIONS;

  PROCEDURE WRITEADJUSTEDLINE;
    VAR
      EXTRABLANKS, NRGAPS, WIDENING: LINESIZES;
      LEFTMOST, RIGHTMOST, POS: LINEPOSITIONS;
    BEGIN
    WITH LINE DO
      BEGIN
      LEFTMOST := 1;
      WHILE COLUMN[LEFTMOST] = BLANK DO
        LEFTMOST := SUCC(LEFTMOST);
      RIGHTMOST := SIZE;
```

```
            WHILE COLUMN[RIGHTMOST] = BLANK DO
              RIGHTMOST := PRED(RIGHTMOST);
            NRGAPS := 0;
            FOR POS := LEFTMOST TO RIGHTMOST DO
              IF COLUMN[POS] = BLANK THEN
                NRGAPS := NRGAPS + 1;
            EXTRABLANKS := WIDTH − RIGHTMOST;
            FOR POS := 1 TO RIGHTMOST DO
              IF (POS > LEFTMOST) AND
                    (COLUMN[POS] = BLANK) THEN
                BEGIN
                WIDENING := EXTRABLANKS DIV NRGAPS;
                WRITE (BLANK : (WIDENING+1));
                EXTRABLANKS := EXTRABLANKS − WIDENING;
                NRGAPS := NRGAPS − 1
                END
              ELSE
                WRITE (COLUMN[POS])
          END
      END (* WRITEADJUSTEDLINE *);

  BEGIN (* WRITELINE *)
  WITH LINE DO
    BEGIN
    CASE STYLE OF
      ADJUSTED:
        WRITEADJUSTEDLINE;
      UNADJUSTED:
        FOR I := 1 TO SIZE DO
          WRITE(COLUMN[I])
      END;
    WRITELN;
    SIZE := 0
    END
  END (* WRITELINE *);

(* - - - - End of the LINE cluster - - - - *)

(* - - - - The TOKEN cluster of subprograms - - - - *)

PROCEDURE SETUPTOKEN;
  BEGIN
  RESET (RAWTEXT)
  END (* SETUPTOKEN *);
```

```
PROCEDURE READTOKEN;
  VAR
    CHARACTER: CHAR;
    I : 0 .. MAXWORDSIZE;
  BEGIN
  CHARACTER := BLANK;
  WHILE NOT EOF(RAWTEXT) AND (CHARACTER = BLANK) DO
    READ (RAWTEXT, CHARACTER);
  WITH TOKEN DO
    BEGIN
    IF EOF(RAWTEXT) THEN
      KIND := ANENDMARK
    ELSE
      BEGIN
      I := 0;
      KIND := AWORD;
      WHILE CHARACTER <> BLANK DO
        BEGIN
        IF I < MAXWORDSIZE THEN
          BEGIN
          I := I + 1;
          SPELLING[I] := CHARACTER
          END;
        READ (RAWTEXT, CHARACTER)
        END;
      SIZE := I;
      FOR I := SIZE+1 TO MAXWORDSIZE DO
        SPELLING[I] := BLANK;
      IF SPELLING = '/PAR/                              ' THEN
        KIND := APARAGRAPHMARK
      END
    END;
  END (* READTOKEN *);

PROCEDURE APPENDWORDTOLINE;
  VAR
    I: WORDSIZES;
  BEGIN
  WITH TOKEN DO
    FOR I := 1 TO SIZE DO
      APPENDCHARTOLINE (SPELLING[I])
  END (* APPENDWORDTOLINE *);

(* - - - End of the TOKEN cluster - - - - *)
```

```
BEGIN (* TEXTFORMATTER *)
(* prepare the processing of lines *)
SETUPLINE;
(* prepare the processing of tokens *)
SETUPTOKEN;
(* read a token *)
READTOKEN;
WHILE TOKEN.KIND <> ANENDMARK DO
  BEGIN
  IF TOKEN.KIND = AWORD THEN
    (* append the word followed by a blank to the current line,
      right-adjust the line and start a new line if necessary *)
    BEGIN
    IF NOT LINEHASROOMFOR(TOKEN.SIZE) THEN
      WRITELINE (ADJUSTED);
    APPENDWORDTOLINE;
    IF LINEHASROOMFOR(1) THEN
      APPENDBLANKTOLINE
    END
  ELSE (* the token is a paragraph mark *)
    (* start a new paragraph *)
    BEGIN
    WRITELINE (UNADJUSTED);
    WRITELN;
    INDENTLINE
    END;
  (* read a token *)
  READTOKEN
  END;
WRITELINE (UNADJUSTED)
END (* TEXTFORMATTER *) .
```

By clustering all the subprograms concerned with LINE, and likewise all the subprograms concerned with TOKEN, we improve the localization of the final program. (Note that the LINE cluster must come first, because APPENDCHARTOLINE in this cluster is invoked by APPENDWORD-TOLINE in the TOKEN cluster and Pascal requires each subprogram to be declared before it is used.) Similarly, the types of the LINE cluster appear together, as do those of the TOKEN cluster.

Ideally, all the constants, types, variables and subprograms of each cluster would be collected together with no intervening material, further improving the localization of the program. Unfortunately this is precluded by Pascal's strict order of declarations within the declarative part of a block.

18.3 Case study IV: transferable vote elections

Problem specification

The transferable vote system is a method of conducting an election in such a way that the successful candidate requires the support of an absolute majority of the voters, even when there are more than two candidates. Instead of voting for just one candidate, each voter is required to complete a ballot placing *all* the candidates in order of preference. In the first count of votes, only the first choice of each voter is considered. If no candidate obtains an overall majority in this count, then the candidate with the *fewest* votes is eliminated, and a recount is carried out in which votes cast for the eliminated candidate are ignored, that is the second choices of those voters who voted first for the eliminated candidate are now counted. Eliminations and recounts are continued in this way until one candidate has obtained an overall majority (or until all candidates still in contention have exactly equal votes, in which case a tie is declared).

For example, suppose the votes cast in a three-candidate election are as follows:

	1st choice	2nd choice	3rd choice
Voter A	3	1	2
Voter B	2	3	1
Voter C	2	1	3
Voter D	1	3	2
Voter E	2	1	3
Voter F	3	2	1
Voter G	1	3	2
Voter H	3	1	2
Voter I	2	3	1

in which the candidates have been numbered 1, 2 and 3. Then in the first count candidate 1 gets 2 votes, candidate 2 gets 4 votes, and candidate 3 gets 3 votes. There is no overall majority, so candidate 1 is eliminated. Both the voters (D and G) whose first choice was this candidate gave candidate 3 as their second choices, so in the recount candidate 2 gets 4 votes and candidate 3 gets 5 votes. Therefore candidate 3 is the winner.

If after any count several candidates have the same, smallest, number of votes, then any one of them may be eliminated.

Write a program to determine the winner, if any, of a transferable vote election. Assume that each ballot is presented as a single line of input, with the candidate numbers arranged in order of preference as above. Assume that these lines are preceded by a line containing the number of candidates. The program must reject invalid ballots, a valid ballot being one on which every candidate has been placed in exactly one position. (For example, with three candidates, 2 2 1 and 3 1 4 are invalid ballots.)

Solution

The problem specification implies that the ballots are liable to be examined repeatedly, once on each count. Our very first deduction, therefore, is that it will not be sufficient to examine the ballots one by one when reading them, unlike the simpler vote-counting problem of Example 11.1. Instead we must first store all the valid ballots.

The heart of the solution will be a loop in which a candidate is eliminated and the votes are recounted as often as necessary. This leads us to Level 1:

Level 1 outline

```
PROGRAM TRANSFERABLEVOTES ( INPUT, OUTPUT );
global declarations;
BEGIN
prepare to count votes;
read all the ballots, storing the valid ones;
count the votes;
WHILE a recount is needed DO
  BEGIN
  eliminate the candidate with fewest votes;
  recount the votes, ignoring eliminated candidates
  END;
report the outcome of the election
END .
```

Testing Level 1

Let us check the logic of Level 1 in all possible cases.

(a) All the candidates have equal votes. In this case we skip the loop; then, since there is no overall majority, we should report a tie.

(b) One candidate has an overall majority. In this case also, we skip the loop; this time we should declare the winner.

(c) Neither (a) nor (b) applies. Then there must be more than two candidates still in contention. In this case, we enter the loop, eliminate one of the candidates, and recount; this must reduce to case (a) or (b), or to (c) with fewer candidates.

When only two candidates are left, either (a) or (b) must apply. Since we eliminate one candidate on each repetition, therefore, the loop must eventually terminate.

Refinements from Level 1

Now we may proceed to refine Level 1. Sooner or later, we shall have to decide how to store the ballots, but we can postpone this decision until we see how to organize the vote counting and recounting.

To count the votes we simply consider each ballot in turn, and credit a vote to the candidate who is the first choice on that ballot. Before rushing ahead with this refinement, we should examine the refinement of 'recount the votes, ignoring eliminated candidates' to see if we can profit from its similarity. Recounting is similar to counting, except that instead of the first-choice candidate every time, we credit the most favoured candidate who has not yet been eliminated.

In fact, counting is just a special case of recounting, since initially no candidates will have been eliminated, so we can use the same piece of program. This will use variables (such as those for accumulating the vote-counts) that will be irrelevant elsewhere, so we should package it as a procedure, COUNTVOTES.

Examining the logic of Level 1, we can see that the following information must be extracted from the vote counting to be used by the rest of the program: (a) the most and least successful candidates still in contention, (b) whether the former obtained an overall majority, and (c) whether all candidates still in contention are tied. This information can be returned from COUNTVOTES through variable parameters.

There are just three possible outcomes of a count or recount: a tie, an overall majority, or a recount. This suggests the use of an enumeration type. We also need a type to represent vote-counts. With these considerations in mind, we see that the global declarations should include the following:

```
TYPE
    VOTECOUNTS = 0 .. MAXINT;
    OUTCOMES =
            (ALLTIED, OVERALLMAJORITY, RECOUNTNEEDED);
VAR
    LEADER, TRAILER: CANDIDATES;
    OUTCOME: OUTCOMES;
    . . .
```

The type CANDIDATES will presumably reflect the specified numbering of the candidates; however, at this state it is unclear exactly how it should be defined.

We can now refine the counting steps in terms of COUNTVOTES.

Refinement 1.1: count the votes

```
COUNTVOTES (LEADER, TRAILER, OUTCOME)
```

Initially, we must consider all candidates as still in contention; this must be arranged by 'prepare to count votes'.

Refinement 1.2: recount the votes, ignoring eliminated candidates

COUNTVOTES (LEADER, TRAILER, OUTCOME)

Refinement 1.3: a recount is needed

OUTCOME = RECOUNTNEEDED

We will introduce a procedure, **REPORT**, to report the result of the election.

Refinement 1.4: report the outcome of the election

REPORT (OUTCOME, LEADER)

We will introduce a procedure, **STOREVALIDBALLOTS**, to read and store the valid ballots.

Refinement 1.5: read all the ballots, storing the valid ones

STOREVALIDBALLOTS

We can also make a start on the refinement of **COUNTVOTES**. This can assume that all the stored ballots are valid ones, because invalid ballots will have been discarded previously.

Level 1 of COUNTVOTES

```
PROCEDURE COUNTVOTES
                (VAR LEADER, TRAILER: CANDIDATES;
                VAR OUTCOMES: OUTCOMES);
    local declarations;
BEGIN
initialize all vote-counts to 0;
prepare to scan valid ballots;
WHILE not at end of ballots DO
  BEGIN
  access the next ballot;
  determine the most favoured candidate on this
      ballot, apart from eliminated candidates;
  add 1 to this candidate's vote-count
  END;
  determine which of the candidates still in contention
      received most votes (LEADER) and least votes (TRAILER);
```

```
    IF LEADER and TRAILER have equal votes THEN
        OUTCOME := ALLTIED
    ELSE
    IF LEADER has more than half the votes THEN
        OUTCOME := OVERALLMAJORITY
    ELSE
        OUTCOME := RECOUNTNEEDED
    END (* COUNTVOTES *)
```

Level 2 of **TRANSFERABLEVOTES** is obtained by substituting these refinements into Level 1. The complete Level 2 program is omitted to save space. Write it out yourself unless you can visualize it clearly. As an exercise, test the complete Level 2 outline using the sample data.

Refinements from Level 2

We cannot proceed any further without deciding how to store the ballots. The most obvious solution, perhaps, is an array each of whose components contains a single ballot. This solution has the disadvantage that, since an array is fixed in size, it would be necessary to fix some arbitrary upper limit on the number of ballots to be accepted, in order that we can declare an array with that number of components. But it would be difficult to choose a suitable limit: 1000 would be too small for many elections; even 100000 might not be large enough for some purposes, but it would be grossly wasteful of space when the actual number of ballots is much smaller.

A little thought suggests a much better solution: a serial file. A file has the decisive advantage of being (virtually) unlimited in size. If we store the ballots in a file, we will be restricted to examining them one by one in a fixed order, but that is perfectly adequate here: examining the logic of procedure **COUNTVOTES**, we can see that each ballot is examined once only per count, and that the order of examination of the ballots is irrelevant. Having generated the file, we may scan it from beginning to end as often as required. So we include among the global declarations:

```
VAR
    BALLOTFILE : FILE OF BALLOTS;
    . . .
```

Each component, of type **BALLOTS**, will represent a single ballot. At this stage there is still no need to decide how to represent individual ballots, so we need not define the type **BALLOTS** just yet. Since the file will be generated by the program for its own use, and will not be retained afterwards, **BALLOTFILE** will *not* be a program parameter. **BALLOTFILE** is generated by the procedure **STOREVALIDBALLOTS**.

Level 1 of STOREVALIDBALLOTS

```
PROCEDURE STOREVALIDBALLOTS;
    local declarations;
    BEGIN
    REWRITE (BALLOTFILE);
    WHILE NOT EOF(INPUT) DO
        BEGIN
        read and check one BALLOT;
        IF BALLOT is valid THEN
            WRITE (BALLOTFILE, BALLOT)
        END
    END (* STOREVALIDBALLOTS *)
```

The local declarations of **STOREVALIDBALLOTS** must include:

```
VAR
    BALLOT: BALLOTS;
    . . .
```

Refinements from Level 1 of COUNTVOTES

While scanning **BALLOTFILE**, **COUNTVOTES** must note the total number of valid ballots in order to be able to compute the number of votes needed for an overall majority.

Refinement 1.1 of COUNTVOTES: not at end of ballots

```
NOT EOF(BALLOTFILE)
```

Refinement 1.2 of COUNTVOTES: access the next ballot

```
READ (BALLOTFILE, BALLOT);
NRVALIDBALLOTS := NRVALIDBALLOTS + 1
```

Refinement 1.3 of COUNTVOTES: prepare to scan valid ballots

```
RESET (BALLOTFILE);
NRVALIDBALLOTS := 0
```

The local declarations of **COUNTVOTES** must include:

```
VAR
    BALLOT: BALLOTS;
    NRVALIDBALLOTS : VOTECOUNTS
    . . .
```

Level 3 of **TRANSFERABLEVOTES** is obtained by substituting these refinements into Level 2. Again, test the complete Level 3 outline with your own data.

Refinements from Level 3

Now we must decide how to represent an individual ballot, that is how to define the type BALLOTS. Each ballot is a sequence of exactly NRCANDI-DATES candidate numbers, where NRCANDIDATES is a variable of type CANDIDATES containing the number read from the start of the input data. The ideal type definition would be:

BALLOTS = ARRAY [1 . . NRCANDIDATES] OF CANDIDATES

but unfortunately Pascal does not allow this, since NRCANDIDATES is a variable. {Some programming languages, such as Algol and PL/I, do allow arrays to have their size determined by variables. Such arrays are called *dynamic arrays.*} If, however, we agree on a fixed limit to the number of candidates, say 10, we can include the following among the global declarations:

CONST
  MAXCANDIDATES = 10;
  . . .
TYPE
  CANDIDATES = 1 . . MAXCANDIDATES;
  PLACINGS   = 1 . . MAXCANDIDATES;
  BALLOTS   = ARRAY [PLACINGS] OF CANDIDATES;
  . . .
VAR
  NRCANDIDATES: CANDIDATES;
  . . .

Only the first NRCANDIDATES components of each array of type BALLOTS will actually be used.

Refinements from Level 1 of STOREVALIDBALLOTS

A ballot is valid if (a) it contains no numbers outside the range 1 to NRCANDIDATES, and (b) each candidate number occurs just once. The latter can be checked easily by declaring:

VAR
  ALREADYCHOSEN: ARRAY [CANDIDATES] OF BOOLEAN;
  . . .

and initializing all components to FALSE; for each candidate number CHOICE on the ballot, we first check that ALREADYCHOSEN[CHOICE] is still FALSE, then we set it to TRUE. Since this piece of program contains details and variables (notably ALREADYCHOSEN) of no interest else-where, it should be packaged as a procedure, READANDCHECKONEBAL-LOT. This will have two variable parameters, one to return the ballot and one to indicate its validity.

Refinement 1.1 of STOREVALIDBALLOTS:
read and check one **BALLOT**

READANDCHECKONEBALLOT (BALLOT, VALID)

Refinement of READANDCHECKONEBALLOT

We can write this down directly.

```
PROCEDURE READANDCHECKONEBALLOT
              (VAR BALLOT: BALLOTS; VAR VALID: BOOLEAN);
    VAR
      CHOICE: INTEGER;
      PLACE: PLACINGS;
      ALREADYCHOSEN: ARRAY [CANDIDATES] OF BOOLEAN;
    BEGIN
    VALID := TRUE;
    FOR CHOICE := 1 TO NRCANDIDATES DO
      ALREADYCHOSEN[CHOICE] := FALSE;
    FOR PLACE := 1 TO NRCANDIDATES DO
      BEGIN
      READ (CHOICE);
      IF (CHOICE < 1) OR (CHOICE > NRCANDIDATES) THEN
        VALID := FALSE
      ELSE
      IF ALREADYCHOSEN[CHOICE] THEN
        VALID := FALSE
      ELSE
        BEGIN
        BALLOT[PLACE] := CHOICE;
        ALREADYCHOSEN[CHOICE] := TRUE
        END
      END;
    READLN
    END (* READANDCHECKONEBALLOT *)
```

Refinement 1.2 of STOREVALIDBALLOTS: **BALLOT** is valid

VALID

Refinements from Level 2 of COUNTVOTES

Refinement 2.1 of COUNTVOTES: determine the most favoured candidate on **BALLOT**, ignoring elimin-
ated candidates

If we make the local declarations:

```
VAR
  BALLOT : BALLOTS;
  PLACE : PLACINGS;
  MOSTFAVOURED : CANDIDATES;
  . . .
```

we can refine as follows:

```
PLACE := 1;
WHILE the candidate placed in BALLOT[PLACE]
      is one who has already been eliminated DO
    PLACE := SUCC(PLACE);
MOSTFAVOURED := BALLOT[PLACE]
```

This is an example of linear search. Notice that the loop does not contain the usual check: PLACE <= NRCANDIDATES. This is unnecessary here because at least two of BALLOT[1], . . ., BALLOT[NRCANDIDATES] will be candidates who have not been eliminated, provided that the ballot is valid. Examination of the program logic shows that only valid ballots are considered by procedure COUNTVOTES.

Level 4 of TRANSFERABLEVOTES is obtained by substituting these refinements into Level 3. As an exercise, hand-test Level 4 using suitable test data.

Refinements from Level 4

The remaining refinements are fairly straightforward. We can keep track of which candidates have been eliminated using the global array:

```
VAR
  INCONTENTION : ARRAY [CANDIDATES] OF BOOLEAN;
  . . .
```

This will be initialized as part of 'prepare to count votes', and updated by 'eliminate the candidates with fewest votes'.

Refinements from Level 3 of COUNTVOTES

Refinement 3.1 of COUNTVOTES: initialize all vote-counts to 0

Refinement 3.2 of COUNTVOTES: add 1 to this candidate's vote-count

Both these refinements can be borrowed directly from Example 11.1. We introduce the local declaration:

```
VAR
  COUNT : ARRAY [CANDIDATES] OF VOTECOUNTS;
  . . .
```

Refinement 3.3 of COUNTVOTES: determine which of the candidates still in contention received most votes (LEADER) and least votes (TRAILER)

This amounts to locating the maximum and minimum of COUNT[1], . . ., COUNT[NRCANDIDATES], ignoring candidates who have been eliminated.

```
LEADERSCOUNT := 0;
TRAILERSCOUNT := NRVALIDBALLOTS;
FOR CONTENDER := 1 TO NRCANDIDATES DO
  IF INCONTENTION[CONTENDER] THEN
    BEGIN
    IF COUNT[CONTENDER] > LEADERSCOUNT THEN
      BEGIN
      LEADER := CONTENDER;
      LEADERSCOUNT := COUNT[LEADER]
      END;
    IF COUNT[CONTENDER] < TRAILERSCOUNT THEN
      BEGIN
      TRAILER := CONTENDER;
      TRAILERSCOUNT := COUNT[TRAILER]
      END
    END
```

LEADERSCOUNT and TRAILERSCOUNT will be local VOTECOUNTS variables. Their initial values have been chosen so that they are certain to be altered, and so that LEADER and TRAILER will receive values. It would be incorrect to initialize LEADERSCOUNT and TRAILERSCOUNT to COUNT[1], as was done in Example 11.1, since candidate 1 may have been eliminated.

The expressions 'LEADER and TRAILER have equal votes' and 'LEADER has more than half the votes' can easily be expressed in terms of LEADERSCOUNT and TRAILERSCOUNT.

Refinement 3.4 of COUNTVOTES: the candidate placed in BALLOT [PLACE] is one who has already been eliminated

```
NOT INCONTENTION[BALLOT[PLACE]]
```

Level 5 of TRANSFERABLEVOTES

This is obtained by substituting these refinements, and one or two remaining minor ones, into Level 4, yielding the Pascal program. As a final exercise, hand-test the complete program with your own data.

```
PROGRAM TRANSFERABLEVOTES ( INPUT, OUTPUT );

CONST
  MAXCANDIDATES = 10;

TYPE
  CANDIDATES = 1 .. MAXCANDIDATES;
  PLACINGS = 1 .. MAXCANDIDATES;
  BALLOTS = ARRAY [PLACINGS] OF CANDIDATES;
  VOTECOUNTS = 0 .. MAXINT;
  OUTCOMES =
    (ALLTIED, OVERALLMAJORITY, RECOUNTNEEDED);

VAR
  NRCANDIDATES : CANDIDATES;
  LEADER, TRAILER : CANDIDATES;
  OUTCOME : OUTCOMES;
  BALLOTFILE : FILE OF BALLOTS;
  INCONTENTION : ARRAY [CANDIDATES] OF BOOLEAN;

PROCEDURE STOREVALIDBALLOTS;
  VAR
    BALLOT : BALLOTS;
    VALID : BOOLEAN;

  PROCEDURE READANDCHECKONEBALLOT
          (VAR BALLOT: BALLOTS; VAR VALID: BOOLEAN);
    VAR
      CHOICE : INTEGER;
      PLACE : PLACINGS;
      ALREADYCHOSEN : ARRAY [CANDIDATES] OF BOOLEAN;

  BEGIN
  VALID := TRUE;
  FOR CHOICE := 1 TO NRCANDIDATES DO
    ALREADYCHOSEN[CHOICE] := FALSE;
  FOR PLACE := 1 TO NRCANDIDATES DO
    BEGIN
```

```
    READ (CHOICE);
    IF (CHOICE < 1) OR (CHOICE > NRCANDIDATES) THEN
      VALID := FALSE
    ELSE
    IF ALREADYCHOSEN[CHOICE] THEN
      VALID := FALSE
    ELSE
      BEGIN
      BALLOT[PLACE] := CHOICE;
      ALREADYCHOSEN[CHOICE] := TRUE
      END
    END;
    READLN
    END (* READANDCHECKONEBALLOT *);

  BEGIN (* STOREVALIDBALLOTS *)
  REWRITE (BALLOTFILE);
  WHILE NOT EOF(INPUT) DO
    BEGIN
    READANDCHECKONEBALLOT (BALLOT, VALID);
    IF VALID THEN
      WRITE (BALLOTFILE, BALLOT)
    END
  END (* STOREVALIDBALLOTS *);


PROCEDURE SETUPCOUNTING;
  VAR
    CONTENDER: CANDIDATES;
  BEGIN
  READLN (NRCANDIDATES);
  FOR CONTENDER := 1 TO NRCANDIDATES DO
    INCONTENTION[CONTENDER] := TRUE
  END (* SETUPCOUNTING *);

PROCEDURE ELIMINATE (CONTENDER: CANDIDATES);
  BEGIN
  INCONTENTION[CONTENDER] := FALSE
  END (* ELIMINATE *);

PROCEDURE COUNTVOTES
      (VAR LEADER, TRAILER: CANDIDATES;
       VAR OUTCOME: OUTCOMES);
  VAR
    COUNT: ARRAY [CANDIDATES] OF VOTECOUNTS;
```

```
      BALLOT: BALLOTS;
      PLACE: PLACINGS;
      MOSTFAVOURED, CONTENDER: CANDIDATES;
      LEADERSCOUNT, TRAILERSCOUNT: VOTECOUNTS;
      NRVALIDBALLOTS: VOTECOUNTS;

 BEGIN
 FOR CONTENDER := 1 TO NRCANDIDATES DO
    COUNT[CONTENDER] := 0;
 RESET (BALLOTFILE);
 NRVALIDBALLOTS := 0;
 WHILE NOT EOF(BALLOTFILE) DO
    BEGIN
    READ (BALLOTFILE, BALLOT);
    NRVALIDBALLOTS := NRVALIDBALLOTS + 1;
    (* determine the most favoured candidate on this
       ballot, apart from eliminated candidates *)
    PLACE := 1;
    WHILE NOT INCONTENTION[BALLOT[PLACE]] DO
       PLACE := SUCC(PLACE);
    MOSTFAVOURED := BALLOT[PLACE];
    COUNT[MOSTFAVOURED] := COUNT[MOSTFAVOURED] + 1
    END;
 (* determine which of the candidates still in contention
    received most votes (LEADER) and least votes (TRAILER) *)
 LEADERSCOUNT := 0;
 TRAILERSCOUNT := NRVALIDBALLOTS;
 FOR CONTENDER := 1 TO NRCANDIDATES DO
    IF INCONTENTION[CONTENDER] THEN
       BEGIN
       IF COUNT[CONTENDER] > LEADERSCOUNT THEN
          BEGIN
          LEADER := CONTENDER;
          LEADERSCOUNT := COUNT[LEADER]
          END;
       IF COUNT[CONTENDER] < TRAILERSCOUNT THEN
          BEGIN
          TRAILER := CONTENDER;
          TRAILERSCOUNT := COUNT[TRAILER]
          END
       END;
 IF LEADERSCOUNT = TRAILERSCOUNT THEN
    OUTCOME := ALLTIED
 ELSE
```

```
IF LEADERSCOUNT > NRVALIDBALLOTS DIV 2 THEN
    OUTCOME := OVERALLMAJORITY
ELSE
    OUTCOME := RECOUNTNEEDED
END (* COUNTVOTES *);

PROCEDURE REPORT (OUTCOME: OUTCOMES;
                  LEADER: CANDIDATES);
    VAR
      CONTENDER: CANDIDATES;
    BEGIN
    CASE OUTCOME OF
      OVERALLMAJORITY:
        WRITELN ('WINNER IS CANDIDATE: ', LEADER:1);
      ALLTIED:
        BEGIN
        WRITELN ('TIE AMONG THE FOLLOWING CANDIDATES: ');
        FOR CONTENDER := 1 TO NRCANDIDATES DO
            IF INCONTENTION[CONTENDER] THEN
                WRITELN (CONTENDER: 20)
        END
    END (* CASE OUTCOME *)
END (* REPORT *);

BEGIN (* TRANSFERABLEVOTES *)
SETUPCOUNTING;
STOREVALIDBALLOTS;
COUNTVOTES (LEADER, TRAILER, OUTCOME);
WHILE OUTCOME = RECOUNTNEEDED DO
    BEGIN
    ELIMINATE (TRAILER);
    COUNTVOTES (LEADER, TRAILER, OUTCOME)
    END;
REPORT (OUTCOME, LEADER)
END (* TRANSFERABLEVOTES *) .
```

18.4 Some general principles

Let us see what lessons we have learned from the case studies, and what general principles can be stated about the practice of programming by stepwise refinement. Refer back to the case studies to see what these principles mean and how they are applied.

Design decisions and refinements

Whenever we choose a particular algorithm to perform some task, whenever we introduce a variable and whenever we choose a type for a variable, we are making a design decision. All but the most trivial programming problems involve a number of design decisions. Moreover, these design decisions are generally inter-dependent, so it is important that they be taken, and documented, in a systematic manner. That is what programming by stepwise refinement is all about.

When we refine a command we are deciding *how* the command is to be performed, having previously been interested only in *what* the command was supposed to do. Refinement consists of breaking the command down into simpler commands, some of which may be Pascal statements.

The decision to introduce a variable, or to choose a type for it, might seem to be so minor that you could take it almost unconciously, especially for a simple variable. Probably you would be more careful about the selection of a data structure, such as an array. Yet all such decisions might be highly significant, and they deserve to be considered carefully.

An example of this kind was the decision, in Case Study III, to keep each line of output in store until it was (almost) filled, and for this purpose to introduce a string field, COLUMN, accompanied by a count of the number of characters in the line, SIZE. This decision influenced the refinements of all the commands concerned with output.

Data structures can be subjected to successive refinement in the same way as commands. Case Study IV provided a good example of this. After studying Level 2 of that program, we decided that the most satisfactory way to store the ballots would be in a file, and on this basis we wrote Level 1 of STOREVALIDBALLOTS and Level 2 of COUNTVOTES. It was neither necessary nor desirable at that stage to decide on the representation of the individual ballots, that is to decide the component type of the file. If we had made the latter decision prematurely, we would have introduced too many details into Level 3.

Introducing details too early is always to be avoided. The whole point of programming by stepwise refinement is to *delay every design decision as long as possible*. It is often possible, for example, to refine many commands without making any commitment on how to store the data on which these commands operate. This allows us to delay choosing the best way to store the data until we can see exactly what operations are to be performed. Again Case Study IV offers a good illustration of this point. If we had rushed into a premature decision about how to store the set of ballots, we might well have chosen a two-dimensional array. By delaying this decision until we were refining Level 2, we were able to see clearly that the ballots would be examined one at a time, in an arbitrary order, and that a serial file would be perfectly satisfactory.

As another example, suppose that the text formatting problem were modified so that the output lines were *not* to be right-adjusted, but were still to be restricted to the specified line width. Even with this modification, Level 1 and Level 2 would be unchanged (except for a rewording of one of the commands). At this point, however, we should realize that there is no need to keep the current output line in store; we can write the words as soon as they are designated for output. This, a decision *not* to introduce a variable, is a design decision as important as any other!

Backtracking and thinking ahead

In Case Study III we saw an example of a situation in which we had to choose between alternative refinements. When it is not immediately clear which refinement is preferable, it is best to try each possibility in turn, refining one or two levels down in each case. This should make it clear which is to be preferred.

Actually, you will often be able to avoid this extra work by thinking ahead a level or two, visualizing roughly the consequences of each alternative, and thus choose the most suitable refinement without trying out inferior ideas on paper. Your ability to think ahead successfully will improve as you accumulate programming experience.

No amount of programming experience, however, guarantees against making refinements which later prove to be unsatisfactory in some respect, for example leading to a program which is wasteful of time or storage space. Then it is necessary to *backtrack*, to isolate the design decision which has proved to be inappropriate and to undo all the refinements consequent upon that decision.

The time spent in backtracking and improving on earlier design decisions should not be regarded as having been wasted; it is part of the essential experience of every programmer. Even the most skilled programmers often find that, having solved a problem apparently satisfactorily, they can devise a better solution by starting again from scratch.

Modifications

Working programs often have to be modified to meet a changed specification. Indeed, professional programmers spend a large proportion of their time doing exactly that. For example, the programs used by a tax authority will require frequent modification in response to changes in the tax laws.

It is also common for a programmer to find that a new programming assignment bears some resemblance to a program previously written, either by himself or by another programmer. In such a case, judicious adaptation of the older program can save a lot of work.

Such modifications must be made in the same systematic manner as correcting errors, and for exactly the same reasons.

Practice

No-one has ever become a good programmer simply by reading about programming methods. (Or, for that matter, by writing about them!) There is no substitute for experience, obtained by solving your own programming problems, all the time consciously practising the methods advocated here.

Do not be tempted to cast off these methods once you consider yourself to be a competent programmer, or if you have to write in a language other than Pascal. The methods presented in this book are of continuing and general usefulness, perhaps especially when programming in a language such as BASIC, COBOL or FORTRAN.

Exercises 18

18.1. Systematically modify **TEXTFORMATTER** so that the procedure **APPENDWORDTOLINE** forms a separate cluster on its own.

18.2. Systematically enhance **TEXTFORMATTER** to support the following features:

(a) the special 'word' /BREAK/ is to start a new line, the current line being written without right-adjustment;
(b) the special 'word' /SPACE/ is to have the same effect as /BREAK/ and, additionally, is to leave a single blank line;
(c) the special 'word' /PAGE/ is to have the same effect as /BREAK/ and, additionally, is to start a new page;
(d) the program is to read, in addition to the line width, the maximum number of lines per page, and a new page is to be started automatically whenever the current page contains that number of lines.

18.3. Why were 'prepare to count votes' and 'eliminate the candidate with fewest votes' refined in terms of procedures in **TRANSFERABLEVOTES**?

18.4. What happens in **TRANSFERABLEVOTES** if *all* the ballots are invalid? What happens if there is only one candidate for election? Systematically amend the program to improve its behaviour in these circumstances.

Programming exercises 18

18.5. Write a program to plot the results of an experiment roughly on a line-printer page. Pairs of *x*- and *y*-values are supplied as input, one pair per line. The plot must include both the *x*- and *y*-axes. The positions of the axes and the *x*- and *y*-scale-factors must be chosen so as to use as much of the page as possible. The scales need not be marked on the axes, but the *x*- and *y*-scale-factors must be printed on the same page.

18.6. A text file **TITLES** contains a list of book titles separated by line boundaries. A number of 'keywords' are supplied as input data, each left-justified on a line. Write a program which, for each keyword, writes a list of all the titles which contain that keyword, aligned such that the keyword always starts in a fixed column, e.g.:

COMPUTER PROGRAMMING FOR ENGINEERS
PROGRAMMING IN PASCAL
SYSTEMATIC PROGRAMMING
AN INTRODUCTION TO DYNAMIC PROGRAMMING
PROGRAMMING AND METHODICAL PROGRAMMING
PROGRAMMING AND METHODICAL PROGRAMMING

If a keyword occurs more than once in a title, the title should be repeated, as illustrated above.

18.7*. Disk files are often used for permanent storage of programs, texts, documents, mailing lists, etc. A program called an *editor* is needed to amend such files as required. Write an editor which reads a text file, **ORIGINALFILE**, and writes an edited copy of this file to a second text file, **UPDATEDFILE**. The input data contains *editing directives*, one per line, whose effect is specified below (where *xyz* and *uvw* stand for any character sequences):

Directive	Effect
C'*xyz*'	Copy the current line and subsequent lines up to the next line containing *xyz*. This line becomes the new 'current line'.
S'*xyz*'	Skip to the next line containing *xyz* (i.e. do *not* copy the preceding lines). This line becomes the new 'current line'.
R'*xyz*''*uvw*'	Replace the first occurrence of *xyz* in the current line by *uvw*.

The 'current line' is initially the first line of **ORIGINALFILE**. When all the editing directives have been processed, the current line and all remaining lines of **ORIGINALFILE** are to be copied to **UPDATEDFILE**.

Part VI
Additional topics

19
Sets

{This chapter may be omitted on a first reading.}

19.1 Sets and programming

The concept of a *set* is one of the most basic in mathematics. A set is best defined, for our purposes, as a collection of distinct objects all of the same type. The objects contained in a set are its *members*. {*June, July, August*} and {3, 5, 7, 11, 13, 17, 19} are examples of sets: the first has three members, which are months; the second has seven members, which are integers. The order in which the members are listed is of no importance: {*August, July, June*} is the same set as {*June, July, August*}. Repetition of members does not affect matters either: {3, 5, 7, 3, 5, 5, 7} is the same set as {3, 5, 7}. A set with no members at all is called the *empty set*.

The following operations are defined upon sets.

(a) Test for membership: a given value either is a member of a given set or is not. Thus *June* is a member of the set {*June, July, August*}, but *May* is not.

(b) Test for inclusion: a set A is included in a set B (alternatively, A is a *subset* of B) if and only if every member of A is also a member of B. Thus {*June, July, August*}, {*July*} and the empty set are all subsets of {*June, July, August*}.

(c) Set intersection: the intersection of two sets A and B is the set of all values which are members of A and members of B. Thus the intersection of {*June, July, August*} and {*December, March, June, September*} is the set {*June*}.

(d) Set union: the union of two sets A and B is the set of all values which are members of A, or members of B, or both. Thus the union of {*June, July, August*} and {*December, March, June, September*} is the set {*March, June, July, August, September, December*}.

(e) Set difference: the difference of two sets A and B is the set of all values which are members of A but not B. Thus the difference of {*June, July,*

August} and *{December, March, June, September}* is the set *{July, August}*.

The use of sets permits a very elegant formulation of many programming problems. The following example illustrates a common situation.

Example 19.1

Suppose we have a variable MONTH, and suppose that we want a statement to be executed only if MONTH has one of the values *April, June, September* or *November*. The 'obvious' solution is:

```
IF (MONTH = April) OR
   (MONTH = June) OR
   (MONTH = September) OR
   (MONTH = November) THEN
   . . . . . . . . . .
```

A much neater formulation is this:

```
IF MONTH is a member of
   {April, June, September, November} THEN
   . . . . . . . . . .
```

Moreover, this formulation can easily be generalized, for example:

```
IF MONTH is a member of MONTHSOFINTEREST THEN
   . . . . . . . . . .
```

where MONTHSOFINTEREST is a *set variable*, that is a variable whose value (in this case) will be a set of months.

19.2 Sets in Pascal

Unlike most other programming languages, Pascal allows the programmer to take advantage of the elegance of set notation. We can declare set variables, and we can compose set expressions using the operations defined in Section 19.1.

Example 19.2

Given the type definition:

```
MONTHS = (JANUARY,FEBRUARY,MARCH,APRIL,MAY,JUNE,JULY,
          AUGUST,SEPTEMBER,OCTOBER,NOVEMBER,
          DECEMBER)
```

we can declare some set variables as follows:

MONTHSOFINTEREST, SUMMERMONTHS: SET OF MONTHS

This declares that the variables **MONTHSOFINTEREST** and **SUMMER-MONTHS** will take values which are sets, and that each member of these sets will be of type **MONTHS**; the latter is called the *base type* of the sets. Alternatively, we may give the set type an identifier by means of a type definition:

SETOFMONTHS = SET OF MONTHS

and then declare the variables as follows:

MONTHSOFINTEREST, SUMMERMONTHS: SETOFMONTHS

The syntax of set types is summarized in Figure 19.1. **SET** and **OF** are both reserved words.

Figure 19.1. Syntax of Set Types

In order to allow an efficient implementation, Pascal imposes the restriction that the base type of every set type must be an *ordinal type*. Moreover, if the base type is **INTEGER** (or a subrange thereof), a Pascal compiler is free to impose limits on the smallest and largest values that can be used.

In Pascal we denote a set value using notation borrowed from mathematics, only replacing the curly brackets by square brackets. For example:

SUMMERMONTHS := [JUNE,JULY,AUGUST]

assigns a set value (with three members) to the set variable **SUMMERMONTHS**. This particular set constructor can be abbreviated. The statement:

SUMMERMONTHS := [JUNE . . AUGUST]

assigns to **SUMMERMONTHS** a set value whose members are **JUNE** to **AUGUST** *inclusive*.

The form $a \,.\,.\, b$ occurring in a set constructor represents all values between a and b (inclusive). If a is greater than b, $a \,.\,.\, b$ denotes no values whatsoever.

We are not restricted to using constants in a set constructor. For example, if I and N are INTEGER variables, we can test whether the value of I lies in the range N to N+6 inclusive as follows:

IF I IN [N . . N+6] THEN . . . . .

which is a neat alternative to the more usual:

IF (I >= N) AND (I <= N+6) THEN . . . . .

(However the set formulation is subject to the limitations stated above.)

The empty set is denoted by [ ]. The syntax of set constructors is summarized in Figure 19.2.

Figure 19.2. Syntax of Set Constructors

The last example has introduced the test for membership, denoted in Pascal by the operator IN. Here is another example of its use, showing how the conditional statement of Example 19.1 would be expressed in Pascal:

IF MONTH IN MONTHSOFINTEREST THEN
. . . .

IN has the same priority as the comparison operators, and like them IN yields a result which is TRUE or FALSE.

The comparison operators '=', '<>', '<=' and '>=' (but not '<' nor '>') may be used with set operands. Let A and B be sets. A = B yields TRUE if and only if A and B have exactly the same members; A <> B is defined in the opposite sense. A <= B means 'A is a subset of B'; A >= B means 'B is a subset of A'.

Set expressions may be composed using the following set operators:

* which with set operands denotes set intersection;
+   ,, ,, ,,   ,,   ,,   ,, union;
−   .,, ,, ,,   ,,   ,,   ,, difference.

A set value may be assigned to a set variable, and sets may be passed as parameters to subprograms. However, a function cannot have a set as its result.

Example 19.3

Assume the variable declaration:

HOLIDAYMONTHS, WETMONTHS, DRYMONTHS: SETOFMONTHS

The following statements illustrate some uses of set expressions:

```
HOLIDAYMONTHS := [JULY . . SEPTEMBER];
(* any month which is not wet is assumed to be dry . . . *)
DRYMONTHS := [JANUARY . . DECEMBER] − WETMONTHS;
IF HOLIDAYMONTHS <= DRYMONTHS THEN
   (* . . . i.e. every summer month is dry *)
   take beachwear on holiday
ELSE IF HOLIDAYMONTHS * DRYMONTHS <> [   ] THEN
   (* . . . i.e. some summer months are dry *)
   take an umbrella as well as beachwear
ELSE
   (* . . . i.e. every summer month is wet *)
   stay at home
```

Example 19.4

Suppose that the departments of an organization are numbered from 1 to 20, and that the organization maintains a file containing details of each of its employees, including his name and the number of the department in which he works. Occasionally it may be desired to create a file containing details only of employees working in a given subset of the departments. Let us write a program to do so, given as input data the numbers of the desired departments, one department number per line.

```
PROGRAM EXTRACT ( INPUT, MASTERFILE, EXTRACTEDFILE );
CONST
   MAXDEPTCODE = 20;
TYPE
   DEPTCODES       = 1 . . MAXDEPTCODE;
   SETOFDEPTCODES  = SET OF DEPTCODES;
   EMPLOYEERECORDS = RECORD
                        DEPT : DEPTCODES
                        (* . . . . . . . . . . . . . . . . . .
                        name and other details
                        . . . . . . . . . . . . . . . . . . *)
                     END;
```

```
VAR
  MASTERFILE, EXTRACTEDFILE : FILE OF EMPLOYEERECORDS;
  ONEEMPLOYEE : EMPLOYEERECORDS;
  DESIREDDEPTS : SETOFDEPTCODES;

PROCEDURE READDEPTS ( VAR DEPTSET: SETOFDEPTCODES );
  VAR
    DEPT: INTEGER;
  BEGIN
  DEPTSET := [  ];
  WHILE NOT EOF(INPUT) DO
    BEGIN
    READLN (DEPT);
    IF DEPT IN [1 .. MAXDEPTCODE] THEN
      (* add DEPT to DEPTSET*)
      DEPTSET := DEPTSET + [DEPT]
    END
  END (* READDEPTS *);

BEGIN (* EXTRACT *)
READDEPTS (DESIREDDEPTS);
RESET (MASTERFILE);
REWRITE (EXTRACTEDFILE);
WHILE NOT EOF(MASTERFILE) DO
  BEGIN
  READ (MASTERFILE, ONEEMPLOYEE);
  IF ONEEMPLOYEE.DEPT IN DESIREDDEPTS THEN
    WRITE (EXTRACTEDFILE, ONEEMPLOYEE)
  END
END (* EXTRACT *).
```

This example illustrates one method of building up a set: in procedure
READDEPTS, the set variable **DEPTSET** is initialized to the empty set,
then members (read from the input file in this case) are successively added
to **DEPTSET** using the set union operator '+'.

19.3 Type rules for sets

The IN operator

If the left operand of **IN** has type *A* and the right operand has type **SET OF**
B, then *A* and *B* must be the same type, or both must be subranges of the
same type, or one must be a subrange of the other.

Compatibility

Two set types are *compatible* if they have the same base type, or if the base types are subranges of the same type, or if one of the base types is a subrange of the other. Two set values may be combined using the set operators, or compared, only if they are of compatible types.

Assignment compatibility

A set expression may be assigned only to a set variable of a compatible type, and every member of the value of the set expression must be a value of the set variable's base type.

Exercises 19

19.1. A group of people have been numbered 1 to N. Write down declarations of variables OLDPEOPLE, MALES, SMOKERS and DRINK-ERS which can take values which represent sets of people in this group. Asssuming that appropriate values have been assigned to these variables, write set expressions whose values will be:

(a) the whole group;
(b) the set of non-smokers;
(c) the set of old smoking drinking males;
(d) the set of those who smoke or drink (or both);
(e) the set consisting of all the old people plus those males who smoke or drink.

Write a statement which outputs the message 'BAD INSURANCE RISK' if a given person PERSON is in set (e).

19.2. Write a function which determines whether a given colour occurs in your national flag or not, by testing for membership of a suitably chosen set of colours.

19.3. Write a program fragment which determines whether a given character is a letter, a digit, a blank, a punctuation, or other. Use sets rather than comparisons.

19.4. Modify program TRANSFERABLEVOTES of Section 18.3 to use set variables instead of the BOOLEAN arrays ALREADYCHOSEN and INCONTENTION. Thus, for example, the condition INCONTENTION [CONTENDER] is to be replaced by something like CONTENDER IN CONTENTION.

Programming exercises 19

19.5. In a strictly hierarchical organization every employee (except for the president) has a single immediate superior. Suppose a small hierarchical organization uses employee numbers in the range 1 to 40. A text file is supplied in which each line contains an employee's number, the number of his immediate superior (or 0 if the employee is the president himself), and other details of no concern here. Write a program which uses this file to produce output showing, for each employee, a list of all employees *subordinate* to him. (Hint: use an array of sets.)

20
Pointers and linked lists

{This chapter may be omitted on a first reading.}

20.1 Pointers

Recall program **SORTNAMES** of Section 15.2, in which a set of names was sorted by inserting each name, as it was read, at its correct position in an ordered list of names. This program served well enough to illustrate the basic idea of insertion sorting.

From the point of view of efficiency, however, insertion sorting using an array is rather unsatisfactory. One reason for this is that inserting an item at its correct position in the array forces us to shift several items along one position. As the list of items lengthens, the number of items to be shifted increases and the program runs more and more slowly. This is likely to be unacceptable if the number of items to be sorted is large (say 100 or more).

The shifting is necessary because the position of each entry in the array is implied by its index: the item in LIST[I+1] immediately follows the item in LIST[I]. So when we wish to insert a new item between these two items, we must place the new item in LIST[I+1], having shifted the item previously in LIST[I+1] into LIST[I+2], the item previously in LIST[I+2] into LIST[I+3], and so on.

A completely different way to represent the list is to make each entry in the list refer *explicitly* to the entry which follows it, as shown here by arrows:

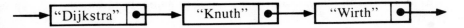

For obvious reasons, these references are called *pointers*. The advantage of using pointers becomes apparent when we update the list by inserting a new item, for example by inserting 'Hoare' between 'Dijkstra' and 'Knuth'. This is achieved simply by: (1) creating a new entry to contain the name 'Hoare' and a pointer to the 'Knuth' entry (which will be the new entry's follower); and (2) redirecting the pointer in the 'Dijkstra' entry to refer to the new entry. The other entries in the list need not be disturbed at all:

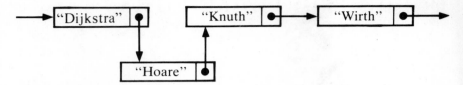

Similarly, it is easy to *delete* an item from such a list, if the problem requires this. To delete 'Knuth' from the last diagram, for example, we need only redirect the pointer in the 'Hoare' entry to refer to the 'Wirth' entry:

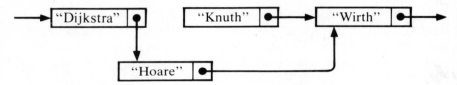

A list of records linked by pointers in this way is known as a *linked list*.

Pointers are data which can be assigned and compared. Thus lists and more complex data structures built up using pointers can be manipulated simply by redirecting the pointers, which is faster than copying bulky data structures.

20.2 Dynamic data structures

When we declare a variable V in the declarative part of a block, we obtain a store location named V:

We can access this store location by quoting its name. For example, if V is a record:

WITH V DO . . .

On the other hand, the store locations in the linked list of the previous section are anonymous. Such locations are accessed not by name, but by means of the pointers which refer to them. Thus, if P is a pointer which refers to a record, the form of the WITH statement must be:

WITH the record referenced by P DO . . .

A named location is created automatically on entry to the block where the variable is declared, and it is destroyed on exit from that block. Anonymous locations have the great advantage that they can be created and destroyed *at any time* while the program is running. Data structures composed of anonymous locations linked by pointers are called *dynamic data structures*, since they can expand and contract freely. A linked list is a simple example.

Thus we see a further advantage in representing a list of varying length as a linked structure instead of an array. A linked list can be made just as long as required. The size of an array, on the other hand, is chosen in advance by the programmer, so an arbitrary limit must be imposed on the number of items to be stored.

20.3 Pointers in Pascal

Suppose we wish to set up a linked list containing items of some type ITEMS. (How ITEMS is defined is irrelevant here.) The type definition:

ITEMPOINTERS = ↑ ITEMNODES

defines ITEMPOINTERS to be a *pointer type*: each value of type ITEM-POINTERS will be a pointer to an anonymous variable of type ITEM-NODES. Each such anonymous variable can represent one entry of the linked list and so must contain not only an item but also a pointer to the next entry in the linked list. Therefore ITEMNODES must be defined as a record type:

```
ITEMNODES = RECORD
            ITEM : ITEMS;
            NEXT : ITEMPOINTERS
          END
```

We can make the field ITEM contain one of the items, and the field NEXT contain a pointer to the following entry in the linked list.

Each entry in the list can thus be accessed from the previous entry, but how can the first entry be accessed? For the purpose we need a variable such as:

LISTHEAD: ITEMPOINTERS

in which we can store a pointer to the first entry. Finally, how can we indicate that the last entry in the list has no follower? For purposes such as this, Pascal provides the special pointer value NIL, which points to nothing at all. (**NIL** is a reserved word.) Thus we can mark the last entry in the linked list by storing **NIL** in its **NEXT** field:

We can represent an empty linked list (i.e. one with no entries at all) simply by storing **NIL** in **LISTHEAD** itself:

LISTHEAD [NIL]

Pointer values in Pascal may be assigned, and they may be compared using the comparison operators '=' and '<>'. (Two pointer values are equal if they are both **NIL** or if they point to the same anonymous variable.) Pointers may also be passed as parameters, and a function may have a pointer result.

If P and Q are pointer variables of some type ↑T, and suitable pointer values (i.e. not **NIL**) have been assigned to P and Q, the anonymous variables to which P and Q point can be accessed by P↑ and Q↑ respectively. For example, if T is a record type, we can write:

WITH P↑ DO . . .

P↑ and Q↑ are examples of *referenced variables*.

It is most important to distinguish between the pointer variable P, which contains a pointer value, and the referenced variable P↑, which denotes the anonymous variable to which P's value points (provided P's value is not **NIL**). The following situation illustrates the distinction, where x and y are values of type T:

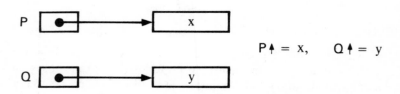

$$P\uparrow = x, \qquad Q\uparrow = y$$

(a) The assignment statement P:=Q assigns a *pointer value*, as a result of which P now points to the same anonymous variable as Q:

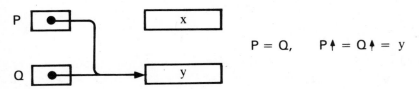

$$P = Q, \qquad P\uparrow = Q\uparrow = y$$

(b) On the other hand, the assignment statement P↑:=Q↑ assigns the value of the anonymous variable pointed to by Q to the anonymous variable pointed to by P. P still points to the same anonymous variable as before:

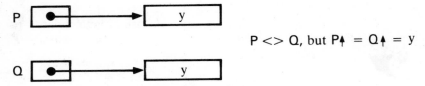

$$P <> Q, \text{ but } P\uparrow = Q\uparrow = y$$

(Both P↑:=Q and P:=Q↑ are meaningless and violate the type rules of Pascal.)

The syntax of pointer types is summarized in Figure 20.1, and that of referenced variables in Figure 20.2. Each pointer type must specify a *domain type*, which is the type of the anonymous variables to which the pointers will point. (The domain type will commonly, but not always, be a record type.)

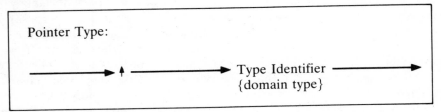

Figure 20.1. Syntax of Pointer Types

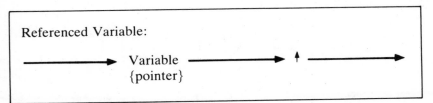

Figure 20.2. Syntax of Referenced Variables

The domain type must be given by a type *identifier*. This type identifier is an exception to the general rule that every identifier must be declared before it is used (see Example 20.3).

The variable declaration:

P : ↑ T

creates a store location for P only. P may subsequently contain a pointer to an anonymous variable of type T, or it may contain the value NIL. However, P's initial value is undefined, just like any other variable:

$$P \boxed{\quad ? \quad}$$

(This does *not* mean that P's value is NIL.)

Anonymous variables are created dynamically using the standard procedure NEW. For example, NEW(P) creates a new anonymous variable of type T and makes P point to it:

The value of this anonymous variable is initially undefined, but a value of type T may subsequently be assigned to it.

If an anonymous variable has outlived its usefulness, for example if we are deleting an entry from a linked list, we can use the standard procedure DISPOSE. DISPOSE(P) releases the storage space occupied by the anonymous variable P ↑ (so that it may later be used for some other purpose), and leaves P undefined. It must be emphasized that DISPOSE does nothing more than this; the redirection of pointers to delete an entry from a linked list (as described in Section 20.1) must be programmed explicitly.

(There are also special forms of NEW and DISPOSE applicable only to anonymous variables which are variant records. See Appendix 3.)

One last point: NEW(P) makes P point to an anonymous variable. There is no way in Pascal to make a pointer variable point to a named variable, so the following situation is *impossible*:

Nor can P ever point to an anonymous variable of any type other than P's domain type T.

20.4 Linked list processing

In this section we illustrate the use of pointers by examples of linked list manipulation.

Example 20.1

Assume the definitions of the types ITEMPOINTERS and ITEMNODES from the previous section. Let us write a function which, given as a parameter a pointer LISTHEAD to the first entry of a linked list of items, returns the number of items in the linked list.

This problem is a simple illustration of serial processing of a linked list. We need a local pointer variable, say REF, which will be made to point to each entry of the linked list in turn. REF will be initialized to the value of LISTHEAD. The serial processing can be performed by a loop which is terminated when REF is NIL. A WHILE loop will allow for an empty list.

```
FUNCTION LISTLENGTH ( LISTHEAD: ITEMPOINTERS ): INTEGER;
VAR
   ITEMCOUNT: INTEGER;
   REF: ITEMPOINTERS;
BEGIN
ITEMCOUNT := 0;
REF := LISTHEAD;
WHILE REF <> NIL DO
   BEGIN
   ITEMCOUNT := ITEMCOUNT+1;
   REF := REF ↑ .NEXT
   END;
LISTLENGTH := ITEMCOUNT
END (*LISTLENGTH*)
```

Within the body of the loop, we can be sure that the value of REF is not NIL, so REF points to a record of type ITEMNODES. Therefore REF ↑ denotes the record itself, and REF ↑ .NEXT denotes the field NEXT of this record. Thus the statement REF:=REF ↑ .NEXT advances the pointer REF from one list entry to the next.

Example 20.2

Assume the definitions of the types ITEMPOINTERS and ITEMNODES from the previous section. Let us write a procedure which, given as parameters an item TARGET and a pointer LISTHEAD to the first entry of a linked list of items, returns in a variable parameter a pointer to the entry containing TARGET (or NIL if there is no such entry in the linked list). We do not assume that the items in the list are in any particular order.

This problem illustrates linear search in a linked list. (Compare Example 11.7.)

```
PROCEDURE SEARCHLIST (TARGET: ITEMS;
                      LISTHEAD: ITEMPOINTERS;
                      VAR TARGETLOC: ITEMPOINTERS);
   VAR
      REF: ITEMPOINTERS;
      LOCATED: BOOLEAN;
   BEGIN
   REF := LISTHEAD;
   LOCATED := FALSE;
   WHILE NOT LOCATED AND (REF <> NIL) DO
      WITH REF ↑ DO
         IF ITEM = TARGET THEN
            LOCATED: = TRUE
         ELSE
            REF := NEXT;
   TARGETLOC := REF (* could be NIL *)
   END (*SEARCHLIST*)
```

Within the body of the loop we know that the value of REF is not NIL, so REF points to a record of type ITEMNODES. The body of the loop processes this record. The WITH clause 'WITH REF ↑ DO' allows us to abbreviate REF ↑ .ITEM to ITEM and REF ↑ .NEXT to NEXT.

Procedure SEARCHLIST could be recast as a pointer-valued function; see Exercises 20.

Example 20.3

Let us modify program SORTNAMES of Section 15.2 to use a linked list instead of an array.

```
PROGRAM SORTNAMES ( INPUT, OUTPUT );

CONST
   NAMELENGTH = 20;

TYPE
   NAMES = PACKED ARRAY [1 .. NAMELENGTH] OF CHAR;
```

```
NAMEPOINTERS = ↑ NAMENODES;
NAMENODES = RECORD
                    NAME : NAMES;
                    NEXT : NAMEPOINTERS
            END;

VAR
  LISTHEAD : NAMEPOINTERS;
  CURRENTNAME : NAMES;


PROCEDURE READNAME ( VAR NAME: NAMES );
  ...................
  ................... (* as in Section 15.2 *)
  ...................

PROCEDURE WRITEALLNAMES;
  VAR
    REF: NAMEPOINTERS;
  BEGIN
  REF := LISTHEAD;
  WHILE REF <> NIL DO
    WITH REF ↑ DO
      BEGIN
      WRITELN (NAME);
      REF := NEXT
      END
  END (*WRITEALLNAMES*);


PROCEDURE MAKELISTEMPTY;
  BEGIN
  LISTHEAD : = NIL
  END (*MAKELISTEMPTY*);


PROCEDURE INSERTNAME ( NEWNAME: NAMES );
  VAR
    REF, REFPREVIOUS, NEWREF: NAMEPOINTERS;
    LOCATED                 : BOOLEAN;
  BEGIN
  (* find the position where the new entry will be inserted *)
  REF := LISTHEAD;
  LOCATED := FALSE;
```

```
WHILE NOT LOCATED AND (REF <> NIL) DO
  WITH REF ↑ DO
    IF NEWNAME <= NAME THEN
      LOCATED := TRUE
    ELSE
      BEGIN
        REFPREVIOUS := REF;
        REF := NEXT
      END;
(* create a new entry for NEWNAME *)
NEW (NEWREF);
NEWREF ↑ .NAME := NEWNAME;
NEWREF ↑ .NEXT := REF;
(* place the new entry in position *)
IF REF = LISTHEAD THEN
  LISTHEAD := NEWREF
ELSE
  REFPREVIOUS ↑ .NEXT := NEWREF
END (*INSERTNAME*);


BEGIN (*SORTNAMES*)
MAKELISTEMPTY;
WHILE NOT EOF(INPUT) DO
  BEGIN
  READNAME (CURRENTNAME);
  INSERTNAME (CURRENTNAME)
  END;
WRITEALLNAMES
END (*SORTNAMES*) .
```

The main program's statement part is unchanged, a direct consequence of the judicious choice of procedures and parameters in Section 15.2. The following changes have been made to the program.

(a) The global variables COUNT and LIST representing the list of names have been replaced by the single global variable LISTHEAD, a pointer to the first entry in the list.
(b) Procedure WRITEALLNAMES has been rewritten to traverse the linked list rather than an array.
(c) Procedure MAKELISTEMPTY now initializes LISTHEAD to NIL.
(d) Procedure INSERTNAME has also been rewritten. The test to ensure that the list is not already full is no longer necessary. The refinement of 'find the position . . .' leaves REF pointing to the entry which will *follow* the new entry. Since the pointer field NEXT in the previous

entry must be redirected when the new entry is inserted (except in the case where the new entry is inserted at the front of the linked list), the procedure uses an additional pointer variable, **REFPREVIOUS**, to point to the previous entry in the linked list. The step 'shift up the entries . . .' is no longer needed, and in its place comes 'create a new entry for **NEWNAME**'. The statement **NEW(NEWREF)** creates a new entry to which **NEWREF** is made to point. The two statements following it store, in the fields of this entry, **NEWNAME** and a pointer to the entry which will follow it in the extended list. The refinement of 'place the new entry in position' redirects the **NEXT** field of the previous entry to point to the new entry, unless the new entry is to be inserted at the front of the list, in which case **LISTHEAD** itself is redirected to point to the new entry.

Convince yourself of the correctness of **INSERTNAME** by working through it by hand, choosing suitable test cases as in Section 15.2.

Example 20.4

Assume the definitions of the types **ITEMPOINTERS** and **ITEMNODES** from the previous section. Let us write a procedure which deletes a given item **OLDITEM** from a given linked list pointed to by a parameter **LISTHEAD**.

The procedure must first locate the list entry which contains the item to be deleted. This can be done by a linear search similar to Example 20.2. Since the pointer field **NEXT** of the *previous* entry must be redirected to bypass the deleted entry, however, we need an additional pointer variable, **REFPREVIOUS**, which points to the entry preceding **REF**. Also we must be careful to cater for the case where the entry to be deleted is the *first* in the linked list, for then it is **LISTHEAD** itself which must be redirected. Thus **LISTHEAD** must be a *variable* parameter.

```
PROCEDURE DELETEITEM ( OLDITEM: ITEMS;
                       VAR LISTHEAD: ITEMPOINTERS);
    VAR
      REF, REFPREVIOUS: ITEMPOINTERS;
      LOCATED: BOOLEAN;
    BEGIN
    (* locate the entry to be deleted *)
    REF := LISTHEAD;
    LOCATED := FALSE;
    WHILE NOT LOCATED AND (REF <> NIL) DO
        WITH REF ↑ DO
          IF ITEM = TARGET THEN
            LOCATED := TRUE
```

```
          ELSE
            BEGIN
            REFPREVIOUS := REF;
            REF := NEXT
            END;
      IF LOCATED THEN
        BEGIN
        IF REF = LISTHEAD THEN
          (* deleting first entry — redirect LISTHEAD *)
          LISTHEAD := REF ↑ .NEXT
        ELSE
          (* redirect NEXT field of previous entry *)
          REFPREVIOUS ↑ .NEXT := REF ↑ .NEXT;
        DISPOSE (REF)
        END;
      END (*DELETEITEM*)
```

DISPOSE must always be used with great care. For example, the statements in DELETEITEM which redirect a pointer to bypass the deleted entry do so by copying the pointer value REF ↑ .NEXT into LISTHEAD or into the NEXT field of the previous entry. It would be a serious error to obey DISPOSE(REF) *before* copying REF ↑ .NEXT, since DISPOSE(REF) makes the record REF ↑ , and therefore its field REF ↑ .NEXT, inaccessible.

Procedure DELETEITEM takes no action at all if no item in the linked list equals OLDITEM. As an exercise, modify the procedure to return, through a BOOLEAN parameter, an indication of whether an entry was deleted or not.

20.5 Type rules for pointers

Assignment compatibility

A pointer value may be assigned to a pointer variable of the same type. NIL may be assigned to any pointer variable.

Comparisons

Pointer values of the same type may be compared with one another or with NIL.

Exercises 20

20.1. (a) Write type definitions describing a linked list whose entries contain integers. (b) Write a function which, given a pointer to the first

entry of such a linked list, returns the sum of the integers stored in the list.
20.2. What happens if procedure **SEARCHLIST** (or procedure **DE-LETEITEM**) is supplied with a list containing duplicate items?
20.3. Write a program which reads a line of characters and writes them in reverse order. Use a linked list, and insert each character as it is read at the *head* of the list.
20.4. Program **SORTNAMES** (Example 20.3) can be improved further if we can avoid searching the whole list to decide where to insert the new name. One way to do this is to have 26 linked lists, one for each initial letter. It becomes necessary to have an *array* of list heads, one for each linked list. Modify the program along these lines.
20.5. Modify Example 16.9 so that the directory is represented by a linked list rather than by an array.

Programming exercises 20

20.6. Write a program which simulates a queue of customers at an office counter or supermarket checkout. A customer on arrival joins the end of the queue. The customer at the front of the queue is served first and then departs.

The times of customers' arrivals and departures are supplied as input data to the simulation program. An arrival is indicated by a line of input data containing the letter 'A' and the time of day (hours, minutes, seconds). A departure is indicated by a line of input data containing the letter 'D' and the time of day. Assume that the input data is ordered by time of day.

The program is to output a histogram showing the number of customers in the queue at intervals of one minute. It is also to compute the mean and standard deviation of the time spent by customers in the queue. (See Exercises 11 for a definition of standard deviation.)

(Hint: represent the queue by a linked list containing one entry for each customer currently in the queue. When a customer arrives, add an entry containing the time of arrival to the end of the list. When a customer departs, remove an entry from the head of the list.)

20.7*. Write a program which maintains a stock inventory held in the form of a linked list. The list must consist of one entry for each different component in stock, each entry containing the component number, the number of units in stock, and the reorder level for that component. The inventory is initially empty. Each line of input specifies an operation on the inventory, the operation being identified by the first character in the line:

Code	Operation requested	Additional data on the same line
'N'	New component	Component number, initial number of units in stock, reorder level.

'D'	Delete component	Component number.
'A'	Add to stock	Component number, number of units added.
'R'	Remove from stock	Component number, number of units removed.
'P'	Print inventory	None.

Invalid and impossible operations should give rise to suitable error messages, and operation 'R' should give rise to a warning message if the number of units in stock falls below the reorder level.

20.8. Modify your answer to exercise 20.7 so that operation 'P' lists the contents of the inventory in order of component number. (The best way to do this is to keep the list ordered at all times, by suitable implementation of operation 'N'.)

21
Advanced use of subprograms

{This chapter may be omitted on a first reading.}

21.1 Recursive subprograms

Any subprogram (function or procedure) may invoke other subprograms. Programmers exploit this possibility to build hierarchical programs, in which the main program invokes subprograms *A1, A2, A3*, . . . to perform subsidiary tasks; these subprograms in turn invoke subprograms *B1, B2, B3*, . . . to perform still simpler tasks; and so on down to any desired depth.

This is by no means the only way of exploiting subprograms. In particular, a subprogram may invoke itself! Such a subprogram is said to be *recursive*. This idea seems paradoxical at first sight, yet recursive subprograms allow very elegant solutions to a certain class of programming problems. The best way to understand this idea is to study some examples.

Example 21.1

Consider the expression A^N, where A and N are integers, N being positive. Let us write this expression, in functional notation, as *power (A,N)*. This function has the value:

$$power(A,N) = A \times A \times \ldots \times A \quad (N-1 \text{ multiplications})$$

Mathematicians avoid this awkward notation by resorting to a different form of definition:

$$power(A,N) = \begin{cases} A & \text{if } N=1 \\ A \times power(A,N-1) & \text{if } N>1 \end{cases}$$

i.e. the function is defined in terms of itself! In fact, the function is defined recursively.

The recursive definition can be transcribed directly into a Pascal function declaration:

```
FUNCTION POWER ( A : INTEGER;
                 N : POSITIVEINTEGER ): INTEGER;
   BEGIN
   IF N = 1 THEN
      POWER := A
   ELSE
      POWER := A * POWER(A,N−1)
   END (*POWER*)
```

where POSITIVEINTEGER = 1 . .MAXINT.

How does this recursive function ever succeed in yielding a result? The answer is that, every time the function invokes itself, its second actual parameter (N−1) is one less than before (N). So, although the function repeatedly invokes itself, it will eventually invoke itself with 1 as its second actual parameter, whereupon the function yields a result directly.

Let us trace the action of the function when it is invoked to evaluate POWER(4,3); this should yield 4×4×4, i.e. 64.

To evaluate POWER(4,3), we obey the statement part of POWER with the value parameters A and N set to 4 and 3 respectively. We can see that the function result will be evaluated as 4*POWER(4,2).

To evaluate POWER(4,2), we obey the statement part of POWER with the value parameters A and N set to 4 and 2 respectively. We can see that the function result will be evaluated as 4*POWER(4,1).

To evaluate POWER(4,1), we obey the statement part of POWER with the value parameters A and N set to 4 and 1 respectively. We can see that the function result will be yielded directly as 4.

Thus 4*POWER(4,1) yields 4*4, i.e. 16.

Thus 4*POWER(4,2) yields 4*16, i.e. 64.

Of course, the function POWER can easily be programmed without using recursion; compare Example 6.1.

Many computations, like Example 21.1, can be programmed either recursively or using a loop. Programmers usually prefer to avoid recursion when they have a choice, because a recursive subprogram tends to use up more space (a complete set of store locations must be allocated every time it invokes itself) and more time (through overheads incurred on entering and leaving the subprogram) than an equivalent non-recursive subprogram.

Nevertheless, there are certain computations which are 'naturally' recursive, in the sense that they are awkward to program without recursion. The following example illustrates such a problem.

Example 21.2

Finding a path out of a maze is a popular puzzle. Let us assume that the maze is a rectangular enclosure divided into squares, each square being either covered by hedge or not. The perimeter squares are all hedge-covered except for one or more exits. You are released somewhere inside the maze, and you have to find your way to an exit. You may move from square to square to any direction (except diagonally), but you cannot cross a hedge.

We could represent the maze in a computer by a two-dimensional character array, for example:

```
H H H H H H H H H H H H H
H . . H H H . . . . H H
H H . . . H . H H H . H
H . . H . H . H . . . H
H H H . . . . H H H H H
H . . . H H H . . . . H
H . H . . . . . H H . H
H H H H H H H H H H . H
```

where 'H' represents hedge and '.' represents walkway

Here is an outline of a computer solution to this problem:

```
(* find a path from square S to an exit *)
IF square S is on the perimeter THEN
    exit from the maze
ELSE
    BEGIN
    try heading East;
    IF no exit found yet THEN
        try heading South;
    IF no exit found yet THEN
        try heading West;
    IF no exit found yet THEN
        try heading North
    END
```

Let us further refine 'try heading East' (the others will be analogous):

```
(* try heading East *)
IF S's eastern neighbouring square is walkway THEN
    find a path from S's eastern neighbouring square to an exit
```

But 'find a path from S's eastern neighbouring square to an exit' is analogous to the original problem 'find a path from square S to an exit'! So let us introduce a procedure, **SEEKEXITFROM**, with the coordinates of a square as its parameters, whose task is to find a path from that square to an exit. This procedure will be recursive.

The following is a complete solution to the problem for a 8-by-12 maze (as illustrated above), omitting only the details of reading and writing a picture of the maze. The coordinates of the starting square are read as input data.

```
PROGRAM MAZE ( INPUT, OUTPUT );

CONST
   NORTHLIMIT = 1; SOUTHLIMIT = 8;
   WESTLIMIT  = 1; EASTLIMIT   = 12;
   WALKWAY   = '.';
   HEDGE     = 'H';
   FOOTSTEP  = 'o';
   PATHMARK  = '*';

TYPE
   LATITUDES   = NORTHLIMIT . . SOUTHLIMIT;
   LONGITUDES = WESTLIMIT . . EASTLIMIT;
   SQUARES    = CHAR;

VAR
   MAZE : ARRAY [LATITUDES, LONGITUDES] OF SQUARES;
   STARTLATITUDE   : LATITUDES;
   STARTLONGITUDE: LONGITUDES;
   EXITFOUND       : BOOLEAN;

PROCEDURE SEEKEXITFROM ( LAT:   LATITUDES;
                         LONG: LONGITUDES );
   (* find a path from square (LAT,LONG) to the exit *)
   BEGIN
   IF (LAT=NORTHLIMIT) OR (LAT=SOUTHLIMIT) OR
      (LONG=WESTLIMIT) OR (LONG=EASTLIMIT) THEN
         (* . . . (LAT,LONG) is on the perimeter *)
      EXITFOUND := TRUE
   ELSE
      BEGIN
      MAZE[LAT,LONG] := FOOTSTEP;
      (* try heading East *)
      IF MAZE[LAT,LONG+1] = WALKWAY THEN
         SEEKEXITFROM (LAT, LONG+1);
      IF NOT EXITFOUND THEN
         (* try heading South *)
         IF MAZE[LAT +1,LONG] = WALKWAY THEN
            SEEKEXITFROM (LAT+1, LONG);
```

```
    IF NOT EXITFOUND THEN
      (* try heading West *)
      IF MAZE[LAT,LONG−1] = WALKWAY THEN
        SEEKEXITFROM (LAT, LONG−1);
    IF NOT EXITFOUND THEN
      (* try heading North *)
      IF MAZE[LAT−1,LONG] = WALKWAY THEN
        SEEKEXITFROM (LAT−1, LONG)
    END;
  IF EXITFOUND THEN
    MAZE[LAT,LONG] := PATHMARK
  END (*SEEKEXITFROM*);

BEGIN (*MAZE*)
read MAZE;
READ (STARTLATITUDE, STARTLONGITUDE);
EXITFOUND := FALSE;
SEEKEXITFROM (STARTLATITUDE, STARTLONGITUDE);
write MAZE;
IF NOT EXITFOUND THEN
  WRITELN ('NO WAY OUT OF MAZE')
END (*MAZE*).
```

The procedure contains some necessary additional details. The statement MAZE[LAT,LONG]:=FOOTSTEP marks each square of the maze as it is visited; this is essential to ensure that we do not go round the maze in circles! The statement MAZE[LAT,LONG]:=PATHMARK marks each square which lies on the path from the entrance to the exit. Thus the final picture of the maze will show this path, and also any blind alleys which were followed during the search. Here is the output obtained when the starting square is (2,2):

```
H H H H H H H H H H H H
H * * H H H o o o o H H
H H * * * H o H H H . H
H . . H * H o H . . . H
H H H * * o o H H H H H
H . . * H H H * * * * H
H . H * * * * * H H * H
H H H H H H H H H H * H
```

where '*' marks a step on the exit path and 'o' marks a step up a blind alley

If the starting square is (3,11), on the other hand, the program will report that no exit path exists.

From these examples we may extrapolate to the following general principles concerning recursive subprograms:

(a) A recursive subprogram must, in at least one degenerate case, perform its task without invoking itself recursively. In Example 21.1, the degenerate case is N=1. In Example 21.2, one degenerate case is when the current square *is* an exit square; in addition, the procedure will not invoke itself recursively when every neighbouring square either is hedge-covered or has already been visited.

(b) A recursive subprogram must invoke itself only in such a way as to approach one of the degenerate cases mentioned in (a). In Example 21.1, the function invokes itself with a second parameter (N) which is positive but smaller than before, i.e. it has moved closer to the case N=1. In Example 21.2, every entry to the procedure marks the current square in such a way that it will not be visited again.

21.2 Functional parameters and procedural parameters

We have already seen that a subprogram may invoke another subprogram. Now, just as a *value parameter* allows a subprogram to work with different given values on different occasions, and just as a *variable parameter* allows a subprogram to work with different variables on different occasions, sometimes we wish to allow a subprogram to invoke different functions or different procedures on different occasions. Pascal makes this possible by providing two additional parameter mechanisms, *functional parameters* and *procedural parameters*.

We illustrate this idea with just one example.

Example 21.3

Let us write a procedure which approximately evaluates the integral of $F(x)$ between given limits A and B, where F is assumed to be a continuous finite real function with a single real parameter.

We can visualize this integral as the area bounded by the curve $y=F(x)$ and the straight lines $y=0$, $x=A$ and $x=B$.

A simple method of approximating the integral is to choose a suitable positive integer N and divide the interval $[A,B]$ into N equal intervals, each of width $W = (B-A)/N$, as illustrated. This divides the area of interest into strips which resemble right-angled trapezia, and it is easy to derive the following approximate formula for the area under the curve:

$$W\ (\ F(A)/2 + F(A+W) + F(A+2W) +\ .\ .\ .\ .\ .\ + F(B)/2\ )$$

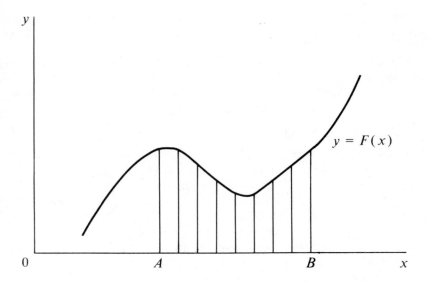

This is called the *trapezoidal rule*.

Since our procedure must deal with *any* given function *F*, *F* will be a functional parameter.

```
PROCEDURE INTEGRATE ( FUNCTION F (X:REAL) : REAL;
                      A, B : REAL;
                      VAR INTEGRAL : REAL          );
  (* evaluates approximately the integral of F(x)
     between limits A and B, using the trapezoidal
     rule with 8 intervals *)
  CONST
    N = 8;
  VAR
    W, SUM: REAL;
    I : 1 .. N;
  BEGIN
  W := (B−A)/N;
  SUM := (F(A)+F(B))/2;
  FOR I := 1 TO N−1 DO
    SUM := SUM + F(A+I*W);
  INTEGRAL := W * SUM
  END (*INTEGRATE*)
```

'FUNCTION F (X:REAL): REAL' is a *functional parameter section*. This specifies that F is a functional parameter, that its result type is **REAL**, and that it has itself a single **REAL** value parameter. (The identifier X here has no significance.) Inside the statement part of INTEGRATE, F is invoked just like an ordinary function, by function designators such as F(A) and F(A+I*W).

When we invoke INTEGRATE by a procedure statement, the actual parameter corresponding to F must also be a function with a REAL result and a single REAL value parameter. For example, to integrate TAN(x) between limits 0 and PI/4, we could use the procedure statement:

INTEGRATE (TAN, 0, PI/4, AREA)

assuming that the function TAN has been declared as in Example 13.1. When this procedure statement is obeyed, the functional parameter F stands for the function TAN. Thus the function designator F(A) actually results in the evaluation of TAN(A); and the function designator F(A+I*W) actually results in the evaluation of TAN(A+I*W).

Functional and procedural parameter sections are similar in syntax to function and procedure headings; see Appendix 1.9.

Every actual parameter corresponding to a functional parameter F must be a function identifier, and that function's heading must be similar to the functional parameter section which specifies F. The only possible variation is in the identifiers chosen for the functional parameter's own formal parameters. (These identifiers may be chosen freely.) A similar rule applies to each actual parameter corresponding to a procedural parameter.

Exercises 21

21.1. Modify function POWER (Example 21.2) to allow its parameter B to be 0, returning the result 1 in that case.

21.2. The factorial function $N!$ may be defined recursively:

$$N! = \begin{cases} 1 & \text{if } N <= 1 \\ N * (N-1)! & \text{if } N > 1 \end{cases}$$

(a) Transcribe this definition into a recursive function. (b) Write an alternative non-recursive version of this function.

21.3. (a) Write a function which returns the number of TRUE values of a given BOOLEAN function F (which takes a single INTEGER parameter), between given limits LOW amd HIGH inclusive. (b) Write a statement which invokes your function to compute the number of prime numbers between 2 and M inclusive. Use the prime-number function of Exercise 13.6 as an actual parameter.

21.4*. Write a procedure which traverses a given linked list of names (defined as in Example 20.3) and applies a procedure P to each entry of the linked list. P is to be a procedural parameter specified by the procedural parameter section:

PROCEDURE P (ENTRYREF:NAMEPOINTERS)

Modify procedure WRITEALLNAMES of Example 20.3 to make use of your traversal procedure.

Programming exercises 21

21.5*. If you have completed Exercise 15.6, modify the procedure which reads the molecular formula so that it accepts parentheses within the formula, such as (Al2(SO4)3). (Hint: on detecting an inner '(', the procedure should invoke itself recursively to read the inner group.)

21.6*. 'The Towers of Hanoi' is a game played with three poles and a set of discs, all differently sized, which fit on to the poles. Initially all the discs are on pole 1, as shown below; the object of the game is to move all the discs on to pole 2. Only one disc may be moved at a time, and no disc may ever be placed above a smaller disc.

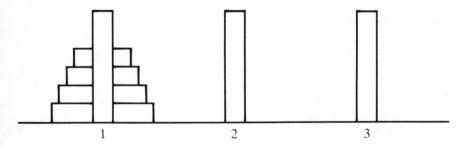

Consider the more general problem of moving N discs from pole SOURCE to pole DESTINATION, using pole SPARE as a spare. This problem can be solved recursively by the following strategy:

(1) move (N−1) discs from pole SOURCE to pole SPARE, using pole DESTINATION as a spare;
(2) move a single disc from pole SOURCE to pole DESTINATION;
(3) move (N−1) discs from pole SPARE to pole DESTINATION, using pole SOURCE as a spare.

Transcribe this strategy into a recursive procedure which writes a suitable message each time a single disc is moved. Write a program which uses your procedure to solve the Towers of Hanoi problem with four discs.

22
The GOTO statement

{This chapter may be omitted on a first reading.}

22.1 Exceptional flow of control

The great majority of programming problems—certainly those which you are likely to encounter at this stage—can be solved satisfactorily without resorting to control structures other than sequencing, selection (**IF** or **CASE**), repetition (**WHILE**, **REPEAT** or **FOR**), and subprograms. Nevertheless, in certain exceptional circumstances we find that the desired flow of control is too irregular to be naturally expressed using only nested selective and repetitive statements.

Such a situation might arise in a program whose input data is somewhat complicated. A high-quality program will check its data as it reads it, and issue appropriate warning messages if it detects any errors. This helps the user to correct any such errors before running the program again. The problem is, how should the program continue after detecting and reporting an error? Some errors are so severe that the program's only recourse is to abandon the task which it is currently performing, perhaps even to halt completely. The cleanest solution in such circumstances might be a direct jump out of the piece of program which detects the error. For such purposes Pascal provides the *GOTO statement*.

22.2 GOTO statements and labels in Pascal

We shall introduce the GOTO statement by an example illustrating the kind of situation described above.

Example 22.1

The following procedure reads an $N \times N$ matrix of non-negative integers and stores it in an array of type:

    MATRIX = ARRAY [1 . . N, 1 . . N] OF 0 . . MAXINT

where N is an appropriately defined constant. If the input data is correct, it should contain exactly N^2 non-negative integers. To guard against the possibility of the input data being incomplete (or of there being too much input data), the matrix elements are followed by a negative endmarker. The procedure checks every datum and, if it detects the endmarker prematurely, it writes a warning message and returns immediately. (Compare procedure READMATRIX of Example 15.1, which performed no error checking.)

```
PROCEDURE READMATRIX ( VAR M : MATRIX );
   LABEL 9;
   VAR
     DATUM : INTEGER;
     I, J: 1 . . N;
   BEGIN
   FOR I := 1 TO N DO
     FOR J := 1 TO N DO
       BEGIN
       READ (DATUM); (* which should not be the endmarker *)
       IF DATUM >= 0 THEN
         M[I,J] := DATUM
       ELSE
         BEGIN
         WRITELN ('TOO FEW MATRIX ELEMENTS');
         GOTO 9 (* stop reading immediately *)
         END
       END;
   READ (DATUM); (* which should be the endmarker *)
   IF DATUM >= 0 THEN
     WRITELN ('TOO MANY MATRIX ELEMENTS');
   9:
   END (*READMATRIX*)
```

There are three aspects to the use of a GOTO statement, which are illustrated by Example 22.1.

(a) A *label declaration* such as LABEL 9 declares that 9 is to be used as a *statement label*, attached to some statement within the same block.

(b) A prefix such as '9:' attaches the statement label 9 to the statement which follows. In Example 22.1, the statement label 9 is attached to a dummy statement preceding the final END of the procedure's statement part.

(c) The effect of a statement such as GOTO 9 is to pass control directly to the statement whose statement label is 9, thereby abandoning whatever was being done before the GOTO statement was obeyed. In example 22.1, the nett effect of **GOTO 9** is to jump out of the nested FOR loops to the end of the procedure's statement part (thus completing the execution of the procedure).

Statement labels look like unsigned integer numbers (with at most 4 digits), but they have no inherent significance. Thus the statement label **9** in Example 22.1 could be consistently replaced by **0** or **1** or **9999** without affecting the meaning of the procedure.

All labels attached to statements in a block must be declared in a label declaration which must be placed at the very beginning of that block (before any other definitions or declarations). No statement label may be attached to more than one statement in the same block (otherwise a GOTO statement referring to the duplicated label would be ambiguous).

Any statement may be labelled, but there are restrictions on the positioning of GOTO statements referring to a given statement label.

(a) No GOTO statement may cause a jump *into* a structured statement (that is a compound, IF, CASE, WHILE, REPEAT, FOR or WITH statement), from outside. For example, the following is illegal:

```
FOR . . . DO
   BEGIN
    . . . . .
   1: . . . . .
    . . . . .
   END;
 . . . . .
GOTO 1
```

Such a jump would have consequences difficult to predict!
(b) No GOTO statement may cause a jump *into* a subprogram from outside. The reasoning behind this is similar to (a).
(c) A GOTO statement may jump *out of* a subprogram, but only to the outermost statement level of an enclosing block. This possibility is illustrated by Example 22.2.

Example 22.2

If the procedure of Example 22.1 were substituted into program **MATRIX-PRODUCT**(b) of Example 15.1, the modified program would print a warning message on detecting an error in its input data, but then it would continue its computation as if nothing were wrong. Its results would probably be useless.

The procedure would be more useful if it had a second, **BOOLEAN**, variable parameter to indicate whether its input data was found to be valid or not. The main program could then use the value returned through this parameter to decide whether to continue the computation. (As an exercise, modify procedure READMATRIX, and the main program of MATRIX-PRODUCT(b), along these lines.)

An alternative solution is to make procedure READMATRIX halt the execution of the program when it detects an input error, instead of just abandoning its own task. This requires the procedure to contain GOTO statements which jump to a label at the end of the main program.

```
PROGRAM MATRIXPRODUCT ( INPUT, OUTPUT );

LABEL 999;   (* end of program label *)

CONST
  N = 10;   (* say *)
TYPE
  MATRIX = ARRAY [1 . . N, 1 . . N] OF 0 . . MAXINT;
VAR
  A, B, P: MATRIX;

PROCEDURE READMATRIX ( VAR M : MATRIX );
  VAR
    DATUM : INTEGER;
    I, J: 1 . . N;
  BEGIN
  FOR I := 1 TO N DO
    FOR J := 1 TO N DO
      BEGIN
      READ (DATUM);   (* which should not be the endmarker *)
      IF DATUM >= 0 THEN
        M[I,J] := DATUM
      ELSE
        BEGIN
        WRITELN ('TOO FEW MATRIX ELEMENTS');
        GOTO 999   (* halt the program immediately *)
        END
      END;
  READ (DATUM);   (* which should be the endmarker *)
  IF DATUM >= 0 THEN
    BEGIN
    WRITELN ('TOO MANY MATRIX ELEMENTS');
    GOTO 999   (* halt the program immediately *)
    END
  END (*READMATRIX*);
```

```
PROCEDURE WRITEMATRIX ( M : MATRIX );
..........
.......... (* as in Example 15.1 *)
..........

PROCEDURE MULTIPLYMATRICES (M1, M2 : MATRIX;
                                VAR PRODUCT : MATRIX);

..........
.......... (* as in Example 15.1 *)
..........

BEGIN (*MATRIXPRODUCT*)
READMATRIX (A);
READMATRIX (B);
MULTIPLYMATRICES (A, B, P);
WRITEMATRIX (P);
999:
END (*MATRIXPRODUCT*).
```

The statement label **999** is attached to a dummy statement preceding the END of the main program's statement part. This statement label must therefore be declared in a label declaration in the main program's declaration part.

The syntax of label declarations, GOTO statements and statement labels can be found in Appendices 1.2, 1.3 and 1.10 respectively. LABEL and GOTO are both reserved words.

22.3 Use and abuse of GOTO statements

It cannot be emphasized too strongly that GOTO statements should be used only when necessary. Overuse of GOTO statements makes a program difficult to understand. Compare the program fragments in each of the following examples.

Example 22.3

```
IF X > Y THEN GOTO 1;        IF X <= Y THEN
MAX := Y;                        MAX := Y
GOTO 2;                      ELSE
1: MAX := X;                     MAX := X;
2: WRITE (MAX)               WRITE (MAX)
```

Example 22.4

```
1: IF R < N THEN GOTO 2;        WHILE R >= N DO
   R := R−N;                        R := R−N;
   GOTO 1;                       WRITE (R)
2: WRITE (R)
```

Each program fragment has the same effect as the one beside it. But which are the easier to understand?

The effect of any selective or repetitive statement can be obtained using only IF statements and GOTO statements. That is of little interest, however, since the selective and repetitive statements are much more convenient to use and much more readable. The reason for this is that their appearance alone tells the reader what he wants to know about the flow of control. Thus the word IF (or CASE) signals a selective control structure, and the word WHILE (or REPEAT or FOR) signals a repetitive control structure. By way of comparison, consider the GOTO statements used in Examples 22.3 and 22.4. We cannot deduce the effect on the flow of control of a statement like GOTO 1 from its appearance alone. First of all we must find the location of the statement label 1. (If that seems easy in these short program fragments, imagine what it would be like in a program extending over several pages!) It turns out that the statements GOTO 1 have markedly different effects in the two examples. In Example 22.3, GOTO 1 is a jump *forwards*, which causes statements to be skipped. In Example 22.4, GOTO 1 is a jump *backwards*, which causes statements to be repeated.

Now, the procedure of Example 22.1 *could* be re-written without any GOTO statement, using nested WHILE statements rather than FOR statements, but it turns out to be awkward to do it this way, and the resulting procedure is no easier to understand. (Try it yourself as an exercise.)

The overriding criterion in this and all matters of programming style is whether a program can easily be understood by its author and by other readers. Nearly always this means that GOTO statements should be avoided, but in exceptional circumstances they are acceptable in order to avoid awkwardness of expression. These circumstances usually involve escapes from loops or subprograms, as illustrated by Examples 22.1 and 22.2.

Exercises 22

22.1. The input data contains a list of integers, one per line, preceded by a line containing the size of the list. Write programs to compute the sum of the integers: (a) using a FOR statement, with a GOTO statement to escape from the loop if end-of-file is reached prematurely; and (b) using a WHILE statement and no GOTO statement.

Which version of the program do you think is more readable?

Programming exercises 22

22.2*. Details of transactions on a number of bank accounts have been prepared, one transaction per line, each line being of the form:

T account-number amount

where the amount is positive for a deposit or negative for a withdrawal. Details of the balances of the accounts are also available, one line per account, in the form:

B account-number balance

Assume that both sets of data have been sorted in order of account-number, and merged so that all the transaction lines for one account are immediately followed by the balance line for the same account. For example:

```
T 2001 +10
T 2001 −20
B 2001 100         (2 transactions on this account)
B 2003 0           (0 transactions on this account)
T 2008 −5
T 2008 −25
T 2008 +3
B 2008 −10         (3 transactions on this account)
```

(a) Write a program which reads this input data, assuming it to be free of errors, and outputs the updated balance for each account. (b) Modify your program to cater for the possibility that the last balance line is missing. (c) Further modify your program to cater for the possibility that transaction lines with different account-numbers occur together, or that a group of transaction lines is followed by a balance line with a different account-number.

Appendix 1
Collected syntax diagrams

Syntax diagrams defining the entire syntax of Pascal, including certain features not covered in the main text, are collected together here.

1.1 The program

Program:

Program Parameters:

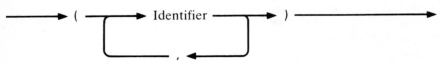

1.2 Blocks

Block:

```
        ──────► Declarative Part ──────► Statement Part ──────►
```

Declarative Part:

Label Declaration:

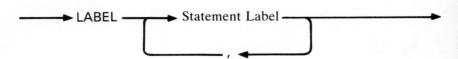

Statement Part:

Compound Statement

1.3 Statements

Statement:

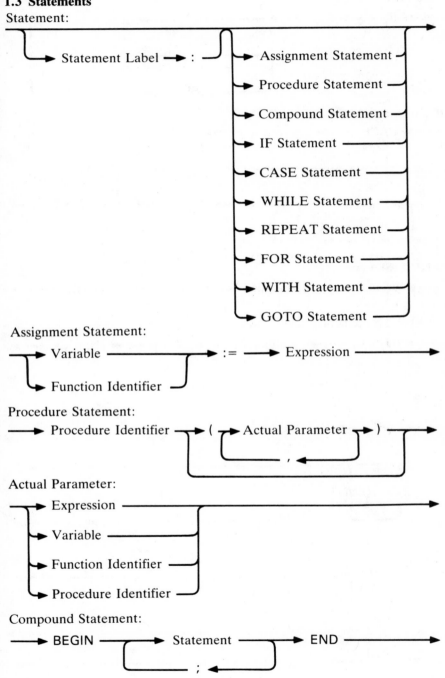

Assignment Statement:

Procedure Statement:

Actual Parameter:

Compound Statement:

IF Statement:

⟶ IF ⟶ Expression ⟶ THEN ⟶ Statement ⟶

⟶ ELSE ⟶ Statement ⟶

CASE Statement:

⟶ CASE ⟶ Expression ⟶ OF

Constant ⟶ : ⟶ Statement ⟶ ; ⟶ ; ⟶ END ⟶

,

WHILE Statement:

⟶ WHILE ⟶ Expression ⟶ DO ⟶ Statement ⟶

REPEAT Statement:

⟶ REPEAT ⟶ Statement ⟶ UNTIL ⟶ Expression ⟶

;

FOR Statement:

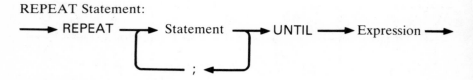

⟶ FOR ⟶ Variable Identifier ⟶ := ⟶ Expression

TO DOWNTO

⟶ Expression ⟶ DO ⟶ Statement ⟶

WITH Statement:

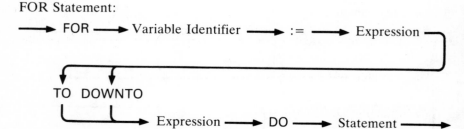

⟶ WITH ⟶ Variable ⟶ DO ⟶ Statement ⟶

,

GOTO Statement:

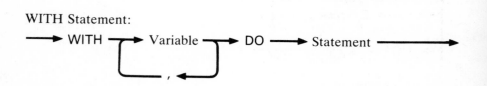

⟶ GOTO ⟶ Statement Label ⟶

1.4 Expressions

Expression:

Simple Expression:

Term:

Factor:

Unsigned Constant:

Function Designator:

Set Constructor:

1.5 Variables

Variable:

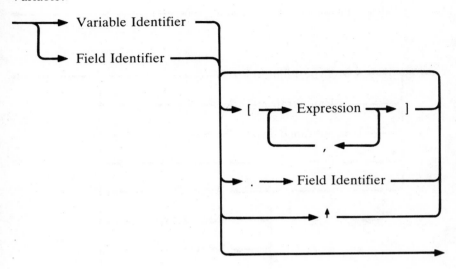

1.6 Constants and constant definitions

Constant Definition:

Constant:

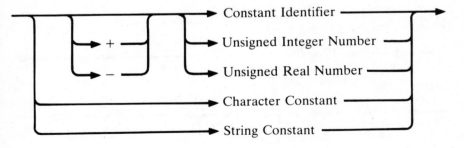

1.7 Types and type definitions

Type Definition:

Type:

Enumeration Type:

Subrange Type:

Pointer Type:

Array Type:

Record Type:

Field List:

Record Section:

Variant Part:

Tag Section:

Set Type:

File Type:

1.8 Variable declarations

Variable Declaration:

1.9 Subprograms

Function Declaration:

Function Heading:

Procedure Declaration:

Procedure Heading:

Formal Parameter Part:

Formal Parameter Section:

```
 ┌──────► Value Parameter Section ──────────┐
 │                                          │
 ├──────► Variable Parameter Section ───────┤
 │                                          │
 ├──────► Functional Parameter Section ─────┤
 │                                          │
 └──────► Procedural Parameter Section ─────┘
```

Value Parameter Section:

```
 ┌──────► Identifier ──────► : ──────► Type Identifier ──────►
 │                     │
 └────────◄────────────┘
          ,
```

Variable Parameter Section:

```
──► VAR ──┬──► Identifier ──────► : ──────► Type Identifier ──────►
          │              │
          └──────◄───────┘
                 ,
```

Functional Parameter Section:

```
──────► Function Heading ──────────────────────►
```

Procedural Parameter Section:

```
──────► Procedure Heading ──────────────────────►
```

1.10 Identifiers, labels and literals

Identifier:

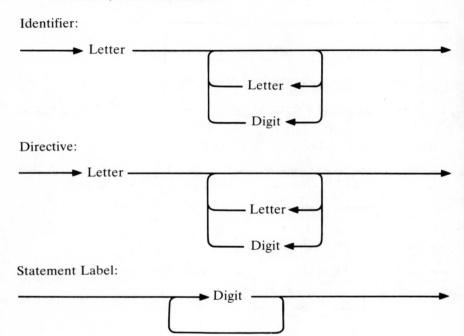

Directive:

Statement Label:

Unsigned Integer Number:

Unsigned Real Number:

Character Constant:

String Constant:

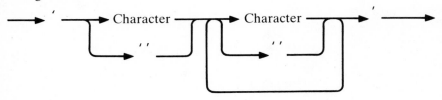

Appendix 2
Reserved words and special symbols

2.1 Reserved words

A *reserved word* is a word which has a special meaning and cannot be used as an identifier. Here is a complete list of the reserved words of Pascal:

AND	DOWNTO	IF	OR	THEN
ARRAY	ELSE	IN	PACKED	TO
BEGIN	END	LABEL	PROCEDURE	TYPE
CASE	FILE	MOD	PROGRAM	UNTIL
CONST	FOR	NIL	RECORD	VAR
DIV	FUNCTION	NOT	REPEAT	WHILE
DO	GOTO	OF	SET	WITH

2.2 Special symbols and their representations

Here is a complete list of the special symbols of Pascal:

```
+      −      *      /
=      <>     <      <=     >=     >
(      )      [      ]      {      }
:=     .      ,      ;      :      . .      ↑      '
```

Some of these symbols have alternative representations, to allow for deficiencies in some character sets:

Symbol:	↑	{	}	[	]
Alternative representations:	^ or @	(*	*)	(.	.)

Strictly speaking, '{' and '}' are the standard representations of the comment brackets, rather than '(*' and '*)'. The latter representations have been used in this book because they are available in all character sets.

Appendix 3
Standard constants, types, functions and procedures

CONST
  MAXINT = the largest positive integer which can be represented in a particular computer (* see INTEGER *);

TYPE
  BOOLEAN = (FALSE,TRUE);
  CHAR   = a particular character set;
  INTEGER = the set of whole numbers, or integers, which can be represented in a particular computer
            (* in effect, −MAXINT . . +MAXINT *);
  REAL   = the set of real numbers which can be represented in a particular computer;
  TEXT   = file of characters subdivided into lines;

(**** Arithmetic functions ****)

FUNCTION ODD (I: INTEGER): BOOLEAN;
  returns TRUE if and only if I is odd;
FUNCTION ABS (A: any arithmetic type): same arithmetic type;
  returns the absolute value of A;
FUNCTION SQR (A: any arithmetic type): same arithmetic type;
  returns the square of A;
FUNCTION TRUNC (X: REAL): INTEGER;
  returns the value of X truncated to its integral part;
FUNCTION ROUND (X: REAL): INTEGER;
  returns the value of X rounded to the nearest integer;
FUNCTION SQRT (X: REAL): REAL;
  returns the square root of X;
FUNCTION ARCTAN (X: REAL): REAL;
  returns the arctangent, in radians, of X;
FUNCTION COS (X: REAL): REAL;
  returns the cosine of X radians;
FUNCTION SIN (X: REAL): REAL;
  returns the sine of X radians;

FUNCTION EXP (X: REAL): REAL;
   returns the value of *e* raised to the power of X;
FUNCTION LN (X: REAL): REAL;
   returns the logarithm of X to the base *e*;

(**** Ordinal functions ****)

FUNCTION SUCC (S: any ordinal type): same ordinal type;
   returns the successor value of S, if such a value exists;
FUNCTION PRED (S: any ordinal type): same ordinal type;
   returns the predecessor value of S, if such a value exists;
FUNCTION ORD (S: any ordinal type): INTEGER;
   returns the ordinal number of S;
   (* The values of an enumeration type, including BOOLEAN, have
   ordinal numbers 0, 1, 2, etc., in order of their enumeration.
   The ordinal number of a CHAR value depends on the character set: see
   Appendix 5.
   The ordinal number of an INTEGER value is itself. *)
FUNCTION CHR (I: INTEGER): CHAR;
   returns the character whose ordinal number is I, if such a character
   exists;

(**** File handling function and procedures ****)

FUNCTION EOF (VAR F: any file type): BOOLEAN;
   returns TRUE if and only if F's reading/writing position is at end-of-file;
PROCEDURE RESET (VAR F: any file type);
   resets F's reading position to the beginning of F, sets EOF(F) to TRUE if
   F is empty, otherwise copies the first component of F into F ↑ ;
PROCEDURE GET (VAR F: any file type);
   (* permitted only if EOF(F) is FALSE *)
   advances F's reading position by one component, sets EOF(F) to TRUE if
   there is no next component, otherwise copies the next component into
   F ↑ ;
PROCEDURE READ (VAR F: any file type;
                 VAR C: component type of F);
      BEGIN
      C := F ↑ ; GET (F)
      END;
(* READ (*f,c1,c2*, . . .) is equivalent to:
      BEGIN READ (*f,c1*); READ (*f,c2*); . . . . . . END *)
PROCEDURE REWRITE (VAR F: any file type);
   makes F empty and ready to be rewritten;
PROCEDURE PUT (VAR F: any file type);
   appends the contents of F ↑ to F, leaving F ↑ undefined;

PROCEDURE WRITE (VAR F: any file type;
                      C: component type of F);
    BEGIN
    F $\uparrow$:= C; PUT (F)
    END;
(* WRITE ($f,c1,c2,$ . . .) is equivalent to:
    BEGIN WRITE ($f,c1$); WRITE ($f,c2$); . . . . . END *)

(* For text file handling functions and procedures, see Appendix 4. *)

(**** Dynamic storage allocation procedures ****)

PROCEDURE NEW (VAR P: any pointer type);
  creates a fresh anonymous variable and makes P point to it;
 (* If p is a pointer to a variant record type which has a case label l,
  NEW(p,l) creates an anonymous variant record which will be con-
  strained to the variant specified by l. (The tag field is not initialized by
  NEW.) This constraint allows the storage space allocated to the variant
  record to be minimized.
  The extended form NEW($p,l1,l2,$ . . .) is available for a record with
  nested variants corresponding to case labels $l1$, $l2$, . . . *)
PROCEDURE DISPOSE (VAR P: any pointer type);
  discards the anonymous variable P $\uparrow$, leaving P undefined;
 (* DISPOSE(p,l) must be used to discard an anonymous variant record
  created by the form NEW(p,l), and thus constrained to the variant
  specified by l.
  Similarly for the extended form DISPOSE($p,l1,l2,$ . . .). *)

(**** Packing and unpacking procedures ****)

PROCEDURE PACK (U: any unpacked array type;
                   I: index type of U;
         VAR P: any packed array type with
                    same component type as U);
      copies U[I], U[SUCC(I)], ... into all the components of P;

PROCEDURE UNPACK (P: any packed array type;
         VAR U: any unpacked array type with
                    same component type as P;
                 I: index type of U);
      copies all the components of P into U[I], U[SUCC(I)], ...

Appendix 4
Text input and output

Legible input and output is achieved through text files, which are character files subdivided into lines by end-of-line markers (see Sections 8.2 and 17.3).

The standard file handling function EOF and procedures RESET, GET, READ, REWRITE, PUT and WRITE, as described in Appendix 3, are all applicable to text files, and are similar in effect. However, when the reading position in a text file t is moved to an end-of-line marker, by RESET, GET, READ (or READLN), a *blank* is stored in $t \uparrow$ and EOLN(t) becomes TRUE.

4.1 The procedure READ

In this and the following section, t denotes a text file, and v, $v1$, $v2$, . . . denote variables of type CHAR or INTEGER (or a subrange thereof), or REAL.

(a) READ($v1$,$v2$,. . .) means READ(INPUT,$v1$,$v2$, . . .).

(b) READ(t,$v1$,$v2$, . . .) means:

BEGIN READ (t,$v1$); READ (t,$v2$) . . . END

(c) READ(t,v), where v is a CHAR (or subrange of CHAR) variable, means:

BEGIN $v := t \uparrow$;   GET(t) END

(d) READ(t,v), where v is an INTEGER (or subrange of INTEGER) variable, reads a sequence of characters from t, consisting of zero or more blanks and end-of-line markers followed by an integer number (possibly signed). This signed integer number is converted to its internal representation, then assigned to v. Afterwards, $t \uparrow$ contains the character immediately following the number.

(e) READ(t,v), where v is a REAL variable, is similar to (d) except that the number may be either real or integer.

4.2 The procedure READLN

(a) READLN(*v1,v2*, . . .) means READLN(INPUT,*v1,v2*, . . .). READLN (with no parameters) means READLN(INPUT).

(b) READLN(*t,v1,v2*, . . .) means:

BEGIN READ(*t,v1*); READ(*t,v2*); . . . READLN(*t*) END

(c) READLN(*t*) advances the reading position of *t* just beyond the next end-of-line marker in *t*, i.e. to the beginning of the next line. EOF(*t*) becomes TRUE if there is no next line.

4.3 The procedure WRITE

In this and the following section, *t* denotes a text file, and *p1, p2, . . .* denote *write-parameters*. Each write-parameter has one of the forms:

e:w   *e*   *e:w:d*

where *e* is a CHAR, string, INTEGER, REAL or BOOLEAN expression, and where *w* and *d* are INTEGER expressions with positive values.

(a) WRITE(*p1,p2*, . . .) means WRITE(OUTPUT,*p1,p2*, . . .).

(b) WRITE (*t,p1,p2*, . . .) means:

BEGIN WRITE (*t,p1*); WRITE (*t,p2*) . . . END

(c) WRITE (*t,e:w*) writes to *t* an external representation of the value of *e*, preceded by as many blanks as necessary to ensure that at least *w* characters are written. If *e* is CHAR or string, its value is written without surrounding apostrophes. If *e* is a string whose length exceeds *w*, only the first *w* characters of the string are written. If *e* is INTEGER, its value is written as an integer number, signed if negative. If *e* is REAL, its value is written in scientific notation, preceded by a sign if negative, or by a blank otherwise; with one digit before the decimal point; and with as many digits after the point as the field can accommodate. If *e* is BOOLEAN, either 'FALSE' or 'TRUE' is written.

(d) WRITE (*t,e*) is similar to (c), except that a suitable default value is taken for *w*. In particular, a CHAR or string value is written without any preceding blanks.

(e) WRITE (*t,e:w:d*), where *e* must be REAL, writes the value of *e* in fixed-point notation, with *d* digits after the decimal point.

4.4 The procedure WRITELN

(a) WRITELN(*p1,p2,* ....) means WRITELN(OUTPUT,*p1,p2,* ...).
WRITELN (with no parameters) means WRITELN(OUTPUT).

(b) WRITELN(*t,p1,p2,* . . .) means:

BEGIN WRITE (*t,p1*); WRITE (*t,p2*); . . . WRITELN(*t*) END

(c) WRITELN(*t*) appends an end-of-line marker to *t*.

4.5 The function EOLN

(a) EOLN (with no parameter) means EOLN(INPUT).
(b) EOLN(*t*) returns TRUE if and only if the reading position of text file *t* is at an end-of-line marker.

4.6 The procedure PAGE

(a) PAGE (with no parameter) means PAGE(OUTPUT).
(b) PAGE(*t*) forces subsequent output on text file *t* to continue on a new page, should *t* subsequently be printed.

Appendix 5
Character sets

The two most common computer character sets are ASCII (or ISO) and EBCDIC. These are tabulated below, each character set in order across the rows. In each table 'b' denotes the blank character, and empty slots are 'control characters', which cannot be printed. The ordinal number of each character may be determined by adding the numbers on its row and column.

5.1 The ASCII character set

	0	1	2	3	4	5	6	7	8	9	10	11	12	13	14	15
0																
16																
32	ƀ	!	"	#	$	%	&	'	(	)	*	+	,	–	.	/
48	0	1	2	3	4	5	6	7	8	9	:	;	<	=	>	?
64	@	A	B	C	D	E	F	G	H	I	J	K	L	M	N	O
80	P	Q	R	S	T	U	V	W	X	Y	Z	[	\	]	^	_
96	`	a	b	c	d	e	f	g	h	i	j	k	l	m	n	o
112	p	q	r	s	t	u	v	w	x	y	z	{	|	}	~	

5.2 The EBCDIC character set

	0	1	2	3	4	5	6	7	8	9	10	11	12	13	14	15
0																
16																
32																
48																
64	␢										¢	.	<	(	+	|
80	&										!	$	*	)	;	¬
96	–	/										,	%	_	>	?
112											:	#	@	'	=	"
128		a	b	c	d	e	f	g	h	i						
144		j	k	l	m	n	o	p	q	r						
160			s	t	u	v	w	x	y	z						
176																
192		A	B	C	D	E	F	G	H	I						
208		J	K	L	M	N	O	P	Q	R						
224			S	T	U	V	W	X	Y	Z						
240	0	1	2	3	4	5	6	7	8	9						

Appendix 6
Implementation variations

Ideally, any Pascal program which runs successfully on one computer should run on any other computer, with identical results. This is not always the case, for two principal reasons. Firstly, different Pascal compilers are not always consistent in their interpretation of the Pascal language. Secondly, there are factors which are determined by the computer system and are beyond the control of the compiler, such as the character set, the range of integer numbers which can be stored, and the representation of real numbers.

A summary of variations from one Pascal implementation to another is given in this appendix, keyed to the chapters in the main text. Gross language variations and extensions are excluded from this list. Before using a Pascal compiler, it may be worthwhile to check these points in the user guide.

Chapter 1

Many compilers ignore all but the first 8 characters of an identifier, so **HYDROGENFLOWRATE** and **HYDROGENTEMPERATURE** would both be treated as **HYDROGEN**. Some other compilers ignore all but the first 10 or 12 or 32 characters.

Some implementations do not provide both upper- and lower-case letters, or do not treat them as equivalent.

Chapter 3

The value of **MAXINT**, and hence the range of **INTEGER** values, vary from one implementation to another.

Some implementations interpret **DIV** and **MOD** wrongly with negative operand(s), for example (-5) **DIV** 3 might yield -2 instead of -1. Many implementations allow **MOD** to have a negative right operand.

Chapter 4

See notes on text input/output (Chapter 8, below).

Chapter 8

The character set, and its ordering, vary from one system to another.

The default field widths for writing **BOOLEAN, INTEGER** and **REAL** values vary from one implementation to another.

Some implementations are very non-standard in their treatment of text input/output.

Chapter 9

The ordinal numbers of **CHAR** values depend on the character set in use.

The control variable of a FOR statement should be a local variable (see Section 13.3), but some compilers do not enforce this restriction. Also, many compilers do not prevent illegal assignments to the control variable.

Some implementations do not treat it as an error for the value of the case index not to match any of the case labels of a CASE statement.

Chapter 10

The range of **REAL** values, the number of significant digits and the set of real numbers represented exactly all vary from one system to another. Some computers round the results of **REAL** operations, others truncate.

Chapter 11

Some compilers use a more liberal definition of equivalence of array types.

Chapter 12

Some compilers ignore **PACKED** altogether.

String ordering depends on the character set ordering.

Chapter 14

Some compilers apply the scope rules incorrectly in certain obscure situations, for example allowing the following (and setting $D = 7$) instead of reporting a violation of the definition-before-use rule:

```
CONST C =7;
PROCEDURE P;
  CONST D = C;
        C = 2;
  ..........
```

Chapter 16

Some compilers do not require *all* possible values of the tag field to be present as case labels in a variant part.

Some compilers ignore **PACKED** altogether.

Some compilers use a more liberal definition of equivalence of record types.

Chapter 17

See notes on text input/output (Chapter 8, above).

The requirements placed on interactive programs vary from one implementation to another. Some implementations have special features to cope with interactive input/output.

Chapter 19

Each implementation imposes its own limits on the range of values of a set's base type. Some compilers restrict all base types (not just **INTEGER**), in some cases excluding even **SET OF CHAR**.

Chapter 20

Some implementations do not allow **DISPOSE**. Some others allow it but ignore it, so that storage space is not reclaimed.

Chapter 21

Some compilers do not implement functional and procedural parameters. Some others do not allow the functional or procedural parameter's own formal parameters to be specified explicitly, and restrict the latter to value parameters only.

Chapter 22

Some compilers do not prevent GOTO statements from jumping into structured statements. Some compilers forbid GOTO statements to jump out of blocks. Some others allow this but do not restrict the jumps to the outermost statement level of a block.

Answers to selected exercises

Specimen solutions to most of the exercises (but not the programming exercises) are given here. Many of the exercises have alternative, equally satisfactory, solutions.

Answers 1

1.1. (a), (b), (c), (e) and (g) are valid.
1.3. (a), (c) and (f) are valid.
1.5. For example: *C1H4, Li1H1, B1H3, He99, C2H4, (C2H2)4C1Li2.*

   Note that (e.g.) *CH4* is *not* allowed by the syntax given, which requires every component to end with an integer number. (What alteration to the diagrams is needed to allow *CH4*?)

Answers 2

2.1. (a) For example: 'is even', 'is zero', 'is prime'.
    (b) For example: 'is a letter', 'is a vowel', 'is a punctuation-mark'.
2.2. (a) REAL, (b) CHAR and (c) INTEGER.
2.3. (a), (f), (g), and (l) are legal.

Answers 3

3.1.

```
CONST
  DAYSINWEEK = 7;
  INCHESPERFOOT = 12;
  CMPERMETRE = 100;
  YARDSPERMILE = 1760;
  METRESPERKM = 1000
```

3.2.

```
VAR
  GROSSPAY, TAX, UNIONDUES, NETTPAY: INTEGER
```

3.3.

UNIONDUES $\boxed{20}$ GROSSPAY $\boxed{4900}$ TAX $\boxed{1633}$

NETTPAY $\boxed{3247}$

3.5. This answer assumes payment in Sterling:

```
VAR
  SUM, FIVERS, POUNDS: INTEGER;
  P50, P10, P5, P2, P1: INTEGER;

  . . . . . . . . . .

FIVERS := SUM DIV 500; SUM := SUM MOD 500;
POUNDS := SUM DIV 100; SUM := SUM MOD 100;
P50 := SUM MOD 50; SUM := SUM MOD 50;
```

(* . . . . . and so on . . . . . *)

Answers 4

4.1.
   8000 −3000 −1000   9000

4.3. For example:

```
WRITE ('Hugh McSporran'); WRITELN;
WRITE ('13 Auchenshuggle Road'); WRITELN;
WRITE ('Campbeltown'); WRITELN;
WRITE ('Scotland'); WRITELN
```

4.4.

```
PROGRAM POWERS ( INPUT, OUTPUT );
VAR
  Z, SQRZ: INTEGER;
BEGIN
READ (Z);
SQRZ := SQR(Z);
WRITE ('NUMBER':12, 'SQUARE':12, 'CUBE':12, '4TH POWER':12);
WRITELN;
```

```
WRITE (Z:12, SQRZ:12, SQRZ*Z:12, SQR(SQRZ):12);
WRITELN
END.
```

4.5.

```
PROGRAM DATE ( INPUT, OUTPUT );
VAR
   DAY, MONTH, YEAR: INTEGER;
BEGIN
READ (DAY, MONTH, YEAR);
WRITE (DAY:2, '/', MONTH:2, '/', (YEAR MOD 100):2); WRITELN
END.
```

Answers 5

5.1.

```
POSITIVE := NUMBER>0;
ZERO := NUMBER=0;
NEGATIVE := NUMBER<0
```

5.2. Either of the following equivalent statements:

```
LEFT := NOT ODD(PAGENUMBER)
LEFT := PAGENUMBER MOD 2 = 0
```

5.3. Either of the following equivalent statements:

```
MONOGLOT := (ENGLISH AND NOT FRENCH) OR
                (FRENCH AND NOT ENGLISH)
MONOGLOT := ENGLISH <> FRENCH
```

5.4.

```
PROGRAM MULTIPLE (INPUT, OUTPUT);
VAR
   I, J: INTEGER;
BEGIN
READ (I,J);
WRITE (I MOD J = 0); WRITELN
END.
```

5.5.

```
PROGRAM CHRISTMAS (INPUT, OUTPUT);
CONST
   DECEMBER = 12;
VAR
   MONTH, DAY: INTEGER;
```

```
BEGIN
READ (MONTH, DAY);
WRITE ((MONTH =DECEMBER) AND (DAY=25)); WRITELN
END.
```

5.6. (a)

LEAPYEAR := YEAR MOD 4 = 0

(b) The following answers are equivalent. Can you see why?

LEAPYEAR := ((YEAR MOD 4 = 0) AND (YEAR MOD 100 <> 0))
     OR (YEAR MOD 400 = 0)
LEAPYEAR := (YEAR MOD 4 = 0) AND
     ((YEAR MOD 100 <> 0) OR (YEAR MOD 400 = 0))

5.7.
$x < y$ is equivalent to NOT x AND y
$x >= y$ is equivalent to x OR NOT y
$x > y$ is equivalent to x AND NOT y
$x = y$ is equivalent to NOT x AND NOT y OR x AND y
$x <> y$ is equivalent to (x OR y) AND (NOT x OR NOT y)

5.8.
$x =$ TRUE is equivalent to x
$x =$ FALSE is equivalent to NOT x
$x <>$ TRUE is equivalent to NOT x
$x <>$ FALSE is equivalent to x

Conclusion—use the simplified forms only, they are easier to read, to write and to compute.

5.9. (a) (a AND b AND c) OR x
 (b) TRUE
 (c) (a OR b OR c) AND (x OR y OR c)
  {Hint: use the fact that c is equivalent to (c AND c) to make the expression symmetrical.}

Answers 6

6.1.
```
*****
****************
*********
******
```
0
 *

6.2. It writes bars of excessive length, which may not fit on a single line. Some computer systems will treat this as an error.

```
PROGRAM DISPLAY ( INPUT, OUTPUT );
CONST
  MAXIMUMWIDTH = 72; (*say *)
VAR
  STARCOUNT, WIDTHOFBAR: INTEGER;
BEGIN
READ (WIDTHOFBAR);
WHILE WIDTHOFBAR >= 0 DO
  BEGIN
  IF (WIDTHOFBAR = 0) OR (WIDTHOFBAR > MAXIMUMWIDTH)
  THEN WRITE (WIDTHOFBAR:8)
  ELSE
    BEGIN
    WRITE ('   ':8);
    STARCOUNT := 0;
    WHILE STARCOUNT < WIDTHOFBAR DO
      BEGIN
      WRITE ('*');
      STARCOUNT := STARCOUNT + 1
      END
    END;
  WRITELN;
  READ (WIDTHOFBAR)
  END
END (* DISPLAY *).
```

6.3. Assume the declaration 'FACTORIAL, I: INTEGER'.

```
FACTORIAL := 1;
I := 2;
WHILE I <= N DO
  BEGIN
  FACTORIAL := FACTORIAL * I;
  I := I + 1
  END
```

6.4. Assume the declaration 'POWEROF10, NRDIGITS: INTEGER'.

```
NRDIGITS := 1;
POWEROF10 := 10;
```

```
WHILE POWEROF10 <= N DO
  BEGIN
  NRDIGITS := NRDIGITS + 1;
  POWEROF10 := POWEROF10 * 10
  END
```

6.5.

```
IF N > 0 THEN
  WRITE ('POSITIVE')
ELSE IF N < 0 THEN
  WRITE ('NEGATIVE')
ELSE
  WRITE ('ZERO')
```

6.6. Assume the declaration 'THISDAY, THISMONTH, THISYEAR, BIRTHDAY, BIRTHMONTH, BIRTHYEAR, AGE: INTEGER'.

```
IF (BIRTHMONTH <  THISMONTH) OR
  (BIRTHMONTH = THISMONTH)  AND  (BIRTHDAY <= THISDAY)
THEN
   AGE := THISYEAR−BIRTHYEAR
ELSE
   AGE := THISYEAR−BIRTHYEAR−1
```

6.7. (a)

```
PROGRAM LARGESTBYCOUNT ( INPUT, OUTPUT );
VAR
  NUMBER, LARGEST, SIZE, COUNT: INTEGER;
BEGIN
LARGEST := 0;
COUNT := 0;
READ (SIZE);
WHILE COUNT < SIZE DO
  BEGIN
  READ (NUMBER);
  IF NUMBER > LARGEST THEN
    LARGEST := NUMBER;
  COUNT := COUNT+1
  END;
WRITE ('THE LARGEST WAS ', LARGEST); WRITELN
END.
```

(b)

```
PROGRAM LARGESTTOMARKER ( INPUT, OUTPUT );
VAR
  NUMBER, LARGEST: INTEGER;
BEGIN
LARGEST := 0;
READ (NUMBER);
WHILE NUMBER >= 0 DO
  BEGIN
  IF NUMBER > LARGEST THEN
    LARGEST := NUMBER;
  READ (NUMBER)
  END;
WRITE ('THE LARGEST WAS ', LARGEST); WRITELN
END.
```

(c)

```
PROGRAM LARGESTTOEOF ( INPUT, OUTPUT );
VAR
  NUMBER, LARGEST: INTEGER;
BEGIN
LARGEST := 0;
WHILE NOT EOF(INPUT) DO
  BEGIN
  READ (NUMBER);
  IF NUMBER > LARGEST THEN
    LARGEST := NUMBER;
  READLN
  END;
WRITE ('THE LARGEST WAS ', LARGEST); WRITELN
END.
```

6.8. (a)

```
PROGRAM LARGESTBYCOUNT ( INPUT, OUTPUT );
VAR
  NUMBER, LARGEST, SIZE, COUNT: INTEGER;
BEGIN
READ (SIZE);
IF SIZE <= 0 THEN
  BEGIN
  WRITE ('THE INPUT LIST IS EMPTY'); WRITELN
  END
```

```
ELSE
  BEGIN
  LARGEST := 0;
  COUNT := 0;
  REPEAT
    READ (NUMBER);
    IF NUMBER > LARGEST THEN
      LARGEST := NUMBER;
    COUNT := COUNT+1
    UNTIL COUNT = SIZE;
  WRITE ('THE LARGEST WAS ', LARGEST); WRITELN
  END
END.
```

Answers 7

7.2. TRAFFIC (b) is more efficient because the interval processing is done only between intervals, rather than at every signal.

7.3. TRAFFIC (a):

Refinement 2.3a': process an error signal

```
ERRORS := ERRORS + 1
```

TRAFFIC (b):

Refinement 1.1b': process a signal or interval and read the next signal

```
BEGIN
IF it is a vehicle signal THEN
  process a vehicle signal and read the next signal
ELSE
  time a vehicle-free interval and read the next signal
END
```

Refinement 2.3b': time a vehicle-free interval and read the next signal

```
BEGIN
note the start of an interval;
WHILE it is a timing or error signal DO
  process a timing or error signal and read the next signal;
note the end of an interval
END
```

Refinement 3.2b': process a timing or error signal and read the next signal

```
BEGIN
IF it is an error signal THEN
```

```
      ERRORS := ERRORS + 1
ELSE
      SECONDS := SECONDS + 1;
READ (SIGNAL)
END
```

Refinement 3.4b': it is a timing or error signal

```
(SIGNAL=TIMINGSIGNAL) OR (SIGNAL>VEHICLESIGNAL)
```

7.4. TRAFFIC (a):

Refinement 2.3a': process an error signal

```
BEGIN
ERRORS := ERRORS + 1;
SECONDS := SECONDS + 1;
INTERVAL := INTERVAL + 1
END
```

TRAFFIC (b): As Answer 7.3(b), except:

Refinement 3.2b': process a timing or error signal and read the next signal

```
BEGIN
IF it is an error signal THEN
      ERRORS := ERRORS + 1;
SECONDS := SECONDS + 1;
READ (SIGNAL)
END
```

7.5. TRAFFIC (a):

Refinement 2.3a': process an error signal

```
BEGIN
ERRORS := ERRORS + 1;
CONSECUTIVES := CONSECUTIVES + 1;
IF CONSECUTIVES = 8 THEN
   BEGIN
   WRITE
      ('THERE HAVE BEEN EIGHT CONSECUTIVE ERROR SIGNALS');
   WRITELN;
   CONSECUTIVES := 0
   END;
check the length of the interval;
INTERVAL := 0
END
```

Refinements 2.1a, 2.2a and 3.7a must all include **CONSECUTIVES:=0**.
Refinement 3.8a must declare **CONSECUTIVES** an **INTEGER** variable.

TRAFFIC (b)

Refinement 1.1b': process a signal or interval and read the next signal

BEGIN
IF it is a vehicle signal **THEN**
   process a vehicle signal and read the next signal
ELSE
IF it is an error signal **THEN**
   process a run of error signals and read the next signal
ELSE
   time a vehicle-free interval and read the next signal
END

Refinement 2.2b': process a run of error signals and read the next signal

BEGIN
note the start of a run of error signals;
WHILE it is an error signal **DO**
   process an error signal and read the next signal
END

Refinement 3.4b': process an error signal and read the next signal

```
BEGIN
ERRORS := ERRORS + 1;
CONSECUTIVES := CONSECUTIVES + 1;
IF CONSECUTIVES = 8 THEN
   BEGIN
   WRITE
     ('THERE HAVE BEEN EIGHT CONSECUTIVE ERROR SIGNALS');
   WRITELN;
   CONSECUTIVES := 0
   END;
READ (SIGNAL)
END
```

Refinement 3.5b': note the start of a run of error signals

CONSECUTIVES := 0

Refinement 3.8a must declare **CONSECUTIVES** an **INTEGER** variable.
Of the amended versions, **TRAFFIC** (b) is significantly more modular.

Answers 8

8.1. Replace the body of the loop by:

```
BEGIN
READ (CHARACTER);
IF CHARACTER = '.' THEN
   PERIODCOUNT := PERIODCOUNT+1
ELSE IF CHARACTER = ',' THEN
   COMMACOUNT := COMMACOUNT+1
ELSE IF CHARACTER = ';' THEN
   SEMICOLONCOUNT := SEMICOLONCOUNT+1
ELSE IF CHARACTER = ':' THEN
   COLONCOUNT := COLONCOUNT+1
ELSE IF ('A' <= CHARACTER) AND (CHARACTER <= 'Z') THEN
   LETTERCOUNT := LETTERCOUNT+1
ELSE IF ('0' <= CHARACTER) AND (CHARACTER <= '9') THEN
   DIGITCOUNT := DIGITCOUNT+1
END
```

and insert declarations and initializations of the INTEGER variables PERIODCOUNT, COMMACOUNT, SEMICOLONCOUNT and COLONCOUNT.

8.2. Assume the variable declarations 'CHARACTER: CHAR; LENGTH: INTEGER'.

```
LENGTH := 0;
WHILE NOT EOLN(INPUT) DO
  BEGIN
  READ (CHARACTER);
  WRITE (CHARACTER);
  LENGTH := LENGTH+1
  END;
WRITELN;
WHILE LENGTH > 0 DO
  BEGIN
  WRITE ('−');
  LENGTH := LENGTH−1
  END;
WRITELN
```

8.3.

```
PROGRAM CUTSPACING ( INPUT, OUTPUT );
```

```
CONST
  BLANK = '  ';
VAR
  THIS, PREVIOUS: CHAR;
BEGIN
WHILE NOT EOF(INPUT) DO
  BEGIN
  PREVIOUS := '*'; (* any non-blank character would do *)
  WHILE NOT EOLN(INPUT) DO
    BEGIN
    READ (THIS);
    IF (THIS <> BLANK) OR (PREVIOUS <> BLANK) THEN
      WRITE (THIS);
    PREVIOUS := THIS
    END;
  WRITELN;
  READLN
  END
END.
```

Answers 9

9.1. (a), (b), (c), (f), (g), (h), (i), (j), (k), (l), (m), (n), (p), (r), (t), (u), (v), and (x) are legal.

9.2. (a)

```
FACULTY: (SCIENCE,MEDICINE,LAW,ARTS)
```

(b) Assume the declaration 'CODE: CHAR'.

```
READ (CODE);
IF      CODE = 'S' THEN FACULTY := SCIENCE
ELSE IF CODE = 'M'THEN FACULTY := MEDICINE
ELSE IF CODE = 'L' THEN FACULTY := LAW
ELSE IF CODE = 'A' THEN FACULTY := ARTS
ELSE
    WRITELN ('INVALID FACULTY CODE: ', CODE)
```

(c)

```
CASE FACULTY OF
  SCIENCE:  WRITE ('SCIENCE');
  MEDICINE: WRITE ('MEDICINE');
  LAW:      WRITE ('LAW');
```

```
  ARTS:      WRITE ('ARTS')
  END
```

9.3. (a)

```
WRITE (DAY:2, '/', 1+ORD(MONTH):2, '/', YEAR:4)
```

9.4. Assume the declaration 'NRDAYSINMONTH: 28 . . 31'.

```
(* determine the number of days in this MONTH and YEAR *)
CASE MONTH OF
  JAN, MAR, MAY, JUL, AUG, OCT, DEC:
    NRDAYSINMONTH := 31;
  APR, JUN, SEP, NOV:
    NRDAYSINMONTH := 30;
  FEB:
    IF YEAR is a leap year (* see Exercises 5 *) THEN
      NRDAYSINMONTH := 29
    ELSE
      NRDAYSINMONTH := 28
END;
(* update DAY, MONTH, and YEAR to tomorrow's date *)
IF DAY < NRDAYSINMONTH THEN
  DAY := DAY+1
ELSE
  BEGIN
  DAY := 1;
  IF MONTH < DEC THAN
    MONTH := SUCC(MONTH)
  ELSE
    BEGIN
    MONTH := JAN;
    YEAR := YEAR+1
    END
  END
```

9.6.

```
FOR STARCOUNT := 1 TO WIDTHOFBAR DO
  WRITE ('*')
```

9.8. Insert WRITE('£') in the initialization sequence. Replace the WRITE statement in the loop body by:

```
IF REMAINDER = NUMBER THEN (* leading zero *)
  WRITE ('*')
ELSE
  WRITE (CHR(QUOTIENT + ORD('0')))
```

9.10 Assume the declaration 'GROUP: 1 . . 5'.

```
IF WEIGHT > 60 THEN
  GROUP := 5
ELSE
  GROUP := (WEIGHT+14) DIV 15;
CASE GROUP OF
  1: CHARGE := 12;
  2: CHARGE := 22;
  3: CHARGE := 31;
  4: CHARGE := 36 + 2 * (DISTANCE DIV 1000);
  5: CHARGE := 40 + 3 * (DISTANCE DIV 1000)
  END
```

Answers 10

10.3. (A+B)+C evaluates to 0.00. (B+C)+A evaluates to 0.004. (In the former case, a significant digit is lost by cancellation.)

X*Y/Y evaluates to 3.89. (The value of X*Y, 15.054, is rounded to 15.1 before division.)

Z+Z+Z+Z+Z+Z+Z+Z+Z+Z evaluates to 3.31. 10*Z evaluates to 3.33. (Cumulative rounding error occurs in the former case.)

10.4. (a) 4/3 * PI * R * SQR(R)
  (b) 2 * (A*B + B*C + C*A)
  (c) SQRT(SQR(X)+SQR(Y)) and ARCTAN(Y/X)
  (d) SQR(V)/R

10.5. Assume the declaration 'S, AREASQUARED: REAL'.

```
S := (A+B+C)/2;
AREASQUARED := S*(S−A)*(S−B)*(S−C);
IF AREASQUARED >= 0.0 THEN
  WRITELN ('AREA OF TRIANGLE IS ', SQRT(AREASQUARED))
ELSE
  WRITELN ('NO SUCH TRIANGLE EXISTS')
```

Answers 11

11.1 (a)

FREE: ARRAY [1 . . NRROOMS] OF BOOLEAN

(b) Assume the variable declarations 'NRFREEROOMS: 0 . . NRROOMS; ROOM: 1 . . NRROOMS'.

```
NRFREEROOMS := 0;
FOR ROOM := 1 TO NRROOMS DO
  IF FREE[ROOM] THEN
    NRFREEROOMS := NRFREEROOMS+1
```

11.3. Assume the variable declarations 'YEAR: 1901 . . 1999; MINRAIN-
FALL, MAXRAINFALL: REAL'.

```
MINRAINFALL := YEARLYRAINFALL[1900];
MAXRAINFALL := YEARLYRAINFALL[1900];
FOR YEAR := 1901 TO 1999 DO
  IF YEARLYRAINFALL[YEAR] > MAXRAINFALL THEN
    MAXRAINFALL := YEARLYRAINFALL[YEAR]
  ELSE IF YEARLYRAINFALL[YEAR] < MINRAINFALL THEN
    MINRAINFALL := YEARLYRAINFALL[YEAR];
WRITELN ('YEARLY RAINFALL RANGE: ',
          MAXRAINFALL−MINRAINFALL)
```

11.5. Replace the constant definition by 'MAXCANDIDATES = 10' and
insert the variable declaration 'ACTUALNRCANDIDATES:
1 . . MAXCANDIDATES'. Replace NRCANDIDATES by MAXCANDI-
DATES throughout the program's *declaration part*, and by ACTUAL-
NRCANDIDATES throughout the program's *statement part*. Insert
READLN(ACTUALNRCANDIDATES) as the first statement of the program.

11.8. (a) Assume the declarations 'SYMMETRIC: BOOLEAN; ROW,
COL: 1 . . N'.

```
SYMMETRIC := TRUE;
ROW := 1; COL := N;
(* traverse the rows from right to left above the main
   diagonal, comparing each element with its mirror-image
   in the diagonal *)
WHILE SYMMETRIC AND (ROW < N) DO
  IF MATRIX[ROW,COL] <> MATRIX[COL,ROW] THEN
    SYMMETRIC := FALSE
  ELSE
    BEGIN
    COL := COL−1;
    IF COL = ROW THEN
      (* hit the main diagonal, go on to next row *)
      BEGIN ROW := ROW+1; COL := N END
    END
```

(b) Similar to (a).

Answers 12

12.3. (a) Assume the variable declarations 'CHARACTER: CHAR; LENGTH: 0 . . MAXINT'. N.B.: the following solution reads up to and including the blank or end-of-line marker following the string.

```
LENGTH := 0;
READ (CHARACTER);
WHILE CHARACTER <> ' ' DO
  BEGIN
  LENGTH := LENGTH+1;
  IF LENGTH <= L THEN
    STRING[LENGTH] := CHARACTER;
  READ (CHARACTER)
  END
FOR LENGTH := LENGTH+1 TO L DO
    STRING[LENGTH] := ' '
```

(b) Insert:

```
WHILE CHARACTER = ' ' DO
  READ (CHARACTER);
```

immediately before the WHILE statement in (a).

12.4. In the declarations of LIST and TARGET, replace INTEGER by PACKED ARRAY [1 . . 10] OF CHAR. No change at all to the program fragment!

12.5. (a) Assume the variable declarations 'HRS: 0 . . 23; MINS: 0 . . 59; TOTALMINS: 0 . . 1439'. N.B.: the following assumes that TIMESTRING has already been checked for correct format.

```
HRS :=  (ORD(TIMESTRING[1])-ORD('0')) * 10 +
        (ORD(TIMESTRING[2])-ORD('0'));
MINS := (ORD(TIMESTRING[4])-ORD('0')) * 10 +
        (ORD(TIMESTRING[5])-ORD('0'));
TOTALMINS := HRS*60 + MINS
```

(b) Assume the same variable declarations.

```
HRS := TOTALMINS DIV 60; MINS := TOTALMINS MOD 60;
TIMESTRING[1] := CHR(HRS DIV 10 + ORD('0'));
TIMESTRING[2] := CHR(HRS MOD 10 + ORD('0'));
TIMESTRING[3] := ':';
TIMESTRING[4] := CHR(MINS DIV 10 + ORD('0'));
TIMESTRING[5] := CHR(MINS MOD 10 + ORD('0'))
```

Answers 13

13.1.

```
N := NRDAYSIN (THISMONTH, THISYEAR+1)
```

13.3. (a)

```
FUNCTION FOURTHPOWER ( X: REAL ): REAL;
  BEGIN
  FOURTHPOWER := SQR(SQR(X))
  END (* FOURTHPOWER *)
```

(b)

```
WRITE (FOURTHPOWER(A+B))
```

13.4.

```
PROGRAM CHARACTERCOUNT ( INPUT, OUTPUT );

. . . . . . . . .

FUNCTION ALPHABETIC ( CH: CHAR ): BOOLEAN;
  BEGIN
  ALPHABETIC := ('A' <= CH) AND (CH <= 'Z')
  END (*ALPHABETIC*);

FUNCTION NUMERIC ( CH: CHAR ): BOOLEAN;
  BEGIN
  NUMERIC := ('0' <= CH) AND (CH <= '9')
  END (*NUMERIC*);

BEGIN (*CHARACTERCOUNT*)

. . . . . . . . . .

  IF ALPHABETIC(CHARACTER) THEN
  LETTERCOUNT := LETTERCOUNT+1
  ELSE IF NUMERIC(CHARACTER) THEN
    DIGITCOUNT := DIGITCOUNT+1

. . . . . . . . .

END.
```

13.6. (a)

```
FUNCTION PRIME ( NUMBER: INTEGER ): BOOLEAN;
  VAR
    DIVISOR: 0 . . MAXINT;
    NOFACTOR: BOOLEAN;
```

```
BEGIN
NUMBER := ABS(NUMBER); (* allows for NUMBER < 0 *)
DIVISOR := ROUND(SQRT(NUMBER));
NOFACTOR := TRUE;
WHILE NOFACTOR AND (DIVISOR > 1) DO
  IF NUMBER MOD DIVISOR = 0 THEN
    NOFACTOR := FALSE
  ELSE
    DIVISOR := DIVISOR-1;
PRIME := NOFACTOR
END (* PRIME *)
```

(b) Assume the declaration 'N: INTEGER'.

```
READ (N); WRITE (N:1, ' IS ');
IF PRIME(N) THEN
  WRITE ('PRIME')
ELSE
  WRITE ('NON-PRIME')
```

13.8. Assume the type definition 'NAMES = ARRAY [1 . . LENGTH] OF CHAR'.

```
FUNCTION INITIAL ( FULLNAME: NAMES): CHAR;
  CONST
    BLANK = ' ';
  VAR
    I: 1 . . LENGTH;
  BEGIN
  (* locate the end of the surname *)
  I := LENGTH;
  WHILE FULLNAME[I] = BLANK DO
    I := I-1;
  (* locate the beginning of the surname *)
  WHILE FULLNAME[I-1] <> BLANK DO
    I := I-1;
  INITIAL := FULLNAME[I]
  END (* INITIAL *)
```

Answers 14

14.2.

```
PROCEDURE SWAP ( VAR X, Y: T);
  VAR
    XCOPY: T;
```

```
BEGIN
XCOPY := X; X := Y; Y := XCOPY
END (*SWAP*)
```

14.3.

```
PROCEDURE READBOOLEAN ( VAR B: BOOLEAN );
  CONST
    BLANK = ' ';
  VAR
    CH: CHAR;
  BEGIN
  (* skip any blanks preceding the Boolean representation *)
  READ (CH);
  WHILE CH = BLANK DO
    READ (CH);
  IF CH = 'F' THEN
    B := FALSE
  ELSE IF CH = 'T' THEN
    B := TRUE
  ELSE
    WRITELN ('INVALID INPUT ON READING BOOLEAN: ', CH)
  END (*READBOOLEAN*)
```

14.5. Assume the type definition 'STRINGS = PACKED ARRAY [1 . . L] OF CHAR'.

```
PROCEDURE READLINE ( VAR LINE: STRINGS );
  VAR
    COL: 1 . . L;
  BEGIN
  FOR COL := 1 TO L DO
    IF EOLN(INPUT) THEN
      LINE[COL] := ' '
    ELSE
      READ (LINE[COL]);
  READLN
  END (*READLINE*)
```

14.6. (a)

```
PROCEDURE MAXMIN ( PROFILE : PROFILES;
                          VAR MAXCENTRE, MINCENTRE: CENTRES );
  VAR
    CENTRE: CENTRES;
  BEGIN
  MAXCENTRE := FRANKFURT; MINCENTRE := FRANKFURT;
```

```
FOR CENTRE := LONDON TO ZURICH DO
  IF PROFILE[CENTRE] > PROFILE[MAXCENTRE] THEN
     MAXCENTRE := CENTRE
  ELSE IF PROFILE[CENTRE] < PROFILE[MINCENTRE] THEN
     MINCENTRE := CENTRE
END (* MAXMIN*)
```

(b) Assume the variable declaration 'SELLCENTRE, BUYCENTRE: CENTRES'.

```
MAXMIN (CURRENCYVALUE[STERLING],
        SELLCENTRE, BUYCENTRE);
WRITELN ('PROFIT ON STERLING DEAL IS ',
        ((CURRENCYVALUE[STERLING,SELLCENTRE]
         /CURRENCYVALUE[STERLING,BUYCENTRE]
         − 1.0) * 100):5:1, '%')
```

Answers 15

15.2. In MATRIXPRODUCT (b), replace the statement part of procedure READMATRIX by:

```
BEGIN
FOR I := 1 TO N DO
  FOR J := 1 TO N DO
    IF I >= J THEN
      READ (M[I,J])
    ELSE
      M[I,J] := 0
END (*READMATRIX*)
```

In MATRIXPRODUCT (a), the refinements of 'read matrix A' and 'read matrix B' must separately be modified in the same way.

The refinement of 'make P the matrix product of A and B' could be modified to be more efficient for the special case of triangular matrices.

15.3. The refinement of 'read a name' becomes simply READ(CURRENT-NAME). Replace the type definition by 'NAMES = INTEGER'. No other changes are needed.

Answers 16

16.1. (a) Similar to the declaration of ONEEMPLOYEE in Example 17.4.

(b)

```
WITH ONEEMPLOYEE DO
  BEGIN
  WRITE (NAME, NUMBER:8, '   ':4);
  CASE GRADE OF
    MANUAL: WRITE ('MANUAL');
    SKILLED:  WRITE ('SKILLED');
    CLERICAL: WRITE ('CLERICAL');
    MANAGERIAL: WRITE ('MANAGERIAL')
    END;
  WRITELN ('£':5, PAYRATE:1)
  END
```

16.2.
```
PROGRAM DATES ( INPUT, OUTPUT );
TYPE
  DATES = . . . .; (* as in Example 16.1 *)
VAR
  TODAY, THATDAY: DATES;

PROCEDURE WRITEDATE ( DATE: DATES );
  BEGIN
  WITH DATE DO
    WRITE (DAY:2, '/', MONTH:2, '/', (YEAR MOD 100):2)
  END (* WRITEDATE *);

BEGIN
WITH TODAY DO
  READ (DAY, MONTH, YEAR);
WRITEDATE (TODAY); WRITELN;
(* determine the date exactly nine months hence *)
THATDAY := TODAY;
WITH THATDAY DO
  IF MONTH <= 3 THEN
    MONTH := MONTH + 9
  ELSE
    BEGIN
    MONTH := MONTH - 3;
    YEAR := YEAR + 1
    END;
WRITEDATE (THATDAY); WRITELN
END (* DATES *).
```

16.3. (a)
```
TYPE
  DEGREES = REAL;
  PLACES   = RECORD
                LATITUDE, LONGITUDE: DEGREES
                END
```
(b)
```
TYPE
  HOURS = REAL;
  . . . .

FUNCTION SOLARTIMEDIFF (PLACE1, PLACE2: PLACES): HOURS;
  CONST
    DEGREESPERHOUR = 15;
  VAR
    LONGITUDEDIFF: DEGREES;
  BEGIN
  LONGITUDEDIFF := ABS(PLACE1.LONGITUDE −
                        PLACE2.LONGITUDE);
  SOLARTIMEDIFF := LONGITUDEDIFF/DEGREESPERHOUR
  END (* SOLARTIMEDIFF*)
```
(c)
```
PROCEDURE READPOSITION (VAR PLACE: PLACES);
  BEGIN
  WITH PLACE DO
    READ (LATITUDE, LONGITUDE)
  END (* READPOSITION *)
```
(e) Assuming the declaration 'A, B: PLACES':
```
READPOSITION (A); WRITEPOSITION (A);
READPOSITION (B); WRITEPOSITION (B);
WRITELN (' HAVE TIME DIFFERENCE OF ',
          SOLARTIMEDIFF(A,B), ' HR.')
```
16.5. (a)
```
SHAPES  = (CIRCLE,RECTANGLE,TRIANGLE);
FIGURES = RECORD
                CASE SHAPE: SHAPES OF
                  CIRCLE:
                    ( RADIUS: REAL );
                  RECTANGLE;
                    ( X, Y: REAL );
                  TRIANGLE:
                    ( A, B, C: REAL )
                END
```

(b)
```
FUNCTION AREA ( FIGURE: FIGURES ): REAL;
   CONST
     PI = 3.14159265;
   VAR
     S: REAL;
   BEGIN
   WITH FIGURE DO
     CASE SHAPE OF
       CIRCLE: AREA := PI * SQR(RADIUS);
       RECTANGLE: AREA := X * Y;
       TRIANGLE: BEGIN
                 S := (A+B+C)/2;
                 AREA := SQRT(S*(S−A)*(S−B)*(S−C))
                    (* . . . assuming the triangle exists! *)
                 END
     END (*CASE*)
   END (* AREA *)
```

Answers 17

17.2.
```
PROGRAM CONCATENATE ( IN1, IN2, OUT );
TYPE
   ITEMS = . . . .;
   FILEOFITEMS = FILE OF ITEMS;
VAR
   IN1, IN2, OUT: FILEOFITEMS;

PROCEDURE APPEND
            (VAR SOURCE, DESTINATION: FILEOFITEMS);
   VAR
     ITEM: ITEMS;
   BEGIN
   RESET (SOURCE);
   WHILE NOT EOF(SOURCE) DO
     BEGIN
     READ (SOURCE, ITEM);
     WRITE (DESTINATION, ITEM)
     END
   END (* APPEND *);

BEGIN (* CONCATENATE *)
```

```
REWRITE (OUT);
APPEND (IN1, OUT);
APPEND (IN2, OUT)
END (* CONCATENATE *).
```

17.3. Assume the type definition 'INTFILES = FILE OF INTEGER'.

```
PROCEDURE SEARCHFILE ( VAR INTFILE : INTFILES;
                             TARGET : INTEGER;
                         VAR FOUND : BOOLEAN );
  VAR
    INT: INTEGER;
  BEGIN
  RESET (INTFILE);
  FOUND := FALSE;
  WHILE NOT (FOUND OR EOF(INTFILE)) DO
    BEGIN
    READ (INTFILE, INT);
    IF INT = TARGET THEN
      FOUND := TRUE
    END
  END (* SEARCH *)
```

17.6.

```
PROGRAM HYPOCRITES
      ( DRINKERSFILE, TEMPERANCEFILE, OUTPUT );
TYPE
  MEMBERS = RECORD
              NAME: PACKED ARRAY [1 .. 16] OF CHAR
              (* .....................
              address and other details
              ...................... *)
            END;

VAR
  DRINKERSFILE, TEMPERANCEFILE: FILE OF MEMBERS;
BEGIN
RESET (DRINKERSFILE);
RESET (TEMPERANCEFILE);
WHILE NOT (EOF(DRINKERSFILE) OR EOF(TEMPERANCEFILE)) DO
  IF DRINKERSFILE ↑ .NAME < TEMPERANCEFILE ↑ .NAME THEN
    GET (DRINKERSFILE)
  ELSE
  IF  DRINKERSFILE ↑ .NAME  >  TEMPERANCEFILE ↑ .NAME  THEN
    GET (TEMPERANCEFILE)
```

```
   ELSE
     BEGIN
     WRITELN (DRINKERSFILE ↑ .NAME, ' IS A MEMBER OF BOTH.');
     GET (DRINKERSFILE);
     GET (TEMPERANCEFILE)
     END
END.
```

Answers 18

18.2. (a,b,c) Replace the IF statement in Level 1 by:

```
CASE kind of token OF
  word:
    append the word followed by a blank . . . .;
  paragraph mark:
    start a new paragraph;
  break mark:
    write the current line without adjustment;
  space mark:
    write the current line without adjustment,
      followed by a blank line;
  page mark:
    start a new page
  END
```

Add **ABREAKMARK, ASPACEMARK** and **APAGEMARK** to the enumeration type **TOKENKINDS**, each corresponding to an empty variant in the record type **TOKENS**. 'Write the current line without adjustment' is refined to:

WRITELINE (UNADJUSTED)

'Write the current line without adjustment, followed by a blank line' is refined to:

WRITELINE (UNADJUSTED);
WRITELN

'Start a new page' is refined to:

WRITELINE (UNADJUSTED);
PAGE

18.4. If all the ballots are invalid, procedure **COUNTVOTES** will set its parameter **OUTCOME** to **RECOUNTNEEDED**, but **LEADER** and **TRAILER** will be left undefined; thus procedure **ELIMINATE** will fail.

If there is only one candidate, procedure COUNTVOTES will incorrectly set OUTCOME to ALLTIED, and that result will be reported.

To correct these errors, replace the statement part of Level 1 of the program by:

BEGIN
prepare to count votes;
read all the ballots, storing the valid ones;
IF there is only one candidate THEN
  report that candidate the winner
ELSE IF there are no valid ballots THEN
  report that the election is null
ELSE
  BEGIN
  count the votes;
  . . . .
  report the outcome of the election
  END
END

'Report that candidate the winner' is refined to:

REPORT (OVERALLMAJORITY, 1)

The condition 'there are no valid ballots' can be refined to NRVALIDBALLOTS=0 provided that the counting of valid ballots is transferred from procedure COUNTVOTES to procedure STOREVALID-BALLOTS and that NRVALIDBALLOTS is made a global variable.

Answers 19

19.1.

TYPE
  PEOPLE = 1 .. N;
VAR
  OLDPEOPLE, MALES, SMOKERS, DRINKERS: SET OF PEOPLE;

. . . .

(a) [1 .. N]
(b) [1 .. N] − SMOKERS
(c) OLDPEOPLE * SMOKERS * DRINKERS * MALES
(d) SMOKERS + DRINKERS
(e) OLDPEOPLE + MALES * (SMOKERS+DRINKERS)

IF PERSON IN OLDPEOPLE + MALES * (SMOKERS+DRINKERS)
THEN
  WRITELN ('BAD INSURANCE RISK')

19.3. The following solution assumes that the upper-case letters are contiguous, and the lower-case letters likewise. Assume the type definition:

```
CHARCLASSES = (LETTER,DIGIT,BLANK,PUNCTUATION,OTHER)

FUNCTION CLASS ( CH: CHAR ): CHARCLASSES;
  BEGIN
  IF CH IN ['A' . . 'Z', 'a' . . 'z'] THEN
    CLASS := LETTER
  ELSE IF CH IN ['0' . . '9'] THEN
    CLASS := DIGIT
  ELSE IF CH = ' ' THEN
    CLASS := BLANK
  ELSE IF CH IN ['.', '!', '?', ':', ';', ',', '(', ')', '"', '-'] THEN
    CLASS := PUNCTUATION
  ELSE
    CLASS := OTHER
  END (* CLASS *)
```

Answers 20

20.1. (a)

```
INTPOINTERS = ↑ INTNODES;
INTNODES    = RECORD
                INT: INTEGER;
                NEXT: INTPOINTERS
                END
```

(b)

```
FUNCTION LISTSUM (HEAD: INTPOINTERS ): INTEGER;
  VAR
    SUM: INTEGER;
    REF: INTPOINTERS;
  BEGIN
  SUM:= 0;
  REF := HEAD;
```

```
  WHILE REF <> NIL DO
    WITH REF ↑ DO
      BEGIN
      SUM := SUM+INT;
      REF := NEXT
      END;
  LISTSUM := SUM
  END (*LISTSUM*)
```

20.2. Procedure **SEARCHLIST** locates (and **DELETEITEM** deletes) the *first* matching entry.

20.3.
```
PROGRAM REVERSE ( INPUT, OUTPUT );
TYPE
  CHARLINKS = ↑ CHARNODES;
  CHARNODES = RECORD
                CHARACTER: CHAR;
                NEXT: CHARLINKS
                END;

VAR
  FIRST, THIS: CHARLINKS;
  CH: CHAR;

BEGIN
FIRST := NIL; (* make the list of characters empty *)
WHILE NOT EOLN(INPUT) DO
  BEGIN
  READ (CH);
  (* insert CH at the front of the list *)
  NEW (THIS);
  THIS ↑ .CHARACTER := CH;
  THIS ↑ .NEXT := FIRST;
  FIRST := THIS
  END;
(* write all characters in the list *)
THIS := FIRST;
WHILE THIS <> NIL DO
  BEGIN
  WRITE (THIS ↑ .CHARACTER);
  THIS := THIS ↑ .NEXT
  END
END.
```

20.4. Replace the variable declaration 'LISTHEAD: NAMEPOINTERS' by:

HEAD: ARRAY ['A' . . 'Z'] OF NAMEPOINTERS

Replace all occurrences of LISTHEAD in procedure INSERTNAME by HEAD[NEWNAME[1]]. Modify procedure MAKELISTEMPTY as follows:

```
PROCEDURE MAKELISTEMPTY;
  VAR
    INITIAL: 'A' . . 'Z';
  BEGIN
  FOR INITIAL := 'A' TO 'Z' DO
    HEAD[INITIAL] := NIL
  END (*MAKELISTEMPTY*)
```

Modify procedure WRITEALLNAMES as follows:

```
PROCEDURE WRITEALLNAMES;
  VAR
    REF: NAMEPOINTERS;
    INITIAL: 'A' . . 'Z';
  BEGIN
  FOR INITIAL := 'A' TO 'Z' DO
    BEGIN
    REF := HEAD[INITIAL];
    WHILE REF <> NIL DO

      . . . . . . . . . .
      . . . . . . . . . .

    END
  END (* WRITEALLNAMES *)
```

Answers 21

21.2. (a)

```
FUNCTION FACTORIAL ( N: INTEGER): INTEGER;
  BEGIN
  IF N <= 1 THEN
    FACTORIAL := 1
  ELSE
    FACTORIAL := N * FACTORIAL(N−1)
  END (*FACTORIAL*)
```

21.3. (a)

```
FUNCTION TRUECOUNT ( FUNCTION F (X:INTEGER): BOOLEAN;
                            LOWLIMIT, HIGHLIMIT: INTEGER )
              : INTEGER;
  VAR
    I, COUNT: INTEGER;
  BEGIN
  COUNT := 0;
  FOR I := LOWLIMIT TO HIGHLIMIT DO
    IF F(I) THEN
      COUNT := COUNT+1;
  TRUECOUNT := COUNT
  END (* TRUECOUNT *)
```

(b)

```
WRITELN ('NUMBER OF PRIMES BETWEEN 2 AND ', M:1,
         ' IS ', TRUECOUNT(PRIME,2,M))
```

21.4.

```
PROCEDURE TRAVERSELIST
              ( LISTHEAD: NAMEPOINTERS;
   (*applying*) PROCEDURE P (ENTRYREF:NAMEPOINTERS) );
  VAR
    REF: NAMEPOINTERS;
  BEGIN
  REF := LISTHEAD;
  WHILE REF <> NIL DO
    BEGIN
    P (REF);
    REF := REF ↑ .NEXT
    END
  END (*TRAVERSELIST*)
```

(b)

```
PROCEDURE WRITEALLNAMES;

  PROCEDURE WRITENAME ( AT: NAMEPOINTERS );
    BEGIN
    WRITELN (AT ↑ .NAME)
    END (*WRITENAME*);

  BEGIN (*WRITEALLNAMES*)
  TRAVERSELIST (LISTHEAD, WRITENAME)
  END (*WRITEALLNAMES*)
```

Answers 22

22.1. (a)

```
PROGRAM SUMINTEGERS ( INPUT, OUTPUT );
LABEL 1;
VAR
  SUM, SIZE, SUMMAND, COUNT: INTEGER;
BEGIN
SUM := 0;
READLN (SIZE);
FOR COUNT := 1 TO SIZE DO
  BEGIN
  IF EOF(INPUT) THEN
    BEGIN WRITELN ('TOO FEW NUMBERS'); GOTO 1 END;
  READLN (SUMMAND);
  SUM := SUM+SUMMAND
  END;
1:
WRITELN ('SUM OF NUMBERS READ: ', SUM)
END.
```

(b)

```
PROGRAM SUMINTEGERS ( INPUT, OUTPUT );
VAR
  SUM, SIZE, SUMMAND, COUNT: INTEGER;
BEGIN
SUM := 0;
READLN (SIZE);
COUNT := 0;
WHILE (COUNT < SIZE) AND NOT EOF(INPUT) DO
  BEGIN
  COUNT := COUNT+1;
  READLN (SUMMAND);
  SUM := SUM+SUMMAND
  END;
IF COUNT < SIZE THEN
  WRITELN ('TOO FEW NUMBERS');
WRITELN ('SUM OF NUMBERS READ: ', SUM)
END.
```

Index